The China Difference

the text of this book is printed
on 100% recycled paper

THE CHINA
DIFFERENCE

EDITED BY
ROSS TERRILL

HARPER COLOPHON BOOKS
Harper & Row, Publishers
New York, Cambridge, Hagerstown, Philadelphia, San Francisco
London, Mexico City, São Paulo, Sydney

The map on pages x–xi is from *China's Changing Map*, revised edition, by Theodore Shabad, copyright © 1972 by Theodore Shabad and adapted by permission of Holt, Rinehart & Winston.

A hardcover edition of this book is published by Harper & Row, Publishers.

First HARPER COLOPHON edition published 1980.

ISBN: 0-06-090757-6

80 81 82 83 84 10 9 8 7 6 5 4 3 2 1

Contents

Note on Romanization

There are various systems of putting Chinese characters into romanized words, none of them fully satisfactory. This book uses the long-established Wade-Giles system, but for the convenience of readers, listed below are some frequently mentioned Chinese words in *Pinyin* romanization system, which is used in offical Chinese government publications.—R.T.

Names

Wade-Giles	*Pinyin*
Chang Chih-tung	Zhang Zhidong
Chang Ch'un-ch'iao	Zhang Chunqiao
Chiang Ch'ing	Jiang Qing
Chiang Kai-shek	Jiang Kaishek
Ch'ien-lung	Qianlong
Ch'in Shih-huang	Qin Shihuang
Chou En-lai	Zhou Enlai
Chu Te	Zhu De
Hua Kuo-feng	Hua Guofeng
Kuomintang	Guomindang
Lao-tzu	Laozi
Liang Ch'i-ch'ao	Liang Qichao
Li I-che	Li Yizhe
Lin Piao	Lin Biao
Li Ta-chao	Li Dazhao
Liu Shao-ch'i	Liu Shaoqi
Lu Hsün	Lu Xun
Mao Tun	Mao Dun
Pa Chin	Ba Jin
P'eng Te-huai	Peng Dehuai
Ssu-ma Ch'ien	Sima Qian
Teng Hsiao-p'ing	Deng Xiaoping
Wang Hung-wen	Wang Hongwen
Yao Wen-yuan	Yao Wenyuan
Yeh Chien-ying	Ye Jianying

Places

Wade-Giles	*Pinyin*
Chungking	Chongqing
Fukien	Fujian
Hangchow	Hangzhou
Kansu	Gansu
Kiangsi	Jiangxi
Kwangtung	Guangdong
Shansi	Shanxi
Shantung	Shandong
Shensi	Shaanxi
Sian	Xian
Sinkiang	Xinjiang
Szechwan	Sichuan
Tachai	Dazhai
Ta-ch'ing	Daqing
Taipei	Taibei
Wusih	Wuxi
Yangtze	Yangsi
Yenan	Yanan

Dynasties

Wade-Giles	*Pinyin*
Ch'in	Qin
Ch'ing	Qing
Chou	Zhou
Sung	Song

List of Terms

CCP—Chinese Communist Party

Central Committee—the decision-making body of the Chinese Communist Party, comprising some two hundred members

Gang of Four—quartet of ultra-leftists (Chiang Ch'ing, Chang Ch'un-ch'iao, Wang Hung-wen, and Yao Wen-yuan) who rose to power in the Cultural Revolution and fell within weeks of Mao's death in 1976

Great Leap Forward—accelerated drive toward socialism begun in the spring of 1958, only partly successful

KMT—Kuomintang

Liberation—the revolution of 1949

May Fourth movement—nationalistic upsurge, with both cultural and political aims, started by students in 1919

PLA—People's Liberation Army (all branches of the military)

Politburo—the ruling body of the Chinese Communist Party, comprising some twenty members, which acts on behalf of the Central Committee

PRC—People's Republic of China

ROC—Republic of China

yuan—about 50 U.S. cents

Acknowledgments

The editor was not a lone star. Robert Oxam, Program Director of The Asia Society's China Council, was an architect and a solid co-worker throughout. Debbie Leonard and Susan Rhodes, of the Council staff, made the difference between having *The China Difference* and not having it. Terry Lautz and Richard Bush, also of the Council, gave their professional advice at key moments, and Barbara Suomi and Kathy Meenan were helpful in many ways.

The ideas in this book were honed in consultations at which, in addition to the essayists, the following people made important contributions: Paul Cohen, Sidney Greenblatt, Joe Huang, Samuel Kim, Andrew Nathan, John Schrecker, and Peter Seybolt.

At Harper & Row, Amy Bonoff, Lisa Morrill, William Monroe and Dolores Simon were as pleasant as they were efficient. The guiding hand was that of Simon Michael Bessie.

Funding for the China Council, which generated this book, is provided by the National Endowment for the Humanities with matching support from private foundations, including the Charles F. Kettering Foundation, the Henry Luce Foundation, Rockefeller Brothers Fund and the Rockefeller Foundation.—R.T.

Foreword

CHARLES W. BAILEY
A. DOAK BARNETT

Co-chairmen of the China Council of
The Asia Society

In the seven years since the reopening of U.S.-China contacts, Americans have begun to rediscover that vast country and to learn something about its society after three decades of Communist rule and revolution. Learning about China is likely to be a long and difficult process; the cultural, ideological, and political barriers to understanding are formidable. But the process will be fascinating and the results will be important.

In the post-Mao period—and especially since the resumption of diplomatic relations between the United States and China—China has opened the door to a great expansion of contacts on many levels between our two societies. Whether such new contacts will enhance mutual understanding or lead to increased frictions remains to be seen.

Understanding a society as complex as China is not easy. In the past Americans have tended to accept oversimplified images and clichés—both favorable and unfavorable—about the Chinese. The authors of this book attempt to probe more deeply and to answer some of the basic questions about what kind of society China is at present and how Chinese of various sorts feel and think. The focus is on China today, but the authors view the present in historical perspective to identify elements of both continuity and change.

The most important questions about China have no absolute answers. Differences of opinion and judgment exist even among the best-informed China specialists, and there will be continuing debate about China's past and future. This book reflects that debate; therefore it presents no homogenized "party line" on China. Partly because of the variety of views represented, it should be an invaluable source of ideas, as well as facts, for the growing number of Americans seriously interested in understanding China. One of its major virtues is that the authors address themselves to the interested general reader, rather than to other specialists.

This book is part of a broader project on Chinese values and the Chinese Revolution, sponsored by the China Council of The Asia Society. Robert B. Oxnam, program director of the Council, played a major role in conceiving both the project and the book. The China Council is a private non-profit educational organization dedicated to raising the level of American interest in, and understanding of, China and U.S.-China relations through a broad educational effort at both the national and local level. It produces a variety of educational materials and programs, and works with affiliated regional councils in various parts of the country to stimulate study and discussion among diverse groups of interested Americans. The Council is a non-partisan group; it takes no position itself on policy questions or other issues. It welcomes participation in its programs by Americans of all kinds who wish to increase their knowledge and understanding of China and U.S.-China relations.

Many of the Council's materials and programs focus on broad themes or topics. To date, those have included U.S.-China relations; American and Chinese mutual perceptions; China and global issues; and Chinese values and the Chinese Revolution. This book focuses on the last topic. We hope and expect that it will stimulate new interest, and provoke further debate, about the nature of Chinese values and the character of Chinese society.

Introduction

ROSS TERRILL

Ross Terrill, born in Australia, came to the United States in 1965 and became an American citizen in 1979. He took his BA at Melbourne University and PhD at Harvard. He is the author of 800,000,000: The Real China *(1972),* R. H. Tawney and His Times *(1973),* Flowers on an Iron Tree *(1975), and* The Future of China: After Mao *(1978). A contributing editor of* The Atlantic Monthly, *his journalistic prizes include the National Magazine Award and the George Polk Award. Terrill was Associate Professor of Government at Harvard University until 1978. Now Research Associate at Harvard's East Asian Center, he devotes himself to writing and speaking. He visited China in 1964, 1971, 1973, 1975, and 1978, and Taiwan in 1970 and 1975. His next book will be a life of Mao Tse-tung.*

One of the first mistakes Westerners made in China was to try to relieve over-supply in their steel industry by selling knives and forks in Canton; it happens that the Chinese have been satisfied with chopsticks for some time.

The two ways of moving food from a plate into the mouth differ intriguingly. The knife is to cut food and is sharp for that purpose; the fork is to spear food and so has prongs. But the function of the chopstick is not written on its face. The two sticks of wood are identical, and have many uses—you may spear, lift, cut, disentangle, stir (even drop). It all hinges on what the fingers do to the chopsticks, not on the design of the implement.

It looks like a case of giving priority to "men over weapons" (to recall one of Mao Tse-tung's military slogans). It also looks like a symbol of the Chinese amateur ideal, in contrast to the functional specificity of the Western mind. One should not go too far. But what is the China difference? Chopsticks are a badge of eternal China, yet it seems that eternal China might now be changing into another China.

China is the oldest civilization to have kept its shape into our era (rather as though Mesopotamia were a great power with nuclear weapons and a seat in the Security Council of the United Nations). But old China was shaken to her foundations in the nineteenth century by peasant revolt and foreign intrusion. The mandarins of Peking made an eleventh-hour effort to reform their dynasty by learning from the West as Meiji Japan had done, but too late. A revolution occurred that sought both to destroy the social system and to turn back all foreign influence except the Marxist idea of revolution. Under Mao all things were made new.

Or were they? Recent shifts have called Maoism into question. Even as

China's influence grows, her moral sheen seems to dim. Three decades after the revolution it is easy for purpose to falter. A new generation is growing up. More involvement with the outside world is bringing a fresh foreign influence to China. What are the priorities, views about the world, ultimate beliefs of the nearly one billion who are Chinese?

The China Difference offers a portrait of the People's Republic of China (PRC) just as it reaches thirty years of age. Our topic is the values, official and unofficial, of the Chinese today—what the French call *mentalité.* * The best American specialists on the subject stand back from their bench and depict Chinese ways of life and thought in broad strokes.

"I still believe that images have a meaning," said Michelangelo Antonioni in 1974, after Peking had denounced his movie about China as showing only the dark side. The Italian director was not repentant and he was not angry. He simply felt that in their wrestlings over texts (in the midst of the "Criticize Confucius" Campaign),** the Chinese ideologists had lost sight of the fact that to photograph China is to find a reality.

Antonioni asked his Chinese hosts to sum up what had happened to China since Liberation. "A new man has emerged," one of them replied. A movie director is in a good position to insist that this man has a face. A way of walking down the street. A way of looking—or looking away. A way of arranging his house that tells you something about him. A way of talking—or not talking, to a foreigner—that is part of what this new man is like.

Antonioni was right. The face of China as twelve thousand Americans have seen it since 1972 is not without a meaning. The authors of this book have between them made more than twenty-five trips to China in recent years. They have all grappled with the Chinese language. *People's Daily* can be read. So can the bulletin board in a tiny lane. And the difference between the two can be noted. One listens to Radio Peking; one overhears snippets of talk at the counter of a department store. The tone and content are not identical.

Knowing the Chinese is also a matter of understanding their historical experience. A proud civilization became dependent on the will of outsiders for a century after the Opium War (1839–42). It should be no surprise that independence now is the key value Peking upholds in its foreign relations. Russia was one of the nations that exploited China's weakness in those decades. Perhaps the brief Sino-Soviet alliance of the 1950s is the oddity to be explained, rather than the split of the 1960s.

---

*The nearest Chinese equivalent to our term "values" is, I think, *shih-chieh kuan*, or "worldview." It is significant that *shih-chieh kuan* suggests more of a conscious standpoint than does the English word "values."
**The campaign is discussed on pp. 65–66.

One theme of this book is that the past is still present in China. Mao did not make all things new. John Fairbank's essay suggests that attitudes toward journalists and foreigners are much the same in the PRC as under the dynasties; Robert Oxnam argues that nowhere more than in China does history matter, and that cultural, national, and revolutionary pasts all weigh heavily on the Chinese today; Holmes Welch offers the surprising view that the religion of Taoism has by no means sunk without trace in the PRC.

I think it is also true that empathy is one important ingredient in perceptiveness. We learned more about China in the 1970s than we did in the 1950s and 1960s because we began to feel that China was interesting, important in Asia, and not as hostile to us as had previously seemed the case.

When China was felt to be a threat to the West, we closed our minds to a number of facts about that country. Now that Russia, not China, is seen as the big threat, we are aware of things once veiled. Who was interested in China's fine public health record when Red Guards were shouting "skin the foreigner"? Who noted that three-quarters of the Chinese people own their own homes in the days when Mao was gloating that capitalist America was a paper tiger?

A New York housewife, Geraldine Resek, kept a diary for UPI of a trip to China a few years ago. "Well," she recorded, after having her first conversation with a Chinese, "this is just another human being like I am." But then she went a bit too far: "I'm not American and he's not Chinese. We are just a man and a woman talking together." Mrs. Resek summed up a lot about American views of China in the 1970s in that eager diary extract.

She had made a simple, necessary discovery of Chinese humanity. But a true encounter between the United States and China cannot occur on the basis of thinking, "I'm not American and he's not Chinese." We have to live with a respect for the differences, as well as seeking as much common ground as can be found for the sake of mutual gain and even survival. This is the task of the 1980s.

The discovery of the PRC by Americans is now an accomplished fact. It is widely accepted that China has made respectable economic progress since 1949 and prodigious social progress; that the Chinese are more interested in developing their own backward economy than in any aspect of the outside world other than what may help them in this task; that patriotism runs deep in China and helps keep the Chinese Communist Party (CCP) secure in the cockpit of power; and that far from being saints on earth, the Chinese may be running out of moral steam.

Our task now is to see how China fits in to the modern world. To be sure, there are a thousand more facts to be uncovered. Military thinking is still veiled from us; the non-Chinese minority races cannot really talk to foreigners about their situation; some areas are closed to nearly all non-Chinese visitors and we cannot be sure to what extent conditions in these places differ from those in places where the eye can supplement the documents.

The authors of this book know very well that it is hard to dig into China and come up with nuggets of certainty. The place is big and complex, and even the new government of Premier Hua Kuo-feng and Vice-Premier Teng Hsiao-p'ing tries to hide some aspects of Chinese life from foreigners. The search for understanding of China is quite an old one—even in the United States—and we are but the latest batch of searchers.

Still, China specialists may have dragged their feet in such evaluation. (My own impression, as one who came to the United States only in 1965, is that until recently memory of the McCarthy era had something to do with this.) "Write about China before you have been there too long," Teilhard de Chardin said to someone who had been in China a shorter time than he had; "later you would break your pen."

Events push scholars far more often than scholars shape events, and that is how it has been with the United States and China. Nixon from the top took a step that led to changed American views of China. He did not wait until the intellectuals had convinced America that China was not, after all, a menace on the march, and then make his trip to China. It is the same at the end of the 1970s. The "normalization" of U.S.-China relations, capped by the American tour of Teng Hsiao-p'ing in early 1979, leads us to ask fresh, more probing questions about the Chinese.

President Carter has insisted that human rights are part of the national interest. But China has not yet been inspected by the light of human rights—whatever that is exactly. How much of what is valued in the United States overlaps with what is valued in China? What are the prospects for mutual cooperation? We have to live with China, and at the same time we have to live with our own consciences.

In the modern era there have been three stages in the intercourse between China and the West. The first was the West's swaggering effort to open China up to the traffic of the time; the idea was for China to "catch up" and jump to norms laid down by the West. The second was a stage of no contact at all. After Mao's victory we pushed China out of sight, and indeed China may have needed a spell of keeping to herself. Traders, students, missionaries stayed home. China and the West were two worlds; the question of influence did not arise.

The sound of Ping-Pong balls heralded the third stage. Traffic resumed between China and the West, but what a different traffic it has been.

Influence is no longer one-way. China is no longer merely the object of great power play, as when Secretary Hay brought forth his Open Door Notes, but an assertive participant in the global strategic triangle. China has begun to have an impact on us, just as our technology begins to have an impact on China.

The game of Ping-Pong itself was a symbol. "Tackle something only when you're sure of success," said the ancient Chinese military thinker Sun Tzu. In Ping-Pong the Chinese could be sure of whatever degree of success they wanted. Since 1972 they have enjoyed a good deal of it at the tables of world politics. Influence makes the voice louder. What we think about the Chinese matters rather less now than in the first and second stages. And what the Chinese think about us now matters quite a bit more.

China is a unique challenge to our social theories because she is the most different of the great powers. A judgment about China's human rights record must be made, but only after choosing our yardstick with care. It is no good looking at our own cherished values, labeling them universal values, then asking if the Chinese are human enough to adhere to such "universal values."

Five mirrors are needed in judging the China difference. We must look at the meaning of Chinese values as reflected in China's own language (as Donald Munro and Victor Li do in this book). We must look at the PRC in the mirror of China's past (as several of this book's authors do). We must look at the PRC's present in the mirror of world history at other relevant epochs (a point Donald Klein stresses). We must look at what the Chinese people—as distinct from the American people—think of Chinese Communist values (a theme of the essays of Richard Baum, William Parish, and Erica Jen). And we must use the mirror of Marxism's own standards (as Maurice Meisner guides us to do).

There is also a moral complication. The evaluation cannot be detached from a hope for common ground with the Chinese. Some will say this is not the task of an evaluation, but the very process of knowing involves caring about what is to be known. And we evaluate in hope because our own fate is ultimately inseparable from that of the Chinese—and the Russians too.

Much remains open-ended in China. Experiments are under way that could veer one way or another. For this reason openness from our side makes good sense. Moreover, U.S. policy will influence to some degree what happens in China into the 1980s and beyond. It is not very startling to say that China needs peace; so does every other country. But not every country gets peace. And Sino-Soviet relations being as they are in 1979, a tacit friendship between Peking and Washington may be China's best single guarantee of peace. We are evaluating a moving target with which we hope to share the planet in a creative way.

Some will dismiss this view as a paralyzed moderation. But I feel that there has been a surfeit of automatic attachment to extremes in reacting to China. Simon Leys, in his critical book *Chinese Shadows,* rejects any fair sifting of the facts in favor of a total rejection of PRC society; yet he does so without telling us that he is rejecting not just the PRC but the entire modern world, for its lack of taste and elitest values. Han Suyin, at the other extreme, can see no wrong until Peking first discovers it—and then makes a new, tight orthodoxy out of criticizing that wrong.

China is neither a distant model whose glow should stoke hatred of our own society nor beyond the pale merely because the walls of Peking have been knocked down and the government is a Marxist one. The country cannot be flung around as an image of what we love or hate about the human condition in general. A billion people live in China—and we don't. We must be hesitant about prescriptions for their welfare. The task is a dual one: first to see the Chinese in their time and place; then to draw up a balance sheet of life in the PRC.

When I speak of values I don't mean theories. China does not lend herself to theory these days. The order of business in Peking is economic development along lines essentially laid down twenty-five years ago. Nor have the theories about China spun by outsiders always been able to bear the weight asked of them. A totalitarian society? Yes, if by that we mean a holistic view of society on the part of the governing elite, and an attempt at regulation of the total scope of social life. No, if it suggests that this view goes unchallenged or that the attempt fully succeeds; or if it suggests that techniques of rule in China are like those in Stalin's Russia or Hitler's Germany.

Is "response to the West" the clue to explaining the PRC? Yes, if it means that the dislocation and challenge brought about by Western assault gave Marxism a head start in the China of the early twentieth century, and that catching up with the West is a deep-rooted aim of the Chinese Communist Party. No, if it denies that China is essentially *peasant* China, that Marxism has been as much changed by its encounter with Chinese culture as eternal China has been canceled out by Marxism.

Modernization? Of course, but one nation's modernity may not be recognizable when put alongside another's. If Mao, Henry Ford, and the rulers of Meiji Japan were all modernizers—as they were—then the term "modernization" does not help us to explain or predict much about patterns of society. The Chinese are not merely treading a path that we trod before them.

Ultimately the values of the Chinese people—their priorities, views about the world, and ultimate beliefs—must be a key testing ground of any theory about China. In this book we have tried to cut the cake from top to bottom in order to look at a cross-section of Chinese values today. It is a humanistic, rather than a social scientific or Marxist approach. We take values more seriously than as a mere tool of analysis. And we take them more seriously than as icing on the cake of class relations.

But if we can and should evaluate China—while recognizing all the hazards involved—it is also well to realize that we do so from shifting ground. Americans see a different China from what they saw a dozen years ago because America has changed over that period.

Richard Nixon once unwittingly summed up some of the changes. "The world cannot be safe until China changes," the Republican candidate declared in 1968. "Thus our aim should be to induce change; to persuade China that it cannot satisfy its imperial ambitions, and that its own national interest requires a turning away from foreign adventures and a turning inward toward the solution of its own domestic problems." If that bears any resemblance to China's situation, it resembles far more what Nixon led the United States to do after he won the election.

I learned in the 1960s that one does not visit China with an open mind. When I went to Peking in 1964, no issue seemed as important to me as the Bomb. And I was a church-goer. On both matters I was critical of the Chinese: they were not anti-war and they closed temples and churches as a janitor might turn out lights. A decade later, when I returned to China on four separate trips, I saw both issues under a fresh lens. I did not put them in the forefront of my view of China and as a result I saw a different China.

What do we bring to the issue of China at this moment? We may have suffered a "loss" of China thirty years ago, but recently the public mind seems to have "gained" a dozen Chinas. Some hawks have found a China that is grist for their anti-Russia mill; others of an even more profound conservative spirit have found in China a traditional discipline and order they contrast with a creeping flabbiness at home. One China that has been found by right-wingers is of a different stripe: a country ripe to be knocked at a time when some Americans need to revivify their faith in a tarnished United States by pointing to far worse places. And now some leftists have found in post-Mao China the latest case of a society abandoning "true" revolutionary values.

The Boeing Company and other firms have found their own China in the form of a technology buyer. Medical personnel and even travel agents, recently, have found their own kind of hope from China. The point is that China now is like a suitcase that has just spilled open.

Looking at the array that emerges, it is hard to believe a neat, monolithic package ever existed.

If we are never truly open-minded, the fragmentation of our image of China suggests that at least we are now not closed-minded. We can no longer afford to be. Setbacks to Western power in Asia have been all too obvious. Ever since Nixon's Guam Doctrine was laid out just ten years ago, it has been clear that the United States would share, no longer monopolize, influence on Asia's affairs. The West as a whole is in sharp relative decline. By the year 2000, according to Zbigniew Brzezinski, the United States will be the *only* Western country among the top dozen powers of the world, and Asia will have 2,150 million more people than now, whereas the United States and western Europe will between them have but 265 million more.

That we do not approach China from a fixed point but from constantly moving ground is a recurrent theme of this book, stressed particularly in the essays of Meisner and Jen.

During World War II it seemed to some observers that the Chinese Communists were modern people who would bridge, if only with Europe's Marxism, the cultural gulf between China and non-China. When the American journalist Israel Epstein went to Yenan, he thought tradition had been blown away in the Yenan dust storms. No more long gowns; a firm handshake instead of a bow; officials who were sunburnt and dressed like farmers. There was a desire to talk back instead of being paralyzed by considerations of "face." Simple folk held up their heads without awe of authority.

The Chinese Communists are not quite as untraditional as Epstein judged them to be in Yenan forty years ago. Yet they are modernizing China, and some steps they have taken seem to bring China and the West nearer. It is not that Teng's new policies are going to make China an economically developed society within a decade or two ; the modernization is slower than that, but in some ways more fundamental.

People's Daily is written from left to right across the page in Western style (papers in Nationalist-ruled Taiwan are still written in the old Chinese style, down the page, starting on the right). Superstitious observances have faded in urban areas during the span of the PRC. No more Dragon Boat Festival, as in Taiwan. Gone is the Ghost Festival, which still grips occupants of high-rise apartment blocks in Hong Kong. The CCP has accepted, more than the Nationalists, that Chinese people who live outside China come under the legal jurisdiction, not of China, but of their country of permanent residence. It has accepted the separation from China of parts of the old Chinese Empire—such as Outer Mongolia—as a permanent fact. Indeed, Peking has fitted itself to a punctilious degree into the system of sovereign states evolved in Europe. The CCP sees China as one nation among others, an historic shift from China's self-image as an entity co-terminous with civilization.

In some respects the PRC seems to outstrip the West in modernity. If a foreigner tries to tip in China he is thought to be reviving a dead practice from a past era. The abolition of tipping is no trivial matter. It touches basic relationships, for the one who receives a tip is accepting inferiority to the one who tips. Such weird and distasteful atavism, which we honor, as if in a dream, has just about succumbed to the hot winds of Marxist modernization in China.

The CCP has broken down fatalism in China. *"Mei yu fa tzu"* ("Nothing you can do about it") is as Chinese as "Come back tomorrow" is Puerto Rican—or was. Today *"Yu pan fa"* ("It can be done") is a theme term of the Chinese Communist era. It is not merely a brittle norm dictated from above, but a phrase on many tongues. A term of can-do buoyancy that smacks of America has replaced one of tired resignation that used to seem endemically Chinese.

Both Peking and Washington are wary of Russian ambitions. The Chinese can talk of stocking up on nuclear weapons "to serve the cause of peace" as nimbly as any other great power. Science has become the rage in Chinese schools just as it did in American schools a quarter of a century ago. Chinese politics can no longer be judged to be a high-minded debate over principles after all the court intrigue that marked Mao's last years. The Chinese had their own Watergate, and worse.

And Chinese and American people *do* care about the same sorts of things. Baum tells us that politics only grips people in China from time to time and when it hits home upon a local concern; that doesn't sound too different from the United States. Parish finds the Chinese worker is no exception to the rule that bread-and-butter considerations are primary.

At the same time, there is much in this book that suggests a yawning gap between Chinese and American ways of doing things. Li shows how the Chinese handling of deviancy is based on a view of the relationship between law and society quite different from that in the United States, and that understanding such differences of context must precede all judgments of human rights performance. Orville Schell warns that in two cultures where the views of "private" and "public" are as different as in China and America, what is admired and damned is unlikely to be at all the same. Jen argues, on the basis of a year and a half's study at Peking University, that cause and effect between education and future social role is entirely different in China.

At times we and the Chinese do seem to be different beings. The surface is so unalike: white is worn for mourning in China; people nod when they don't mean yes; the Chinese smoke like chimneys, with little of the mingled guilt and fatalism of American smokers. Authority in the United States is a uniform and a gun. In China, authority is baggy pants and a fountain pen. The only commercial street sign I have seen in both countries is "People's Bank"; it is everywhere in China's cities and there is a bank of that name in Florida.* When America experiences a setback in the world, there is often panic and breast-beating. When China does so, she typically says: "The situation is excellent" and: "We have friends all over the world."

"Serve the people" was the topic of a talk I had in Peking with a young official with whom I spent six weeks in 1971. Liu was convinced about the importance to society of an ethic of service. After a while I wanted to go beyond service. What about love? It had been an ingredient in the wave of progressive thought from which Marxism was distilled after World War I. Does love also make society go round? Liu would concede only two spheres for love: within marriage, and love for one's country. I was struck by this, for in the West justice has had a vital, if indirect link with love. By 1979 China's press began in a gingerly way to discuss love as a literary and philosophic theme. This was new. But the Chinese still find Western views of love fundamentally strange in ways that Schell and Harriet Mills explain.

In the late 1960s and early 1970s, when Chiang Ch'ing, Mao's last wife, rode high in the arts—Mills, Roxane Witke, and Michael Sullivan discuss her role—there were only nine approved items performed on China's national stage. Such a straitjacket over the mental life of hundreds of millions of people seems amazing to a Westerner. Why did the theater-loving Chinese people put up with it? Again, we can glimpse the size of the gulf between Chinese values and our own by considering one of *their* questions: How can a people with the traditions of the American Revolution tolerate the cruelty and inefficiency of having some 7 percent unemployed?

Red Guards smash the fingers of a pianist because he has been playing Beethoven's music, which they find decadent. To a Westerner who expects to be able to do his own thing, such action suggests a tyranny without equal in history. In New York City, two old folk die of cold because the gas company turned off the heat in the face of an unpaid bill of $20. To a Chinese, who honors the elderly, it seems callous beyond belief.

To be sure, it is very hard for us to measure the feelings of the Chinese people on any issue. They do not all see things the same way, any more than all Westerners do. Many Chinese were appalled by the assault on the pianist and many New Yorkers by the fate of the two old folk. The authors of the "Daily Life" section of this book have necessarily been tentative

---

*In the 1960s there used to be a notice at the beach resort of Peitaiho that made the Westerner feel different: "Sea bathers must wear dark-colored swimming suits. The mentally defective should be kept from sea bathing. To promote the spirit of friendship and mutual help, collective sea bathing is recommended."

in assessing grassroots attitudes. Still, it is the beginning of wisdom to face frankly the enormous differences between China and America. Only after doing so, it seems to me, can we grasp that there are also important common values, and perhaps some forces at work that will bring the two societies a bit closer together.

We and the Chinese differ because of the past. When Couve de Murville, the former French premier, came back from China in 1972 and said: "China is big and old," scholars laughed at his simplicity; but in fact, these are the two most vital facts about China. China has a long past, we have a brief one. Just as the United States was rising to be the supreme power in the world, earlier in this century, the Chinese nation was in the pit of humiliation. China is not "eternal China" but the product of experience.

Some of that experience is very ancient and some of it is very recent. In the 1790s, when the British banged on China's door with surplus goods to sell, a China demure in its self-sufficiency could tell a startled King George that "the Celestial Empire possesses all things in abundance and has no need of the manufactures of outside barbarians." As recently as Andrew Jackson's presidency, even an educated Chinese did not know, or feel the need to know, where America was. When Liberation came, hundreds of millions of Chinese did not know Marx from Jesus, and thought Mao Tse-tung and his military chief Chu Te were one amazing bandit called Mao-Chu.

China and the United States also differ by choice. The Chinese are different because they want to be different—or are happy to remain so—just as America wanted to be different from Europe. They had a bad time from foreign business and gunboats and they swung to the left; not all of them, just as not all Americans like the capitalist system, but enough to carry the day. Old China was dismantled because large numbers of influential Chinese believed in Marxism.

But if China and America have chosen such divergent social systems, can the quest for real cooperation lead to anything other than disillusion, even now (perhaps especially now) that full diplomatic ties exist? It is hard to say which is the greater—the pressure to find common ground or the many obstacles to doing so.

Nuclear weapons will more likely than not incinerate millions unless an international order with teeth begins to appear soon. Issues of resources and environment—suddenly seen to be vital for the life of all nations and classes—do not appear solvable except by international action that will crack the sanctity of national sovereignty. The United States has already learned since 1971 of the benefits of a China that you talk with, rather than speculate about as a crimson phantom of nightmare's imagination. The danger of war does not exist between China and the United States, as it did in the 1950s and 1960s. The whole of Asia is more relaxed because of this. Only the Marxist regimes now squabble among themselves, and this, tragic as it is in human terms, does not harm American or any other non-Communist interests.

But the negative goals are easily forgotten once attained. And in truth the tasks of positive cooperation will be difficult—more so than Washington's gradual acceptance during the 1970s that China is not a threat to the United States, and its sudden acceptance in 1978 that the Chinese civil war is over and that Mao Tse-tung, not Chiang Kai-shek, won it.

We can safely say that objective forces alone will never make one world. People do choose to be different and always have. Yet they also choose to accommodate in order to survive. A will toward common ground will be at least part of the means to attaining such accommodation.

It is important to assess the future of Marxism as a faith in China. "Convergence" does not occur, any more than history moves, independent of the minds of men. Do the people and government of post-Mao China still believe in Marx? To Welch, Marxism as a religion has not taken hold of the Chinese mind as the old religions once did. Meisner argues that the role of Marxism in China has been one of modernization. It is implied, I think, that as modernization is achieved, Marx will not retain the same hold over a Party that turned to him *when and because* China was not modern, and not the mistress of her own house. But several authors point out that, whatever the fate of Marxism in China, the Chinese future is going to be very Chinese, not a copy of anything from abroad.

There is a hunch in some quarters that China, after all, is pretty much like Russia. This was a very common view in the 1950s. In the 1960s, there seemed to be many reasons to conclude otherwise. Mao switched on his very un-Russian Cultural Revolution. Peking talked "revolution" as Moscow talked "peace," which led not a few people to the illusion that China was an expansionist power and Russia not. And there was the "lean" and "fat" theory about Communists: the advanced ones turn moderate; the ones that are still poor remain militant.

The idea of Russia-China convergence appeals, I think, because "big government" is not popular, and Russia and China seem linked by being big governments *par excellence.* Yet China is not at all like Russia.

The Chinese Communist Party is paternalistic toward the people, but it lacks Moscow's heavy-handedness. Russian communism is an edifice of rule. Chinese communism is that, but also a social morality. Its values, most of the authors of *The China Difference* believe, have been accepted in significant part by a lot of the Chinese people.

We should not overestimate the importance of the issue of Sino-American convergence for the future of our relations with China. Whether nations live the same way or not is by no means the chief clue as to whether they can live in peace with each other. Affinity is like a bridge— either friendship or domination may walk across it. The last century of Japan-China relations has shown what diverse traffic can make use of a bridge of affinity. Nations usually want very little from each other.

China has wanted from the U.S.: the removal of American military presence from China's doorstep (mostly done); leverage against the U.S.S.R.; some trade and technical know-how; and to be taken seriously as a great power (in a way, her biggest wish). The Chinese don't really want intimacy.

The opening up of China in the 1970s has taught us a few things about ourselves. It emerges that we are more interested in the Chinese than they are in us. That should remind us Americans of our tendency to reach out to other cultures with an assumption that what is liked here will also be liked elsewhere. (The Chinese, like the French, are the opposite; they assume their own uniqueness.)

We have learned a bit about the recent past in Asia. A PRC now reckoned to be too busy with domestic tasks to go off on foreign adventures was in fact always much like that. American expansionism, not Chinese, was the prime mover in the international politics of Asia during the fifties and sixties. Washington was trying to "contain" the most self-contained major nation on earth.

How seriously should we take official China? First, we have to take into account that the public record is a different animal in China and the West. *People's Daily* sets out the norms; it does not report the news. In a sense the Chinese people don't take official China all that seriously. They know *People's Daily* is not a reflection of Chinese reality. On the other hand they know—as the foreigner may not—that it is not *meant* to be. They take it seriously only as a stylized catechism of what their government wants China to be like.

Richard Nixon could publish his memoirs, and have millions of people read them, because there is intrinsic interest in his story. In America the printed word is not only a statement of society's norms, but also an extension of individual opinion (people outside my window are wearing T-shirts printed with sayings that each has presumably selected as expressive of his or her attitudes).

In China the jostling of individual opinions—of which there is plenty —has little link to the printed word. John Fairbank tells us that it has long been considered wrong to step on a piece of paper with printed characters on it. That is not quite the case today, but the principle behind it endures. The printed word is a technique of rule in China.*

Paradoxically, then, unofficial values are of particular importance in China. Even within the government the unofficial point of view is allotted a regular function. Publications are issued—on a limited basis but in millions of copies—that contain "wrong opinions," but also information the Politburo considers should be reasonably widely known.

Any portrait of China must note the strong value attached to family ties, the deep apoliticism of a people long used to honoring social bonds above the claims of the state, the great stress placed upon security by the ordinary Chinese (which Parish reminds us of), and the tension between Mao's insistence on struggle and the Chinese penchant for harmony and compromise (a theme of Munro's conclusions).

Values do not really exist independent of behavior. What people do, taking all levels of conduct into account, adds up to what they care about. Here we have a clue as to how much tension exists between official and unofficial values. You cannot rule hundreds of millions of people year in and out and achieve the tranquility of the PRC—it has only been untranquil when Mao from the top willed it so—if the gap between what is said and what is done is too vast.

As Li argues, the PRC simply could not have made the strides that it has over thirty years if a great deal of willing cooperation had not been forthcoming from the grassroots. There must be many shared values in a nation that fought the Korean War on its doorstep without major strains for three years just after an entirely new regime had come to power; defied both superpowers simultaneously during tense years (the late 1960s) when both were hostile to it; feeds itself though it contains nearly a quarter of the world's population and can cultivate only 11 percent of its land; and raises industrial output by about 10 percent per year.

Beyond that one can only state an opinion: patriotism has given wings to the Communist Party. Tens of millions of Chinese (maybe more) do not agree with the tenets of Marxism, but a lot of those salute the Party for having reactivated the Chinese nation and restored a flash of pride to the Chinese eye. Simple love of China is the large common ground between official and unofficial values in the PRC.

That common ground may erode, simply because the 400 million-odd

---

*This is made easier by the nature of the Chinese language. The characters have a potency that comes from their being semi-pictures. Four strokes represent "grass"; a sign of a pig under the sign for a roof means "home"; a character meaning "day" or "bright" includes a *picture* of the sun. Four ideograms—or even two—can carry a universe of meaning, with an ambiguity that is useful in a slogan or a piece of higher wisdom. Moreover, the characters are difficult to master. To write them correctly taxes the memory; to write them with style is considered an art. Chinese who can do neither have an awe of those who can do both. So the door is thrown open to manipulation by an elite.

born since 1949 have no memory of the bitter past from which the CCP has helped rescue the Chinese people. In this respect Jen's experience at Peking University is instructive; students are being asked to struggle against an evil of which they have no direct knowledge.

One area where China and the United States do differ radically, although the gap will gradually lessen, is over the vital question of space for the individual to be him- or herself.

"I am master of my own ship, after God," cried a young Chinese worker. *People's Daily* condemned him as an anarchist.* In China the individual is not meant to be master of his own ship. There are three good reasons for this: tradition, Communist Party rule, and nationalism.

In old China the line that separated the individual from society was hardly to be discerned. "Self" indeed meant selfishness. Traditionally, fulfillment of the individual personality was conceived of solely in terms of fitting in to society. No sanction existed for individual legal rights. This is still fairly true of the PRC. The term for "everybody" in Chinese is "big family." It's not a bad summary of China today. A social network gathers people together almost as in a vast family.

The second barrier in the way of individualism as the West knows it—Communist Party organization—joins forces with the first. The individual cannot decide on the truth for himself because the Party is supposed to be the guardian of all truth. Here Chinese tradition and Leninism reinforce each other, except that the CCP has broken down lineage ties.

In the West, the nature of the individual (e.g., as a child of God, or as a being possessing "natural rights") is the starting point. In China, his function in society is the starting point. In a democracy, the individual is believed capable of changing his own outlook and fate. In China, change is believed, now as in the past, to take place by experience in a group. No one is alone with God; no one is asked to pick himself up by his own bootstraps; no one is expected to plot great schemes from the recesses of her own spirit. Even a couple's decision on when to have a baby will likely issue from a group discussion with CCP officials and neighbors.

The demands of the nation have also subdued the individual. At its birth, Chinese communism set out to emancipate both the individual and the nation. It is fair to say that the second drive has eclipsed the first. Mao as a young man wrote passionate articles about the "freedom to love" that old China had denied and a new China would offer. But securing the "wealth and power of the nation" (a famous old phrase) soon occupied him much more.

The balance among these three constraints on the autonomy of the

*The paper drew a veil over the youth's unusual mention of God, or Heaven—*t'ien.*

individual is going to be quite different tomorrow. A new political culture is gradually emerging in China. It comes out of the CCP's success in modernizing Chinese society and making the Chinese nation secure. Yet the Party may not find its own children easy to deal with. To emancipate a people is one thing; to govern an emancipated people is quite another.

People are the only mediators of a living tradition. This makes *social* modernization more potent than other forms. Tens of millions of Chinese can read and write who could not before; 35 million belong to the Party and grow used to taking account of the sophisticated information Party members get. Women speak up to men—thanks to the eclipse of feudalism—and children come out quickly from under the shadow of their parents. Superstitions are gone that used to make rural people see themselves as a mere stick or bird, rather than an aware individual who takes his life into his own grasp. A whole upper working class of skilled technicians has emerged in the cities.

Knowledge, mobility, an end to awe—these are the sinews of social modernization. They pack a bigger punch than does an interesting "Long March Playground" that exists in a park in Shanghai. The Long March shaped the lives of a "generation of heroes." There is no way to summon new heroes into existence by mere simulation of a past experience. Nothing can count for today's generation as much as its own experience.

Politics does not remain the same in such circumstances. In old China, *cheng* (politics) and *chiao* (doctrine) were fused. For the early Mao they also were. But by the time Mao died three years ago, the two were pulling apart from each other. Politics has ceased to be the reign of a demigod over undifferentiated masses. It has begun to be a process of give and take, in which the people's interests and opinions are an ingredient. Truth and power may be drifting apart.

The rash of wall posters about "democracy" in late 1978 was a straw in the wind. "The ordinary people will be making fresh demands," I wrote in early 1978 in *The Future of China: After Mao,* "and seeking a larger say in decisions that affect their lives." That has indeed occurred over the past year.

It is not a question of democracy in our sense of the word: a periodic choice between competing sets of leaders. Constitutionalism is really all that is being demanded, and that mainly in the cities. The wall poster writers of 1978 criticized arbitrary authority. They asked for laws to protect them, and to which officials will be accountable; for more open and credible decision making; for a steady period when what is "revolutionary" in the morning is not declared to be "counterrevolutionary" by evening.

Underlying this trend is a social change. The individual emerges from the rubble of tradition. That same individual, who owes much to the CCP after thirty years of social progress, cannot be treated as a tame sheep by the Party. Meanwhile, as China's international position improves, the total subordination of individual will to national will is called into question.

A few years ago an Australian girl was teaching in the city of Sian. She fell in love with a Chinese man at her institute. They decided to marry and approached the authorities to arrange for it. But permission was denied. It has never been easy for a citizen of the PRC to marry a foreigner. The Chinese nation is still too close to its trauma at the hands of imperialism to feel at ease with the idea of a Chinese making his or her life with a non-Chinese. The prime minister of Australia took up the girl's case personally with Chairman Hua Kuo-feng. Still the answer was no. But Hua gave a reason: the boy's father was a soldier. *No offspring of a People's Liberation Army (PLA) man may marry a foreigner.* Otherwise, the Australians were told, the marriage could have gone ahead.

This sad story sums up how a nationalistic imperative takes away from the autonomy of the individual, in a nation that has been under siege. All the ghosts of a century of assault from abroad (plus some ghosts from China's earlier isolation too) danced around Hua's explanation of why the couple in Sian could not marry.

Yet some change is under way. In the past, even Chinese other than the offspring of PLA fathers were not allowed to marry non-Chinese. Hua's answer implies that this may no longer be the case. Moreover some mixed marriages have recently been permitted. The case of the Australian girl itself has a happy ending: after the fall of the Gang of Four she married the Chinese man and the couple now lives in Shanghai.

Within Chinese society, the PLA cannot hold forever to its near-sacred image, as its magnificent exploits of the 1930s and 1940s recede into the history books. The siege is basically over. In war, the whim of the individual counts for nothing. In peace, it can be given some play without doing much harm.

Yet the myths of a glorious past are tenacious. Change will be slow and it will not make China like the United States. But it will make post-Mao China different from Mao's China.

So in looking to the future I keep my eye on China's social modernization and on her march from weakness. This does not go against my earlier explanations for the China difference: that we perceive different meanings in things, that our pasts are far from similar, and that China has chosen a social system that she sees as history's judgment upon our own. On the contrary, it puts those explanations in perspective.

No value is so fundamental that it never undergoes change. Rather, we should seek out the law by which such change is likely to occur. I think social modernization and national recovery are the twin keys. The CCP wanted to set China free from a double past of backwardness and dependence. Its instrument—nationalistic Marxism—is gradually doing the job in its own way.

In the first place the gap in meanings between China and non-China has been reduced by China's partial adoption of a European philosophy.

Second, Marxism is the great self-destructor among ideologies. It holds that thought derives from social reality. Yet—like Calvinism—it does not quite believe in its own deterministic claim. It seeks, as Calvinism did, to change the world. Nowhere more than in China has this been its mandate. And as it succeeds in making a new social reality, it saws off the branch on which as an *ideology* it sat. So even to take the Marxist character of China seriously, as I do, is also to see the PRC as being on a treadmill of change that carries it away, not only from its feudal past, but also to a degree from its recent Maoist past.

In the third place, the anti-imperialist passion of modern China—an envelope for its Marxism—also self-destructs. The CCP chose Marxism, not out of pure metaphysical delight, but to serve two purposes. One was to give the people a better life by modernizing the country. The other was to rescue China from the era of imperialist assault. This second job has been well done (better than the first). Marxism was a means, after all, not an end.

People's Daily often hits out against Mencius's idea that "man's nature is good at birth." For that doctrine does not fit in with the Marxist idea that "good" and "bad" are always relative to social class. But what about when class has gone and socialism is ready to yield its place to communism? Will man's nature be good at the birth of communism?

What are the bases for a moral society? Self-fulfillment of the person. Shared values among all of the people. In my view, all rights and duties stem from one or the other. Each individual needs to insist on the first as much as he can. But without the second, there could be no obligation of one to the other, and ultimately no order upon the earth.

In the United States we have clung to the individual as the entity of moral significance. For the Chinese a collective rescue operation has been the entity of moral significance. That remains the great difference between us. I have suggested that there are seeds of change on the Chinese side. There may be a seed or two of change on our side too.

Enough from me. On to our banquet of fifteen courses.

The Mind
of China

Private Life in a
Public Culture

ORVILLE SCHELL

Orville Schell examines the twilight zone that lies between public and private values. He has a keen eye for the asymmetry and the quirks in the Sino-American encounter. More than most writers he is able to take a detached view of it and see the oddities on both sides. In the Chinese mirror he discovers, and wonders at, the all-embracing nature of American individualism.

Much of what Schell has to say is based on his experience during 1975 as a worker in a Shanghai factory and on a commune. He asks how different is China in the handling of deviancy and discovers Chinese heroes who are models of conformity. He looks into the realm of love and the emotions and finds there a crucial reason why Americans and Chinese sometimes pass each other like ships in the night. He asks some interesting questions about attitudes toward leisure and aesthetics—and finds that as sealed-off sectors of life, they hardly seem to exist in China.

All in all the public wins hands down over the private in China, in Schell's view, and he finds China and America to be very different indeed.

Orville Schell, born in 1940, lives in rural northern California. He divides his time between looking after cattle and hogs, and writing on a variety of topics. His **In the People's Republic** *(1977) was the story of his stay in China. He has also edited the anthology* **China Reader,** *and written* **Modern China,** *a short history. Most recently Schell is the author of* **Brown,** *a book about the governor of California. He revisited China in 1978 and 1979.*

—R.T.

It was not long ago that most people in the United States looked upon the Chinese Revolution with fear and scorn. It was assumed to be a phenomenon so contagious that any mention of it that was not critical or derisive might infect an unwary soul with its disease, communism.

But times have changed. And as we reach the eighties, we see China through new eyes. Once we reviled the Chinese and their political experiment; it is now acceptable, even fashionable, to turn toward China with more benign intent. A mad scramble to obtain a visitor's visa followed Nixon's "Ping-Pong" diplomacy in 1972. An increasing number of people began to travel to China. Ten or fifteen years ago it was those who traveled to China who became outcasts (their passports were revoked by our government). Now the unfortunates who cannot obtain visas find themselves left behind. One can hardly contemplate this reversal without wryly recalling Mao Tse-tung's own conviction of the unity of opposites.

Nixon seemed to adore China. Conservative columnists and congressmen journeyed to Peking to return home fascinated with the clean streets, the discipline, the absence of crime. Leftists, too, made the pilgrimage, certain to find their land of Canaan—the perfect embodiment of all the political principles and visions they had been discussing and struggling for during the late sixties and early seventies. It was an odd specter. China, at first the poor pariah of the world, then the red menace, seemed to have evolved into an example, if not of Utopia, at least of some hope for the future organization of society on the planet Earth.

But there was an unreality to many of these new perceptions, too. There was again an adolescent quality to the way we as Americans were appreciating China. Perhaps our intrigue was simply a fad; an extension of our "in" and "out" mentality, which often seeks to put value on what is bizarre or forbidden. A trip to China was indeed a kind of prize calculated to imbue the lucky traveler with prestige and an aura of the elect. (I have often wondered if the Chinese appreciated this aspect of visa giving.)

Perhaps our sudden rush to embrace the Chinese Revolution is only an extension of the physics principle that every force has an equal and opposite reaction; the 1970s were our hour to embrace rather than reject.

And there was an adequate water table of guilt, accumulated from the Opium Wars (1839–42) through our débâcle with Chiang Kai-shek, to increase the fervor of our new infatuation.

As a sophomore in college in 1958, I sat in a Harvard survey course taught by Professors John K. Fairbank and Edwin O. Reischauer on Asia, humorously dubbed "rice paddies" by the students. I remember Fairbank up at the podium trying to make some sense out of the Communist Revolution (then only eight years old) for the lecture hall full of introductory students.

"The Chinese Revolution was not made for *you*," he would say, almost comically, to the assemblage, like a father trying to explain that coffee and cigarettes are not for children. "The Chinese Revolution was made for the Chinese. The *Communist* Chinese. The peasants! Not you!"

We students laughed. It seemed such an obvious point. But Professor Fairbank, in stressing the evident, was actually suggesting the profound: that however (or whenever) we chose to interpret the Chinese Revolution, it was essential to remember that not only was it not made for us, but that it was improbable that any such revolution would ever come to be an integral part of our lives. It was conceivable that some revolution might come to pass in our country, but it would not be the Chinese Revolution. It would be our own revolution—one that would doubtless prove as confusing to the Chinese as their own is to us.

For students of China, and visitors to Peking, it will never be easy and probably rarely possible to understand the Chinese Revolution as it must appear to a Chinese peasant. Our experiences are simply too divergent.

The kinds of experience that we as Americans have had in growing up, being educated, and working, are radically different from those of my young benchmates in the Shanghai Electrical Machinery Factory, with whom I worked while I was in China for several months in 1975. They are differences that were not immediately apparent to me as we worked and went about our daily routine. They did not begin to come into relief until one night during a farewell meeting when I looked over to Chang Yuan-kang, the man with whom I worked. He sat in his blue tunic, blue cap, and sneakers. It was later in the evening than he was used to staying up. He was yawning as our official goodbyes droned on. I wondered if I would ever see this man again. I thought about it for a moment. It seemed clear that unless I returned to China, to Shanghai, to *this* factory, I would not see him again.

I tried to imagine my new friend in America. Perhaps in my house, in my town, watching "All in the Family," eating a Big Mac and a diet soda at the drive-up window of McDonald's, going to the movies or bowling, a ski weekend.

The idea seemed almost unthinkable. For the rest of this formal occasion of leave-taking, I found myself staring up at the portrait of Chairman Mao on the wall, lost in a catalogue of characteristics that apparently divided China and America like separate galaxies.

We are men and women who have grown up unalterably on the private side of the great public/private divide. Not only do we own private property, but we thirst for individuality. We cherish our private lives. And if you doubt the deep importance of the part of our lives that we call private (our friends, our lovers, our wives, husbands, and children, our private thoughts, cherished possessions, and aesthetic preferences), one has only to open any great work of Western literature to find a saga of the interior life. Love, and the romantic notion of finding happiness and contentment in conjugation with *one* other person, is a concept at once so deep and so all pervasive in our society that those who sought other solutions traditionally have been branded as deranged heretics and perverts. When we are young, we are taught to be imaginative and unique as individuals; to differentiate ourselves from the others and the group. To stand out. In fact, to compete and surpass others in our quest to "be ourselves."

Regardless of what lofty political ideas and theories we might hold, most of us are at bottom creatures so imbued with the sense of individuality that we cannot turn back. We are in fact prisoners of the French Revolution, of Rousseau, John Locke, Thomas Jefferson, and James Madison. And it is precisely this heritage, this passion for ourselves as individuals, that runs headlong into contradiction with the Chinese dedication to mass consciousness.

The Chinese are not brought up "free to be you and me." They are not brought up to be nonconformists. For a Chinese, the means of experiencing and expression is the group. He learns in a group, works in a group, lives in a group, and most of the things around him (land, housing, machines, transportation, etc.) are owned by the group. It may sound contradictory, but the revolutionary Chinese does not now define himself by rebelling individually. While there was a tradition of individual rebellion tinged with suggestions of romanticism, during the twenties and thirties, and then again during the Cultural Revolution of 1966–69, it is now the revolutionary with a cause, in the context of a revolutionary society and mass movement, who is the understandable hero in China; not the isolated rebel without a cause or the lone outlaw.

Singular heroes hold a deep fascination for us. There is an attraction to the maverick, even the misfit, that I think is perplexing for the Chinese. Even in China, Americans insistently probe for information about these elements of society, elements that the Chinese clearly view as aberrant.

Repeated and fervent questions by Americans to their Chinese hosts about homosexuality, the mentally ill, slow learners, juvenile delinquents, criminals, premarital sex, and artistic renegades attest to our abiding fascination with deviance; with individuals who spurn the precut patterns. These are our heroes. But they are not the Chinese heroes, who tend to be cast in the mold of the youth hero Lei Feng.

Born a poor peasant in 1939, enduring a life of oppression, but ultimately joining the army and being admitted to what one Chinese account refers to as the "Glorious Communist Party," Lei Feng became a model of revolutionary commitment in the fifties and sixties. It would be safe to say that there is almost no one in China unfamiliar with the story of Lei Feng's model life. His rectitude and squareness would surely make him the laughing stock of most American teenagers. No sex, drugs, rebellion, or treason for Lei Feng, who spent his years earnestly "serving the people" until he was felled by a telephone pole in an untimely accident. Lei Feng was a youth dedicated to the people, not his own self-expression or welfare.

The Chinese seem to tolerate our endless probings through this supermarket of deviant concerns with a certain resignation. One can only wonder what odd image the Chinese form from us, people who seem so resolutely dedicated to probing all the ways a human can be antisocial rather than social.

One area of deviance the Chinese are grudgingly willing to talk about now is mental health. Interestingly enough, mental illness is largely treated as a social disorder, rather than as an individual problem. Treatment, crudely stated, consists in trying to put the patient back into the nurturing fabric of socialist society through constructive work. The image that comes to mind is of putting a cast around a shattered bone to set it and allow healing to take place. Schizophrenia, paranoia, delusions are all diagnostic terms for a *"psychiatrist"* in China. But the mode of treatment is not to take a patient further out of context, lay him on a couch, goad him into a laborious personal recounting of his childhood relations with his parents. It is precisely this realm, which we might refer to as "personal," that the Chinese choose not to underscore or accentuate. Thus it is not surprising that the Chinese have very low regard for Western psychiatry, which attempts to treat illness by trying to isolate and heal the individual psyche apart from the context of a larger group.

"We can't explain psychosis on the basis of conflict between the conscious and the unconscious," Dr. Wu Chen-yi, chief of psychiatry at Number Three Hospital attached to the Peking Medical College, told me on a recent visit. "Mental disease is the outcome of material forces."

China has mental hospitals and "psychiatrists." But here the similarity with our own system ends. Just as mental disease is viewed as the product of social and political forces, so must it be solved in this context. Mental health is a public problem rather than a private one in China.

Without exploring in depth the very interesting question of the Chinese approach to mental disorders, it may be helpful to use it as a kind of metaphor for the larger thrust of Chinese society, toward the "public" rather than toward the "private." I think that in trying fully to grasp the magnitude of difference between our own society and theirs, it is instructive to reflect momentarily on those institutions and theories that we so matter-of-factly accept as given here at home. For we do not live in a world where public participation and commitment are esteemed more highly than private life. We live in a world where it is considered noble to sacrifice for the common good, but where finally it is the well-being of a person's inner soul and his or her material well-being that we are encouraged to attend to first. For us, the individual is sacred; for the Chinese, it is the group which is sacred.

It has long been a conviction of mine that if one is truly interested in unraveling the intricacies of another society, one must pose exactly those questions that seem to most bedevil the people of his own society. Another society cannot possibly live for an American (or perhaps for any Westerner) unless we are able to see how it addresses the problems and breakdowns that we know firsthand. And with the possible exception of anxiety over finances, there is no area that seems to absorb our energy more than that of interpersonal relations.

What does love, considered one of the most private, intimate expressions in our society, mean in China? What role do the Chinese ascribe to the emotions? It would seem to me that any explication of the differences between our two countries must ask these questions of the Chinese (whether they can be conclusively answered is another question), lest we arrive at an account of the Chinese as flat and meaningless as one of our own country taken from an eighth-grade civics text.

It is not until one has been in China for some time, living, eating, and fraternizing with Chinese, that one fully realizes how much we relate to each other sexually and emotionally in our own society. There is a constant, pervasive innuendo of sexuality in almost all of our relationships; this strikes us as so natural as to be hardly worthy of reflection. We are raised to see ourselves as prey or hunters in a game of sexual hide-and-seek. Blue for boys, pink for girls. Aggressive machismo for men, and retiring femininity for women. We are exhorted to define and perceive ourselves through a sexual image; through clothes, manner, body shape, facial features. We seek to be individually attractive and alluring, judging ourselves against some grand cosmic standard projected by movie stars, commercials, and foldouts. We are a nation fixated on our sexual desirability, sexual expression, and sexual competition. We are a nation slavishly devoted to sexual success and failure, flip sides of an impulse deeply implanted in the constellation of our self-esteem. I think it would not be unfair to say that our fortunes with the opposite sex goad us into emotional extremes—bliss or deep depression. One of the most valuable currencies that we as a people trade in is sexual and emotional currency. There is little *angst* apparent in China. I think it is the absence of this emotional flamboyance and sexual innuendo that often leaves Americans with the feeling there is something flat about Chinese life—some important part of our familiar landscape missing.

The Chinese speak of making a "new man." Clearly this is a somewhat sweeping abstraction of composed features, all of which obviously have not come to pass in the youth of China. But just the notion of a "new man" does intimate that the Chinese are headed off in a direction different from our own. The most striking feeling in being with young people in China is of the absence of focus on intimate feelings. Although since the fall of the Gang of Four, matters of love and courtship are discussed more openly, there is virtually no pressure for pairing off, and little sexual game playing going on. One enters a room full of young comrades without feeling the underground hum of sexual energy; people are not preoccupied in casting furtive glances around the room, checking out members of the opposite sex, undressing likely candidates in their minds and making a quick inspection of legs or breasts. There is a greater degree of concentration on the task at hand. One does not feel that those who might attend a meeting of young people are there as part of a search for sexual partners. They may be enjoying the company of the others, but not in an overtly titillating or salacious way.

And so, questions from curious Westerners about intimate matters are not received with great enthusiasm, and they seldom, even in private, elicit much response. One older, quite sophisticated official with whom I did talk at some length one night during a long bus ride in Shanghai, told me that while there had been a revolution in China, there had emphatically not been a "sexual revolution"; that it was an area deemed incompatible with the attainment of such urgent goals as industrialization and modernization. He said that he realized sex was one of the few areas in which China really has made no pronouncements, an area that has essentially remained static since 1949, when new laws were promulgated forbidding arranged marriages and allowing divorce.

There was a lull in the conversation. Then he added, "We are busy with other things before we marry, although there are cases, particularly during the Cultural Revolution. But can you imagine what China would be like if everyone was running around worrying about the opposite sex all the time?"

In China one rarely senses that complicated webs of individual emotions are the governing force. People do get angry, they become sad and happy, and do fall in love. There is even depression and suicide. It is not so much that the Chinese are emotionless, but that they are not as careless with their emotions as people often are in Western society. There is not an acceptable political framework provided in which one can wantonly act out a daily psychodrama. There is little of the permissiveness in China that engenders such statements as "Let it all hang out." Whereas we find it acceptable, and are often even encouraged, to vent emotions toward some cleansing catharsis in our own society, the Chinese tend to view such displays as disruptive. Emotional outbursts are not written off in China as healthy ways of releasing tension. Like overtly sexual advances, emotional extravagance gets little support.

One of the most impressive aspects of China is the way it has provided men and women with a new standard by which they can prove and define themselves. The standard is not predominantly a sexual or emotional one. Whereas in our own life finding the right clothes, make-up, and hairstyle can be an almost all-consuming task, in China people tend to measure their image in terms of their work, their political commitment, and social responsibility. It is not simply recited propaganda when a young woman tells you that she does not wish to get married until she is thirty, so that she can spend the best years of her life building socialism, and that then she wants to marry a man with high political consciousness, who is dedicated to his work and "serving the people." This is not the full story, of course, but it is as much of the story as that of the young American pompom girl who tells you that she is passionately in love with the football captain. The important question here is the models a society holds up for its young people to emulate.

Neither men nor women in China expend great energy on fashion. (Children dress rather colorfully. But for an adult, to be neat is "correct.") To stand out from the group in the ways fashion engenders is considered to be individualistic and distracting from the greater purposes at hand. Although recently there has been more evidence of self-expression in dress, clothes are still, by and large, plain and functional. It is often difficult to tell at first glance if someone is male or female, much less if their physiognomy is comely or not.

"All the better," a cadre might say. "What does it matter what the shape of someone's body or face is? These are matters of little significance, when there is a country to modernize."

Insofar as a women does pay attention to her sartorial appearance, she might take special pains to wear a colorful shirt beneath her tunic, with pretty buttons. She might even have a special tunic taken in slightly at the waist. In the summer time she might wear a skirt or get a "permanent" if she lived in one of the larger cities. Such subtleties are not without significance. But the whole emphasis on individual appearance is so muted as to pale in comparison to our own obsession with it.

There is some premarital and extramarital sex in China. Chinese do "fall in love." But again this expression, "fall in love," has a vastly different connotation. The Chinese, particularly among the peasantry, have never had a deep tradition of romantic love—the notion that goes back to medieval chivalric times of affairs between men and women that are deeply and exclusively attractions of the individual soul. I sensed in talking to people in China that marriage and courtship are more practical matters than in our own country; almost a contract between two people who found each other interesting and acceptable to share the process of having children. There is less temptation to believe that finding the right mate is *the* answer to life. The "home" itself is hardly the center of an average Chinese person's universe. Whether married or not, a person has other responsibilities, such as work, politics, and community affairs. Far from being viewed as necessary but barely tolerable forms of drudgery, these pastimes are seen as vital contributions. They demand attention, dedication, and seem to channel much human energy into productive labor, energy that might otherwise be spent in more leisurely and indulgent pastimes.

"Leisure" is a word that seems to barely exist in modern Chinese. If the Chinese do not define themselves in terms of being sexual or emotional men and women, they are even less likely to view themselves in terms of "leisure-time identities." The Chinese are not a hedonistic or indulgent people. They do not revel in weekend culture, recreational pilgrimages, gourmet eating, resort life, or even highly individualistic sports. There are no ski weekends. There is no Las Vegas, no Merv Griffin, no Disney World.

Leisure without good purpose is still a concept that has little sanction in China. This is not to say that there are no lazy people, but rather that laziness, or leisure, are not traits people feel entitled to, or through which they might constitute some part of their sense of identity. China is still a poor country, wrestling with fundamentals like adequate food, clothing, and shelter for her people. It is easy to forget this as the Chinese recite the litanies of their progress, but it is not a country that shows any inclination or that can afford to sanctify idleness as a right and privilege. One gathers that this is not even a goal in China, although it could possibly come to be one as China develops.

In comparison to ourselves, the Chinese appear as pointedly purposeful people with little proclivity or opportunity for frivolity. People by and large take politics seriously, and since they also define themselves as human beings in a political sense, it is not surprising that they ascribe political meaning to all endeavors. Things do not exist in a value-free atmosphere. Enjoyment as an end in itself is not a primary goal.

Art and entertainment, prime leisure activities in our own society, have a predominantly different purpose in China. Americans who have gone to Chinese movies, ballets, or operas craving a little entertainment or divertissement have often found themselves bored by what is derogatorily referred to in our own culture as "propaganda."

But in China, the word "propaganda" is not one with sinister connotations. It is a word that evokes the notion of teaching and learning. It is commonplace to meet Chinese who proudly and unabashedly proclaim that they are in a local work brigade or factory "propaganda team," whose role is to go throughout the unit performing works of redeeming social and political importance. Propaganda teams are not indiscriminate in what they teach. Their calling is to incorporate the thoughts of Marx, Lenin, Engels, Stalin, and Chairman Mao into an art form. The object of these works is not to help you "escape the surly bonds of earth," or to transcend the mundanity of your daily existence for a moment of fantasy. (I can hear the words of John Fairbank echoing.) The object is to take the viewer or listener and resolutely plunge him back into the world of political verities and class struggle. As Mao is quick to point out in his short discourse, *The Yenan Talks on Art and Literature* (1942), any work that is escapist in nature is bourgeois and counterrevolutionary. The function of art is not to divert people's attention from the realities of political life and grant them a moment of surcease, but to redirect their attention with new insight to the task of revolution.

I recall one incident. We were visiting the county town of Tachai near the famous Tachai Model Work Brigade in northwest China. Our bus disgorged us in an empty lot. Right in front of us was a large brick wall covered with the tattered remnants of posters from the innumerable political campaigns waged throughout China over the past three decades. The wall was a collage of shreds, colors, and brick. In the middle of this shaggy field was one gleaming, defiant proletarian face in blues, reds, and yellows, some vestige from a long-departed political poster. There was something about the colors and textures of this tableau that I found irresistible, completely apart from any political meaning it might impute.

I raised my camera to photograph it, only to encounter the disapproving countenance of one of our guides. Not wishing to cause any ill feeling, I relented for the moment.

But returning to it several hours later, I was again struck by this inadvertent work of art, which reminded me of something Robert Rauschenberg might have done. I again raised my camera to photograph it. Suddenly out of nowhere popped up the same comrade, registering even more severe opprobrium. Making a split-second decision, I decided to persevere and shot a number of slides in spite of the clear message I was getting from my host. I then walked over to him, pondering what I might say to convey my real intentions.

"Why do you wish to take pictures of dirty walls?" the guide asked.

I realized that although this man had been abroad, he probably did not have any deep appreciation of an art that had no political significance.

"You may not grasp what I'm going to tell you," I parried, "but I do not see a dirty wall there. I see some textures, color combinations, and designs on that wall that I found interesting and appealing. That is why I took the photographs."

My explanation did not seem to impress my Chinese host, whose fears that I might be trying to belittle China seemed to remain undeterred.

It occurred to me later that one reason aesthetics *per se* may have little place in China today is that such judgments must be of a highly individual nature. Whereas one can lead or even legislate political points of view, doing so in art is somewhat more problematic. Aesthetics are more difficult to define and analyze. The championing of one set of color complements or textures over another, let us say, is a much more arbitrary proposition than declaring the truths of Maoist social analysis, or the need for modernization, which are at least purported to have been arrived at through a scientific method of social inquiry.

Like the world of feelings, emotions, and sexual attraction, artistic questions of beauty are not easy for a nation such as China to engage in. In modern Chinese literature there is an absence of the kind of personal torment or even personal commentary that is the hallmark of almost all Western novels. Such themes are neither a part of China's revolutionary tradition, nor her Confucian tradition, which stressed the need to maintain correct relationships between men of all kinds, rather than the well being of the individual soul. Their absence does not indicate that the Chinese are feelingless robots, but rather that all of these questions are really the expressions of keenly emphasized individual consciousness. They are expressions that the Chinese are either loath, or unable, to deal with, remembering back to the lamentations of the great Chinese essayist and short story writer Lu Hsün. Surveying the plight of an atomized China in the 1930s, he described his country as a "dish of loose sand."

And so Chinese art and literature remain heavily didactic, as a means of binding up all the grains of sand of this once disparate land into a unified whole. There are few divisive and illicit scenes of love and passion such as we find in Flaubert's *Madame Bovary*. No tortured, soul-stricken martyrs who raise suffering to a virtue such as we find in Dostoevsky. Art is at once didactic and collective, so that not only are political themes stressed, but the rise of certain artists to positions of prominence is discouraged. As in sports, "stars" are not singled out of an art troupe and placed on a pedestal. For this phenomenon, too, is considered destructive to the overall attempt to even out the discrepancies between people and classes of Chinese society.

Wherever one turns in China, one encounters efforts to channel this energetic society toward what I have referred to as the "public" rather than the "private." Whether one looks to the problem of deviants, the mentally ill, interpersonal relations, leisure, or art, one sees the hallmarks of a society that, up until now, has been attempting to aim itself in a direction almost diametrically opposite to that of our own. In China one has become a member of "the people" (we might say, "a good human being") by fitting into the group, not by endeavoring to separate oneself from it and establish one's own identity. One may be ambitious—there are ambitious people in China. But the acceptable paths of such striving have been in the public rather than the private domain. And in the next few years, if the post-Gang of Four liberalism should continue loosening the screws on political militancy and allowing more freedom of expression, it will be fascinating to watch and see what new chemistry develops between the world of the "public" and the "private."

The Shape of Chinese Values in the Eye of an American Philosopher

DONALD MUNRO

Donald Munro takes us to the heart of Chinese values. We see the ideas that heavily influence the individual: selflessness, understanding how your work fits in with that of others, the desirability of being a jack-of-all-trades, self-reliance. We see a further set of values that attach to society as a whole: equality of status, order (not always easy to reconcile with equality), listening to the views of the people, struggle, peer respect. Munro ends with a shrewd assessment of how much of all this is likely to endure into the 1980s.

Munro comes to the topic with training in both philosophy and classical Chinese. He is the author of The Concept of Man in Early China *(1969) and* The Concept of Man in Contemporary China *(1977). A third volume of the triology, on the medieval period, is under way. Munro, who is professor of philosophy at the University of Michigan, visited the PRC in August 1973, April 1979, and again in December–January 1979–80.*

—R.T.

People's motives are mixed. Many of us assume that others are motivated only by a desire to increase their wealth or their power. These are significant incentives, but it would be unwise to assume that there are no others. Yet this is exactly what many journalists and diplomats did in 1966 when they explained China's Cultural Revolution as merely a power struggle between Mao and President Liu Shao-ch'i. And it is what a number of economists did after 1958, when China initiated new economic policies at the same time that she turned away from Soviet-style practices in several areas. The economists reacted only to the "irrationality" of the Maoist criticisms of material incentives (such as money bonuses) and failed to evaluate fairly the preferred Maoist incentives. (In this essay, "Maoist" refers not to the radical faction that implemented the Cultural Revolution but to basic doctrines in Chinese Marxism as reflected in writings of Mao Tse-tung.)

There was much truth in these Western accounts of the place of power struggle and of Maoist illusions about the degree to which monetary incentives can be shunned. But the Western reporting of China was inaccurate because it ignored the fact that most of us also pursue ideals. The Cultural Revolution only comes alive if we take account of a Maoist ideal. That ideal is the quest for some level of status equality in China— a reduction of the gap between officials and ordinary people.

Even the most cursory consideration of one Maoist substitution for material incentives, "knowing the meaning of your work," reveals that it is based on acceptance of goals and ideals. "Knowing the meaning of your work" refers to understanding how your daily work is connected with other tasks in the factory, farm, or other enterprise, and how all the tasks together help to realize accepted local or national goals. Along with group respect, this is also "moral encouragement," as Premier Hua Kuo-feng used the term in discussing incentives in his 1978 speech to the Fifth National People's Congress: "moral encouragement and material reward must go hand in hand, with the emphasis on the former."

These incentives are not mysteriously Eastern. Effective, though embryonic, counterparts fall within commonplace American experience. Perhaps we assume that people are selfish, interested only in maximizing their own personal wealth or power, because of our "original sin" legacy, translated by philosophers into a portrait of man the hedonistic pleasure calculator and by psychologists into a picture of man with his innate aggressive instinct. While remaining mindful of the strength of money and power, in this essay I wish to round out the statement of human motivation, by portraying some ideals or intrinsic values that have also served as powerful goals. I will distinguish those values that the individual can embody as character traits from those that are sought for society in the aggregate, with special attention to China. I will trace value roots in Confucianism, the guerrilla experience, Marxism-Leninism, or elsewhere. The depth and contours of such values come into relief as they are compared with the values of the "individualism" that has long symbolized cardinal ideals in liberal democratic societies such as America and England.

Values of the Individual

Watch the train pull into the old city of Sian in 1976. Across the front of the engine in huge red letters is painted: "Serve the People," and everyone knows that means "rather than yourself." Look at the headline of the newspaper that person on the bus is reading: "Lei Feng Destroyed the 'I.'"

Selflessness, to which both of these statements refer, is one of the oldest values in China, present in various forms in Taoism and Buddhism, but especially in Confucianism. The selfless person is always willing to subordinate his own interest, or that of some small group (like a village) to which he belongs, to the interest of a larger social group. Foreigners have often encountered it in the parrot-like responses they have received from many students all over China to the question: "What do you want to do when you leave school?" Answer: "Whatever the People wish me to do." As a result of post-Mao policy changes aimed at increasing China's science capability, students are less reluctant to speak also about their personal educational interests, arguing that public service and the pursuit of personal academic interests can be congruent.

In Confucianism, the individual was always perceived as part of a network of related social positions. Confucians usually spoke not of single social positions but rather of hierarchical sets, such as father–son, younger brother–older brother, and husband–wife. The positions in any set were defined in terms of the duties and legitimate expectations that each had toward or from the other. Thus a person was not defined in terms of his own immediately perceived interests or abilities, but rather as the son of X, the father of Y, a peasant of Z village that had certain relations with other villages.

The harsh facts of economic survival usually lay behind the obligation of individuals in the family to subordinate their own personal interests to those of the larger clan to which they belonged. Forego an education yourself, so that the brightest member of the clan can be educated—money available for education being limited. He in turn will look out for the clan's financial well-being if he is successful in the civil service examinations. Today the social networks still include families. They also include basic production units like "teams" and "brigades" (brigades being equivalent to one or several villages), and, in the city, neighborhoods (which make up districts). In addition, they include social classes—thus a person may be defined, among other things, as a ' poor peasant." The social classes bear specific relations to each other. At the very least, a unit as vast as a class provides the member with certain expectations about how he or she will be treated by other members of the same or other classes in the society. For example, a man linked to one of the former landlord families knows that he might have certain problems marrying off his daughters to the most desirable young men, although this runs counter to official policy.

All ethical systems rely on untestable moral intuitions as the source of an underlying standard for deciding which goods should be prized over other goods. In Confucianism, the intuition was that fulfillment of the duties of your social position in the largest relevant social group had top priority (for example, the extended clan took precedence over the family; the center over the regional bureaucratic office). In imperial China as well as contemporary China, obedience and discipline to the chief relevant authority have often been taken as signs of selflessness, since the leaders of any organization always claim to work on behalf of the interest of the largest whole.

Our own history has no shortage of self-sacrificing persons who have been suitably honored for their work among the poor or their heroic battle deaths. But the idea of identity through group relations and of expected subordination of personal interests (including the individual's rights) to those of the group are absent in our view of self-sacrifice. Thus, Chinese selflessness conflicts with the first of several values we can subsume under individualism: the exercise of natural rights. (Indeed, in Chinese, the term "individualism" suggests selfishness, understood as the unnatural attempt to isolate the self from the group and to place personal interests over those of the group.)

We Americans speak of people being "endowed by their Creator with inalienable rights," which means that people possess rights as individuals apart from society, which has an obligation to protect them. The rights derive from their dignity or worth as individual "children of God." (Some Westerners argue for universal rights as necessary to the maximum happiness of all people; they do not accept the argument that rights come from God.) In the Chinese case, people are not conceived of apart from social groups. They only have characteristics that they take on by living in society.

Americans also believe with few qualifications that it is legitimate for the individual to pursue his own beliefs (the right to freedom of conscience), without concern for the impact of his choices on society as a whole. When we ask a student about his or her career plans, we expect an answer something like, "I intend to be a painter and follow my interest in art," and that is the end of it. If the key Chinese ethical values revolve around the duties adhering to various social positions, and to the largest relevant social group, the key American value is individual rights.

The Chinese constitutions of 1954, 1975, and 1978 contain references to rights. These include the right to freedom of speech and press, and the right to work, to education, to pension, to support in case of illness, and so forth. Does this mean that the Chinese are accepting a doctrine of individual rights akin to that which is so important in liberal democracies? Probably not. The rights that are important in Western liberal democracies are natural in the sense that individuals are said to possess them from birth. Other people can neither bestow them nor have license to interfere with them. These rights are different from the legal rights that can be granted by any organization to its members. (A store grants its employees the right to participate in a pension plan.) The rights cited in the Chinese constitution, especially those that are welfare-oriented, have more this latter quality of legal rights: they are features of the social system that can change as the political climate changes (a new constitution, a modified list of rights); they are not unchangeable properties that a Chinese individual possesses from birth. There is also the question of enforcement. In Western theory and practice, the identification of rights in a constitution has been closely associated with independent enforcement mechanisms, like our Supreme Court. There is no mechanism that plays this role in China.

In China, in the matter of free speech, there also has been a difference between constitutional principles and competing ultimate authorities. Faced with a specific case, officials regularly have invoked Mao's "six political criteria" in determining if a piece of writing and its author should be condemned, passing right over the matter of free speech. (The list begins: "Words and actions should help to unite and not divide the people of our various nationalities. They should be beneficial and not harmful to socialist transformation and socialist construction.")

There certainly are Chinese who get angry when their freedom of expression is abused. In the big cities, some people even hang up wall posters condemning abuses of their right of expression, as occurred in

Peking in November and December 1978. However, the consequences of repression of a right like freedom of speech are less likely to set off civil disturbance in China than they would be in America. We have here a good example of an area where central American and Chinese values do not converge: the doctrine of rights is not a part of the core of Chinese ethics, as we have shown.

A second idealized character trait of the individual is "knowing the meaning of your work." The educational process that ensures this learning usually takes place in one's small political study group, made up of co-workers, and it involves teaching something about the interrelatedness of tasks; for example, how a rural agricultural product is used by a city factory in order to make a substance required by the state to produce a weapon for national defense. Confucians regarded knowing the relation between subordinate tasks and ultimate goals as "knowing the difference between branches and roots." They held such knowledge as the key to tranquility.

We have experience with the cultivation of a comparable trait in certain elite military units noted for their high esprit de corps. Contrary to the views of some Marxists, the productive zeal in the Chinese work organizations and in the U.S. military units may not require participatory democracy. Nor does it require the elimination of routine, or of repetitive assembly-line-type work on part of a product (such as affixing hubcaps). Rather, it requires an acceptance of the group's goals and an understanding of how one's own routine tasks relate to them.

So far we have been talking about contemporary values that are rooted in Confucianism. Another infusion, derived from Marxism-Leninism, is the idealized character trait known as "all-round development." The Chinese are fond of citing a famous passage from *The German Ideology* in which Marx describes the new man who will emerge in Communist society after the elimination of the division of labor:

> . . . society . . . makes it possible for me to do one thing today and another tomorrow, to hunt in the morning, fish in the afternoon, rear cattle in the evening, criticize after dinner, just as I have a mind, without ever becoming hunter, fisherman, shepherd or critic.

Marx conceived this trait in almost Leonardo da Vinci-like terms: the all-round person has a multitude of disparate talents, including the artistic ones (the critical critic), and he has the ability to give expression to them all.

In contrast, the Maoist view of all-round development has been more limited. It has meant an ability and willingness, especially in youth, to do manual and mental labor and to regard both as equally worthy. This reformulation derived in part from the political need for unity and the consequent need to minimize status inequalities. In imperial China, the major status division had nothing to do with the Marxist idea of classes based on property ownership or lack of it. Rather, the classes were split between Confucian scholar-officials ("mind workers") and peasants ("hand workers"). In attempting to combat the continually lingering status gap, Maoists sought to enforce some role switching: students, teachers, and desk workers were sent for manual labor experience to farms and factories (or, in the case of students, school shops). And manual workers were in turn offered spare time education and low-level managerial participation (a form of mental labor). This reformulation of Marx's Leonardo ideal was also influenced by the manpower needs of a country that is modernizing economically. One of these needs is for technicians who have escaped the rote style of learning appropriate for classical studies and instead are able and willing to apply textual knowledge to the solution of practical problems. Thus the ability to combine mental and manual labor has also meant an ability and willingness to make the transition from theoretical knowledge (mental) to practical application (manual).

A Taiwan handicraft firm once lost business making lampshades for elegant American stores because the designers and executives, who were among the educated upper class, never went to the villages where the lampshades were made. The "mind workers" stayed at their desks with their pens and paper. No one ever explained to the hand-working villagers what they were making, and no one ever monitored whether or not the products conformed to specifications. Each lampshade was a different shape and size, with no quality control. Mainland Chinese factories had engineers who refused to leave their drawing boards for the workshops where the lathes are: the result was a perpetuation of design errors. China's all-round development plans have aimed at altering the habits stemming from the historical mental-manual gap that gives rise to such incidents.

Because fostering the ability to go from theory to practice, or from book to machine, helps promote the acquisition of technical skills, it continues as a pedagogical principle. However, a role switching labor requirement for teachers, desk workers, and university students is disruptive of technical training and professional work. This particular aspect of the pursuit of all-round development is unlikely to endure. The mixing of a manual labor experience with mental work continues principally at the primary and middle school level. In 1972 Chou En-lai exempted some students with extraordinary mathematical, artistic, and linguistic talents from the required two-year labor stint after middle school graduation. Today, most universities draw students directly from middle schools, and those students will not have additional factory or farm experience (unless it is academically justified for a given course).

Unlike "selflessness," the ideal of "all-round development" does not conflict with any of the values associated with Western individualism. Indeed, it is quite compatible with American ideals that have roots in the progressive education movement, beginning in the 1890s. John Dewey's attempts to introduce manual training and field experience into the American schools had two aims: one was to introduce the student to the whole range of occupations encountered in an industrial society and thereby cultivate positive feelings about the worth of many different occupations (this was not done in the traditional school, with its focus on the genteel arts and classics); the other was to promote problem-solving ability by "combining learning and doing," or texts with application. In this case the American and the Chinese ideals converge.

A third individual trait, self-reliance, emerged from the guerrilla experience of the 1930s and 1940s. It is a societal value as well. The exemplary guerrilla made his own rifle out of scrap wood and metal, and he poured his limited powder into shells himself, when he could not capture the factory item from the Japanese or KMT. The exemplary peasant similarly repairs his work team's tool and his own dwelling with scrap material, even though he may be entitled to material from public stores. This self-reliant trait is in periodic tension as attempts are made to minimize distributional inequalities by raising the living standards of the least prosperous peasants. (There are rich and there are poor communes as a result of differences in soil, weather, or water over which the inhabitants may have little control.) Those peasants on the low end of the material scale, working the less productive farm areas, may be more likely to remain poor as long as they are encouraged to make do with what they have, rather than ask for goods from the distribution center, which would have to take them from the wealthier areas. The value of self-reliance is promoted primarily in domestic behavior. In foreign policy, it is set aside as China's new leaders borrow foreign capital as part of rapid economic development plans.

Values of Society

In 1965, China ordered the elimination of overt signs of rank on military uniforms. Soldiers addressed each other as Old Wang, not Sergeant Wang; Old Li, not Colonel Li. Some recent visitors to China have noticed renewed use of titles denoting rank; however, even if there are aberrations from the principle of status equality, the ideal that lay behind it is likely to endure because equality of treatment in one form or another is the strongest and most nearly universal value in our world in the latter half of the twentieth century. One sign is the fact that leaders of many countries feel obliged to give reasons for treating some people differently (unequally) from others. We may agree or disagree with their stated reasons for doing so. We may agree that conviction of a crime of violence is grounds for unequal treatment (convicted felons lose certain rights that other citizens enjoy), while disagreeing that having parents who were factory owners is also a valid reason for forfeiting rights. But this is not the core issue.

The crucial issue here is the universal assumption that treating people equally needs no justification, no reasons. It is assumed to be intrinsically desirable. Only a hundred years ago, rulers would have had to justify equal treatment of their subjects. The assumption would have been that to do so was inconsistent with the natural hierarchies in human society, which derived in turn from the hierarchy God established in nature (God–angels–man–other animals–inanimate objects), or some other variation on this theme.

Several forms of egalitarian treatment have been stressed respectively in different societies: protection of equal rights, promotion of equal opportunity (primarily through education), equal distribution of wealth or income, and equality of status. The first two are less significant in China than the latter two. The leaders who succeeded Mao would argue that they are realizing equality of opportunity by increasing the number of middle schools; in 1978 there were four times as many students in such schools as there were in 1966. They would also claim that they advance that value by using written examinations that insure admission to college on the basis of competence rather than favoritism. And they assert that, with prosperity from modernization, those educational opportunities will continue to increase for the currently disadvantaged rural folk.

The Maoist value of equality of status has been a matter of attitude, which means that, with a few exceptions, people are not to be judged as more or less worthy or valuable to society because they come from one region or another, or because they engage in one kind of occupation or another (such as doing blue-collar or white-collar work).

Besides being intrinsically desirable, status equality has been regarded as essential to the realization of political order, which is another goal of society. The argument has been that the cohesive pursuit of common goals—whether economic, social, or patriotic—is only possible in the absence of serious social cleavages. Herein lies a contrast with the past. Confucian doctrine required social hierarchy as a means of ensuring order. The *Analects* says, "Let the prince be a prince, the minister a minister, the son a son . . . ," meaning that people should stick to the duties and expectations appropriate to their hierarchical social positions.

Practically speaking, status equality in China today has been expressed by a close interaction between occupational supervisors and workers or farmers, both in contact and ease of verbal communication; by a degree of shared lifestyle (on the surface, clothing is fairly uniform); and concurrently by the minimal use of blatant rank symbols. And yet, no ideal is devoid of tensions. There are qualifications: although from one perspective status equality and order are compatible, from another they conflict at times. For best efficiency, clear distinctions are often required between those who issue directives and those who receive them.

This difference is reflected in the simultaneous use of limousines and buses, available respectively for those who issue and those who receive directions. At the railroad station across the Hong Kong border, expecting that he has just arrived in egalitarian China, many a foreigner has been shocked to hear the Chinese request his group's protocol list. And when the foreigners reach Canton, there will be limousines for the delegation's leaders and buses for the other delegates, or two types of cars, a black Red Flag for the leader and gray Shanghais for others in the delegation. In administrative hierarchy lies ease of mind, and the Chinese are more comfortable when they can rank-order their foreigners. From a different perspective, then, administrative status is central to how a person is treated.

There will be additional strains on the egalitarian ideal as the Chinese seek to create a corps of high-level scientists and technicians. Passengers in limousines may soon include members of the scientific elite in addition to the administrative elite.

The ideal of status equality has some vitality in the United States. Politicians often feel compelled to claim humble origins even if they do not possess them. We frown on cultivated accents. But there is regional variation with roots reaching back to the eighteenth century: favored church pews were passed on from generation to generation in the families of the Southern elite, whereas in New England practice, the pews changed hands (seats?) every few years. In any case, in America status equality has never had the prominence as an ideal that it has had in Maoist China. Instead, Americans have been most concerned with equality in the form of the principle of equal rights (life, liberty, or freedom of belief, happiness, property).

The peasant's poster on the bulletin board near the commune headquarters attacks an official by name for irrationally assigning farming tasks without regard for the distance the individual peasants must travel to get to the various fields. When Chinese officials have tolerated citizen criticism, they have not invoked the natural right of freedom of expression; rather, they have justified the criticism by what they call the "mass line," which has some association with status equality.

When an official is encouraged to "go down to the villages and squat on a point," he is not receiving an obscene insult. Squatting on a point describes the first part of the principle of the mass line: "from the masses and to the masses." The "point" stands for a place within a larger area that has characteristics typical of the entire area. The language comes from the guerrilla period of the 1930s, when the Communists were head-quartered in northwest China and battled first the Japanese and then the Kuomintang troops.

The message is for the official to leave his desk and go spend time mingling with the local people who will be affected by a policy about to be formulated or modified. Eat with them; visit with them at work; find out how they really feel, and see if they have helpful suggestions. If a bridge needs to be built, for example, the people may have useful knowl-edge about local building materials, traffic patterns, or stress factors. Or the official may gain some insight into popular judgments about com-mune, provincial, or state policies, or about policy reform.

He then returns to his office (or military headquarters in guerrilla days) and, in consultation with others, decides on the best way to formulate a policy. "To the masses" refers to this process in which directives that reflect popular wisdom and the official's own ideas are explained to the people before they are enacted. The Chinese perceive this somewhat like the testing of a hypothesis; the directive may be modified on the basis of new information. "To the masses" is also the reminder that the central authorities give the directives, in spite of the democratic spirit that pre-vails during information gathering.

The mass line is significant from the Westerner's standpoint because it is the closest the Chinese come to the ideal of government by represen-tation in our own political system; some officials, like congressmen, are supposed to represent our views and be responsible to us. To enforce the mass line is to enforce a means for making officials responsible to the people over whom they have authority. But the practice of the mass line is also significant in being distinctive among Communist societies.

In Russia, from the early 1900s until 1917, the urban Bolsheviks ope-rated secretly in small cells. Important decisions were made by a few people without consultation among the rank and file. There was little alternative: to operate in the open or to widen the consultative base was likely to expose the leaders to identification and arrest by the Czarist secret police. The revolutionary work style became the method of gov-erning after 1918. In China, by contrast, after the initial débâcle of the 1920s in the cities, the Communists operated openly in the northwest. They were dependent on the rural villagers for intelligence concerning the movement of Japanese or Kuomintang troops, and for supplies in order to avoid long supply lines that were vulnerable to enemy sabotage. They had to interact closely with the villagers in order to sustain these services, and the mass line developed in this context. After 1949 Mao insisted, with varying intensity, on officials observing this principle in their peacetime functions.

The tension between the two aspects of the principle—democratic (from the masses) and centralist (to the masses)—is reflected in periodic policy fluctuations. One shift has occurred between centralized and decentralized decision making. Another shift has been between democracy (letting people speak out or have a voice in the selection of their leaders in lower-level work units) and centralism (the withdrawal of these rights in the name of the Party's maintenance of order and stability). There is, too, some tension between the ideal and the practice of the mass line, as suggested by the regular criticisms of officials for arrogance. The strength of the ideal is highlighted by drawing attention to the lapses in the practice. But this particular tension is also what gives an American most pause, for in spite of its flaws, his own brand of representative government has built-in institutional safeguards that can be used to get rid of officials who are not responsive to their constituents. These safeguards are election and impeachment. Most Americans have faith that laws will protect them against their rulers. They would feel naked without the legal barriers set up between various branches of government that prevent a dangerous concentration of power in the hands of one individual. Judging by citizen statements made in the Peking rallies of November and December 1978, some Chinese people desire institutional safeguards, which China has lacked. The official Chinese position has been to put primary faith instead in educating all citizens to respect and demand the mass line. Of course, it is possible that the rulers who succeed Mao will experiment with legal protections, what we would call civil rights. But they do not have much of a tradition here on which to build.

Harmony, or the avoidance of conflict, especially in the area of social relations, was a Confucian ideal of considerable strength. Maoists tried to replace it with the value of justifiable struggle. A short story written several hundred years ago reveals the potential for an acrimonious, sword-and-dagger dispute between two families over a property boundary. Both claimed the same piece of paddy field and both had some reasonable arguments. For one side to give in directly to the other would have shamed the entire yielding clan. However, throughout the life of the dispute, the surface relations between the two families remained cordial. The men could sit in the same market town teahouse, exchange greetings, and listen to the storyteller. The explanation? Hostility was deflected through a middle person who sought to reach a compromise between the two clans, endlessly suggesting, carrying threats from one side to the other, bargaining and conciliating. When one remembers that the principal contenders would have to live near each other for the rest of their lives, the argument was strong for mediating the dispute in this way rather than bringing it to a magistrate's court. In any case, it is an example of the Confucian ideal of harmony, as applied to social relations.

The same pre-modern ideal also applied to relations between man and nature: poetic themes reflected the wisdom of adapting to the natural events (death) that come one's way rather than attempting to control or fight them; similarly, planning daily acts (such as selecting different-colored clothes) to correspond with appropriate seasons, and placing one's dwelling in proper relation to the configurations of hills and streams, reflected the ideal of harmony. And it applied to man's internal psyche, where breath control and meditation helped foster a balance of *yin* and *yang* ethers within the body, with consequent tranquility.

The very strength of this traditional ideal of harmony is partially responsible for the virulence of the campaigns from 1949 until Mao's death to replace it with the ideal of struggle: the struggle of man against nature, when the need for a dam means slicing off a mountainside; and struggle within the psyche, against negative attitudes. But most of all struggle as an ideal in society, a class struggle between the progressive and the reactionary groups in China, no matter how these groups are defined. This is an ideal that derives from Marxism-Leninism, with its theory that antagonistic relations between classes lead to historical change. But it was reinforced by the experience when foreigners attempted to carve up China, and Chinese felt that the national penchant for harmonious compromise inhibited a strong response to the foreign enemy.

During Mao's life, intellectuals from "bourgeois" backgrounds frequently were the targets of class struggle campaigns. In a 1956 speech, Chou En-lai made two statements that differ considerably in spirit:

> Despising labor, the laboring people and government workers who come from families of working people, (intellectuals) refuse to mix with workers and peasants. . . . They have enormous conceit, thinking themselves Number One in the world, and refusing to accept anyone's leadership or criticism.

and:

> We should make suitable adjustments (upward) in the salaries of intellectuals on the principle of remuneration according to work, so that their earnings are commensurate with their contribution to the state.

These statements reflect the Maoist ambivalence toward China's intellectuals. Such intellectuals are untrustworthy, because they come from capitalist backgrounds; but China needs their skills, so she must encourage their reeducation and cooperation. In the cyclical policy fluctuations dating back to Yenan guerrilla days, the intellectuals have been the targets of some intense class struggle campaigns. The campaigns have been characterized by public verbal assaults on teachers, scientists, or their friends in the bureaucracy; by forced confessions of past attitudinal deficiencies or more serious deviant acts; and by removal to rural areas for labor, political reeducation, and sometimes loss of job. The periods of struggle have been followed by periods of reduced constraints on the books intellectuals may read and on the way in which political viewpoints must be stated in public writings. Sometimes teachers were reinstated in their former positions.

As of 1977, there was a new orientation in the Party's approach to the problem of intellectuals, dictated in part by the desire to enlist them in rapid economic modernization. In essence, the claim was made that most intellectuals, who are said to number 20 million, are now either from the worker or peasant classes or, if not, at least identify with those classes, and will willingly accept reeducation to correct their ideological deficiencies. In sum, no more anti-intellectual class struggle for a while.

Americans have no trouble identifying with the value of struggle. It has an early root in Western civilization, going back to the pre-Socratic Heraclitus ("War is the father of all and King of all," and "All things take place by strife"). In child-rearing practices, the value is manifest in the reinforcement of aggressive traits, especially in male children, and it is expressed in the esteem we place on athletic and sports competition. However, the focus on *class* struggle is alien to Americans, in view of the ideal of the value of individual dignity; it precludes raising or lowering the worth we assign to a person solely because of the social group (class) to which he belongs.

Advanced scientific and technical ability has been prized by members of all factions in China's political scene. But since the early 1960s, some of China's leaders have been willing to wait longer than others to attain a capability comparable to that of the advanced Western countries. They have tended to favor policies that hindered its rapid realization. After Mao's death, their opponents turned speedy modernization into a moral value, linked to patriotism and citizen welfare with the full weight of the country's moral education machinery transferred to it.

In 1966, as a result of conflict on the issue of the social costs of modernization the "key schools," which received better equipment than others and enjoyed special prestige, were condemned as "little treasure pagodas" (housing the nation's treasured students and providing them with a ladder to success), and terminated, only to be revived in 1977. Their revival is tied in with recognition of the urgent need to produce students able to acquire high-level scientific skills.

The question of the degree of speed with which to seek scientific capability is also intertwined with the issue of mass line, as it affects the locus of authority in education. Those favoring a rapid pace have tilted toward ultimate control by the Peking Ministry of Education over textbook content, curriculum, and criteria for student advancement. This is because they wish to retain quality control. Those willing to delay the attainment of an advanced industrial economy are in favor of enhanced equality of opportunity for students in poorer areas, and prefer decentralized authority, with local control of admissions. In spite of the conflict, there are political limitations now on the policies that either side may pursue. As a result of the Cultural Revolution, rural people have high expectations about the availability of education; to withdraw support from the ideal of universal education would be political dynamite. Hence the government of Hua and Teng has committed itself to the goal of universal, compulsory eight-year education in the rural areas by 1985.

One final ideal, with roots in traditional doctrine and practice, emerges with respect to society's responsibility to control its members. Rather than focusing on fear of judicial punishment for breaking penal law, this ideal approach employs the concept of peer respect (and, secondarily, avoidance of disrespect) to enforce compliance with rules or to motivate efforts toward the goals inculcated by education.

Several years ago a provincial newspaper in China carried a story about a four-year-old child who gave up his own playtime in order to pick up pig droppings for use as vegetable field fertilizer. He became an expert, and was awarded a plastic flower, a red rubber ball, and the title "Droppings-collecting Model." Chinese readers no doubt were as amused by the event as we are. But they would also recognize in it an expression of the value of peer respect.

The boy's title is significant. In principle, honor itself is intrinsically good, and other bounties are less important. Indeed, radical Maoists voiced fears that monetary awards help foster selfish traits. Thus from 1958 until 1977 the trend was to bestow mainly group honor on exemplary persons in all occupations. Peer respect was being used both as a prize for the individual on whom it was bestowed, and as an incentive for others who might be moved to greater efforts in hopes for the accolade. Factory workers would receive T-shirts, tea mugs, or pens with the title "Advanced Producer" emblazoned across them, or a banner for their work stations listing their accomplishments. They would be selected for these honors by the factory administration every three months from a slate proposed by their workshop mates. In spite of the expressed problems about material rewards, monetarily valuable goods were still made available to advanced producers without publicity, in such a way as to cloud any relationship between being a model and receiving the goods.

Advanced producers got first crack at factory-owned housing units, preferential admissions for themselves or their children to desirable schools, and financial bonuses (though not awarded at the time of selection as a model).

The opposite control technique is peer disapproval. It is difficult to forget the photographs of Teng Hsiao-p'ing riding around Peking on the back of a truck wearing a dunce cap during his period of disgrace in 1966. (Teng was then General Secretary of the Central Committee of the Chinese Communist Party. He was formally rehabilitated and made First Vice-Premier of the State Council in 1975, purged in April 1976 of all rank except Party membership, and reinstated to all posts in July 1977.)

In cities, factories, and schools, most Chinese belong to small groups that meet at least weekly. These are vehicles for the transmission of values through group study of texts. Participants might study the value of selflessness by reading Mao's essay on the Canadian doctor Norman Bethune, who treated wounded guerrillas and died of gangrene contracted in the course of his work. Or they might try to understand a new policy by reading and discussing a newspaper account of it. These small groups are also places where control over the individual through peer respect or disrespect can be rapidly and regularly exercised. The American "encounter group" and "T group" bear some faint resemblance to such Chinese organizations.

To some degree the Chinese authorities have no other choice than to use some nonmaterial incentives, because the country is not wealthy enough to permit large wage payments. However, respect and disrespect are highly effective techniques of social control in any society. And there are special conditions, among them the minimal mobility of the average Chinese, that make the application of positive and negative forms of group pressure especially effective there. In addition, the Confucian ideal of the importance of the individual's position and identity in a larger society helps to make such group pressure techniques very effective.

In the United States, if I like to leave my garbage scattered about my lawn, I may be inviting neighborhood disapproval in the form of spray-can graffiti. But even if this disrespect hurts my feelings, I need not overly fear it. I can always move to another neighborhood, perhaps choosing one more accepting of my style of living. In China, where I may have to look forward to a lifetime among the same neighbors or co-workers, there is much stronger reason for me to be sensitive to their opinions and attitudes. The potential flaw in the use of peer approval or disapproval in China is the increased occupational or geographical mobility that may come with industrialization and the large-scale movements of people to areas or districts of economic growth.

Americans are not unfamiliar with peer respect, but they encounter its systematic application much less frequently than do the Chinese. There is the occasional notice with appropriate photograph in *The New York Times* financial section honoring someone for selling $1 million worth of insurance. This is one of the "embryonic counterparts" of the Chinese use of nonmaterial incentives that falls within American experience. In China, however, the extent of the systematic application is staggering. As far back as 1959, some 3 million "advanced producers" were selected in the country, and this is not the only category of models.

The use of peer approval or disapproval as a control technique may often conflict with a second value included in "individualism"—privacy. Classical liberal thinkers such as J. S. Mill first made the point over a hundred years ago: Human progress is most facilitated when all of people's beliefs remain their private business, and when no one interferes with the cultivation of their own interests, however bizarre a lifestyle may seem in the eyes of the majority. Any official sponsorship in the United States of the use of peer respect to control people would be distasteful to many Americans.

How Much Will Last?

A number of the individual and societal values such as selflessness, knowing the meaning of work, and peer respect are deeply rooted in Chinese culture. Others, anchored in Marxism-Leninism, such as all-round development, will endure because they are associated with traits that promote economic growth. Equality of status and of educational opportunity are consistent with global sentiments at this time in history and therefore are reinforced by some amount of international favor, expressed by foreign newspapers and conveyed by groups visiting China. However, the existence of two groups which receive special privileges will continue to buffet severely this egalitarian ideal: the intellectual elite whose skills are needed in the modernization drive, and the occupants of the upper reaches of Party and administrative hierarchies, whose presence is required by the competing value of social order. And as the children of these groups regularly gain most of the places in the best middle schools and universities, opponents of the new policies will acquire arguments to question the scope of actual equality of educational opportunity.

The ideal of limited democracy in its Chinese sense will endure because of deep roots in the pre-"Liberation" massline policy and because of its utility in heightening work motivation. But again, a conflict with the competing ideals of order and stability, ensured by tight Party control, is inevitable.

The value most likely to change is class struggle, when it takes the form of nationwide campaigns purportedly involving people with different economic backgrounds. The violent struggle campaign is not congruent with traditional moral principles, which favor harmony and the avoidance of conflict. There is no evidence that mass struggle campaigns are required to solve China's development needs: they disrupted productivity by encouraging factory workers to attack managers and frequently to put down their tools to attend political meetings. The highly educated suffered the kind of verbal abuse that creates apathy and a lack of willingness to work. These mass class struggle campaigns were usually initiated and supervised by Mao himself, and Mao has gone. The elimination of campaigns need not undermine other means of minimizing the gaps in privilege between people of different occupations.

If many of these values do indeed endure, what can we say about the prospects for future convergence of American and Chinese ideals? It is a mixed bag. Our value of privacy draws double strength. It is basic to American popular morality; we want a private car and a personal lawn mower so we can go places or cut grass on our own schedule, not that of the neighbors. It is our own business whom we share our beds with and what we wear. And privacy is also enforced by law, as evidenced by the outcry over wire tapping and mail opening. Serious acceptance of this value by the Chinese is unlikely, given their view of the primacy of the social group. Similarly, selflessness as conceived by the Chinese will remain for many of us a remote and unfamiliar notion, fraught with images of asceticism and manipulation by rulers intent on coercing people in the name of the people's "deeper interests."* On these issues we will remain as far apart as Ursa Major and the animal that likes honey.

In other ways, China is just next door. The insoluble conflict between many of her values is mirrored in our own lives. China seems unable to satisfy her interest in ensuring academic standards for future scientists and in providing compensatory education opportunities for her peasant youth. So she abolishes entrance examination to universities, fills classes with unqualified students, and graduates "scientists" with an eighth-grade technical level. Then, just as abruptly, she moves to reestablish academically elitist schools and to bring back the tough examinations. America may not bump and jerk into the policies the way the Chinese do, but it has the worthy, competing claims of the advocates of affirmative action for women and minorities, and of the advocates of the maintenance of standards in its college and medical school admissions or corporate hiring.

If we share with the Chinese some of these perplexities about our ideals, at the same time we are both committed without qualification to

*Cf. Erica Jen's experience, p. 157.

one principle. The world has seen enough esoteric learning by nobles, priests, and scholars. If you have studied a physics textbook, you should be able to fix a light circuit; if you have read social philosophy, you should understand the implications of continuous warfare. Mao Tse-tung and John Dewey would both be comfortable to call this new form of education a combination of theory and practice. Mao spoke of the American "practical spirit" that is worth duplicating in China. This is another way of saying that we agree that it is a good thing for people to be self-reliant and to be able to solve technical problems. This is not a trivial matter on which our values converge, not an insignificant base for sharing some of the roads ahead.

The Past Is Still Present

ROBERT OXNAM

We turn for a moment to a broad and very Chinese theme. Robert Oxnam asks what is the Chinese view of the past, and shows in what large measure the past is still present. History does matter—and nowhere more than in China. Oxnam finds several pasts: cultural, national, revolutionary (itself now growing gray with time). He keeps in mind the difference between elite and grassroots feeling about the meaning of the past. He reminds us that the Chinese can be arcane about history, on occasion, as well as highly emotional, on other occasions.

There is a sense of purity to China's view of the recent—anti-imperialist —past, for the Chinese were on the receiving end. This raises an intriguing question as to whether the Chinese can go on clinging to that pure self-image while at the same time becoming a major world power. Moreover, as the generations pass, who can "speak bitterness" about the past?

In the end, perhaps surprisingly, the past seems to take a beating for the sake of the present moment and a hope for the future. Oxnam warns, however, that there is much in the Chinese memory that could quickly come to the surface if a major international crisis should confront Peking.

Oxnam is program director of the China Council of The Asia Society, from which this book derived, and he himself suggested the topic for **The China Difference.** Born in Los Angeles in 1942, the China Council's guiding force took his BA from Trinity College and his PhD in Chinese history from Yale. His major book, **Ruling from Horseback** (1975), is a study of the Manchu conquest of China. With Michel Oksenberg of the National Security Council, he also co-edited the recent **Dragon and Eagle,** the best up-to-date overview of Sino-American ties. Oxnam visited China in 1975, 1977, and 1979, and Taiwan in 1976.

—R. T.

A visitor with a camera can take a short stroll in today's Peking and record the simultaneous presence of "new China" and "old China." The "new China" is evident in the ubiquitous red propaganda banners and colorful billboards, the brick apartment complexes under construction, the myriad bicyclists in egalitarian garb of muted blues and grays, the recently planted trees on main thoroughfares, and the new seventeen-story Peking Hotel.

But a slight shift of the camera reveals the weathered appearance of "old China," with dusty alleys, small gray-walled residential compounds, tiny shops on the side streets, old men with wispy beards, old women with bound feet. A clever photographer can capture both the "old" and the "new" in a single scene—I recall a remarkable photo of an old woman clasping two grandchildren in front of a poster with Mao's slogan: "Women hold up half the sky."

It is much more difficult, however, to capture what the "new China" *thinks* about the "old China." What does the past mean to today's Chinese? What values are derived or reinforced by their views of the past? How different are Chinese views of their past from American views of history? What is happening as the Chinese become further removed not only from the dynastic period but also from much of their revolutionary past?

The past weighs heavily on the Chinese partly because there is so much of it. Even within living memory there are several pasts to reckon with: the collapse of a two-thousand-year-old imperial tradition in the face of colonialism and revolution; the emergence of Chinese nationalism; the clash between Communist and Nationalist revolutionary movements; the successful growth of a Communist state and society; the Maoist search for continued revolution; and the beginnings of a post-Mao era. Each of these successive epochs has left its distinct imprint on present-day China.

The impact of the past on the present, however, is due to more than just the sheer magnitude and turbulence of Chinese history. Contemporary Chinese seem to have a consensus about China's historical importance. It is a "we're number one" attitude that is expressed in a quietly confident way to outsiders. The consensus grows out of uniquely Chinese roots, with few clearcut parallels to the American experience. It is reinforced by three broad "lessons of history" in contemporary China: national and cultural lessons (the meaning of being Chinese in historical perspective); Chinese Communist lessons (the place of the CCP and the PRC in Chinese and world history); and popular lessons (the ties between ordinary Chinese and the broader sweep of history).

At the same time that we seek to understand this consensus, we must also observe that it seems to be losing some of its force and coherence in the post-Mao era. Nowhere is this phenomenon more apparent than in our last topic—the past in the eyes, and the hands, of China's leaders. China is still shuddering with the aftershocks of the deaths of Mao Tse-tung, Chou En-lai, and other elders of the Communist movement. Many of yesterday's heroes have become today's villains. Historical records have been tailored to suit new leaders and new goals. Cynicism is beginning to tear away at the tapestries woven in Mao's China.

So today's Chinese, although their eyes appear to be on the future goal of "comprehensive modernization by the year 2000," still confront some tricky problems in dealing with their past. What can they salvage of the consensus that helped propel Mao's movement for a half-century? Indeed how will Mao's legacy be treated now that his successors run China? Will there be new respect for the cultural and artistic achievements of China's four thousand years of pre-modern history?

National and Cultural Lessons

Shortly after a foreigner arrives in China, he begins to sense something of what the Chinese feel about their country. There is a powerful national pride that goes far beyond the routine propaganda statements. It is a gut feeling, which filters through almost every encounter, whether with ranking officials at a banquet table or with peasants on a commune. Much of this Chinese nationalism is derived from looking at present conditions and future aspirations in historical perspective.

History is bittersweet for contemporary Chinese. Over the course of their hundred-year revolution, the Chinese have had a special set of historical encounters that contribute to their sense of uniqueness today. They see themselves as having slowly released the powerful grip of the world's most long-lived ancient civilization. They see themselves as having survived the most fearsome combination of domestic chaos and foreign imperialism in modern experience. They see themselves as selectively using aspects of their traditional and modern historical experiences to create a society that has been unusually successful in combining modernization and revolution. In short, when the Chinese look at their past, they see the basic factors of rejection, survival, and creation behind the Chinese Revolution.

Mao Tse-tung (1893–1976), whose early life spanned the waning years of imperial China, played a major role in shaping contemporary Chinese views of the traditional period. His maxim, "Use the past to serve the present," requires an active involvement with history: one cannot simply appreciate the past, nor simply reject the past, but must use the past to suit the needs of the present. Mao's view, derived more from his experience as a Chinese Nationalist revolutionary than from his study of Marxism, was perhaps best captured in his poem, "Snow," written in 1936. The first stanza expresses Mao's deep love for the Chinese land:

> This is the scene in that northern land;
> A hundred leagues are sealed with ice,
> A thousand leagues of whirling snow.
> On either side of The Great Wall
> One vastness is all you see.
> From end to end of the great river
> The rushing torrent is frozen and lost.
> The mountains dance like silver snakes,
> The highlands roll like waxen elephants,
> As if they sought to view in height with the lord of heaven,
> And on a sunny day
> See how the white-robed beauty is adorned with rouge,
> Enchantment beyond compare.

The second stanza places historical accomplishments in Mao's revolutionary perspective, emphasizing the greatness of today's heroes compared to past emperors:

> Lured by such great beauty in our landscape
> Innumerable heroes have rivaled one another to bow in homage.
> But alas, Ch'in Shih-huang and Han Wu-ti
> Were rather lacking in culture,
> T'ang T'ai-tsung and Sung T'ai-tsu
> Had little taste for poetry,
> And Genghis Khan
> The favorite son of heaven for a day
> Knew only how to bend his bow to shoot great vultures.
> Now they are all past and gone.
> To find heroes in the grand manner
> We must look rather in the present.

This Maoist view of the past is symbolized in Chinese outlooks on monuments from the imperial era. In Peking, for instance, much of the magnificent architecture, walls, and gates have been destroyed by successive waves of invaders, warlords, and revolutionaries (including the Communists). But a few monuments—the Forbidden City, the Temple of Heaven, the Summer Palace, the Ming Tombs—have been restored by the present regime. These national landmarks, formerly the private preserve of the imperial elite, are now open to the general public. Tour guides and well-posted signs teach the "correct" view of the monuments, describing both the enormous costs in human terms and the enormous cultural achievements. In a burial vault at the Ming Tombs, for instance, an impressive chart shows the expense in terms of millions of man-hours of conscript labor and millions of silver bars.

The message is clear: Reject the elitist society that sponsored these monuments; revere the genius of the workers who created them. The message may appear sterile on the chart, but it seems alive to some of the Chinese visitors who come to these monuments by the thousands. The pleasure of a holiday picnic is enhanced by the splendor of these once-forbidden places. Watching children climbing up Ming Dynasty stone camels and soldiers listening to transistor radios in the Forbidden City, it appears that the Maoist view is indeed a popular view. Even without reading the signs, the Chinese visitors are rejecting the old society, appreciating ancient creativity, not to mention having a good time.

Another historical factor behind Chinese national pride stems from the Chinese experience with Western imperialism. Chinese see their history from the 1840s onward as filled with threats from every quarter—the British, French, Russians, Japanese, Americans—and filled with Chinese efforts to resist the foreigners and protect the integrity of their nation. Memories of this imperialist past strongly influence contemporary Chinese views of the world. Their continued sense of vulnerability to foreign pressure stems from their sense of the pervasiveness of imperialist threats in an earlier era. And their sense of resilience arises from the fact that the Chinese succeeded in their effort to avoid becoming anybody's colony.

But there is a major difference between Chinese views of the imperialist past and the outlooks of many other peoples who have confronted foreign domination, such as the Russians, the Japanese, and the Americans. From a Chinese perspective, each of these countries has moved from a threatened position to becoming an imperialist power itself—the Russians from Lenin's revolution to Brezhnev's 1968 invasion of Czechoslovakia, the Japanese from their Meiji restoration to Tojo's invasion of mainland Asia, the Americans from Washington's revolution to LBJ's intervention in Vietnam.

By contrast the Chinese feel a sense of purity. They see themselves as having been wholly on the receiving end of Western and Japanese imperialism, without having had imperialist ambitions of their own. It is an historical outlook which carries a ton of suffering but not an ounce of guilt.

Views of the imperialist past influence the ways in which contemporary Chinese deal with foreigners. The slogan, "self-reliance," and the relatively autarkic economic approach it represents, express the Chinese conviction that they will never again come under foreign economic domination. Although Chinese foreign trade has more than quadrupled since 1969, they are very careful to keep that trade diversified among several countries to prevent dependency on a single source (memories of severe economic dislocations after the Sino-Soviet split in 1960 are particularly acute in China). The Chinese place limits on visitors to China, not only in numbers but also in where and how they travel, even to the point of keeping Chinese and foreigners in separate dining rooms and on separate floors. And most foreign expatriates living in China find that they are still denied PRC citizenship and still kept apart from many political activities.

Arising from a combination of Chinese views of the traditional past and the imperialist past is a strong sense of destiny in world affairs over a long span of time. Confidence is reinforced by the remarkable staying power of the traditional Chinese civilization and the equally remarkable resurgence of the Chinese Revolution against the forces of imperialism. The Chinese believe that time and the thrust of history are on their side.

With this sense of national destiny comes patience, a most unusual characteristic among revolutionaries. Sun Yat-sen once commented to a group of frustrated Russian revolutionaries that he did not expect the Chinese Revolution to succeed for a hundred years. Mao often spoke in time frames of hundreds and even thousands of years. Indeed he once said that Marx, Engels, Lenin, and Stalin will probably "appear ridiculous" in a thousand years.

But patience must not be confused with complacency. The modern view of Chinese destiny has been shaped by active involvement in a revolution. It is a far cry from the traditional "Middle Kingdom" concept which portrayed China as the sophisticated center of civilization deserving homage from the rest of the "barbarian" world. China is now seen as part of the third world, but a leading part because of the special nature of her twentieth-century history and her size. The Chinese capacity to turn backwardness into revolutionary strength leads to the Chinese belief that other third world countries will learn from her experience.

Armed with this new concept of destiny, the Chinese interpret their recent history with growing confidence. New measuring rods are employed to gauge China's rising stature in the world, among them the Chinese atomic bomb, first exploded in 1964, the PRC's seating in the United Nations in 1971, and full relations with Japan and the U.S.

The despair of the early twentieth century, prompted by the collapse of the old order and the encroachments of imperialism, has been replaced by confidence in China's role as a world power. A new mix of values—

cultural pride, anti-imperialism, and national destiny—has come together out of contemporary Chinese views of past and future.

Chinese Communist Lessons

Today's China is portrayed as the rightful heir to the concepts of national and cultural identity. Just as the revolution has swept away much of the old society, the Communists have rewritten the history of the dynastic period. The new history is designed to give legitimacy to the victors in the Chinese Revolution—the CCP and the popular forces behind the revolution. The Communists have rejected the old views that the "golden age" was in the past, that emperors and officials dominate history, that history is a story of Confucian concepts in action, and that history records the glories of an imperial "Middle Kingdom."

Instead, the new history is based on Chinese Marxist concepts: history is a record of progress toward a future age of communism, a story of the masses and their popular leaders, a scientific tool that describes material forces in action. The only similarity between the new set of concepts and the old one is that both are based on the Chinese belief that history teaches profound lessons, which must be taken to heart.

The new concepts give contemporary Chinese a sense of a place in both Chinese and world history. The Chinese see themselves as part of a living historical process in which the PRC is a critical link between past and future. History is relevant because the PRC is relevant. This notion of national importance in a world historical continuum, of knowing what one is for and what one is against, seems vaguely reminiscent of American outlooks in the 1940s and early 1950s, before Vietnam and Watergate began to cloud the proud self-image.

The belief in an historical continuum prods the Chinese to keep grappling with their past. They adjust historical interpretations to suit new political lines, constantly fiddling with the rear-view mirror as it shifts course between the road to rapid economic modernization and the road to continued revolutionary zeal.*

Such fiddling means that historical debates and political debates are intertwined in China. Prerevolutionary history, for instance, has caused trouble for the PRC. The trouble arises from the growing recognition that old practices and beliefs still persist among the Chinese people even after the Communist victory. Mao's concern about historical counter-revolutionary forces was one more important cause of that violent era in

---

*Unlike dynasties of old, the PRC has not developed an official "comprehensive history" of China or the Chinese Communist movement. The PRC leadership is well aware that such "comprehensive histories," always written by new dynasties to justify their takeover, can freeze a new regime's view of itself and offer a target for opposing factions.

the late 1960s known as the Great Proletarian Cultural Revolution. With Mao's blessing, millions of Red Guards went on a rampage, seeking to root out anything resembling traditional China. The Red Guards took the "four olds" as their enemy ("old customs, old habits, old culture, old social thought") as they toppled statues, burned books and buildings, ransacked museums, and humiliated teachers, scholars, poets, and artists. The Cultural Revolution sought to kill the ghosts of the Chinese past, once and for all. It failed to achieve this goal, but the Cultural Revolution left deep imprints on contemporary Chinese.

One such imprint is found in the "brief introductions" given to foreign visitors at various institutions—described elsewhere by Orville Schell. The Cultural Revolution slogan, "Emphasize the present," is evident in the Chinese reluctance to give detailed accounts of the past. Instead, one hears a terse rendition of institutional history, centered on three dates (1949: Liberation; 1966: Cultural Revolution; and 1976: Purge of the "Gang of Four"), and after each date things are perceived to be much better than before. The distant past is ignored and the recent past compressed in a rush to focus on the present.

A less violent effort to deal with traditional legacies was the "Criticize Confucius" Campaign of the early 1970s.* This campaign brought a systematic reassessment of the traditional era, pointing out the negative and positive forces that still had a grip on contemporary China. The movement reflected Mao's belief that history is filled with conflict between the bad guys who supported "class restoration" and the good guys who supported "class struggle," and that modern political conflicts were closely connected to ancient historical conflicts. Mao believed that post-1949 China was in a critical Marxist transition period, between "capitalism" and "socialism," and thus he felt that understanding the ancient transitions, particularly between "slave" and "feudal" periods, had considerable contemporary relevance.

The campaign's arch villain was Confucius, the fifth-century B.C. philosopher whose beliefs in a hierarchical society dominated by intellectuals was revered by Chinese scholar-officials throughout most of the imperial period. But in Mao's view, the Confucians were malicious reactionaries who slowed down the Marxist train of history by trying to restore "slave society." The heroes in the campaign were the followers of the Legalist School, which had its origins in the fourth-century B.C. and contributed to the building of the first Chinese Empire under Ch'in Shih-huang in the third century B.C. Mao portrayed the Legalists, traditionally seen as cruel tyrants obsessed with laws and punishments, as

---

*Later in this essay I explore the leadership struggle behind this campaign and the changed outlook on Confucius in the post-Mao era.

enlightened progressives who sought to propel China through the Marxist "feudal society."

On this level the campaign looks like a rather strained academic debate, as if Westerners were told to look at their history as one long struggle between the outlooks of Hamilton and Jefferson, or between Gladstone and Disraeli. On the contrary, my impression during a visit to China in 1975 was that the "Criticize Confucius" Campaign had widespread impact—perhaps more far-reaching than any educational movement besides the Cultural Revolution itself.

Museums, which are considered important educational institutions in China, were revamped to illustrate the ongoing Legalist-Confucian tensions throughout history. Archeology, a highly touted field in China, enlivened the museum exhibits and pinpointed the dividing line between "slave" and "feudal" societies (continuing the ancient Chinese obsession for precise historical periodization). Evil Confucians and enlightened Legalists were described in the major magazines and newspapers, in hundreds of high-circulation pamphlets, in a rash of new comic books and posters. People read these publications with what seemed like biblical devotion in bookstores, in classrooms, in factories, in communes, on the streets, on buses. Even kindergarten children were brought into the act as they performed anti-Confucian dances with wooden swords to slash away at the villains of the past.

Once again, as in the Cultural Revolution, Mao had launched a campaign that touched sensitive nerves among a substantial part of the Chinese population. Although Confucian civilization died with the end of the last dynasty in 1911, many Confucian traits persisted: the quest for privileged positions and "soft" lifestyles, the unquestioned respect for elders and those in authority, the subordinate role of women in a male-dominated society, and the esteem for intellectuals rather than workers and peasants. Thus the "Criticize Confucius" Campaign vividly highlighted the ongoing struggle between traditional and revolutionary values.

While the Chinese Communists have discovered enduring—and often ominous—signs of life in traditional history, they have seen the more recent history of the nineteenth and twentieth centuries as the most lively of all. It is a history with direct connections to the Chinese Communist Revolution—a living past, filled with demons, heroes, and saints.

The demons of the recent past are neatly catalogued as "enemies of the revolution" in CCP terminology. They include imperialists, comprador merchants (those who worked for foreigners), Chinese Nationalists, warlords, big landlords, big capitalists. Although these categories fill the pages of PRC high-school texts in rather bland fashion, they come alive at night in movies, plays, operas, and dance dramas. These performances feature stock villains: the slinking Nationalist agent in a trenchcoat, the fidgety Japanese colonel in his too tight uniform, the drunken loud-mouthed landlord.

The audience usually laughs at the sight of the familiar villain, but it takes many of his lines quite seriously. The villain is not only a reminder of recent history, but also a symbol of the "bad elements" in today's China. The PRC regime holds that a "handful of bad elements" (sometimes numbered at 5 or 10 percent of the population) still exists and seeks to bring back the pre-1949 society. The most oppressive reflection of this view, at least in Western eyes, is the continued practice of recording the "class background" of every citizen of the PRC. The children, grandchildren, and even great grandchildren of former "bad elements" still suffer the sins of their forebears. They face discrimination in admission to higher education, entry into the army, membership in the Party, and employment in cadre-level positions.*

The classic demon to emerge from the recent past is the "revisionist" who commits the unpardonable sin of pretending to support communism while wanting to restore capitalism—a Marxist equivalent of the "Uncle Tom" or "Oreo" to black Americans. Since the Sino-Soviet split of the early 1960s, the Soviets have been tagged as "revisionists" and seen as China's most serious threat. Mao came to see the Soviet model of development not only as irrelevant to China's needs, but also as a sellout of Marxist-Leninist principles. Increasingly, Mao also saw the Soviets as "superpower imperialists" who threatened China's sovereignty, an outlook that was confirmed in Chinese eyes by the 1969 Sino-Soviet border hostilities.

The allies in the continuing battle against demons are the heroic rebels of Chinese history. Unlike the Chinese Nationalists, who follow the traditional practice of vilifying most peasant rebels, the Chinese Communists applaud the rebels as bold precursors of the Maoist revolution. Elementary-school textbooks relate the romantic adventures of ancient Chinese Robin Hoods and recount tales of the nineteenth-century Taiping rebels and the Boxer rebels of 1900. The same heroic rebel message is conveyed to high-school students and adults. For example, a dance drama called *The Small Sword Society* portrays a valiant but unsuccessful uprising in Shanghai in the 1850s. The hero and heroine, a handsome couple with romantic as well as revolutionary intentions, battle a wide array of imperialist demons (including an American who looks like Simon Legree), before suffering defeat and death.

*This policy is currently under review by the Hua Kuo-feng administration and it is possible that such discrimination will be lessened in the years ahead; Munro and Li discuss this possibility in their essays.—R.T.

This heroic rebel theme, focusing on two thousand years of peasant uprisings, is significant to contemporary historical outlooks. Mao's break-through was his discovery that a nationalist peasantry could be organized into a revolutionary movement. Until Mao, everyone—including Marx and Lenin, as well as Sun Yat-sen and Chiang Kai-shek—had seen the peasants as subordinate forces in a revolution. Mao's new concept, once it was organized into a full-scale peasant revolution, brought a dramatic change in history lessons. The losers in a five-thousand-year history—the peasants and most of the peasant rebels—now achieved their posthumous victory in the Maoist revolution. Ironically, now that Mao is gone, peasants may actually find their lot improving in the agricultural modernization program, though their revolutionary status may be declining.

Mao's concept of peasant revolution brings us to the most exalted chapter in Chinese lessons about history: the Communist movement itself. The CCP is portrayed as the link between the present and all the past that preceded it, as the organizing force that gave the Chinese the capacity to realize the peasant rebels' dreams and the energy to cope with the demons of past and present. In this view, the specific details are less important than the general spirit of the Chinese Communist movement (indeed the details have been distorted badly by CCP leaders over the past fifty years). Thus the Chinese popular view centers on a sequence of dramatic moments and towering leaders, much as popular American history sees a progression centering on the Pilgrims, Washington's revolution, Lincoln's Civil War, and FDR's New Deal.

And during the 1960s and early 1970s, the popular outlook was filtered through a sort of Maoification. The man and the myth were blurred together as Mao assumed saintly stature. Mao was portrayed as an historical figure of unparalleled significance—the man who realized the revolutionary potential in twentieth-century China by selecting from history, both Chinese and Western, the variety of ideas and organizational techniques called "Mao Tse-tung thought."

Mao's life became a religious history, a story of revealed truth over time. Too sacred for the mass media of film, drama, or opera described by Roxane Witke, Mao's life was revealed through his own writings, the "little red book" of *Quotations* as well as the five-volume *Selected Works,* and through shrines commemorating famous places and eras in his career. At Mao's birthplace, Shaoshan in Central China, people still line up by the thousands each day to walk through his home and to have their pictures taken as a souvenir. Most of the visitors pass more rapidly through the Shaoshan museum of photographs and Mao memorabilia; and perhaps only Western Sinologists note the remarkable distortions, inaccuracies, and omissions in recording the history of Mao and the CCP (despite what museum labels indicate, for instance, Mao did *not* achieve paramount leadership in the CCP until 1935).

The Cultural Revolution brought the Maoification of Chinese Communist history to new heights of intensity. On one level, the Cultural Revolution was Mao's effort to recreate his own life and the Long March atmosphere for a new generation of Chinese who had grown up since 1949. He was seeking to turn a classroom memory of a revolutionary past into a living reality of the revolutionary present. Behind the Cultural Revolution and the "Criticize Confucius" Campaign was Mao's hope that vital links to the past would not die with him.

Today Mao's status in the Chinese Communist Revolution seems a bit shaky. The corpse of Mao has begun to wither away and so has his reputation. Indeed some have suggested that 1976 represented a smashing of the "Gang of Five" with Mao being the unnamed fifth member. At the very least, we are seeing another spin in the wheel of rewriting history to "serve the present."

Popular Lessons

What about the ordinary person in China? Many of the beliefs discussed so far, under the labels of national/cultural lessons and Chinese Communist lessons, appear to be shared by much of the Chinese population. They are concepts that move the Chinese to respond knowingly when they see an historical play or ballet, when they watch an historical film, when they read an historical pamphlet or wallposter.

But the fact that the concepts are shared does not mean that they are based on a detailed knowledge of history. At museums, for instance, a curious and bewildered crowd is sure to gather if a foreigner starts to recite dynasties or emperors. Most Chinese know as few details about their history as most Westerners know about theirs.

For people in both societies, the past comes alive only when there is some kind of personal connection, an emotional entry point that gives history relevance. Occasionally that connection occurs on a national level, such as the Anti-Confucian Campaign in China or the television series "Roots" in America. But more often the link to the past is limited to a specific group, a specific region, or a specific generation. In the West, one learns a lot on an anecdotal and emotional level by listening to people directly affected by the Depression, Hitler, the world wars, and race riots. The same is true in China concerning experiences with the Warlord era, the Anti-Japanese War, the Shansi Famine, land reform, or the Civil War.

But there is one major difference—the Chinese have made a much more organized effort to relate personal historical experiences to national historical outlooks. On this point the Maoists agree with a traditional Chinese view: personal experience must fit into a national system of beliefs.

The cement in the bonding process between individual history and general history is the belief in personal sacrifice for the revolutionary cause. The belief in sacrifice gives a sense of meaning to the otherwise meaningless human tragedies of twentieth-century China. It thus turns personal and family losses into revolutionary gains, bringing individual experience to the national/cultural and Chinese Communist lessons about the past.

One approach to linking personal feelings with general lessons, widely used by the Chinese Communists for over fifty years, is known as "speaking bitterness." I have attended a few of these public testimonials designed to create a sense of shared historical pain among young and old. A grizzled Shanghai dockworker tells a group of younger longshoremen about the bad old days of pauper's wages, sixteen-hour days, corporal punishments, company stores, company scabs, and broken strikes. A former prostitute and opium addict describes her childhood abduction, her Japanese pimps, her brutal beatings, her attempted suicides, and eventually her painful withdrawal from addiction after Liberation. Sometimes the younger generation "speaks bitterness" as well. A young woman in Hupei describes her father's strong objections when she wanted to do "man's work" on a team tending high-tension electrical wires. With considerable conviction, the woman acknowledges that she really did not understand the Anti-Confucian movement until her father firmly refused and uttered an old saying, "Expecting that woman can do man's work is like hoping that the rabbit's tail will grow longer." Finally, with some persuasion from the Hupei Women's Federation, her father relented and now she is a member of an all-women high-tension wire team.

It is too easy for a foreigner to dismiss this "speaking bitterness" with cynicism. That cynicism must be tempered by the recognition that these sessions have become an important part of everyday life in China, a way of linking oneself with a larger whole, perhaps not altogether different from the mixture of ritual and conviction that some Catholics bring to a daily confessional.

Such techniques for relating the personal to the national, and the past to the present, take on heightened significance when one considers the generation gap in China. A person would have to be about forty today to have any substantial personal recollections of pre-Liberation China. A rough guess would place some 600 million Chinese under age forty and perhaps 400 million Chinese under age twenty, out of a total population of one billion. Just as a personal knowledge of history now begins with Watergate and the end of the Vietnam War for American high-school students, Lin Piao's assassination attempt on Chairman Mao is probably the personal starting point for many Chinese middle-school youth. The new generation in China lacks any direct experience with revolution and imperialism, or even with the Cultural Revolution and the Sino-Soviet border conflicts of the late 1960s.

How can such limited personal experience be transformed into shared national experience in the post-Mao era? Mao's notion of "permanent revolution" required that the deep-seated belief in personal sacrifice, a key value for the founders of the Chinese Revolution, would be passed on to generations of successors. Mao's worries that sacrifice would be forgotten were clearly expressed in a poem written to Chou En-lai in 1975:

Loyal parents who sacrificed so much for the nation
Never feared the ultimate fate.
Now that the country has become red, who will be its guardians?

Our mission unfinished may take a thousand years.
The struggle tires us, and our hair is gray.
You and I, old friends, can we just watch our efforts be washed away?

China's Leaders Struggle over the Lessons of History

The generation of Mao Tse-tung and Chou En-lai spanned the whole course of the Chinese Revolution. They shaped the national, cultural, Communist, and popular lessons about the past. They were makers of history in part because they were so deeply aware of the history that preceded and surrounded them. They seemed to have a capacity to leap back into the past, take a critical look around, and come back to the present with a new sense of energy and purpose. Knowing that history, they seemed to be able to use it for revolutionary ends without being seduced by the lure of the past.

The Chinese Communist leadership has long seen its own history as a "struggle between two lines." While we outside China may view PRC political battles as power struggles apart from ideology, the leadership has never shared this viewpoint. Although power struggles are clearly involved, the winners and losers in Chinese Communist politics both contend that they are perpetuating a "correct line." By "line" they mean not only a set of policies, but a general ideological thrust that has a genealogy back through history. It is a genealogy that extends through Mao, through a set of "correct" CCP leaders, further back through to Stalin, Lenin, Engels, and ultimately Marx. Since Marxist history is dialectic, there are always "two lines" operating, a correct line and an incorrect line, a progressive line and a reactionary line.

At this point, the non-Marxist foreigner tends to find his credulity stretched a bit by a tautology. Since the winners are always representing the "correct line," the losers are always painted as demons, and history is rewritten each time around.

History must be rewritten to serve present needs; what else is history for? Here most Westerners differ sharply with the Marxist viewpoint. Of course, our own historians are rewriting history under the name of "historical revisionism" (a term that will bring a smile to Chinese lips). And of course, we have some classic cases of politicians distorting their memoirs to justify their policies.

But those schooled in non-Marxist Western traditions reserve a strong sense of outrage for tampering with the past, corrupting facts, distorting the truth. New ideas, new contemporary issues, and new sources of evidence may change our outlooks on the past—but very few would argue that the truth is served by ignoring facts and twisting a record to suit a new political line. Indeed, "using the past to serve the present" might well be grounds for the dismissal of a journalist, the public criticism of a politician, or the ostracism of an historian in the West.

But what about the Chinese people? How do they view their historical clashes at the top? From reports in the 1960s and from a few observations in the early 1970s, it appeared that many people shared the general viewpoint of the leadership. The new interpretations, offered in *People's Daily* and other periodicals, were discussed, debated, and personalized in many institutions and homes in China. But there has been so much topsy-turvy historiography, keeping rhythm with Chinese politics, that a creeping cynicism is emerging in certain quarters. One example is a 1976 wall poster in Canton that draws on the history of Vice-Premier Teng Hsiao-p'ing, who has twice been purged and twice restored in the past dozen years. The wallposter reflected the "correct line" of the time: "Fiercely Criticize Teng Hsiao-p'ing." But in the interest of economy and cynicism, the wall poster still remained in late 1977, with three new words written over it so that it then read: "Fiercely Criticize the Gang of Four." An ingenious example of "using the past to serve the present."

The protagonists in the "struggle between two lines" often use difficult historical metaphors and allegories in their debates. Here the Chinese Communist leadership is perpetuating an ancient tradition of playing factional politics by talking in historical imagery, "Using the mulberry to point to the ash," as the old Chinese expression has it. This tricky game of political backbiting in historical code, a game with deadly significance for losing players, was often played late in Mao's life.*

---

*The most complex historical allegory game was played in the early 1970s around the "Criticize Confucius" Campaign. While the campaign dealt with issues of revolutionary *vs.* traditional values at the popular levels, it was actually a fierce contest among political personalities and policies at the highest levels of PRC leadership. Mao was clearly equated with Ch'in Shih-huang, the good guy in the campaign. But who was Confucius? As the

But why do the Chinese do this at all, why drape political conflicts in historical garb? One possible reason is a Chinese penchant for subtlety, particularly when dealing with explosive issues. The 1970s battle was clearly a succession contest. Mao and Chou were dying and their possible heirs, both the radical and moderate factions, were fighting for leadership. In a Chinese view, it would be unseemly to acknowledge that they were fighting over two near-corpses. Another reason is that historical allegory permits a game to be played on several levels, each level with its own political significance. It permits a political faction to initiate a debate as a "trial balloon," seeing how and whether opposing factions will respond to the initiative. It permits a period in which the top leaders can try to rally support among subordinate leaders, the "inner court" reaching out to the "outer court" in traditional parlance, before bringing the whole struggle out into the open. And it eventually permits the leadership to develop a public education campaign around the issues and personalities involved. The historical allegories are a contemporary use of the past that parallels a traditional use of the past in form but not in content.

Since Mao's death in September 1976 the Chinese have continued the patterns of seeing things in "two lines" and using historical imagery. For many Chinese, Hua Kuo-feng's rise to power must seem like a replay of successful "dark horse" emperors in traditional history—complete with a battle over Mao's will, a fight over Mao's body, a palace coup by Mao's bodyguard, a purge of Mao's widow and her faction, and a public campaign for legitimacy by the Hua leadership. The late 1976 "Smashing of the Gang of Four" (Ms. Mao and three radical colleagues) appears like a chapter out of Ming or Ch'ing Dynasty court history: a quick removal of the leaders of an opposing faction, a clear indication of new and more "moderate" policies, and the creation of new villains for the Chinese people in a period of anxiety. In pushing the "Smashing of the Gang of Four" Campaign to the limit over 1976–77, Hua and Vice-Premier Teng Hsiao-p'ing have missed few opportunities to blacken the reputations of the purged foursome with historical parallels. In national publications and colorful wall poster cartoons, for instance, Ms. Mao was likened to the "grasping, crafty, greedy" Empress Wu of the T'ang Dynasty (note alas, this very traditional view of the Empress Wu has done little to

campaign began, it appeared that the more radical leaders (now called the "Gang of Four") were equating Confucius with Chou En-lai, both seen as reactionaries from a radical point of view. But as the campaign progressed, Chou En-lai counterattacked by adding the name of the dead defense minister Lin Piao, once a radical leader but disgraced by trying to assassinate Mao, and equating Lin Piao with Confucius (thereby taking the heat off Chou and turning the attack on the radicals). Thus Chou won the contest by expanding the "Criticize Confucius" Campaign into the "Criticize Lin Piao, Criticize Confucius" Campaign.

promote Chinese confidence about women in politics).

A major problem for the post-Mao leadership is how to deal with Mao himself now that he too is part of history. Like any charismatic leader with a long career, Mao left a complex legacy open to a variety of interpretations and political uses. How then to contain Mao, to prevent Mao's ghost from roaming wild like Confucius' ghost? Physically and symbolically, Mao is now at rest in a crystal coffin in a mausoleum in T'ien-an-men Square. But how can Hua make it clear—it is not very clear in the historical record—that his leadership has the complete blessing of Mao?

In 1977 huge posters were put up in China depicting a benign, seated Mao looking gently at Hua and handing him a note that reads: "With you in command, my heart is at ease" (an episode that is alleged to have taken place on April 30, 1976). One is reminded of Michelangelo's ceiling of the Sistine Chapel where God infuses Adam with similar energy. To support Hua's strong emphasis on rapid modernization, great fanfare has accompanied the posthumous publication of Volume V of Mao's *Selected Works,* which covers the years 1949–57, the period in which Mao devoted himself to building a strong state and economy. And to disassociate the late Chairman from the last Ms. Mao (his fourth wife), the Hua regime is paying reverent attention to Mao's first chosen wife, who was executed by the Nationalists in 1930. A new dance drama concerning this young martyr has a surrealistic finale in which her ghost flies over the heads of the Chinese people who are celebrating the "Smashing of the Gang of Four."

At present, therefore, we seem to be watching selective de-Maoization in the name of Mao Tse-tung himself (indeed Mao has been declared 70 percent correct and 30 percent incorrect by Teng Hsiao-p'ing). Whether these trends will eventually lead to total de-Maoization is a matter of conjecture. A hint of this possibility, again using historical imagery, emerged in *People's Daily* in a November 1977 article entitled "Ch'in Shih-huang Did Not Belong to the Communist Party" (Mao equals Ch'in Shih-huang in the allegory game). Throughout much of 1978, Chinese publications began to rescue the name and image of Confucius: noting that his "educational methods are worthy of being learned in some respects" and that he gave special stress to "seeking truth from facts." The revival of Confucius, like the downgrading of Ch'in Shih-huang, have become allegorical symbols of the new leadership: giving new emphasis to the intellectuals and holding the more radical legacies of Mao at arm's length. By late 1978, wall posters seemed to begin focusing the attack on Mao himself, noting that he had become somewhat "metaphysical" and "senile" in his later years.

Whatever the long-term fate of the late Chairman's memory, it is apparent that Mao's death symbolized the end of the senior generation of leaders in the Chinese Communist movement. The Mao generation played key roles in bringing together the three broad Chinese lessons of history—shaping the national and cultural lessons, creating the Chinese Communist lessons, and nationalizing the popular lessons. The confluence of these lessons contributed to the growing consensus that helped make and sustain Mao's revolution.

During the Maoist years, the revolutionary consensus included general agreement about history. The national/cultural lessons taught the Chinese to adopt a love-hate relationship toward the dynastic past and the foreign imperialist past. The Chinese Communist lessons used Marxist historiography to show the importance of the CCP and the PRC in Chinese and in world history. The popular lessons prompted all Chinese to see themselves as part of a momentous historical moment.

But now the future of the Maoist consensus is in question. A new post-Mao era is opening, further and further removed from the origins of the Chinese Revolution. Mao once warned that China could "change its color" (i.e., lose her revolutionary "redness") and it is possible that Mao's greatest fear will come to pass—the China of the year 2000 may indeed begin to reflect certain aspects of today's Soviet Union, especially the growth of a rigid bureaucracy, a "new class" of educated elites, and increased demands for consumer goods. If trends continue in these directions, then Chinese values may become more similar, for better or worse, to those of other developed countries. Indeed rapidly increased Chinese contact with the West and Japan, spearheaded by trade and cultural exchanges, will probably accelerate this trend.

Under these circumstances, Chinese views of the past are sure to change. But in what directions? What will happen to the widely shared beliefs in the lessons of history? Perhaps some aspects of the past will become more revered, just as the Japanese had a traditional revival in the 1890s and the Soviets a more selective revival of prerevolution literature in the 1950s and 1960s. Although the dynastic civilization is gone for good, the Chinese might find new inspiration in certain facets of the aesthetic tradition. After all, by the year 2000 few Confucian-educated Chinese will be around any more, and an eclectic use of traditional painting and architectural styles would run little risk of bringing back the Confucian value system.

What about views of the revolutionary past? One possibility is that China will follow the pattern of other revolutionary societies in which the revolution seems more and more remote from daily life, something to celebrate on Bastille Day, July Fourth, October Day. Under this pattern, the mix of Marxism and nationalism will persist as a key determinant of Chinese values, but more as a routine expression of beliefs than as part of a live revolutionary atmosphere. The routinization of revolutionary values is most likely among the younger generations, particularly those of post-Cultural Revolution vintage.

So far the scenario seems familiar to Westerners—a loss of vitality behind the values that inspired a revolution. But it's not the only possibility in China. We often have misread China in the past. We have responded positively to perceived periods of "moderation" and "pragmatism" (nice English and American words), only to find ourselves baffled by new rounds of Chinese "revolutionary radicalism" (somewhat scary words now that we are several centuries removed from our own revolutionary heritages).

Links to the revolutionary past may be weakened by the death of the Mao-Chou generation, but they are not yet severed. Indeed new crises, domestic or foreign, might rekindle a fiery revolutionary nationalism among postrevolutionary Chinese. The new generation is still taught the Maoist dictum, "To rebel is justified," and might put those words into action in future political struggles. It is worth noting Chairman Hua's suggestion that China might have a "second Cultural Revolution" in the future.

A strong link to the revolutionary past is the anti-imperialist aspect of Chinese nationalism. Although warfare around China's rim has abated in the 1970s, the potential for conflict remains. Even in the age of détente, the United States and Russia are still seen as "imperialist superpowers" bent on domination of third world countries, including China. It is an outlook that could have volatile implications. A crisis could erupt—over Korea, Taiwan, the Soviet border, the Indian border, Indochina—and could lead China and America back to more belligerent postures reminiscent of the era before "Ping-Pong diplomacy." In a crisis atmosphere, the anti-imperialist "lessons" of Chinese history from the Opium Wars onward would take on immediate relevance for today's Chinese.

Perhaps there is a lesson here for the West and China alike. 1970s détente, and particularly U.S.-China détente, emerged because both sides saw more advantages in limited cooperation than in the mutual hostility of the cold war era. Détente began with a candid recognition of our differences. It has progressed to the point of normalized diplomatic relations because we have developed a mutual respect and mutual interests in spite of our differences. It will persist only if we continue to explore the cooperative potential, rather than the combative potential, in the gaps between our two societies.

China and America *are* different. We have different histories and different views of the past. We are at different stages of historical development. We cannot remake China in an American image—that was an illusion of the early twentieth century. Nor should the Chinese assume that America is on its way to a Marxist revolution—that is a projection of their ideology onto America.

Both societies take pride in their revolutionary heritages; but those heritages are quite different. America's revolution engendered pride in the liberty of the individual, while China's revolution produced pride in social egalitarianism and collective economic development. Both outlooks have relevance to the human condition in the late twentieth century. In this philosophical sense, the Sino-American relationship is an important test case of whether two societies, with such different views of man's past and man's potential, can find common ground.

Tradition
and Change

Self-Expression in China

JOHN KING FAIRBANK

John Fairbank goes back into the past in order to throw light on the present. He depicts the old society in which the boundary lines that separated politics and morals from other things were not sharp, and both were connected with all facets of life. To Fairbank, there are two ways to fit China into our own understanding of the world: as a latecomer to a universal process of modernization; or as a unique culture that has its own future as well as its own past.

Although Fairbank finds himself in between, he is nearer to the second theory than to the first. He pursues his subtle inquiry into China's special ways by probing how people speak in public and the meaning of what they say. This puts in perspective the Chinese view of journalists, of foreigners, and of their own current ideology. Fairbank does not rule out that the PRC could yet pull some surprises, but he feels they would be within Chinese tradition rather than efforts to copy something non-Chinese.

John Fairbank first went to Peking in 1932, last in 1972, and in between he became a great force for promoting the understanding of modern China in the United States. His classic The United States and China *(1948 and 4th edition 1979), his guidance of successive generations of students, and his role as a bridge between the specialty of China and the affairs of the community have given him a unique influence that shows no sign of abating. Among his other books are* Trade and Diplomacy on the China Coast *(1954),* China: The People's Middle Kingdom and the U.S.A. *(1967),* China Perceived *(1974), and* Chinese-American Interactions *(1975).*

—R.T.

For word-users in all lands self-expression is a primary concern. As a right in the United States it includes the individual's freedom of speech, together with some freedom of assembly, of worship, and of publication, subject to the constraints of public order, laws of libel, and the like. Like all our rights, self-expression receives primarily a legal definition. But a comparison with China, if we go only by the legal definitions that most typify American culture, will crash on takeoff. We must begin more broadly with a glance at the social-cultural context in which literate self-expression has occurred in China and how it developed there.

Let us agree on a first point, that political self-expression cannot easily be disentangled from self-expression in general because "political" will usually include whatever people in power believe it includes. A poem that seems to criticize them becomes by that fact a political statement, whether so intended or not. China's Marxist rulers of today tell us that all writing betrays a class viewpoint and that this is an era supremely characterized by class struggle. This Chinese belief is at once and in itself part of the problem we face—a point of difference.

The Chinese Marxist claim that all self-expression is part of class struggle may serve as a useful point of departure: it reminds us that one of the Western philosophers' observations about Chinese classical cosmology has been that it favors organicism, a view of the world in which all things are not only interrelated but interactive. Indeed, Chinese philosophers saw the world in a very flux of interaction in which cognate aspects wax and wane like the alternation of night and day, or of *yin* and *yang*. It follows that moral acts are situational, and proper conduct is not a thing by itself but is other-related. As a result, moral man is primarily a social animal, to be socially judged; but more than that, the cosmos is a great unity, not a pluralism of the type we usually assume.

From this Chinese philosophical position it naturally follows that conduct in the sense of how one appears to others is all-important, and therefore daily life is an arena of moral action. One's worth depends on one's behavior, and so all aspects of behavior are subject to scrutiny and moral evaluation. A proper Confucian, we now infer, was in a constant state of moral tension, and a proper Communist should be so today. As a result, morality pervades Chinese life even more than it does Western life. In the West large sectors like science and art, sometimes even law, are considered to lie outside the moral sphere. This is not the case in the People's Republic—another point of difference.

Let us begin by asserting that these different assumptions about political self-expression in China—that all such expression involves a class viewpoint and a moral posture—have been inherited from China's long history.

There are two ways to put China in context with ourselves and world history: either as a backward case, a latecomer to a universal process known as modernization; or else as a deviant, a unique other culture going its own way. Both views are valid, but only up to a point. They suit respectively the familiar and the unfamiliar aspects of Chinese society and culture. Economic development—the combination of industrialization and agronomic technology that Vice-Premier Teng Hsiao-p'ing now calls for—is familiar to us from our own experience. For instance, we understand the need for chemical fertilizer, its cost and its potentialities. Measured on this technological scale, the People's Republic is still underdeveloped. It is low in railroad mileage, oil consumption, and standard of living generally; but it is going in the same general direction as ourselves.

Yet if we think back only a decade to Mao Tse-tung's Cultural Revolution of the late 1960s, we see in China some things very strange and unfamiliar. There was not only an extraordinary degree of popular fanaticism among hordes of teenage Red Guards in numbers that only China could produce, but also a moralistic condemnation of the West. This included denouncing the Western concern for individualism as a social trait unfit for the world's future, and denying the propriety of material incentives. Such views bespoke a utopian collectivism in action on a scale never seen before in history. This difference in degree makes China an exception to the general experience of people elsewhere. China's size alone, soon a billion people in one nation, raises the question: How does such a mass of people hang together? Thus there are mysteries in China that set her apart.

The latecomer approach to China's condition is a theory of delayed progress along lines that are supposed to hold good for all countries. This has appealed to Chinese Marxists who dislike to see themselves as quaint and curious exceptions. They much prefer a self-image of socialist China at the head of world progress, especially now that the Soviets seem to them revisionist backsliders even worse than the Americans floundering in their capitalism. China's tardiness in developing can be blamed on the twin evils that Marxist-Leninists see in world history, feudalism and imperialism.

The other approach, that China is a unique problem for cultural study, naturally appeals to China specialists who live off the idea. But it also makes sense to historians at large, who are born area specialists and comparativists because they generally deal, at least in their doctoral dissertations, with concrete particulars of the past and leave the broad model-making to political scientists. Chinese history in the West is just in its infancy. It is a quite specific story and explains what Mao's revolution has been about. History of course is not quite everything, but certainly it is the best starting point for the study of cultural idiosyncrasies.

Bearing in mind both the latecomer and the deviant interpretations of China's development, let us look further at the record. The massed labor that tamped the Shang capital's city walls hard as cement at Chengchow near the Yellow River about 1850 B.C. was already a lower class directed by an upper class. This lower class continued to constitute about 85 percent of the Chinese people for the next 3,800 years, down to the establishment of the People's Republic at Peking in 1949. During that time the Chinese upper class, constantly invigorated by talent rising from the common people, created Chinese civilization: the imperial state unified in 221 B.C.; the early bureaucracy of the Han; the poetry of the T'ang; Sung painting and philosophy; and a society that by A.D. 1100 was really far ahead of Europe in size of population, food supply, ship-building and navigation, commerce, city life, fine arts, paper and printing, porcelain, and the civility of upper-class existence.

One secret of this success, while 85 percent of the people continued largely illiterate in their hoe culture, was the development of the examination system after A.D. 600. This invention was as important as the printed books on which it depended. State examinations open to talent were held annually at the lowest level and triennially at the provincial and metropolitan levels in conditions of strict anonymity for the candidates' written papers. The system produced a special class of self-indoctrinated degree holders or "gentry." This group formed an elite reservoir from which through further examinations officials could be selected with some assurance that they would know the rules, remain loyal to the system, and have the wit to keep it going. Degree holders who did not make it into officialdom could become great compilers of records, aesthetes, philosophers, and pillars of their communities, holding local society together. Because mastery of the classics was a full-time job for any youth, these literati almost all came from landlord families. They were not a free-wheeling intelligentsia prone to criticize, but on the contrary had a prescribed and often genuine faith in the familial and Confucian social order. This rested on a hierarchy of statuses that conferred authority on fathers, husbands, and rulers, and expected obedience from sons, wives, and subjects. It also gave the scholar, whose labor was mental, preeminence over the soldier, farmer, and artisan, who relied on their muscles, and over the merchant, who merely moved things around from place to place.

A ruling class that could perpetuate itself by written examinations, at a time when European scholars were still engaged in oral expostulation, also knew how to co-opt talent from all quarters. It could borrow money from merchants while controlling their licenses, praise the farmer while taxing and conscripting him, and make warrior conquerors dependent on using Chinese as scribal administrators. All this kept the universal kingship of imperial Confucianism going until A.D. 1912, the year Woodrow Wilson became President of the United States and Mao Tse-tung went to middle school in Changsha.

The Confucian order had its seamy underside, and if it had continued in the twentieth century it would still have left 85 percent of the Chinese people hoeing their fields with muscle power. Mao and his modern generation could easily see the enormity of their task in trying to create a new and modern China. The Chinese reformers and revolutionaries of the twentieth century have all labored in the shadow of China's long history, trying to use some elements of their heritage against other elements, pulling hard on their bootstraps. Many stimuli have been offered from outside China, beginning with British invasion and Chinese humiliation in 1840–42 and ending with Japanese invasion and Chinese humiliation in 1937–45. In between there came to China much good advice, the menace-cum-promise of Christianity, the demonstration effect of steamships and factories, and a whole series of foreign invasions and border wars interspersed with peasant rebellions.

These foreign stimuli and domestic events all contributed to irreversible changes that became a revolution, but the revolution was still *within* Chinese culture. Many journalists and other specialists in short-term history and contemporary events have noted that the revolution speaks in a new vocabulary and condemns the old pre-Liberation China before 1949. This we can all applaud as a necessary effort to break free of tradition and see China in new terms. But we should not be misled. This attack is the least that Mao could do if he was to have any effect at all. But it doesn't certify complete success in breaking free of the past.

For example, the denunciation of parents as bourgeois and deserving rebuke or reform by their newly liberated children horrified Chinese spectators at show trials of the early 1950s. To rebuke a parent was a good deal more heinous than the "mother fucking" used as a radical epithet in America a decade ago. Filial disrespect under Confucianism had been a capital crime. In law a father was entitled to kill a truly impious son, since the son was his social responsibility and filiality was the most important social bond. Parent-denouncing in the 1950s therefore testified to the real strength of the old family system that impeded, and still continues to impede, the community effort at revolution. As Mao, the Great Helmsman, recedes into the past, more and more of his campaigns and programs may appear in retrospect as efforts only partly achieved, battles half-won, business unfinished. This indeed was his own view, the basis for his doctrine of Continuing or Permanent Revolution.

The long-term view is therefore essential to understanding China's future. Chinese developments cannot be expected to break sharply with past tradition, simply because of the enormous mass of the society and because of the inertia created by a long history. China is the most distinctive separate culture in the modern world and has been until recently the most distant from Europe. Her style of individual self-expression must first be seen in historical context and in her traditional forms. Only later can we try to appraise how far this style has continued and how far it has been changed.

Traditional Limitations on Political Self-Expression

The Chinese polity was a steep pyramid topped by the emperor. Political self-expression diminished rapidly as one descended from his level. Of course he had tutors in youth and ministers when on the throne, but they were well advised to be conservatives and promote orthodoxy. The Golden Age was in the far past. If only one could get back to it!

Confucianism taught conservative conduct in the interest of preserving the social order. It was of course the doctrine of the ruling elite, but its teachings spread downward and permeated the society. For the educated persons who knew the rules of civility and etiquette, Confucianism provided a code of behavior. For the illiterate masses, however, more was needed, and here the doctrines of the Legalists—the school of administrators who were rivals of Confucius—were applied in the form of rewards and punishments. If the masses could not be moved by the upperclass morality that filtered down to them, then they could properly be coerced, but Chinese ideas of coercion were from the first sophisticated. One of the primary teachings of the Confucian doctrine was the belief expressed most fully in the classic *Mencius* that man is naturally well intentioned and that people can be led to better conduct by exhortation and the power of example, not merely by threats and punishments. In theory, anyone could aspire by sincere and unremitting self-cultivation in classical studies to master his own nature and become a cultivated or "superior" man *(chün-tzu)*, and so enter the small upper class.

Through the examination system the class structure was both preserved and ensured, for degree status could also be purchased; and yet those who, like merchants, bought the official degrees were never more than about one-third of the total, and this ensured the supremacy and prestige of the written examinations as the main path of advancement. The main achievement of the massive examination system was to produce a ruling class conscious of its prerogatives and cultural role, but above all obedient to the state on which it depended for major employment. The scholars who did not secure official positions remained subordinates and hangers-on of the scholar-officials who held office. These latter possessed both political authority and social prestige, and through office they gained material wealth, since the state revenues were collected by tax farming, that is, an official collected enough to meet his quota and more to maintain his establishment, with no questions asked unless his collections seemed excessive and produced violent popular dissent.

Now self-expression in print was a public act that might affect the social order for which emperor and officials were primarily responsible. Among the ruling class there was a rank order of written self-expression descending from the Son of Heaven. Officials in practice had certain duties of self-expression, but only in this hierarchic context. The masses generally found channels of written expression only to the degree that literati could be induced to assist them. When rebellion flared up, the most urgent question was whether literati had joined the rebels to give voice to their claims, perhaps even to help them set up a civil government that could finance and perpetuate their military power. Only with scholar-officials on their own side could rebels hope to rival a ruling dynasty.

The officials' style of operation was authoritarian in a hierarchic chain of command. At the apex the emperor played a unique role, not only as commander, sage, and high pontiff, but also as the spot where innovation might be brought into the system. An official with a good new idea could bat it up to the emperor, but only the latter could make it effective. Ordinary emperors performed ritual acts while the bureaucratic machine kept on its established course. Able emperors, of whom there were quite a number, sometimes made innovations. Typically their role was to rise above routine and, by the selection of talent for appointment, maintain the quality of officialdom. Their methods of control included a built-in unpredictability since the emperor could easily give himself to sudden wrath, inconsistency, and unforeseeable whims, beyond ordinary comprehension. The higher an official rose, the more likely he was to be disciplined by his master. The emperor answered to no one but Heaven and his ancestors.

The Chinese bureaucratic style *vis-à-vis* the masses was highly manipulative. An official properly versed in statecraft—the art of administration for the benefit of society or the preservation of the social order—could judge whether to try to kill bandits or enroll them in the police, whether to attack smugglers at all points or leave them to operate on the circuitous and difficult routes. In this system the official's use of force was a confession of failure to persuade, or at least to secure results by nonviolent means. The people's so-called right of rebellion was simply a desperate act of protest against intolerable conditions.

Out of this complex of traditions one can discern a whole series of factors militating against free speech and freedom of expression in writing and publication. First, the printed word had a particular sanctity. One did not step upon printed characters or even handwriting. They represented the classical learning and its sacred teachings. The orthodoxy proscribed certain taboo characters and certain heterodox ideas and doctrines. The use of characters in writing was thus a trust to be handled circumspectly by any writer. The best-known illustration of how this worked is the literary inquisition of the Ch'ien-lung emperor in the 1770s. Following earlier precedents that went way back to the unifying First Emperor of the Ch'in, this Manchu ruler conducted a census of extant literature and a house-to-house search for proscribed works. Some 2,300 works were listed for total destruction as containing seditious or abusive language. "None may remain to later generations," the emperor declared, "in order to cleanse our speech and make straight the hearts of men." Out of many cases, let us note only that of the unfortunate dictionary maker Wang Hsi-hou, who had printed taboo characters: he was executed, while two sons and three grandsons were sent into slavery.

In short, print was to be used in the service of orthodoxy as judged by the political authorities. Poetry could be as seditious as prose. Meanwhile the reading of novels was considered unseemly and was done only in private.

Another complex of practices was related to the self-expression of officials when they had authority. Within the ruling strata, scholars were people of prestige but little power, for power depended upon office. High officials regularly patronized able scholars to do works of compilation for them. Even an ordinary magistrate customarily had as his specialized advisers scholars who had not made it into office and were employed by him as his "tent friends" *(mu-yu)* or brain trust. In the late eighteenth century the great philosopher Tai Chen made his living as a tutor or editor in the homes of leading officials, while the great historian Chang Hsueh-ch'eng spent his life as a compiler of local gazetteers or director of academies dependent on the patronage of officials who befriended him. There was little chance of a career for an independent scholar, least of all for a social critic.

Among officials in office the Ch'ing Dynasty established the strict rule that policy matters were not to be discussed except in the direct line of duty. For officials to gather of their own accord and discuss policy was a serious offense. They were not to form groups or *tang* (now the word for parties), but each official was to remain the loyal servitor of his imperial master and the others above him in the hierarchy. Policy discussions even among officialdom were thus circumscribed. When the emperor sought official advice, he declared the "path for statements" or *yen-lu* to be open, and thereupon officials of a sufficiently high level might offer opinions on a given subject. But when the *yen-lu* was declared closed, even this was improper.

Criticism was not unwanted, for it could assist the exercise of power. Only it must be helpful—"constructive criticism"—not negative or ill-intentioned, and whether it was really constructive was to be judged by the official recipient.

Censors were officials appointed for terms of service as investigators and critics. In ancient times the censors had performed a duty of remonstrating with the ruler, as well as impeaching other officials for misconduct. But as the monarchy became more despotic in the early modern period, remonstrance became a risky act and the custom withered. The major models for speaking out that can be adduced in modern times are famous censors, who sometimes paid a heavy price for simply doing their job. As censors they had no extra security and were mere temporary appointees. Over the centuries the censorial function did not grow in strength, and it was just that—an official function not expected of other officials or, least of all, commoners. The presenting of commoners' petitions to officials provides another slight strand of popular self-expression for modern citation, but it failed to become a major institution in the process of government.

Under the empire before 1911 the closest approach to modern schools of thought about policy was probably made by bureaucratic factions or cliques. Of course the throne always had leading officials whose judgment and suggestions it relied upon, like the Empress Dowager's relying on Li Hung-chang or Chang Chih-tung in the late nineteenth century. But to offer spontaneous policy advice, unsolicited and from outside the web of official responsibility, was a dangerous move. The formula was to invoke the loyal scholar's ancient duty, on the basis of his acquired wisdom, to offer its fruits to the ruler *as an act of loyalty and moral responsibility.* Such policy advice was therefore usually wrapped in the Confucian equivalent of the flag and motherhood, couched in highly moral terms that, if accepted, might give the author some immunity, or at least a claim to selfless sincerity. It was best, of course, to say something the ruler wanted to hear. One seldom tried to get an imperial decision reversed, only better applied or further developed.

Less cynically, we must acknowledge that China's bureaucratic politics was often powered by schools of thought or opinion among officials and high gentry, who sometimes took strong moral stands and supported one another in pushing their views. One classic example is the scholars and ex-officials associated with the Eastern Forest Academy at Wusih on the lower Yangtze during the declining years of the Ming Dynasty in the early seventeenth century. These academics wanted to eschew the eclecticism of contemporary thought and reassert the old-time Confucian morality in official life. They attacked high officials at Peking and particularly a notorious eunuch who had subverted the court and acquired enough corrupt power to purge them in return, blacklisting some seven hundred Eastern Forest supporters. Out of this struggle the "six heroes" emerged as martyrs, who became the prototype of fearless men of principle who would speak out, come what might. Another such group of six eminent figures demanded publicly in the 1930s that Chiang Kai-shek stop his anti-Communist Civil War and stand up to the Japanese encroachment. They were known as the Six Heroes, of course.

Probably the most spectacular faction of the nineteenth century was the "Party of the Pure" (the young Chang Chih-tung was one of them), who began beating the drum of anti-foreign bellicosity in the late 1870s. They were top scholars and eloquent armchair strategists, who voiced the general Chinese ruling-class şense of outrage at Russian and French border aggressions and demanded that they be summarily chastised. Their militancy suited the needs of the Empress Dowager as an offset to the practical Westernizers who were trying to save China by arms, which were so much more expensive than words. The moral righteousness of this strident faction was given the name "pure discussion." Erudite and impeccable, but above all, righteous, the practitioners of "pure discussion" had considerable influence at court until the hostilities with the French in the 1880s made the going tough and they in turn were defeated.

Taken by and large, the long record of China's official history is replete with expressions on policy but only (or almost only) within channels, by officials to officials. The basic concepts of organized and hierarchic responsibility set those limits. Behind them lay the fact that high policy was imperial and therefore secret in origin, not the business of the officialdom, much less of the scholar class or the common people.

This concept of the political role of print and its proper use only in the service of authority derives from one of the main features of the old Chinese polity—the fact that it was maintained in part by an imperial leadership, if not monopoly, of morality and ethics. The government depended in part upon the preservation of a moral climate of loyalty in print if not in practice. Emperor Ch'ien-lung's literary inquisition was only an offshoot of his great project to compile an imperial compendium of all Chinese literature in its four forms—classics, history, philosophy, and belles lettres. This vast project took twenty years and employed as many as 15,000 copyists to produce a work of 36,000 Chinese volumes.

Evidently the emperor owned Chinese literature, or at least had a duty to look after it. This was because the moral teachings of the sages and their exemplification in the pronouncements of emperors preserved an atmosphere of moral exhortation toward right conduct in the service of social order and the state. Authority was threatened when this monopoly or atmosphere was damaged.

The maintenance of the Chinese government's central prestige could be likened to a film of surface tension. If one break in it was allowed, it would collapse.

This explains the recurrent imperial crusades against impious literature or any writings casting aspersion upon the established regime. Word of mouth could not be entirely controlled, but print was less evanescent and stood witness to any infractions that made their way into publication. The ruling class, and particularly those in authority, were therefore much concerned to preserve the written record in the proper form. Appropriate expressions of praise and blame were meted out by the official historians sitting in judgment upon the past, but always with a wary eye out for the authority of the moment. As each dynasty took on the responsibility of writing the history of its predecessor, it saw to it that praise and blame were bestowed in a moralistic manner so that history would set an example of both proper and improper conduct and their just rewards. History was thus filtered through official lenses and the bestowal of epithets upon losers was customary practice. The old saying was that the rebel, if he succeeded, would be emperor, but if he failed, a bandit. The worst punishment was meted out to those whose names were expunged from the record entirely so that they did not thereafter exist.

One result of these complex practices was an extraordinary sophistication in the symbols, signs, and Aesopian language that might give political indications without overt explicit statements. The conveyance of views by indirection, by allusion and esoteric references, became the fine art it remains today. Thus the slightest lack of warmth or deviation from customary usage might rouse suspicion. The Soviet custom of indicating power in the bureaucracy by rank order on a rostrum is only a pale reflection of the similar Chinese practice. Mao's Great Proletarian Cultural Revolution was triggered in 1965 against a play concerning a loyal official of the Ming period, some four hundred years ago, who ventured to remonstrate with his emperor. It seemed to refer to Mao.

It is quite in keeping with the traditional emphasis upon proper conduct that the proper use of words, especially in printed form, should be an index of the individual's attitude and political position. The well-schooled official makes his position known by inaction or omission even more easily than by the kind of overt affirmation or denunciation customary in Western politics. To say nothing at the appropriate moment can be a form of self-expression that may carry with it the least danger.

The Modern Problems of Journalists and of Foreigners

The tradition that policy is the prerogative of those in power and capable of making it dies very hard and makes modern Chinese journalism a very dubious activity.

Ordinary people do not know the many considerations entering into policy decisions, so they can hardly be expected to participate, and since they do not participate, they do not need to be informed. This self-perpetuating stultification of an informed citizenry goes back to Confucius' dictum that sometimes the people should be told only the ruler's decision and not the reasons for it. Trying to break this tradition of government-as-manipulation, Sun Yat-sen and others advocated a transitional stage of "tutelage," when the common people could be gradually taught to participate in policy formation. This idea paved the way for the Leninist type of party dictatorship set up by the Kuomintang and the Chinese Communist Party. Trusting the rabble has seldom commended itself to statesmen. The elections for Chinese advisory provincial assemblies and for a parliament early in the century followed the initial European custom of a very restricted electorate, highly qualified by education, property, or status—in effect, an electorate drawn from the ruling class. Nationalism naturally aroused the Chinese citizens' interest in affairs of state, but tutelage and dictatorship tended to keep this interest limited to discussion of policy decisions already made, not those still under consideration. The acme of this informing of the citizenry *a posteriori* was probably reached when General Lin Piao, minister of defense, number two to Mao, and his designated successor, suddenly and mysteriously died in Mongolia in September 1971 and the first official account of his death was given out to the Chinese public in August 1973. Investigative reporting has never been applied to the incident.

With public information considered an exceptional act of grace, not a right, journalism has been a slow transplant and has needed special protection. The modern press in China is barely a century old. It grew up first in the British colony of Hong Kong, where the pioneer Wang T'ao began publishing a Chinese newspaper with political opinions in the 1870s. Other papers, like the *Shen-pao* at Shanghai from 1872, got started in the foreign shelter of the treaty ports. In the Chinese time scale the profession of journalism is recent and still of questionable respectability. Foreign reporting from within China often seems to be regarded by Chinese authorities as almost equivalent to spying.

It follows that journalists are people who ask for trouble. Without representing the authorities, they make statements concerning the actions of the authorities. This can only be considered, from the traditional point of view, both irresponsible and dangerous to public order, particularly when journalists spread bad news that damages public morale or describe improper behavior that may inspire others to the same impropriety. Like other observers of the American media, Chinese note that TV reporting of bizarre crimes may stimulate a rash of such crimes. Thus hijacking and abduction seem to feed off the news. The fact that we Americans have not yet worked out a stable balance between the public's need to know and the media's need for restraint leaves this as still another unresolved point of disagreement in Chinese-American relations. The problem becomes most acute in the case of foreign journalists in China.

Chinese rulers have long had to deal with foreigners not entirely under their control. They have of course developed age-old methods to control or influence the expression of such people. Dealing with people they could not coerce directly in war or politics, the Chinese created a repertoire of threat and intimidation, ingratiation and persuasion, plus friendship and outright purchase, that became very full and sophisticated.

The model for influencing foreigners may be seen first in the old tribute system. Tribute envoys coming from foreign rulers to represent their homage to the Chinese court were guests of the state and proceeded to the capital by the imperial post, to be lodged in the imperial hostels for tribute envoys. Thus they remained guests, and their Chinese hosts retained the commanding position in the relationship. This tradition lies behind the generally enjoyable guided tours of today, when the honored guest from abroad is treated with civility and etiquette as a means of bringing him within the Chinese moral sphere. This rests on the fact that the basic principle of human relations in the Confucian order was that of reciprocity. One who receives the entertainment and amenities of being a guest is thereafter obligated in the nature of things to return this civility.

Ideally this should deter foreign visitors from unfriendly criticism. Since almost all criticism in Western guise would seem to be unfriendly criticism in Chinese terms, this has put Western journalists and other travelers on their guard. Mao's original biographer, the late Edgar Snow, for example, made a point of paying his own way when he went to China as a reporter. Even outside the Chinese realm it sits poorly on the human conscience to receive the hospitality of a regime and then give it adverse criticism. Manipulation of the foreign press in this fashion is only a latter-day application of old principles.

This amounts to a denial of the institutional role of journalism as practiced in the Atlantic community. In Chinese thinking, friendship is the basis for international relations, as it is for personal. To be a guest is a first step toward becoming a friend, and toward accepting obligations of reciprocity. Journalists, like other foreign critics, are therefore anathema to a tradition-bound Chinese, who sees them as simply ungrateful, unaware of the most elementary principles of civility. In the personal world of Chinese group relationships there is little middle ground. The individual foreigner must be categorized as for or against, either a "friend of China" or an enemy. To remain on middle ground is to be a moral trimmer or opportunist.

The foreign critic on the penumbra of China is still part of her moral universe, and if he is an adverse critic he is thus against morality. Just as a Chinese official who loses out in a policy struggle becomes an immoral person, so the foreign critic may be seen to have a faulted character. At the least he is an ingrate who is not conscious of the bonds of friendship and will not repay civility with loyalty. Those who are morally wrong in this way may well deserve denunciation like those who wind up on the losing side in Chinese politics.

Among the means available for the persuasion or disciplining of foreign critics is the withholding of contact, a practice reminiscent of the occasional stoppages of trade to coerce the foreign traders at Canton two hundred years ago. Whatever is of interest to the foreigner is the means by which he may be moved, either by gratitude for its receipt or by the threat of withholding it. Would-be muckrakers and whistle-blowers have seldom returned to the People's Republic.

Chairman Mao's Mixture

Individual political criticism has flourished in the West as an ingredient in the political process. It reached a high point in the columns written over the years by Walter Lippmann, who was above all things independent in idea and opinion. As he would have been the first to say, his function as a commentator was the end product of a long historical development. No comparable development had occurred in China before 1900, up to the time that Liang Ch'i-ch'ao and others began to write their editorials in exile in Tokyo, and the necessities of revolution in recent decades have not called it forth. On the contrary Mao Tse-tung, when struggling at Yenan to unify a movement that could win power and remake Chinese society, demanded that literature and art like all other activity should serve the cause embodied in the Party (and in his leadership). Mao's talks at the Yenan forum on literature and art in 1942 denounced art for art's sake and warned all writers to toe the Party line.

In place of individual self-expression, Mao advocated the practice of the "mass line," by which an interaction between Party and masses would permit popular desires to be ascertained and answered. The aim was to bring the rural 85 percent of the Chinese people into political activity as eventual participants in building up China and fashioning a good life for themselves. Leading the people to effect changes through the mass line is a practice suited to their current situation, because it presupposes the mediation of a large and well-trained elite of Party members and cadre-activists who are in touch with both the masses and the Central Committee leadership. "From the masses, to the masses" works through the cadres as the collectors of mass opinions and the purveyors of central decisions.

One is reminded of how in a far simpler day the Yung-cheng emperor in the early eighteenth century used to get local intelligence from his officials through the palace memorials submitted to his eyes alone, and so kept in touch with his government. How far things have come! Yung-cheng could check on grain supplies stored defensively against famine and attendant rebellion. Mao was intent on getting greater production. Yet both could function only through a ruling elite, by directives that were partly public, like edicts distributed empire-wide through the Peking *Gazette*, and partly secret, like palace memorials or restricted circulars for Party information only. Just as intelligence was a tool of administration, so information was a tool of government in general, the property not of the public but of the state to use in its own interest. Thus news in China today is part of the government's wherewithal in the continuing tradition of political manipulation. It is distributed rather like intelligence, on a need-to-know basis: some millions of officials get a full summary of world news, which however does not turn up on street corners for the masses. China's domestic news is made edifying today in the same way that novels were considered unedifying formerly, by the ruling authority's application of what it considers its responsibility to maintain moral-political standards.

Since the PRC has inherited the need for great bureaucracies through which to govern and has added its own determination to make great changes through mass mobilization campaigns, it has remained in the position of the sage-manipulator who must show the people the proper way to go and help them move along it. The nature of Mao's problem could be seen in the campaign of 1952, which tried to recondition the bureaucrats who had been taken over from the Nationalist era: their continuing functions were essential but their traditional values could torpedo the revolution. Mao differed from former emperors less in his moral claim to instruct the people than in his having a new teaching for them, which required more strenuous efforts to instruct them.

There were similar problems with revolutionary writers left over from the 1920s and 1930s. Their former style of vigorous social criticism now had to change and become edifying—uplifting, not critical. They were increasingly whipped into line by citation of Mao's dictum of 1942 at the

Yenan forum that art and literature must be purely tools of politics. Modern writers have ever since resented this, or been hamstrung by it even if they didn't resent it. But if we look back only to yesterday, the Ch'ien-lung emperor patronized and controlled art as well as literature, putting his big red personal seal on every ancient painting he could get into the imperial collection. His collecting and winnowing of all Chinese literature has already been noted. Chinese art and literature he viewed as part of his empire. It was not so outlandish for Mao, 150 years later, to view them as part of his revolution. A moralizing revolution was now in charge of all such things, in fact more in charge than the empire had ever been.

The greatest ambivalence in Mao's eyes attached to higher education and the foreign-educated modern scholars left over from the first half of the twentieth century. Their skills could be of essential help, but their values had the bourgeois taint of pronounced individualism. Their expertness gave them a sanction, even a necessity, to exercise their individual judgment and make final decisions within their spheres of competence. This was in Chinese terms very close to a revival of the ancient Confucian scholar's claim to know what was proper, wise, moral, and just, independently of the ruler. Mao's moral revivalism would have none of it. The revolution could not speak with many voices, not his revolution. The proof came in Mao's second and more messianic uprising, the "Great Revolution for a Proletarian Class Culture" (a liberal translation of the Chinese phrase) of the late 1960s. Its first move was to close the universities and keep them closed.

Mao Tse-tung seems to have decided, in short, that if he was going to induce political self-expression among the 85 percent, he would have to stifle it among that part of the 15 percent who retained a double consciousness of the scholar elite's traditional prerogatives and the Westernized student's special competence. Unlike Chou En-lai, Chu Te, and most of his Central Committee colleagues, Mao had never become a returned student with a foreigner's view of China. He didn't like the breed as such nor trust it to understand the peasantry.

As one means for political self-expression during the Cultural Revolution of the late 1960s, Mao made use of the big character poster. This reminds one of the sheets of paper with a message to the reader that missionaries used as religious tracts in their nineteenth-century efforts to give the word of God to the common man in Protestant style. Since missionary tracts were printed, they were something like the printed Chinese newsbills or handbills that circulated in commercial centers. Meanwhile the handwritten poster put up in the marketplace was the same potent device by which the anti-Christian gentry had denounced missionary improprieties when they became ostentatiously obnoxious on the local scene after 1860. Scholar-gentry posters touched off many anti-missionary riots. It took upper-class literacy and calligraphy to rouse the common people and give them a sanction for violent action in defense of their common interests and moral values.

The big character poster with which Mao in his own hand in 1966 urged the Red Guards to "bombard the headquarters" thus had a long social history behind it. Monitored by foreign journalists as well as Chinese, handwritten wall posters have become a major institution of political expression. Their quality of cheap and instant publication, available to all who can get them to stay on the billboards, makes them worth studying as a distinct genre.

These notes have tried to suggest the richness of China's traditions of political expression as well as their influence on the present. If we posit that political self-expression has grown in Western countries along with private property and personal affluence, then we should not expect it to flourish in the relative poverty of today's PRC. But let us not foreclose the future nor sell the Chinese people short. Many more changes lie ahead of them. The recent expansion of Chinese politics to include the great mass of the people—Mao Tse-tung's achievement—implies that they must become informed and express themselves, if only to show their sincerity as participants in the mass line. Moreover, they are the heirs of the scholarly tradition of indirect and Aesopian expression, a sophisticated art; and their class interest and moral sense are regularly appealed to by the leadership.Out of this mix of inherited ways and current issues, we can expect political self-expression in China to achieve considerable vigor, even if it is not in the Western style.

Marxism and Chinese Values

MAURICE MEISNER

↑

Maurice Meisner undertakes the difficult task of distilling the main Marx-
ist values still held by the Chinese. His argument centers on a point of great
significance: Marxism has served to narrow the gap between China and the
West. It is the bourgeois virtues—hard work, struggle—that Meisner sees
upheld in the PRC. The American who goes to China often likes it, because
what he sees resembles America's receding past.

At the same time we see that Marxism in China has been savage toward
much of the Chinese heritage. Even here Meisner finds the Chinese experience
quite understandable in Western terms; modernization in the West was also
destructive of what went before it.

It is not that Meisner believes China to be heading for the same goal as
we are. But there is a very blurred quality to the Chinese future. What will
come to pass tomorrow is uncertain, Meisner suggests, because the values of
modern industrialism, with which China is presently smitten, do not always
mesh with the values of socialism the Chinese expect to be able to hold on to.

Mao saw this, and tried to find a Chinese Way to escape the dilemma.
Meisner grants him a large degree of economic success. He also sees a large
degree of political failure, and he expects the shadow of authoritarianism to
lie on China for some time. But much of Mao's legacy will help—not hinder
—the modernization drive now going on under the government of Hua and
Teng.

Maurice Meisner, born in Detroit in 1931, took his MA and PhD at the
University of Chicago. He is currently professor of history at the University
of Wisconsin, Madison. A leading scholar in the field of the history of ideas
in modern China, Meisner is the author of Li Ta-chao and the Origins
of Chinese Marxism *(1967) and many articles on socialist thought in*
China. His most recent book is Mao's China: A History of the People's
Republic *(1977), and he is now at work on a book about utopianism and*
Maoism.

—R.T.

John K. Fairbank once suggested that it does no good for foreign observers of China to echo Professor Higgins's plaint in *My Fair Lady,* "Why can't *they* be more like *us?*" But whatever its utility or futility, the question is still asked by scholars and laymen alike, and no doubt will continue to be posed by those who seek to understand China in our time.

It is usually assumed, of course, that one of the main reasons that the Chinese Communists are "different" from "us" is not only because they are Chinese but also because they are Marxists. Yet it may well be that it is precisely the Marxism of the Chinese Communists that is making China and the Chinese less "Chinese" and more like "us." For it should be remembered that Marxism is a Western doctrine, not one that twentieth-century Chinese intellectuals found in the millennial Chinese tradition. And it may be the historical case that the world view and values Chinese Communists have derived from Marxism are serving to make the "new China" more like the Western nations from which they originally borrowed the ideology today officially canonized as "Marxism–Leninism–Mao Tse-tung Thought." It is that paradoxical case that will be suggested in this essay.

Maoism and Modernization

The Chinese Communist Revolution implicitly rejected many central tenets of the Marxist-Leninist theoretical canon that the leaders of the Chinese Communist Party officially proclaimed, and which they claim Mao Tse-tung raised to a higher stage of universally valid revolutionary theory. Whereas Marxism taught that socialism (and socialist revolutions) presupposed modern capitalism and industrialism, the Chinese Communists undertook their revolutionary efforts in a largely precapitalist agrarian land with little modern industry. Whereas Marxism identified the modern industrial working class as the main agent of revolution, Mao and his followers looked to the revolutionary potentials of the peasantry. While Marxism assumed that the cities would lead the countryside in the making of modern revolutions, the Maoist revolution was made by harnessing the forces of rural revolt to "surround and overwhelm" the conservative urban centers. And while Marxism taught that a socialist revolution must be part of an international revolutionary process, the Chinese Communists appealed to popular Chinese patriotic sentiments; in a country so long humiliated and impinged upon by foreign intruders, it was a revolution that assumed as much the form of a war for national independence as a Marxist-guided struggle for social class revolution.

Yet however unorthodox a revolutionary path the Chinese Communists pursued, however far they departed from the theories of Marx and Lenin, they remained committed to achieving the Marxist socialist goals, values, and visions they had adopted at the beginning of their revolutionary careers. And that commitment molded the history and values of postrevolutionary Chinese society in the years after 1949.

If the Chinese Communist victory of 1949 confirmed the unorthodox Maoist belief that a socialist-oriented revolution could triumph in a precapitalist land on the basis of peasant support, neither Mao Tse-tung nor any other leaders of the Chinese Communist Party believed that a socialist society could be constructed in conditions of perpetual economic backwardness. For Mao, the transition to socialism demanded modern economic and industrial development, even if social changes in a socialist direction did not necessarily presuppose the prior existence of a highly developed industrial economy. Thus, once having achieved power in a wretchedly impoverished country almost entirely lacking the Marxist-defined material prerequisites for socialism, the Chinese Communists saw as their first and most essential task the creation of those very prerequisites. In their efforts to bring about the modern industrial transformation of the economically destitute land they had come to rule, the values that the Communists fostered and practiced during the revolutionary decades of the 1930s and 1940s (especially the celebrated Yenan era) have played a key role—both during the early years of the People's Republic when the Chinese followed the Soviet pattern of economic development, and when they later abandoned the Russian model in favor of a distinctively Maoist developmental strategy.

Most of the values conveyed by "the Yenan spirit" are essentially ascetic values, ones that demand a highly disciplined and selfless orientation. Among them, none has been emphasized more highly than the value of struggle, as Donald Munro has shown in an earlier essay.

The Maoist notion of struggle corresponds in part to the original Marxist concept of class struggle—the struggle of the exploited masses against their exploiters. But perhaps in larger part, Maoism emphasizes struggle as a process of inner spiritual transformation, a process of internal ideological struggle against "incorrect thoughts," which, in turn, is regarded as the first and essential prerequisite for correct social behavior and proper political action.

Closely associated with the value of struggle is the value of "activism." Maoism is a doctrine that rests not on any real Marxist faith in the workings of objective historical laws but rather on the faith that the truly decisive factors in history are conscious and active people imbued with the proper moral and political values. Such spiritually remolded people, Maoism teaches, are able to conquer nature and mold social reality in accordance with their ideals and values. This activistic impulse is reflected in such popular Maoist maxims as "Men are more important than machines," and "The subjective can create the objective." The widely publicized Maoist ideal is the self-reliant guerrilla leader of the Yenan era who "became one" with the people, who combined "ability with virtue," who was always prepared to sacrifice his life for the revolutionary cause, and who practiced the virtues of struggle, self-denial, frugality, and the rural values of "plain living and hard work."

This ideal (and idealized) Yenan revolutionary was the prototype for the post-1949 Chinese conception of "the new communist man," who exemplifies these ascetic values and revolutionary commitments. Such people, who have internalized the values drawn from a romanticized revolutionary past, are, according to Maoist theory, to be the bearers of the socialist and communist future. Whether the values that Maoists prize will bring about a socialist future remains to be seen. But from the perspectives of the present, it would seem that the Maoist version of Marxist values has contributed to the modernization of China over the past three decades much as similar values contributed to the modernization of the Western world over the past three centuries. Indeed, it is ironic that many of the Chinese Marxist values that emerged from the harsh conditions of revolutionary struggle in the backward rural hinterlands of a tradition-bound land have proved to be eminently Western in character and modern in function.

Although the question of the role of values in modern economic development is a highly controversial one, there is widespread agreement that the ascetic religious values that flowed from the Protestant Reformation were intimately linked to the rise of modern Western capitalism and industrialism. Sects such as Calvinism created among their believers an extraordinary tension between the ethical demands of a transcendental God and the sinfulness of a mundane world, a tension that could be relieved only through an activistic and ascetic orientation that aimed to seek grace and salvation by transforming the world in accordance with God's will. Such life orientations dictated the adoption and practice of values that we today take for granted as both morally and economically desirable—diligence, frugality, self-discipline, honesty, unselfishness, and especially the ethical value of hard work. These values originally were accompanied by ascetic attitudes toward consumption, attitudes that

made expenditures (or, at least, extravagant expenditures) morally suspect, and a feeling that the desires of today should be subordinated to
the needs of tomorrow. These values and attitudes were, of course, conducive (and some would argue essential) to the modern economic and
industrial transformation of the Western world in its modern capitalist
form.

In many respects, Maoism in China has served as a secular ideological
equivalent of the religious world views identified with the rise of capitalism in the West, for the ideology that is called "Marxism–Leninism–Mao
Tse-tung Thought" generates similar internal tensions by contrasting the
ideal and the real. It is an ideology that produces comparable feelings of
guilt by pointing to the political, ideological, and moral deficiencies of the
members of Chinese society; and it is an ideology that conveys a remarkably similar set of values. The point might be briefly demonstrated by
drawing a composite picture of the innumerable Maoist personalities who
have been widely propagated as models for emulation over the last three
decades.

The ideal "new communist man"* is not only inspired by a deep sense
of mission "to serve the people" but also burdened by a self-imposed
feeling of guilt and sin. Thus he must continually employ "the weapon
of self-criticism" to examine his consciousness "for the presence of bad
thoughts," and always struggle against "shortcomings and mistakes." He
must carry out "a life-long revolution in his mind," for he has an eternal
obligation to serve the Party, society, and the "thoughts of Mao Tse-
tung." His burdens can be relieved and his obligation fulfilled not simply
by faith in the thoughts of Mao but by the practical demonstration of that
faith in his self-disciplined, self-reliant, and diligent pursuit of Maoist-
defined revolutionary goals and values. His disciplined activity is under-
taken not in order to achieve happiness for himself or his family, but to
serve the larger collectivity of the laboring masses. He thus recognizes
that manual labor is the source of all social wealth and "the prime want
of human life"; labor and laborers are "noble," and if he is not already
a worker or peasant, he regularly engages in manual labor and fosters a
"fervent love of labor." He feels that work is not a burden, but rather a
joy that carries its own rewards. Indeed, the dominant social value per-
sonified by the model Maoist "new communist man" is the ethical value
of hard work.

He also embodies unselfishness—"the selfless spirit of heroic struggle
for state and collective interests," and "the Communist spirit of altru-
ism." He subordinates all personal pleasures to the duty of service, for

---

*The quotations are drawn from various articles in the periodical *China Youth* over the years
1958–66.

the only true source of happiness is struggle on behalf of, and together with, the people; such selfless struggle is "saintly and divine," and from it one derives inner spiritual strength and joy. He lives "the frugal and simple style" of life of the masses of workers and peasants, for he knows that self-denial and thrift are virtues, whereas indolence, luxury, and waste are sins. Material waste is sinful but waste of time even more so, because "time is something cunning" and "if one does not grasp it, it will slip away." Thus what is demanded is a highly activistic and methodical patterning of one's life, based on ascetic Maoist moral values.

The propagation of ascetic values is by no means confined to didactic popular writings. It appears as the most prominent theme throughout the writings and speeches of the highest leaders of the Chinese Communist Party. In his concluding speech to the Seventh Party Congress in 1945, for example, Mao Tse-tung retold the ancient fable "How Yu Kung Removed the Mountains" and how "God's heart" was touched by Yu Kung's "perseverance." He concluded the speech by drawing a contemporary lesson from the traditional tale: "We must *work persistently, work ceaselessly,* and we too may be able to touch God's heart." And in his celebrated 1957 speech on "the Correct Handling of Contradictions Among the People," to take one of innumerable examples, Mao emphasized that "We must spread the idea of building our country through hard work and thrift. . . ." Indeed, asceticism is the major theme in the best-known work of the man who was to prove Mao's most formidable political foe, Liu Shao-ch'i. In his 1939 treatise *How to Be a Good Communist,* widely read in China in the years prior to the Cultural Revolution, Liu stressed the virtues of "ceaseless struggle" and the need for "self-cultivation in developing the style of hard work and persistent struggle."

The ascetic values so ardently promoted in Chinese Communist ideological pronouncements, both theoretical and popular, are presented as attributes of a "communist consciousness." Yet they are eminently bourgeois virtues and values. The ethical value of hard work, diligence, frugality, thrift, self-denial, self-discipline, honesty, and unselfishness—and indeed all the ascetic values conveyed by Maoist ideology—are precisely the values associated with the rise of capitalism in the West and ones deeply imbedded in modern Western thought and morality. Thus it is hardly surprising that so many Western visitors to the People's Republic return to praise the moral spirit and values of contemporary Chinese society, for the values they perceive are part of their own Western heritage and still evoke positive responses in Western minds, even in a perhaps "post-bourgeois" Western age that places a higher premium on the pleasures of consumption and the virtues of leisure than on the ethical value of work.

But if Westerners find the ascetic values of Maoism intelligible and often appealing, this is not generally the case with the profoundly antitraditional values that Maoism conveys. To most Westerners, the virulence of the Chinese Communist critique of the Chinese cultural heritage and its rejection of traditional values seems no less than an assault on culture in general and an attack against the very fabric of civilization itself. One need only note the uncritical acceptance of Simon Leys's depiction of Maoist "aggression against culture" and his proclamation of the "death" of Chinese intellectual life.

Yet when viewed from broader historical perspectives, Chinese Communist antitraditionalism can be seen as no less essential a modernizing force than the ascetic values and bourgeois virtues that Westerners find morally acceptable, or at least not unduly unsettling. It should not be forgotten that the modernization of the West both promoted and presupposed fundamental breaks with traditional Western values, particularly the rigid traditions of the Middle Ages, and that modern capitalism itself was a profoundly antitraditional force.

The rise of capitalism in Europe involved the destruction of the old family system, the ascendency of universal ethical values over particularistic kinship values, the freeing of the individual from traditional family obligations, and the emergence of the modern nuclear family within the larger disciplinary system of modern political structures. It was closely associated with the rise of modern skepticism, rationalism, and science— and consequently demanded a radical devaluation of all traditional magical, superstitious, and mystical beliefs and values. Capitalism (and the "spirit of capitalism") brought fundamentally new attitudes toward work. The notion that work was a burden to be carried on at a leisurely pace and for the purpose of subsistence was replaced by the view that work is an ethical duty and a moral obligation, an orientation highly conducive to the new and disciplined work patterns that modern capitalist forms of production required. Such are some of the many profoundly antitraditionalist features of the modern Western historical experience generally regarded as the necessary prerequisites for, and consequences of, "modernization."

Chinese Communist antitraditionalism has played a strikingly similar modernizing role, albeit in different historical circumstances and by different means. Just as the ideal of "Christian fellowship" of the Protestant sects broke apart the traditional Western family and its values, so the Maoist ideal of "serve the people" has undermined the sacred values of the traditional Chinese family system. In both cases the social result has been the consolidation of the nuclear family within larger social and political frameworks, with individual family members free and able to participate in modern secular work and vocations.

Perhaps most importantly, and much in the fashion that the modernization of the West presupposed the modern work ethic, Chinese Communist ideology prizes "the dignity of labor," manifesting itself most forcefully in an attack on the sharp distinction between mental and manual labor that was so deeply ingrained in the traditional value system. A typical Maoist hero is an educated youth who goes to labor among the peasants in the countryside and emerges with a "dark skin and red heart."

If Maoist antitraditionalism, so similar in nature and function to Western capitalist antitraditionalism, appears to take the form of a wholesale assault on traditional culture, then this is because persisting traditional cultural forms convey values that are perceived as incongruous with modern economic and political development. For example, Communists attack the traditional Chinese opera not necessarily because they dislike the singing and music, but because traditional operas have been an especially powerful popular means to reinforce old social practices and values, particularly the values of kinship institutions.

To be sure, antitraditionalism in China has taken a far more extreme form than its earlier Western counterpart. For one thing, the old Confucian heritage was a much greater barrier to modern economic development than the pre-modern Western tradition. In a cultural and intellectual tradition lacking almost entirely the element of prophecy, traditional values emphasizing the virtues of social harmony and adjustment to nature were much more deeply ingrained than conservative values in the Western tradition. And there was far less in the Chinese tradition that could be salvaged to serve modern economic and political needs.

But the more important factor is one of timing. In the West the break with traditional values was a relatively gradual process, spanning several centuries and accompanying the relatively gradual growth of modern forms of economic life. In China, the processes of modern economic and cultural change have been telescoped into several decades, rather than centuries, and thus the break with the past has been a far more traumatic experience and one that has assumed a more radical character.

There is little that is socialist about the ascetic and antitraditional values that occupy so large a place in Chinese Communist ideology. For Marx, such ascetic values as self-denial, frugality, and hard work were appropriate to the early stages of capitalist industrialization, but they were seen as repressive values, reflecting the conditions of "alienated labor" that the capitalist mode of production imposed. By contrast, socialism, which for Marx presupposed the prior existence of a high level of capitalist economic development, meant a process whereby the laboring masses would liberate themselves from alienated conditions of labor as well as from the repressive and ascetic values that accompanied those conditions.

There are, to be sure, elements of Marxist theory that Maoists have drawn upon to provide theoretical support for their emphasis on ascetic values; one might mention, for example, the Maoist theory of the universality of contradictions, a theory derived in part from the Marxist notion of dialectical materialism and one that offers a quasi-philosophic basis for the value of struggle and, by extension, the value of productive work. But the ascetic values that are praised as attributes of a "communist" consciousness and morality are, from the perspectives of Marxist theory, essentially bourgeois values corresponding to a capitalist stage of socioeconomic development that Marx assumed would have been relegated to the "dustbin of history" with the transition to a socialist society.

Perhaps it should not be surprising that many Chinese Communist values seem more "bourgeois" than "socialist," for any effort to construct a socialist society in an economically backward land demands as its first and foremost task the building of the modern industrial basis for the hoped-for new society. The ascetic and antitraditional values of Maoism are favorable for realizing that universal industrial end, just as such values played a similar role in the modern economic development of the West in earlier centuries. They are the appropriate values for a society that is doing the economic work an abortive Chinese capitalism failed to accomplish under earlier regimes.

Yet it cannot be assumed that the eventual historical result of contemporary Chinese development will be a modern industrial society on the Western model. There are different routes to modernization and a modern industrial economy is compatible with different social and political systems. Moreover, similar values existing within the framework of different ideological world views may tend toward different socio-historical results. In the case of the People's Republic, the "bourgeois" values of Maoism are part of a larger world view derived from Marxism, which proclaims and prophesies socialist and communist goals. And it is that broader (and rather murky) realm often referred to as "the Maoist vision" that now must be taken into account the better to understand the nature and function of Chinese Communist values.

The Vision of the Future

If Maoism—and Chinese Communist theory in general—conveys bourgeois values, at least in very large measure, such values are not presented to the Chinese people as ends in themselves. Rather, they are set forth as the necessary means of the present to realize the Marxist goals of a "post-bourgeois" communist society historically located in the future. Just as Calvinism and Puritanism demanded an ascetic pattern of life as an ethical obligation to serve the glory of God and to establish the future Kingdom of God on earth, so the practice of the ascetic social values demanded by Maoism is justified by the highly utopian vision of the future prophesied in Marxist theory. The message carried in popular Chinese moral tracts is a rather simple and familiar one: Struggle, sacrifice, and hard work in the present will be rewarded in the communist utopia of the future.

The advent of that utopia sometimes has been presented as a long-term historical process, as in Chou En-lai's oft-repeated promise that China will be a "powerful modern socialist country" by the year 2000. At other times, when the more utopian aspects of the Maoist mentality held sway, the arrival of communism was perceived and presented as more or less imminent. The popular rallying cry during the early phases of the Maoist-inspired Great Leap Forward campaign, for example, was that "three years of struggle" would lead to "a thousand years of communist happiness." In the first case, one struggles in the here and now for the sake of future generations; in the second, there is a chiliastic conception that a communist utopia is being realized in the here and now. In both cases, the ascetic values of struggle and hard work receive their ultimate ethical sanctification in the vision of a "truly human life" derived from classical Marxist writings.

The Maoist vision of a future communist society, beyond reinforcing the prescribed ascetic values that are to guide social behavior in the present by making them morally meaningful in terms of a larger historical world view, also has served powerfully to reinforce the modern Western notion that change is desirable and indeed the historical norm. It conveys to the Chinese people a strong sense of hope and optimism, the promise that the future will be both different from and better than the present, the notion that there lies ahead a life of greater material abundance as well as one that will be morally and socially superior. Nothing from the classic Marxist texts is more frequently quoted in Chinese Communist writings than the famous passage in *The German Ideology* where Marx took one of his rare glimpses into the future and foresaw a communist society

> . . . where nobody has one exclusive sphere of activity but each can become accomplished in any branch he wishes, (where) society regulates the general production and thus makes it possible for me to do one thing today and another tomorrow, to hunt in the morning, fish in the afternoon, rear cattle in the evening, criticize after dinner, just as I have a mind, without ever becoming hunter, fisherman, shepherd or critic.

The passage not only conveys an idyllic vision of the future, but also serves to reinforce a Maoist preference for the values of the ideologically pure generalist over those of the professional specialist.

Perhaps more importantly, the utopian Marxist vision propagated in

Chinese Communist ideology poses a fundamental challenge to traditional values. For Chinese thought largely lacked a tradition of ethical prophecy; in striking contrast to the Judeo-Christian tradition of the West, the Chinese world view was not one that demanded of all men the ethical duty to build a new and perfect world in accordance with God's will. Instead, social harmony was the primary Confucian value (and indeed the popular Chinese value), and it fostered patterns of thought and behavior that favored accepting the world as it existed. It was Marxism, more than any other Western ideology, that brought to China a particularly powerful prophetic element. By contrasting the ideal communist society of the future with the grim realities of the present, Marxism (especially in its visionary Maoist form) conveys values which demand that the world be mastered, values which teach that one need not reconcile oneself to things as they are, but rather that one can and must struggle to transform nature and change society in accordance with higher ideals.

Yet the "Maoist vision" does not convey an unmitigatedly optimistic view of the future. Chinese Communist thought, at least in its Maoist form, is marked by the lack of a typical Marxist faith in the historical inevitability of socialism. Intermingled with optimistic hopes for a socialist and communist future were pessimistic fears of the ever-present possibility of historical retrogression. For Mao, the question of whether China would move forward to socialism or slide back to capitalism was never definitively settled; in his later years he was obsessed by fears of regression, warning in 1962, for example, that "a country like ours can still move toward its opposite," and indeed even turn "fascist." And the Maoist mentality of the Cultural Revolution was characterized more by a fear of the reassertion of the forces of the past than it was by a positive utopian vision of the future. In the Maoist view, the question of whether China was to be socialist or capitalist was not left to the workings of history, but ultimately was dependent on the consciousness and activities of people. Here the enormous emphasis on the value of struggle once again comes to the fore, for it was only the social and ideological struggles of dedicated people that could bring about a favorable historical outcome. And it was here, in the sense of historical indeterminateness which generally characterizes the Maoist mentality, that Maoists drew upon the more activistic strains in the Marxist tradition, emphasizing the Marxist premise that "men make history," that people change their own nature by acting on and changing the external world, and that the emergence of the new socialist society presupposes the "emergence of new men."

Less easy to reconcile with Marxism is the Maoist vision of the future communist society itself. On the one hand, it is a standard Marxist vision of a classless society where the age-old distinctions between mental and manual labor, between town and countryside, and between workers and peasants have been abolished—and where the state "withers away." On the other hand, it is a vision that foresees a future of contradictions, conflicts, and struggles that are ↩ndless and eternal. Even after the advent of communism, Mao prophesied, "ideological and political struggles between men and revolutions will continue to occur; they will never cease. . . . The theory of cessation of struggles is sheer metaphysics." Whereas Marx (and Marxists generally) viewed communism in terms of the overcoming of all conflicts, Mao was opposed in principle to any conception of a future characterized by the absence of conflict. The "Maoist vision" precluded a final resolution of contradictions and precluded, as both undesirable and impossible, the very notion of any perfect social unity. Indeed, the ultimate Maoist vision extended the notion of "the universality of contradictions" well beyond communism, as when Mao speculated:

> Capitalism leads to socialism, socialism leads to communism, and communist society must still be transformed, it will also have a beginning and an end. . . . There is nothing in the world that does not arise, develop, and disappear . . . in the end, the whole human race will disappear . . . the earth itself will also cease to exist . . . the sun too will grow cold. . . . All things have a beginning and an end. Only two things are infinite: time and space.

These strands in "the Maoist vision" projected into the communist (and "post-communist") future the conflicts and the dominant value of struggle in the present. It is a vision that reflected the extraordinary emphasis placed on the value of struggle, converting struggle from a means to achieve ultimate ends into an ultimate end as such. And it served to provide an absolute ethical sanction for the value of struggle to achieve social and economic change by making change and struggle absolute and eternal cosmic laws.

The Dilemma of the Means and Ends of Socialism

The more idiosyncratic aspects of Mao's vision of the future, the speculations about the time when "the sun too will grow cold," hardly have any meaningful relationship to the present. For the imaginable future the communist promise, at least as popularly conveyed to the Chinese people, is an essentially Marxist vision of a socially egalitarian and materially abundant socialist society, albeit one that involves continuous ideological and political struggle. Yet the vision of a China both modern and socialist has long been a source of tension in the People's Republic, for the values of modern industrialism and the values of socialism do not always coincide. It was in the mid-1950s, during the course of China's First Five Year

Plan of economic development, that Mao and Maoists were first forced to confront the dilemma of the means and ends of socialism.

The First Five Year Plan of 1953–57, emphasizing the development of urban heavy industry, succeeded in doubling China's modern industrial capacity. But like the earlier Soviet counterpart upon which it was largely modeled, the Chinese plan brought consequences that seemed to clash with the socialist ends modern industrialism was originally intended to serve. Instead of reducing the differences between rulers and ruled, centralized economic planning required enormous bureaucratic structures that accentuated those differences. Rather than promoting social equality, the drive for modern industrial development produced new forms of inequality; a new political elite of bureaucratic administrators and a new economic elite of industrial managers, scientists, and technicians emerged to occupy privileged positions in the new society, enjoying economic and social benefits not afforded to the common people. And far from narrowing the gap between the modern cities and the backward countryside, the First Five Year Plan widened the differences between the urban and rural populations, for the industrialization of the cities was largely based on the exploitation of the peasantry. What was called "the transition to socialism" was not a process that was diminishing social differences, much less creating a classless society.

As industrialization produced increasingly complex bureaucratic structures and a new hierarchy of ranks, the values of organizational efficiency and strict obedience to authority vitiated the Maoist preference for administrative simplicity and local popular initiative. The technician and the engineer replaced the revolutionary cadre as the new social model for emulation, and vocational ethics overshadowed the Maoist political ethic. "Rationalize, systematize, and regularize" was one of the popular slogans of the time and it reflected the temper of the times. Socialist goals were still ardently proclaimed, and no doubt still believed, but the real operative values in Chinese society were becoming the values of modern industrialism—the values of economic rationality and bureaucratic efficiency.

It was against these social and ideological consequences of industrialization, against the dominance of values and social tendencies that seemed so incongruous with both the envisioned socialist goals of the future and the revolutionary heritage of the past, that Mao Tse-tung rebelled. And it was from that rebellion against Soviet-style industrialization that there emerged a new and distinctively Maoist strategy of socioeconomic development, a strategy designed to reconcile the means of modern economic development with the ends of socialism. At the heart of that strategy was an attempt to reestablish the primacy of political values over economic values and a revival of the old revolutionary populist faith in the moral values and political consciousness of the masses, especially the peasant masses.

The new Maoist strategy of development, which began to take shape in 1955 and which received its fullest practical expression in the Great Leap Forward of 1958–60, was a wholesale rejection of the orthodox Soviet assumption that a crash program of industrial development under Communist political auspices would more or less guarantee the arrival of a socialist society. The Maoist assumption, by contrast, was that social and ideological change must precede economic change if the socialist and communist goals of the revolution were to be realized. Under Chinese conditions, Mao proclaimed in 1955, "technical reform will take longer than social reform."

It was further assumed that the socialist transformation of society and the "communist" transformation of popular consciousness must take place in the here and now, in the very process of constructing the economic foundations of the new society, and not after a lengthy process of modern economic development—a notion reflected in the widely publicized Maoist formula that "proletarianization" was to precede "mechanization." The Maoist strategy also rested on the belief that the key to modern economic development was the full utilization of China's greatest resource, the labor power of the Chinese people, and that belief, in turn, rested on the assumption that the masses were (or were to be) spiritually transformed in accordance with the proper Maoist social, political, and moral values.

These various beliefs and assumptions received their main theoretical formulation in the doctrine of "permanent revolution," a doctrine that demanded rapid and continuous processes of ideological, social, and economic transformation and placed an enormous emphasis on the values of change and struggle. "The revolution must advance without interruption," Mao declared in setting forth the doctrine on the eve of the Great Leap Forward. "The theory of cessation of struggles (in a socialist society) is sheer metaphysics."

Closely associated with the notion of "permanent revolution" was the dictum: "Politics takes command." This formula for the general politicization of values found its most popular expression in the "red and expert" notion, which occupied so prominent a place in Chinese Communist thought and ideology in the years after 1957. The ideally portrayed "red and expert" not only exemplifies the ascetic and antitraditional values deemed necessary in the present, but is also the bearer of the communist consciousness and values that will bring about the utopian social goals proclaimed in the Marxist vision of the future. As typically described, the "red and expert" person is the model for a new generation of "all-round men who combine a capacity for mental labor with a capacity for manual labor"; he is a politically conscious "jack-of-all-trades," who is able to master modern science, technology, and culture, as well as diligently engage in physical labor; he is capable of combining civilian with military affairs, theory with practice, "brain work with brawn work," and willing and able to switch from one job to another as the needs of society dictate. The "red and expert," in short, was the prototype and bearer of the values of the "new communist man" who would realize the Maoist dream of a whole nation of "socialist-conscious, cultured laborers."

In the Maoist view, the popularization of the values associated with the "red and expert" notion were seen as essential for the success of the distinctively Maoist policies and programs introduced during the Great Leap Forward era and after: the rural people's communes, originally envisioned as the embryonic social and political units of the future communist society; the obligation of officials and intellectuals to engage regularly in productive labor together with the masses in factories or on farms, celebrated as a way to promote the dignity of labor and reduce the distinction between leaders and led; educational policies that emphasized the combination of learning and productive labor, hailed as a step in eliminating the separation between mental and manual labor; and programs for rural industrialization, popularized as a means to narrow the gap between town and countryside and between workers and peasants. It was through such collectivistic policies and programs, and through the egalitarian values they presupposed and were to foster, that Maoists hoped to reconcile modern economic development with the modern Western-derived ideal of socialism.

From the perspective of the Chinese Communists' own socialist goals and standards, the results of the Maoist strategy have been both positive and negative. On the one hand, the effort to reconcile economic means with socialist ends has mitigated the growth of bureaucratic elitism and the extremes of social inequality that early industrialism invariably fosters. Moreover, in striking contrast to most "developing" countries, it has kept within tolerable bounds the social and economic gap between the modern cities and the backward rural areas. And perhaps most importantly, Maoism kept alive the socialist goals and values of the revolution, forestalling the universal tendency for revolutionary goals and ideals to become empty rituals in the postrevolutionary era.

At the same time, Maoism did not prove incompatible with modern economic development. Although immediate economic gains were sometimes sacrificed to political and ideological considerations, most observers agree that the basic foundations for a modern industrial economy were laid during the quarter-century Maoist era in the history of the People's Republic. Indeed, the ascetic and antitraditional values conveyed by the Maoist version of Marxism have played a highly significant role in modernizing the world's most populous land.

While Maoism conveys profoundly anti-bureaucratic values, neither in theory nor practice did it foster the popular democratic institutions that are so essential in the Western Marxist conception of socialism. The political deficiencies of Maoism can be traced back to the celebrated Yenan era of the Chinese Communist Revolution. The Yenan period was a time when Chinese Communists forged a tradition of egalitarian values and practices that encouraged popular participation in social and economic life. But it was also a time when Mao and Maoists set down rigid dogmas for the conduct of political and cultural life and relentlessly suppressed those who dissented from their orthodoxies. There was a glaring contrast between the values that pointed to liberation from the socioeconomic oppressions of the past and the ones that supported political-intellectual repression in the present. And this incongruity remained to mark and mar Maoism in the postrevolutionary history of the People's Republic.

The Future of Maoist Values

In the period since the death of Mao Tse-tung, his successors have tended to portray Mao more as a great modernizer and nation-builder than as a builder of socialism. The new portrait has been drawn to support policies that place an increased emphasis on the need for modern scientific and technological development and a more rapid pace of economic growth. Yet far from repudiating the Maoist legacy, the new rulers of China will likely champion it, albeit selectively, since the ascetic and antitraditional values that occupy so large a place in the Maoist version of Marxism are highly conducive to the goal of modernization. If the more iconoclastic aspects of Maoism are likely to be muted, new celebrations of the traditional cultural-historical heritage will likely take place in "the silence of the museum," while the basic antitraditional thrust of Maoist values will be retained. In the political realm, it is probable that the emphasis will be on the more authoritarian values of Maoism rather than on the populist values that lend themselves to the disruptions of mass campaigns. This may make Chinese political life appear more "rational" in Western eyes, but it is not likely to make China more democratic. In general, Maoist values in the post-Maoist era will probably play the same modernizing role that they did in the years when Mao was alive.

Yet Marxism and Maoism are not simply ideologies of modernization. The Maoist aim, derived from Marxism, was to make China both modern *and* socialist. The leaders of post-Maoist China are certainly committed to making China modern. And they undoubtedly desire to make China socialist as well. But the historical question yet to be answered is whether the new rulers of China will be as concerned as were their predecessors with reconciling the goals of modernization and socialism. Where the two aims are in conflict—or are perceived to be—it seems likely that the egalitarian and collectivistic values of Maoism will be subordinated to an emphasis on the ascetic Maoist values favorable to modern economic development. While the future of Chinese society cannot easily be predicted, it might be suggested that as long as China's modern transformation takes place under the auspices of Marxist theory, the history of the People's Republic will continue to be influenced significantly by a doctrine that conveys essentially modern Western, and not traditional Chinese, values and goals. And in this sense China is becoming a modern nation in a world of modern nation-states—a distinctive nation to be sure, but distinctive in the way in which modern nations differ from one another. As an eminent historian of China once speculated:

> . . . the spread of a common technology, though it may destroy the world materially, may actually create that Hegelian fantasy, a world-spirit. And China, then, would differ from Russia and England not as the Confucian civilization differed from the Christian, but as nations, in keeping their own historical *personae,* differ from one another—yet exist in a single many-coloured, more-than-national civilization.*

---

*Joseph R. Levenson, *Confucian China and Its Modern Fate* (1965), vol. 3, p. 123.

The Fate of Religion

HOLMES WELCH

Holmes Welch takes up what looks like a bleak topic. He goes to fundamentals by starting and ending his essay with attitudes toward death (a theme that Mao mentioned a great deal in his later years). In this respect he finds the Chinese people today not all that different from what they used to be, which means very different from Americans.

In brief strokes Welch sums up the main Chinese religious traditions and then examines their institutional fate in the PRC. The author knows too much about Chinese religions to build walls between Confucianism, Buddhism, and Taoism, or to draw firm and rapid conclusions, but in general he finds that the first two have suffered near-total eclipse as institutions. Politics has fatally invaded most of the various religious establishments of China. About Taoism as a practice, Welch strikes a surprising—and perhaps controversial—note of optimism, based on reports in the Chinese media and on evidence from refugees from Hong Kong.

Islam seems to be flourishing, in part for international reasons. Welch also argues that Maoism has at times functioned as a religion in China, though he doubts that it will do so in the future. He regrets the passing of the old, but his regret is flecked with a hopeful suspicion that the past is sometimes still present. If there used to be a bit of all three religions in each Chinese— and later Christianity too—perhaps that makes the demise of religion more problematic than it would be in a culture where a church is exclusive.

Holmes Welch has long been a scholar of Chinese religions. His books include Taoism: The Parting of the Way *(1957);* The Practice of Chinese Buddhism, 1900–50 *(1966);* The Buddhist Revival in China *(1967);* Buddhism Under Mao *(1972); and* Facets of Taoism *(1979). Born in 1921 in Massachusetts, where he still lives, Welch worked in the U.S. State Department and Foreign Service during 1942–45 and 1957–61. In recent years he has taught at Harvard and held research appointments under a variety of auspices.*

—R.T.

Death is inevitable, even in a progressive society. Education in dialectical materialism or in the importance of class struggle cannot eliminate death. The ways of coping with death give important clues to the nature of a society, including that of contemporary China.* Death is one of the cornerstones of religion. I cannot think of a case where it is not; and so it will be my first topic.

My second topic will be organized, institutional religions. Only one of the four major ones in China (Confucianism, Taoism, Buddhism, and Islam) is comparable to a religion in the United States—and that is Islam. This is not to imply that the United States is a religious monolith, stable and uniform. Change is rapid, and God knows where it will end. Too many Americans seem to have forgotten the words of Jesus: "False prophets will arise and show great signs and wonders." The other pasture looks greener. In the United States, however, one is free to try grazing there openly.

In China, Muslims alone belong to a church in the sense that many Americans do. Most Chinese were formerly said to be "Confucian in office, Taoist in retirement, and Buddhist as death approached." There was much truth in this saying. Committed lay Buddhists did exist, of course. They had taken the lay vows and some, particularly women, lived in so-called vegetarian halls (places where elderly and unmarried women dwelt—supposedly observing the rule of chastity and practicing Buddhism in order to prepare for their eventual death).

There were laymen who seriously practiced Taoist self-cultivation, which was comparable to the practice of lay Buddhists, and even comparable in one of its aims—the perfection of the self—as well as to the non-Buddhist pursuit of physical immortality. I know of very few Chinese who were not deeply affected by Confucian social ideals, particularly the ideal of social order and the family. Yet Confucianism and Taoism had little following abroad and hence have not been factors in foreign policy. Even the Chinese form of Buddhism is largely autochthonous.

*The attitude toward death in China is discussed more fully in my *Buddhism Under Mao* (1972) and in books by Simon Leys, Ross Terrill, and many others.

Another common saying was that Ch'an (Zen) Buddhism was really Taoism in Buddhist dress. Islam, on the other hand, is a foreign religion —the religion of countries that are important in China's international relations. This is the reason why Islam has survived particularly well and received government backing.

To what extent have Buddhism, Taoism, Islam, and Confucianism survived as institutions? It is a complicated question. I think that Buddhism and Confucianism have not really survived. Until recently I did not think that Taoism had survived. Islam is another matter. It is, after all, the religion of a national minority and its treatment, as I have said, affects relations with many foreign countries. The Chinese press for several years (1967–75) gave religious coverage to little but Islam—such as how the Bairam and Corban festivals (the two most important festivals of the year for Chinese Muslims) were celebrated in Peking during October and December. Such stories contrast with reports of how certain mosques have been closed, abandoned, or converted to other uses. (Leys cites an example of one that he saw in 1972.) It would be oversimplifying to say that Islam has survived whereas Confucianism, Buddhism, and Taoism have not; the case of Taoism is particularly complex.

My third topic will be the extent to which Maoism has become a religion. I believe that it was one for a while. During the Cultural Revolution Maoism was, I think, clearly a religion—or the functional equivalent of a religion. This statement may grate on the nerves of readers who accept the Marxist and Maoist view that religion is bad, but I fear that they must face the facts. Robert J. Lifton's *Revolution Immortality* (1968) offered valuable evidence of how Maoism became a religion during the Cultural Revolution. The burial of the Chairman in a glass case like Stalin's has, since 1976, offered further evidence.

This will lead us back to where we started: the way death is regarded and handled in China today. The Chinese people are now not supposed to fear death. It is a fact of life that they are told to accept. Any attempt to cope with it by religious means has been condemned as "superstition." Gone is the comfort of a Buddhist service for the dead—the main source of income for most Buddhist temples in China before 1949. Gone seems to be the comfort for the intellectuals of Taoist writings about physical immortality—writings that have played a role in China for two thousand years or more. As for Islam, it offers comfort to the 1–2 percent of the population who are officially said to be Muslim.

The Treatment of Death

What are the important moments in the everyday life of the Chinese? One is death. Funeral and burial practices have changed since 1949. My impression is that cremation has become as customary for Chinese Communist leaders—Mao was the exception—as it used to be for all Buddhist monks; that most of the rural population are buried, as used to be normal for non-Buddhist Chinese; and that cremation is winning widespread acceptance among ordinary city dwellers.

But just where country folk are buried has changed. In the 1950s there was a series of campaigns to move the graves that used to lie in the middle of cultivated fields throughout much of China and interfere with cultivation. There was touching evidence of the people's resentment against this moving of their ancestors. In China the animal soul of the dead person was supposed to linger about the corpse for three years, but at the festival of "Clear and Bright" (Ch'ing Ming), which occurs close to Easter, it was customary to visit the graves of one's ancestors, to sweep them, to tidy up around them, and to perform a ritual—eating a simple meal and offering a share to the spirits of the ancestors, individually and collectively.

Wolfram Eberhard, probably exaggerating one-sidedly, wrote in 1958 of the effect of moving graves: "Chinese Communist reforms . . . would have rather drastic results. The last source of firewood and lumber of North China would disappear, and how could the peasant then feed his only cow or a couple of goats that graze on the grasses that grow around the tombs?"* The answer is, of course, that the state has taken over responsibility for both agriculture and feeding the rural population.

The festival of "Clear and Bright" also used to be an occasion when the family came together, even from distant places. Probably the family plays less of a role in China than it used to play. It was perhaps the most important thing in life, now theoretically replaced by the Communist Party and collective organizations. Therefore the impossibility of usually getting together for the "Clear and Bright" Festival means less than one would otherwise expect. The immediate family still tries meeting to celebrate the New Year, that is, the lunar New Year (which is called the "Spring Festival"). The solar New Year used to be considered by a few people to be "more progressive," although it was Western and therefore conflicted with the spirit of nationalism.

Between Hong Kong and Canton, 80 odd miles apart, there is considerable traffic connected with death. For example, some devoutly religious women in Hong Kong go to Canton, taking incense with them secretly (or at least it was secret a few years ago). Once in Canton three hours later, they would light it at the graves of their ancestors. Then they would try to get the lighted incense sticks back to Hong Kong secretly, which was even more difficult than it had been to bring them *from* Hong Kong. This traffic was, of course, one-way.

The practice of burning sticks of incense before the tablets of ancestral

*Wolfram Eberhard, *Chinese Festivals* (1958), p. 116.

spirits is today discouraged, if not forbidden, in China. A soul tablet is a small oblong plaque—say 2 by 12 inches—kept on an altar. Its principal inscription is the name of the deceased, whose soul is believed to come to enjoy his worship, the food offered, and the prayers for advice and help. Such tablets were also, until recently at least, sternly discouraged. Yet ancestor worship has been one of the most important features of Chinese religious life for several thousand years.

According to Chinese custom, offering food, burning incense (or candles), and praying for ancestral advice and help is done at the grave as well as at the soul tablet. I heard of one case in which a Hong Kong woman melted down red "spirit candles" and made them into little figures that could be safely taken across the border. Once in China, she had them remelted into candles, which were then burned before the graves of her relatives.

Yet another practice has been to "lead the spirits of the dead" back from their graves in Canton to soul tablets that had been set up in Hong Kong at a special altar where they could receive regular offerings of food, incense, and the recitation of scriptures. The recitation of scriptures is another religious practice that is discouraged in China, but it is an old Chinese custom and gives comfort (and wisdom, perhaps) to the living.

The following story involves "passports" *(lu-p'iao)*—slips of paper on which are written the names and addresses of dead relatives in China. In Hong Kong such a "passport" is burned before a soul tablet that some Hong Kong resident has paid to have set up and given "perpetual care" by a Hong Kong temple. I call it a "passport" because to a Chinese believer such a slip of paper, when burned in this way, serves as a ticket of admission for the soul to move from Canton to Hong Kong (or get into what Buddhists call the Western Paradise).*

A variant in the use of "passports" is suggested by the story of an old woman in Hong Kong who had decided to return to China to die. She purchased a soul tablet for herself (presumably because she had no children who would have purchased it for her after her death) and arranged to have it set up in a vegetarian hall. She had a "passport" made up that would enable her soul to return to her tablet in Hong Kong after she herself had died in Canton. She sewed it into her clothing, hoping that the customs officials would not spot it. Her plan was that, once she had finally died, her relatives in Canton would burn the "passport" so that her soul might return to Hong Kong. This illustrates that "where there's a will, there's a way."

*W. E. Soothill, *A Mission to China* (1907), gives a somewhat different explanation of *lu-p'iao.* He says they are passports with which the soul of the deceased can enter the Western Paradise.

Such examples may or may not be typical of what happens in China. The proximity of Canton and Hong Kong is unique in the relations of China with the outside world. Yet I think these reports suggest what may be typical of the attitudes of many older Chinese in areas further north. The reports also suggest the ingenuity with which common people (not merely those from Hong Kong) get around the resolve of the People's Government to "eradicate superstition."

Taoism Disappears?

The fate of Taoism as an institution has apparently been far more severe than that of Buddhism, to be discussed below. In 1950–53 Taoist organizations—both genuinely Taoist and pseudo-Taoist—were suppressed in the campaign against "heterodox Taoist sects." There is an obvious reason for this. Most of the important rebellions in Chinese history have been connected with Taoism, beginning with the Yellow Turban rebellion in A.D. 184, which so weakened the Han Dynasty that it fell three decades later. In 1957 a Chinese Taoist Association was established. This did not mean that the government had relaxed its efforts to fight "heterodox Taoist sects" or "superstition." Almost no organized Taoism apparently remained alive. I do not know of any counterpart to *Modern Buddhism* or the other Buddhist periodicals.

The headquarters of the Chinese Taoist Association were in the White Cloud Monastery (Po-yün Kuan), a famous Taoist center in Peking. The site goes back to the T'ang Dynasty. In the thirteenth century its abbot, Ch'ang-ch'un, was made head of all the religious people and organizations in China by Genghis Khan, an absolute ruler who was admired by Mao Tse-tung. (Ch'ang-ch'un and Genghis Khan both died in A.D. 1227.) Of course, the Mongols then only controlled a small part of China. In 1756 the emperor Ch'ien-lung had extensive repairs made to this monastery and gave it an image of the first Taoist "Pope," who had lived in the second century.

Despite its illustrious history and the fact that it became the seat of the Chinese Taoist Association in 1957, I have been unable to find any reference to this monastery in Chinese guidebooks to Peking published there in 1956, 1957, and 1960—either in the Chinese language or in English. In 1972 it was being used as an army barracks, according to Simon Leys, who lived only ten minutes away by bicycle. Apparently the Taoist association always got far less attention, both favorable and unfavorable, from the Religious Affairs Bureau than did the Buddhist association. Again, this must be because there are few Taoists outside China, especially in countries with which the Chinese government considers relations to be important.

In 1973 Professor and Mrs. Ivan London interviewed a refugee who had come from living on a commune in Fukien.* The refugee said that on his commune, which he left in 1972, funerals were still being performed, but not by Buddhist monks. Instead, they were performed by Taoist priests, who lived in the village inconspicuously, anonymously. Yet everyone knew who they were, and, when a death occurred, the family would ask a priest to perform the traditional Taoist rites dressed in his ceremonial robe, but without the traditional headdress. (Thus it was like similar rites performed today in Taiwan.) The authorities, of course, discouraged all this. They even stopped funerals occasionally on orders from authorities higher up. On those occasions, "everyone was so very angry, even people looking on in the street. . . . The commune authorities knew they were looking for trouble," said the refugee. A member of the Communist Party in the production brigade would sometimes ask a Taoist priest to perform a funeral ceremony for his father.

The refugee began talking about all of this in response to a question about lumber production: Who paid for the wood from which coffins were made? The family did, he said. It would rather go into debt than bury one of its members in a cheap coffin if it could avoid doing so. The prices ranged from $25 to about $100. The fee of the Taoist priest was only $2.50, but he was also given a meal. During the Cultural Revolution the several Taoist priests in the village had all been paraded and struggled against. This seems to have had no effect on their performing funerals *after* the Cultural Revolution.

The refugee also offered interesting information about the survival of private enterprise in the production of objects having a religious use. Coffins, joss sticks (incense), and token paper money to burn at a funeral were all made in people's homes. The traditional concern for "face" had, of course, continued. People used to worry on the commune about what their neighbors would think if they tried to carry out Party policy, which was (as many other sources confirm) not to waste time, money, and materials on an expensive funeral. A picture of the deceased was still kept in front of the coffin. There was no picture of Mao anywhere nearby.

In April 1978 the Hunan Province press and radio reported an extraordinary event. It was the funeral of the father of a Communist Party member named Liu, who was deputy chief of the county labor wage bureau. His father had died on April 18, 1977. The three sons, all of whom were members of the Communist Party, invited a Taoist priest to conduct the funeral, and a geomancer to pick an appropriate time and

*See *The Revenge of Heaven* (1972) by Ken Ling. Simon Leys calls this work, which is a collaboration between the Londons and the former Red Guard, "without doubt the most important book to be born out of the Cultural Revolution." The Londons have for many years carried on systematic interviewing of Chinese refugees.

place for the funeral and temporary burial. The brothers gave the two religious specialists money and gifts to reward them. At the memorial service on April 19, "members of the family, old and young, circled the coffin three times to indicate that they would carry lanterns at the funeral." The temporary burial took place on April 20. According to the Hunan radio report,

> . . . the coffin was covered with a cloth and a photograph. . . . Some fifty to sixty wreaths were carried in front of the coffin. . . . Musicians played drums and gongs in front and behind. Some three hundred people attended the funeral. . . . The funeral procession passed two communes, four production brigades, and fourteen production teams. . . . During the journey the Liu family also distributed money to passers-by. . . . On the day of the burial forty tables of food were set up for lunch. Some thousand catties of grain and three hundred catties of pork [about 600 lbs.] were wasted. Expenses reached 790 yüan [about $400]. . . . Liu also exploited his position and power to order a vehicle and tractor to take his relatives and friends to the funeral. . . . He accepted more than seventy scrolls and over 420 feet of cloth from the people who attended the funeral.

A year passed before the Party took punitive action. On March 29, 1978, it placed the eldest son on a year's probation and dismissed him as deputy chief of the county labor wage bureau. A serious warning was given to the vice-chairman of the county CCP committee, who had helped the Liu family with the funeral "during the busy season of transplanting early rice seedlings."

A similar event was reported from Anhwei in March 1978. Here the deceased had himself been the deputy secretary of the CCP county committee. His "memorial services" were "large-scale and magnificent." There was a forty-man funeral committee, of which the members included the Standing Committee of the CCP County Committee, the County Revolutionary Committee, and all the directors and deputy directors of county government departments. The funeral was held in the courtyard of the CCP county committee. Party members stood by the coffin day and night, and communes were asked to send funeral wreaths.

Protests were made about this to the CCP county committee, which ignored them. Finally the CCP Anhwei Provincial Committee issued instructions to the whole province on how to handle such matters. "Party committees at all levels were asked to grasp the rectification of the Party's work style as a major issue and resolutely to check the evil wind caused by the Gang of Four and their agents in our province." *Plus ça change, plus c'est la même chose.*

What this all means is that Taoism has apparently replaced Buddhism as the principal source of care for the dead—at least in some areas of the countryside, far from the eyes of foreigners. In that case Taoism may not have disappeared except in the cities. This would make sense, for country people have always been more conservative than city people, and more ingenious in finding a way to get around the wishes of the central government. In other words, here the net effect of the Cultural Revolution was to preserve—but in an altered way—Chinese culture in the countryside.

There is also evidence that here and there Taoist temples survive in the city if they are considered cultural monuments worth showing to visitors. In 1977 two American visitors to Kunming were shown "a great Taoist temple" outside the city and allowed to photograph it in detail. Such phenomena are not to be confused with the survival of Taoism as a widespread institutional religion, which remains a question mark.

Buddhism Fades Away

Let us turn now to the fate of Buddhism in China—a topic equally hard to research and to summarize. Until the Cultural Revolution began in 1966, the Chinese government followed a carefully thought-out policy. First, it tried to reduce the influence of Buddhism *inside* China. Second, it nevertheless tried to use the same persons for the purpose of building good relations with Buddhist countries and Buddhist leaders abroad. Destroying Buddhism as a faith did not mean destroying it as a cultural heritage. A lot of public money was spent in renovating the few "living" monasteries—those that were still permitted to have monks in residence.

This contradictory policy was moderately successful, although it was hard on the Chinese Buddhists involved. They had to cooperate in the use of Buddhism to destroy Buddhism. As to foreign Buddhists, some were taken in, perhaps because they wanted to be taken in. It served their own domestic purposes. A good example is Amritananda, a leading Nepalese Buddhist monk who ran a boys' boarding school near Katmandu. He used China in order to get financial support as well as publicity for the school and himself. He went to China in July 1959 and again in December. In that year, when the Lhasa Uprising (or Tibetan rebellion) took place, the Chinese said that "Nepal persisted in its correct stand of non-interference in China's internal affairs."

Amritananda has been called, by an unfriendly person, "the most valuable to the Chinese of all the toadies among foreign Buddhists." I myself found his motives hard to understand when I visited his school in October 1962. The Chinese in Peking had published his book *Buddhist Activities in Socialist Countries* the year before. On the other hand, some foreign Buddhists were less impressed than he by the red carpet that the Chinese government rolled out for them—and by other things. Indeed, some were privately very critical of what they had seen on their guided tours.

A Chinese Buddhist Association was set up in 1953, run by a layman named Chao P'u-ch'u, a well-known poet and calligrapher. I met him in 1961 at the Sixth Conference of the World Fellowship of Buddhists (WFB), in which both the PRC and the Republic of China (Taiwan) were represented. I even, through a peculiar quirk of fate partly described in *Buddhism Under Mao,* led the Hong Kong Buddhist delegation. I talked several times with Chao P'u-ch'u, who impressed me as being wary and a little tortured in his manner. After the Cultural Revolution, Japanese Buddhist visitors to China reported that Chao was in the hospital with heart trouble. Yet in November 1974 there was a news item in the *People's Daily* about how he had greeted a Japanese delegation. In October 1977 a national daily published a poem he had written about the birthplace of Hua Kuo-feng, the Chairman of the PRC since 1976. This town in Shansi happened to be the site of one of the most famous monasteries in China and a mecca for all Pure Land Buddhists in Japan. In April 1978 Chao P'u-ch'u led a delegation of Chinese Buddhist monks to Japan. It was like old times.

What has happened to the Chinese Buddhist Association? Specific information about what is really going on—or has really gone on—is extremely hard to get (I apologize for this litany). For example, a national census was taken in 1953. Neither then nor later was it revealed how many monks and nuns there were in China.* Nor was it revealed after 1949 how many active monasteries and nunneries there were in China. (I would define them as those having at least one monk or nun in residence.) Nor have any figures ever been given on the number of monks and nuns being ordained.

Let me give another illustration of how hard it is to get the facts about Buddhism. In 1958 several articles in the Chinese press criticized monks who "swindled money from people on the pretext of chanting scriptures." The nature of this "swindling" has never been legally defined. Also in 1958 the abbot of the most famous monastery in southern China was arrested on several charges. One was that he had failed to give the police the names of all the people who came to worship. The real intention of this charge was never explained. Again in 1958, *Modern Buddhism* stated that Buddhists "must kill the war-provoking devils in defense of world peace." Already in 1951 (during the Korean War) it had said: "To wipe out the American imperialist demons who are breaking world peace is, according to Buddhist doctrine, not only blameless but actually gives rise to merit." All of which raises questions about the values that the government has been trying to teach Buddhists.

*In 1930 there had been 738,000, according to a survey made by the Chinese Buddhist Society and accepted by the Nationalist government in 1947.

Now let us return to the first part of Chinese government policy under Mao: to reduce the influence of Buddhism in China, to eliminate it as a source of competition for the people's loyalty to Mao Tse-tung. The most illustrious Buddhist monastery in China is probably the T'ien-t'ung Ssu, which lies in the countryside approximately 14 miles from Ningpo (southeast China). It was built about A.D. 300. At this monastery Dogen experienced enlightenment and went back to Japan in 1227 to found the Japanese version of the Ts'ao-tung (Soto) sect of Ch'an (Zen) Buddhism —the second main sect of Ch'an. Here also for a time lived Sesshu (1420–1506), "the greatest painter, or at least the greatest landscape painter, that Japan has produced."* Before Liberation, the T'ien-t'ung Monastery had about four hundred monks (there had been about five hundred in A.D. 1225). In the spring of 1957 there were 151 monks in residence, who lived partly off farming their own land and partly by charging fees for their performance of rites for the dead. Before Liberation this monastery had had enormous landholdings, which it rented out to farmers or which the monks cultivated entirely themselves (sources differ). In any case there was more rice than the monks could eat; the surplus used to be given to needy monasteries nearby. Whatever landholdings remained after 1950, when most were probably lost, must have been confiscated in 1958 or 1966.

By June 1962 the number of resident monks had dropped to a little over a hundred. I have been able to get no information about what happened to the T'ien-t'ung Monastery during the Cultural Revolution. Foreign students living in Shanghai asked in 1976 if they could go to Ningpo. They were told that there was nothing there worth seeing.

More specific recent information is available on the Monastery of Broad Help (Kuang-chi Ssu) in Peking, which became the headquarters of the Chinese Buddhist Association when the latter was set up in 1953. By this year the Chinese government had coped with its most urgent tasks. The time had come to formalize a policy toward organized religion. Already in 1950 it had taken a preliminary step when it allowed Buddhists to start publishing a monthly, *Modern Buddhism,* in Peking. The first issue was dated September 1950, "the 2515th year of the Buddhist era."** The editor of *Modern Buddhism* was a monk, Chü-tsan, who was destined to play a leading role in the government's effort to tame Buddhism. The name of the layman who later became the most prominent in this effort —Chao P'u-ch'u—did not even appear in the first issue.

In January 1951 the beginning of what was to become in 1954 the

---

*Heinrich Dumoulin, *The History of Zen Buddhism* (1963).
**This meant that the Buddha was born in 565 B.C.—about the same date as is accepted by many Western scholars. Curiously enough, one traditional Chinese Buddhist chronology, still in use in the 1950s, had the Buddha born in 446 B.C.

Religious Affairs Bureau (RAB) was set up under the State Council. Thus it did not get its orders from any government department but from the Central Committee of the CCP itself. Because the RAB's work was going to be so delicate and many-sided, the Party wanted to keep the RAB under its direct control. The heads of its branches throughout China, as they were set up, were Party members of long standing.

In 1953 the national association held its inaugural conference from May 29 to June 3. It adopted almost the same name as its predecessor before Liberation and became the Chinese Buddhist Association. It had to have a headquarters where *Modern Buddhism* could be edited and published. For some reason an obscure monastery in Peking was picked for this purpose—the Monastery of Broad Help. Before 1953 this monastery had been so obscure that it is not even shown on a large map of Peking enclosed with the best English guidebook of the city, published there in 1953. But once it got the attention of the Religious Affairs Bureau, it was handsomely renovated and enlarged. The number of resident monks rose to "more than fifty" in 1959. In 1961 the abbot, Chü-tsan (who was also in Cambodia for the Sixth WFB Conference), told me that it had "about forty monks." Its income, he said, was derived partly from rents on its real estate, which was managed, along with the real estate of other Peking monasteries, by the Temples Management Committee of the Religious Affairs Bureau. In August 1967 a Japanese Buddhist went to the Monastery of Broad Help alone, after his interpreter had evaded questions about it. He found that the name outside it had been effaced and the main gate was closed. (Since then the name has been restored.) There was a lay receptionist at another gate. The Japanese asked him if he could interview the monks. The reply was: "They are not here." He asked if he could worship in the ordination hall, on the grounds that he himself belonged to the Vinaya sect (the "ordination sect"), and so did the monastery. The reply was: "No, because you do not have an introduction from the Religious Affairs Bureau." The Japanese was not allowed to enter the premises, but he could see from the gate that many youngsters were hanging about the monks' living quarters on the left and right of the central axis. The walls of the shrine halls were covered with big cartoons. It seemed to him that the monastery had been taken over by Red Guards and its monks expelled. In 1968 other Japanese visitors had similar experiences there.

Today, a decade later, the eventual fate of the Monastery of Broad Help is uncertain, as is the fate of the Chinese Buddhist Association. Apparently no final government policy has been determined with regard to Buddhist monasteries that have not become "cultural monuments," as most of the famous ones did during the Cultural Revolution. But at the end of 1978 their future looked better than it had since 1964.

Islam Survives

As I pointed out at the start, not only are there foreign countries to which the fate of Islam in China may be important, but also there are national minorities who are (whenever possible) practicing Muslims. So both foreign and domestic policy is involved in the treatment of Chinese Muslims. Yet the same can be said of the treatment of Tibetan and Mongolian Buddhists. Muslims particularly were involved in the century-old competition with Russia for control of central Asia. Sir Aurel Stein has vividly described the Russian efforts in 1900 to dominate western Sinkiang, the gateway to Chinese Turkestan—and to China.*

A Chinese Islamic Association was set up in 1953. It too published a monthly. Many mosques in China are still in use for worship. Foreign observers have recently seen worship under way, or have been told that it was under way regularly. In contrast to this are reports that some mosques are only showpieces. As usual, it is hard to arrive at a balanced conclusion based on adequate facts.**

Most Muslims in China were Sunnites, divided into "traditionalists," "reformists," and "modernists." The traditionalists adhered to the sinicized form of Islam that developed in China. The reformists advocated a return to orthodoxy and observance of the Koran. The modernists emphasized ethics more than doctrine and ritual. The Chinese government has refused to recognize such a division. All Muslims come under the Chinese Islamic Association, which was headed from its establishment by a Uighur named Burhan. At its inaugural meeting there seems to have been no mention of Allah or Mecca; at the time of its second meeting in 1956 the Suez crisis was on, and so it declared its support for Egypt.

Muslim youth are given Islamic education nowhere except at the Institute of Islamic Theology in Peking. At school young Muslims are taught politics. Everywhere, except perhaps at the Institute of Islamic Theology, the Cyrillic alphabet has replaced the Arabic alphabet. In Sinkiang and probably elsewhere, the government has abolished *purdah* (the seclusion of women). In Sinkiang, according to an unverified 1959 report, loudspeakers blaring political propaganda were being turned on during prayer meetings, and attendance was decreasing. During the late 1950s

---

*See Jeannette Mirsky, *Sir Aurel Stein, Archeological Explorer* (1977), and M. Aurel Stein, *Sand-Buried Ruins of Khotan* (1903) and *Ancient Khotan* (1907).
**There is even a question about how many Muslims the government considers there are in China. They may be divided into two main groups: the Hui (about 6 million Chinese-speaking Muslims who live in many areas); and the Uighurs (about 3.5 million Muslims in northwest China).

there was a government campaign against "local nationalism." In the case of Muslims the existence of local nationalism does not seem surprising.

There has been widespread confiscation of mosque lands, although initially the government respected the Agrarian Reform Law of 1950, which provided that land belonging to mosques was to be left in their ownership. The flying of the Islamic flag at mosques is (or was) forbidden on Muslim feast days.

Opposition to the government has reached the point of open revolts by Muslim minorities, such as those in 1952 by the Kazakhs in Sinkiang and the Hui in Kansu. Nor has the government's efforts to use Islam in foreign relations been entirely successful. In 1955–56 delegations from China succeeded in reaching Mecca, but they spent less time there than in other Muslim countries, where they presumably carried out government orders to promote better relations with China.

Tibet

Does Tibet lie outside the focus of this essay? What does it have to do with religion in China? The Dalai Lama is head of the Gelugpa sect of Buddhism, which is the "reform sect" established in the fifteenth century. He is often referred to as the "God-King" of Tibet. His rival, the Panchen Lama, has been a Chinese pawn for a long time—even before the present Panchen. He has had his ups and downs in playing this role. In 1964 he was dismissed as deputy chairman of the National People's Congress (according to one report, he was placed under house arrest or disappeared). In 1978 he was again in the good graces of Peking, reappearing in March as a delegate to the Chinese People's Political Consultative Conference. One NPC delegate was a Tibetan Living Buddha from Chamdo, the area in eastern Tibet that adjoins China, where revolt has smoldered since 1959.

The government's concern for Buddhism did not prevent it from doing terrible things to the Tibetans after the Lhasa Uprising of 1959.* India sided with the Tibetans, giving shelter to the Dalai Lama, and there was fear of war. In 1964, when the Seventh WFB Conference was held in India, the Chinese Buddhist Association withdrew from the WFB, protesting its "illegal activities." Chao P'u-ch'u, as a vice-president of the WFB, was quoted on this by the New China News Agency on Novem-

---

*Anyone interested in the history of Tibet can turn to a source that is presumably unbiased: the International Commission of Jurists in Geneva. It has published two books on the Tibetan question: *The Question of Tibet and the Rule of Law* (1959) and *Tibet and the Chinese People's Republic: A Report to the International Commission of Jurists by Its Legal Inquiry Committee on Tibet* (1960). The committee concluded that Chinese authorities had, among other things, committed "genocide against Buddhists in Tibet."

ber 17, 1964. On December 3 the Chinese Buddhist Association issued a specific statement:

> We have of late learned that . . . the headquarters of the World Fellowship of Buddhists has blatantly convened in India a seventh conference . . . has flagrantly invited the "Buddhist delegates" of the Chiang Kai-shek clique . . . and has brazenly admitted to the conference the ringleader of the Tibetan rebel clique, Dalai, who has been openly carrying out activities of betrayal of his motherland under the wing of foreign countries [meaning India and the United States] for several years past.

I sympathize with Chinese friends who consider that Japanese imperialism in China was worse than Chinese imperialism in Tibet. Yet it seems to me that imperialism is imperialism, regardless of its source. Only small countries do not seem to have often engaged in it.

The Religion of Maoism

The effort to make Mao Tse-tung into an object of worship seems to me undeniable, particularly during the Cultural Revolution. George Urban's book *The Miracles of Chairman Mao* (1971) offers extraordinary excerpts from the Chinese press and radio. Particularly striking are the items entitled:

Resurrecting the Dead (1969)
Faith Saving (1969)
Class Love Overrides Wife's Death (1968)
Martyr Posthumously Received into the Party (1968)
Vexed by Unclean Spirits (1969)
The Power of Chairman Mao's Image (1967)
The Recitation of Chairman Mao's Words (1969)
Immortality and Rebirth in Chairman Mao (1967)

Maybe someday there will be devout Maoists who say that his was a virgin birth or that, like the Buddha, he came from his mother's side. In the glass case his corpse is, unfortunately, said to be looking poorly. Perhaps, like Lenin's, part of it will have to be amputated.

Let me give one quotation in full. It is called "The Memorial Meal" and was broadcast by Peking Radio on June 1, 1969:

> It has been customary to eat meat dumplings on the first day of the Spring Festival, but I purposely made steamed corn rolls. I said to the children: "We take this meal so as not to forget the past sufferings, so as to let you know that our great leader Chairman Mao has brought us today's happi-

ness, and so as to make you become good children nurtured by Mao Tse-tung's Thought."

There is nothing particularly religious about this. The Spring Festival used to be the most important time of the year for almost all Chinese families. For centuries they had looked forward to eating meat dumplings together on New Year's Day. To me it seems needlessly cruel and destructive to promote a change to steamed corn rolls—although it would save meat.

"One Chinese provincial newspaper," wrote a Soviet observer, Yakovlev, in 1968, "reported that on holidays peasants install a picture of Mao in the middle of the village. Peasants go out to the fields carrying Mao's picture. Sometimes the field where they may be working will be fenced off with Mao's pictures. Tibetan peasants have placed next to effigies of Buddha large and small busts of Mao Tse-tung and sanctified towels [scarves] are presented as a votive offering in the same way as to Buddha." Yakovlev ends his piece by speaking of the "new-style zealots," who are inflating "great-khan chauvinism for their own ends."

"Great *Han* chauvinism" (or the feeling of superiority of Han Chinese toward other nationalities) was, of course, one of the cardinal sins denounced in Peking during the rectification movement of 1956–57, two or more years before the Lhasa Uprising. The denunciation was intended to assuage the Mongolians, Hui, Manchus, Uighurs—and the Tibetans. How rapidly government policy changes in China! The jack-in-the-box career of Teng Hsiao-p'ing since 1966 is only one example. With such a system in control, it is hard to write an essay on religion in China that might not be obsolete in a short time. The possibility exists that there will be a new Mao, deified despite the efforts of soberer heads.

The Future of Religion in China

If there should be a new Mao, Chinese culture, which was so impressively battered during the Cultural Revolution, will receive yet another blow. It might even disappear almost as completely as have the city walls of Peking, which looked so solid and indestructible only thirty years ago. It is my guess that the poorest rickshaw puller in Peking once felt, subconsciously, that he was living in a mandala, a magic diagram, which connected Heaven and Earth, the past with the present. (Perhaps this is one reason that the walls had to go in the early 1950s.) He may have felt, despite his hunger and poverty, a little comfort in the security of that architectural mandala. There are no more rickshaw pullers in Peking, but the city still has poor people. I suspect they have a feeling, which they would never dare express to foreign visitors and probably are not consciously aware of themselves, that the new sense which the Communist Party gives their lives is not a satisfactory substitute for the sense that once was there.

Now I hope I may be forgiven for saying something purely personal. Here and there I may have sounded a little anti-Chinese and so lost some of my best friends. May I remind them of the great tradition of the Censorate? This was, so far as I know, unique to China among the major countries of the world. Some censors—famed in history—lost their lives for doing their job, which was to criticize even the emperor. Po Chü-i, the great T'ang poet, got into trouble this way. More recently people have gotten into trouble for criticizing the government in many Chinese areas, including both Taiwan and the mainland. Some have lost their lives.

Yet 1978 was a year of rapid and dramatic change for the better. Admirers of the "Gang of Four" would call it a year of "counterrevolution." Chao P'u-ch'u, as mentioned earlier, led a delegation of Chinese Buddhist monks to Japan in April. In addition to Buddhist leaders, the chairman of the Chinese Catholic Patriotic Association and the former deputy secretary-general of the All-China Conference of Protestant Churches attended the Fifth Chinese People's Political Consultative Conference in May. For the first time in a long while, foreign visitors began to be shown Christian churches, in which they found small congregations on Sundays. An even more striking development took place in April 1978, when the Institute for Research on World Religions was revived within the Chinese Academy of Sciences and held its first forum, attended by 110 persons. The press report on this forum contained a surprise. In 1963, it said, Mao Tse-tung had written a "marginal note" that it was necessary to study, from a Marxist point of view, "the world's three great religions—Christianity, Islam, and Buddhism." (Hinduism, the ancient religion of India, did not qualify.) In line with Mao's instructions and "under the personal supervision" of Chou En-lai, "China's first scientific institute for the study of religion and Marxism—the Institute for Research on World Religions—was established in 1964."

News of its creation was not published. "It did not have a sound footing and functioned abnormally." This was attributed by the press to Lin Piao and the Gang of Four. "For more than ten years newspapers and journals rarely carried articles on the study of religion and the popularization of atheism."

This use of a "memory hole" (in George Orwell's phrase) ended with the forum of the Institute for Research on World Religions in 1978. First in the name list of those who took part was Hsiao Hsien-fa, long the head of the Religious Affairs Bureau. There were many other members of the Communist Party, as well as some well-known religious figures. The institute's task was "to develop the study of religion with Marxism in the struggle to criticize theology."

Here we may see exemplified the Chinese talent for screening with orthodoxy what is really innovation. "To write work of scientific value," said NCNA, "it is also necessary to do a great deal of work in compiling reference materials and to translate and explain with footnotes all kinds of classical religious documents." This would be welcomed by scholars all over the world.

The publication of "classical documents" had begun at least four years earlier. In November 1974 the journal *Wen-wu* reprinted the oldest known text of Lao-tzu, found in a Han dynasty tomb called Ma-wang-tui. (The Te chapters on "virtue" come in it before the Tao chapters on "the Way.") It is interesting that this, the seminal text of Taoism, was chosen for publication then. In April 1977 it was republished in book form, but still there was no one's name attached to the preface and postface. A year later, individuals engaged in the scientific study of religion had lost their shyness. "Counterrevolution" (academic and religious freedom) seemed to be in full swing. In saying this I differ from observers who have visited China often, which I have not. For example, in August 1978 Tim Brook, a Canadian student who had lived in Peking and Shanghai in 1974–76 and who had visited China twice in the first half of 1978, wrote an excellent article for *Commonweal,* the Catholic bi-monthly, with the title "Dying Gods in China." Brook is my friend, informant, and collaborator. Yet, when he wrote his article for *Commonweal,* he was unaware of the official radio and newspaper reports from Hunan and Anhwei that have been cited above to show how Communist Party members and organizations have been directly involved in religious practice and its support. Nor was he aware of the establishment of the Institute for Research on World Religions, headed by Jen Chi-yü, whom he does mention as an historian of Buddhism during the T'ang Dynasty. Fluctuations and reverse swings have been so common in China since 1949 (and before) that I hesitate to say now (in late 1978) either that the gods are dying or that religious freedom is sure to be in full swing for long.

There has been news of such rapid religious change in 1978 that the following five paragraphs are written "stop-press."

One day in May a Western student visited a famous Buddhist pagoda in Shantung province. He was the only foreigner there. He saw many schoolchildren. Money offerings were being left by the public in front of the four statues in the adjacent hall. In September 1978 a national daily printed an article about the Moon Festival, which falls on the fifteenth of the eighth lunar month. The article discussed the festival "in a cheerful, non-scientific way." Such an article has not appeared for many years, so far as I know.

In October and November 1978 there was news about how Islam was flourishing in China. Some of this news was carried by the Chinese radio. On November 11 television crews filmed the celebration of Id al-Kabir in the main Peking mosque. This was the first time in the memory of Muslim diplomats that such a thing had happened. They saw about a thousand worshipers in the mosque, including a hundred Chinese, many of them young. Official figures in 1977 gave the number of Muslim residents in Peking as 160,000. They had their own restaurants and butcher shops.

In Muslim areas of northwest China the flourishing of Islam was reported even more strikingly. At Urumchi, the capital of Sinkiang province, there were said to be 22 mosques. Most of the worshipers there in the autumn of 1978 were over sixty, but a few looked no older than fifteen (despite the fact that all Muslim schools in China were closed down in 1950).

Government money was being used to support Muslim religious activities. Imams (prayer leaders) were getting state salaries 50 percent higher than the average Chinese salary. All Muslims were given three days off for Ad al-Fitr, the festival at the end of Ramadan. In the capital of Ninghsia a slaughter house was handling 4,000 cattle a day. Following Muslim custom, imams alone could do the slaughtering. On a local commune new houses were being built for Muslims. They even had special washing facilities, as required by Muslim custom. A mother told the NCNA correspondent: "Our people's commune and its subdivisions never interfere with our religious life." Han Chinese peasants there had special eating vessels reserved to use for their Muslim guests. Han peasants did not draw water from wells used by Muslims.

So far as I know, no practicing Muslim may join the CCP even today; and the printing of the Koran is not permitted in China. Yet in 1978, for the first time since 1949, an old mosque was being restored in Turfan, which until then had not had a single religious building.

Let us return to where we started: the attitudes toward death. How much is left in China of what Robert Lifton recounted in *Revolutionary Immortality?* How many people still derive an "individual sense of immortality" from following the words and example of Mao Tse-tung? And what about the future? Mao once quoted Ssu-ma Ch'ien, the first great Chinese historian (Han Dynasty) and then said: "To die for the people is heavier than Mt. T'ai [weighty and good], but to work for the fascists and die for the exploiters and oppressors is lighter than a feather [inconsequential and bad]." Lifton speaks of "the replacement of prior modes of immortality (especially the biological one provided by the Chinese family system) with the newer revolutionary modes [such as] those of the biosocial revolutionary 'Family.' "*

Some Chinese will say that all Chinese were once Confucian in their social thought and behavior. I would agree. Some Taoists will say that all Chinese were Taoists without knowing it: Zen Buddhism is, they would say, only Taoism in disguise. I would agree. Some Chinese will say that Buddhism had the most profound influence on Chinese thought and behavior, on painting, on sculpture. I would agree. I am reluctant to accept the statement that there were once 100 million Buddhists in China. I prefer the old saying that I used earlier: ' Confucian in office, Taoist in retirement, and Buddhist as death approached" (now apparently, it is *Taoist* before death in some places). Except for the Muslims, the Chinese tend not to belong to a religion in the same way that some of us do. So the difference that communism or Maoism has made in China is this: the people are not free to follow their traditional religious inclinations. In the United States people are free to do so, although many of them are "turned off" by traditional religion. This fact may be part of the answer to the question: How different is China?

*Lifton, *Revolutionary Immortality*, pp. 67–71.

Daily Life

An Experience with Peking Youth

ERICA JEN

Erica Jen's essay is a reflection on her experience as a student at Peking University. She wished to live for a while in China, but a university was not her idea of the best place to be located. To her surprise, the world of students turned out to be a crucible of most of the value struggles of life in China today.

Jen warns that a vast gap yawns between the aims of American and Chinese education, as also between assumptions about how education relates to social change. She is harsh about American education and ambivalent in an illuminating way about Chinese.

She shows us that education is not a ladder in China. Even putting the terms "elitism" and "social mobility" into clear Chinese phraseology that her classmates could understand was a difficult task. Instead, she found the Chinese college to be low key in mood and strictly functional in the role it plays in the lives of those who attend it. In her view, Chinese students do really believe that workers and peasants are the cutting edge of Chinese society in the present epoch.

But she finds tensions. Most seem likely to continue, for they are classic tensions between the outlooks of teacher and taught, and between generations whose social experience is different. With all the uncertainty that Jen has about overall conclusions, and despite the possibility that she has idealized what she saw, her experience as an American in China amounts to a fascinating encounter between individualist values and collectivist values.

Erica Jen, a Chinese-American born in 1952 at Washington, D.C., holds a BS in mathematics from Yale and an MS in applied mathematics from SUNY at Stony Brook, where she is now writing a PhD thesis on partial differential equations. Her stay in China during the early 1970s lasted one and a half years. At Peking University she was the first foreign student since the Cultural Revolution (1966–69) and the first U.S. student since the Liberation of 1949. At the China-Cambodia Friendship People's Commune, where she lived for two months, she was the first American ever.

—R.T.

When I went to China in June of 1972, I wasn't really interested in education. Having grown up in the United States, I automatically thought of education as an institution with a lethal craving for abstraction. I wanted to see socialism in practice, not theory. Hoping to work in a Chinese factory or commune, I was a little disappointed at being admitted instead to Peking University.*

Once at the university, however, I came to realize that the educational experience is perhaps the best introduction to the values and goals of Chinese society. Superficially, Chinese schools function as "knowledge factories" just as do U.S. schools—students live on campus, attend lectures, specialize in majors—and yet they do not. As I was to discover, the Chinese are emphatic in viewing the educational structure as being derived from, and changing in response to, the continuing economic and political struggles of the society. In objectives, content, and methodology, Chinese education differs from that in the United States to the same extent that Chinese economics and politics differ from their counterparts here.

For U.S. visitors to China, the expectation of benefiting from the Chinese experience in education carries the seed of potential misunderstanding and disappointment. Reformers look to China for models of progressive education, and instead find schools whose emphasis on "proletarian values" and the "correct line" contradicts their images of a liberating educational process. Chinese education often seems dogmatic and overly politicized in its methodology and content, not at all suited to producing an open-minded, broad-based, technically skilled leadership corps.

Such disappointment is perhaps the natural consequence of trying to assess Chinese education by the criteria and values implicit in the conventional U.S. model of education. It is dubious, for one thing, whether the Chinese consider the production of a leadership corps to be one of the primary objectives of the educational system. Secondly, the Chinese be-

*I would like to express my thanks to my teachers and friends in Peking, who gave me an education both within and outside the classroom, and to my parents, who were my first and best models of the strength and character of the Chinese people.

lieve that education can reinforce, but certainly not revolutionize, the basic structure of their society.

In the United States, on the other hand, education is often seen as the key to wide-reaching social change (for better or for worse), and especially to the elimination of social and economic inequality. People here believe in education as a source of social mobility and as the cornerstone of a social meritocracy. Educational reform then is seen as a crucial tool in the remaking of society.

Even in the United States, however, there is a growing dissatisfaction with the conventional perception of education. Empirical evidence suggests that it is not education that shapes the future of individuals in U.S. society, but their social and economic standing, which in turn determines the quality and content of the education they receive.* Comparison of schools for lower-, middle-, and upper-class students indicates a deliberate compatibility between the norms stressed by a school—including discipline, dependability, technical expertise, individual initiative, leadership skills, etc.—and those required in the occupations already open to such students.

Because of its close relationship to the existing economic structure, education in the United States actually serves to reinforce the present class barriers and to promote an acceptance of oppressive work situations. The strict discipline and rigid teaching methods characteristic of working-class schools prepare their students for the demands of the blue-collar work place, and effectively preclude them from middle- or upper-class jobs requiring greater independence and initiative. For such students (and to varying degrees, for students of other class backgrounds as well), the emphasis on grades and the threat of failure anticipate the use of salary increases and the threat of firing, rather than the intrinsic pleasure of work. Attempts to provide minorities and underprivileged students with a more "open" education flounder when it is realized that such training makes them misfits in the job market.

I believe that the failure of U.S. reformers to achieve a progressive educational system is not unconnected with their difficulty in fathoming the workings of the educational system in China. Both reflect a misreading of the relationship between a society's educational and economic structures.

The Meaning of Chinese Education

In trying to understand what Chinese young people believe to be the purpose of their education, I fell back on the U.S. perception of education as providing social mobility. Assuming that education in China has the

*See Samuel Bowles and Herbert Gintis, *Schooling in Capitalist America* (1976).

responsibility for training the society's future leaders, I tried to interpret the continuing movement to revolutionize the university as a struggle over the class nature of the educated elite. Were they to comprise an oligarchy divorced from the common people; or were they to act as a "proletarianized" leadership, whose interests truly reflected those of the people?

My classmates at Peking University insisted that this approach to Chinese education was wrong. Education represented to them the promise not of social mobility, but of an enhanced ability to contribute to their country's development. They claimed that they could expect neither increased political responsibility nor higher social status as a result of their education.

Students simultaneously denounced the "education is useless" thinking (what's the point of leaving the countryside to go to school, if you just return to the countryside afterwards?) and cited its prevalence as evidence of the unchanged state of their ambitions. Their argument was supported by my experiences later in a factory and commune where, even while attempting to demonstrate their goodwill toward intellectuals, the workers and peasants indicated that there is still suspicion of the "knowledge and experience" acquired at universities. The fall of the Gang of Four and the recent emphasis on technical skills notwithstanding, a diploma from Peking University is certainly not seen as a necessary or a sufficient qualification for leadership.

I believe that my classmates' dismissal of the value of social mobility and their lack of concern over elitism stemmed from the fact that neither concept has relevance to the present-day struggle in Chinese economic relations.

I would have thought that both "elitism" and "social mobility" would be mainstays in Chinese political terminology, with a straightforward interpretation of the former as the divorce of leaders from the masses, and of the latter as the rise of workers and peasants into positions of leadership and authority in the society. Unfortunately, any time I tried either of these two translations on my classmates, the response was a blank stare (though not quite as blank as when I tried to explain hypnotism).

In the case of "elitism," it seems that the difficulty lay in my definition of the word in terms of the pyramid-like shape of U.S. society. I understood "elitism" to refer not only to an objective structure that elevates a select few to positions of prestige and power, but also to a conviction of superiority on the part of the elite group. In both subjective and objective terms, it is the selectiveness of the criteria for membership in the elite, as well as the general acceptance of the superiority of the elite, that is integral to elitism.

But in China the "brightest and best" qualities are seen to be those of the broad masses of workers and peasants. The concept of an elite as the select few thus loses much of its meaning. Nevertheless, a form of elitism does exist in Chinese society. Its existence is implicitly recognized in the criticism of worker and peasant youth who believe themselves to be automatically superior by virtue of their class background, and in the debates in the university over the merits of dividing students into classes on the basis of their abilities. Such forms of elitism, however, lack an objective base in society. In each case, the characteristics of the "elite" —whether they be "good" class background or high technical competence—are not regarded by the society as a whole to be in themselves justification for a sense of superiority. The Chinese will perhaps in the future invent a term for "false elitism."

In the United States "social mobility" simply refers to movement upward on the social ladder; moreover, it carries strong connotations of the desirability of doing so. The Chinese social hierarchy, on the other hand, is much more ambiguous, with incentives and rewards of a predominantly moral rather than monetary nature. Becoming head of a commune may bring increased authority and responsibility, but it also means working harder than anyone else, taking the worst living quarters, and sacrificing one's own wood, food, cotton, or other material goods in times of scarcity. It certainly brings none of the perquisites associated with a rise in position and power in the United States.

When I was living in a commune outside Peking, a cadre there talked for an entire afternoon about her ambivalence toward her position, without once mentioning a personal struggle over elitism or vanity or any of the other traditional trappings of power. Her concern was solely with the negative aspects of her position, which she perceived to consist of political vulnerability, sacrifice of time away from her family, extended hours of physical labor. Against these she balanced a desire to contribute to the socialist cause without which, in her words, she "probably wouldn't even have a family today." It was clear that she had become a cadre because she felt it to be her duty, rather than in her personal interests, to do so.

In looking at the effects education in China has on students' futures, it might be useful to replace the concept of education as providing social mobility with that of education as a supporting mechanism in the continuing movement to eliminate the "three differences" between worker and peasant, town and country, mental and manual labor. Social groups are encouraged to aspire not to change their social status, but to assimilate the progressive viewpoints and skills of their complements. Such a policy could become a mechanism for freezing the people's, and especially the peasants', aspirations and opportunities; but it in fact represents a fundamental struggle to change the criteria by which individuals judge the value of their work.

In China the emphasis is on making a contribution to society, and on developing a personal satisfaction in doing so. The potential for making a contribution exists regardless of the specific nature of one's work. The category of a "service profession" as it is understood in the United States to refer specifically to those in the medical, social work, or related fields does not exist in China. All professions are seen to be potentially "serving the people." The Chinese people's perception of themselves as the "masters of society" forms the basis of a belief that all labor, whether it be in the university, the factory, or the fields, can be directed so as to benefit the masses.

The Chinese recognize, however, that the traditional association of prestige and social standing with particular types of work is difficult to overcome. One aim of the campaigns sending the urban population into the countryside has been to illustrate the truth of Mao's claim that "great contributions can be made in the countryside." The prestige and personal satisfaction for individuals working in the communes have grown as the rest of the country has come to a better appreciation of the difficulties and rewards of agricultural labor. Intellectuals who go to the countryside discover that their technical know-how can lead to surprisingly large increases in production. More importantly, it is only in the society outside the university that they can acquire the political understanding that will inspire and direct significant research.

For the most part, my classmates at Peking University seemed to respond enthusiastically to the importance of making a contribution to society, rather than attaining a particular social standing. They defined themselves not in terms of their present status as students, but in relation to their previous work outside the university. They were not so much students receiving an education in preparation for some unknown future occupation, as workers and peasants who would eventually return to their original work units with enhanced skills.

My roommate once broke into tears because she realized that she had fallen into the university pattern of napping for two hours in the afternoon. She remembered how, as a peasant, she had used the daily break to do extra work in the fields, and wondered if her dedication had been undermined by the relatively easy life of the university. Another time, I came across a big-character poster criticizing other students for wasting food in the dining hall. The poster appealed not to students' sympathy for the workers and peasants producing the food, but to their sense of the need to preserve their own integrity as past and future agricultural workers. In their studies as well as in their lifestyles, my classmates seemed intent upon ensuring that their educational experience did not effect a shift in their social class allegiance.

A group of Peking University students went to the countryside to help with the wheat harvest. I was one of them. It was a hot summer day, 110° in the shade, and we were exhausted from working continuously with bent back and dull sickle. (I felt so miserable I remarked to my roommate: "Now I know what it was like to be on the Long March," and although she must have felt as bad as I did, she looked at me with outrage at the presumption of the comparison.) Three students passed out from the heat and exertion, which seemed perfectly natural to me, but not to my schoolmates. After returning to the university, they organized a spontaneous self-criticism session. They were upset over the effects that a year at the university had had on their physical stamina, and worried about how they would adjust to their eventual return to the fields after graduation. Their decision was to escalate the morning exercise routines and increase the weekly physical labor sessions.

In getting to know my classmates at Peking University, I found it important to remember the circumstances under which they came to the university. Most of them had worked in a factory or commune believing that they would be doing so for the rest of their lives. Upon being nominated for study at the university, the decision to accept was often a difficult one, made more so by the knowledge that there were many young people from the same work units who had refused such offers in order to continue working. Some of those who chose to leave were doubtless glad at the opportunity. Others sincerely regretted leaving, and did so only because they saw the prospect of using an education to "serve the people" as the best means to justify, and in some sense repay, the confidence, trust, and energy invested by the people in them.

The Weaknesses of the Educational Process

The Chinese students recognize, and are determined to fight against, the possible negative effects of the educational experience. They see themselves as workers and peasants, and they are aware that they represent a progressive force within the university, but they are also sensitive to their vulnerabilities. Again, these vulnerabilities are defined in terms of their relation to the society's economic and political struggles. The problem is not just that of being away from manual labor and succumbing to the easy life of a university student. The real problem is that of being removed from the political realities and succumbing to the easy extremism of all talk and no action. As my classmates themselves pointed out, the history of political struggles—in particular, the Cultural Revolution and the misguided anti-Teng Hsiao-p'ing campaign of 1976—have demonstrated that students can play the crucial role of sparking a political movement, but in the end it is the workers and peasants whose leadership is needed to clarify the issues, define the real targets, and formulate new policies.

Like their counterparts in U.S. campus movements, Chinese students are more eager for, than adept in, political struggle. They are quick to accept change and progressive ideas, but often dogmatic, extremist, and self-righteous in imposing them on others. They know that the real heroes of the country are the peasants who toil day in, day out for an entire lifetime; but they tend to identify with the revolutionary who sacrifices himself in a sudden burst of glory, the miner who covers a bomb with his body to protect his comrades, the youth who plunges into the rapids to recover telephone poles for his commune. As a result, their political thinking sometimes demonstrates more sincerity than sense, as I found during a physical labor session when my classmates persisted in digging a ditch despite a rainstorm, believing the discipline to be more important than the actual results.

Chinese students recognize their own detachment from, and inexperience in, struggle, and they look to the workers and peasants for guidance. A Canadian foreign student and I followed their example, and went to work at Peking No. 1 Machine Tool Parts Factory, after having spent seven months at the university. We worked for two weeks in the foundry with an Iron Women's Team, a group of eighteen- and nineteen-year-olds who had requested upon graduating from middle school to be assigned to the "dirtiest, hardest" work in the factory. The work was excruciating and yet exhilarating. (The topper was the daily basketball game during the "rest period.") After two weeks, we asked for our stay in the foundry to be extended. Our request was denied, and we were sent instead into the assembly workshop and the demoralizing task of fastening nuts and bolts.

For the first few days, I resented the workshop terribly. The workers seemed dull and the work wasn't even tiring. When the study sessions started, however, my opinions began to change. The discussions were much more enthusiastic, much more intelligent than those I had heard either at the university or with the Iron Women's Team. It almost seemed that the very monotony of their work brought a vitality to these workers' thinking. In discussing Lenin's *State and Revolution,* one woman even took the side of the renegade—something I had never witnessed before in China—agreeing with Ferdinand Lassalle that the socialist system of distribution should persist even after the transition to a Communist society.

It was not only during the study sessions that the assembly-line workers demonstrated a liveliness greater than that of students and young workers. Far from being automatons on the job, they spontaneously proposed revisions in the workshop floor plans and participated in implementing changes in the work flow. Many showed up for work half an hour early every day, and voluntarily put in extra time after hours with no compensation.

One young worker was especially dedicated to her work of inserting nuts and bolts in a machine part. She explained to me that her willingness to work extra hours derived from the time she contracted a near-fatal disease, but was cured after the state sent her for treatment at China's top hospital. The cost to the state was tens of thousands of dollars, and she felt deeply that it was only under a socialist system that such expense would be incurred to save the life of an ordinary worker.

Learning from the Peasants

Perhaps even more than workers, it is the Chinese peasants to whom the students look for guidance in overcoming their own weaknesses. After a year's stay in Peking, including ten weeks at the factory, I came to the conclusion that life in the countryside occupies a central place in the consciousness of all Chinese young people. Everything I had experienced in Chinese society—casual conversations with friends, the reorientation of the university, the whole of Chinese art, music, and literature—seemed to say that the countryside represents the heart and soul of socialist China. In June of 1973, when I was scheduled to return to the United States, I applied for my stay to be extended another six months, and to be allowed to go to work at a commune.

I was assigned to the China-Cambodia Friendship People's Commune, southwest of Peking. The village I lived in had been one of the poorest in the Peking area before 1949, so poor that it had had no landlords and only two rich peasants. The villagers believe that their extreme poverty before collectivization is one reason they have been so successful in implementing socialist change.

I found adjusting to life in the countryside much more difficult than adjusting to either the factory or the university. Part of my problem was my total ignorance of agricultural production, and the villagers' ignorance—much greater, I thought, than that of people in the cities—of life outside China. There seemed little basis for comparison or exchange of experiences. I had to learn a new vocabulary of agricultural terms and countryside slang, and before doing so, it was impossible even to ask the questions which would open communication. Compounding my problem was the fact that the production brigade, which is one step below the commune in organizational structure, is a much more tightly knit social unit than is any single factory or university. The brigade has its own school, store, first-aid center; its finances are to a large extent independent of the rest of the country. The peasants in the brigade work together in the fields by day, and spend most of their evenings visiting neighbors. Living in the village, I felt more an outsider that I had elsewhere in China.

My own difficulties in adjusting made me appreciate that for Chinese students, who have grown up in the cities, going to the countryside involves a deeply emotional struggle over the "three crises" of labor, lifestyle, and ideology. The most troubling question for these students is whether they would be willing to remain permanently, whether life in the countryside is acceptable only when sweetened by the fact that their stay would be temporary. For me, the knowledge that I would be leaving soon made me regard skeptically even my most sincere efforts at arduous labor and plain living.

My classmate told me that since the early sixties, the purpose of sending students to the countryside has shifted with the changing perception of the role of the peasants in the political process. Before the Cultural Revolution, it was the importance of adjusting to the manual labor and living conditions which was stressed to city students preparing to go to a commune. These students then tended to evaluate their progress in terms of how well they succeeded in emulating the peasants in diligence, generosity, dedication, and so on. In the years since the Cultural Revolution, however, their own difficulties in struggling against the thinking of Liu Shao-ch'i, Lin Piao, and the "Gang of Four" have given Chinese intellectuals a new sense of the superiority of workers and peasants in matters of political consciousness. Many students now feel that they must go to the countryside because it is there that they can best appreciate the importance and difficulties of political struggle.

After working two months at the commune, I began to understand the meaning of the famous slogan, "Politics in command." The peasants believe wholeheartedly that it is their political choices that determine the economic and moral well-being of their village.

One day, during a break from the rice harvesting, I asked a group of people for their analysis of why our village was leading the area in individual incomes. One peasant said, "Good soil," another suggested, "Good leadership." Then a sixty-year-old woman said, "Good politics."

The woman went on to explain that our village had been consistent in making agricultural production the basis for its economy, even at the expense of short-range profits. It had done so in response to Mao's call for communes to place the country's agricultural needs ahead of their own individual commune's interests. The neighboring village, on the other hand, had invested a large portion of its funds in buying horses and carts, and then transporting goods from other villages to the city for pay. For a while their investments paid off, and their incomes exceeded those of our village; but then the need to import grain, wood, and cotton for their own use caused incomes to drop. Since then they have returned to grain production, but they still lag far behind. Later that day, we walked over to the boundary line between our village and the neighboring one, and sure enough, the rice on our side was standing strong and tall, while theirs was mottled and drooping with disease.

For the two months I was in the countryside, I followed the practice of Chinese students and attended weekly briefings on the commune's history since 1949. The briefings were in reality a study of the relationship between the political line and the success or failure of the commune. The peasants cited grain production statistics that showed a gradual increase during the collectivization campaigns of the middle and late fifties, a huge upsurge after the formation of the commune, a setback during the 1959 period when it was believed that communism had arrived, further setbacks under the influence of Liu Shao-ch'i's policies, and so on. They supplemented these statistics with stories characterizing their own emotional state of mind during each of these periods. During the collectivization period, villagers were filled with a sense of confidence and cooperation. One peasant pointed to his house, and told me how the entire village had chipped in to help build it. During the "false communism" year, however, laziness set in. The dining halls were serving free food, and one day at the height of the wheat harvest there were only two people in the fields, with the rest of the village gorging themselves on fritters.

The peasants laughed when they told these stories, but it was clear that they were completely serious in believing their welfare to be in large part governed by the correctness of their political thinking.

I found the political consciousness of the peasants strikingly different from that of people in the university. The sense of politics determining the community's welfare is present, but much less distinct, in the academic environment. Of course, it is difficult to measure the quantity and quality of academic "production," and then relate it to political line. A more important factor seems to be the difference between the economic and political history of the commune and that of the university, both before and after 1949.

Almost all of the villagers I talked to had suffered terribly before 1949. Memories of their past misery, starvation, and desperation form an emotional basis from which they fight to maintain and improve the socialist system, and they value these memories accordingly. But the peasants have learned from experience that a gut-level emotional commitment to socialism is not enough. Distinguishing between the socialist and revisionist line on a daily basis requires emotional commitment directed by intelligent analysis. Directives passed down from top-level leadership are not always correct, and the individual must be capable of assessing political implications by himself or herself. Having seen the disastrous results of politically bad policies on their personal lives, the peasants keenly feel the necessity of heightening their own political consciousness and involvement. As many villagers put it, "Being a hardworking mule only makes matters worse if you're pulling in the wrong direction." It is this intense personal commitment to politics, derived from a clear appreciation of the significance of politics to one's personal life, that I felt was the most important lesson for students going to the countryside.

Reorienting the University

The focus of present-day Chinese universities is outward, away from themselves and toward the political and economic realities of Chinese society. Students look to workers and peasants for guidance in overcoming their weaknesses. Similarly, the university as a whole looks toward the political struggle for direction in deciding the correct content and methodology of education. If the educational system is to serve the needs of the society, then it must be the values and ideology of the working-class people that are to direct and inform the educational process. Education in China presupposes the values implicit in the socialist economic base.

In the sciences the influence of society's needs on course content is obvious. Students laugh about many of the scientific theses written before 1949 and even up through the Cultural Revolution. Some of the topics were so esoteric it seems that the only point was to be "original" by writing about something no one had ever bothered to consider. The emphasis in science courses and research now is on those aspects of basic and experimental science which are seen as fundamental to the modernization of Chinese society. Particularly in introductory courses, priority is given to research which can be verified and which has applications outside the laboratory. In this spirit, some of my classmates in the Biology Department at Peking University went to a commune to ask the peasants what problems they could suggest for a term research project. They came back with samples taken from diseased cattle, and returned to the commune four months later with their preliminary results. Others in the Botany Department were asked by villagers to check whether a highly touted grain hybrid would be suitable for their particular soil and weather conditions.

In the humanities and social sciences, the influence of society is felt as much on the style of learning as on the content. A classical study of Confucius would concentrate on the internal structure and logic of his work, but a modern-day analysis must also assume the viewpoint of the oppressed classes in considering his role in influencing philosophy, morality, and politics throughout Chinese history. At one point, some classmates in the History Department organized a debate over Napoleon's status as a historical figure. Was he a reactionary because his aim was to conquer the Western world, and because he was responsible for widespread death and suffering? Or was he a progressive because the effect of his rule was to break down existing feudalistic structures and to promote the spread of revolutionary ideas?

At the time, I was somewhat startled by my classmates' willingness to decide definitively on Napoleon's moral and political stature. In the United States the consensus is that there are no easy answers to such questions, and that the desire to find them is a sign of intellectual laziness or immaturity. I found that for Chinese students, however, the search for answers or the "correct line" is not a denial of the plurality of existence, but a refusal to become paralyzed by its complexity.

Socialist ideology insists on an active approach to human phenomena, no matter how complex. The underlying theme in the classes I attended was to stress the inadequacy of pure analysis, and the necessity of taking stands. In all their studies—whether they be of philosophies, political systems, works of art or literature—students are urged not only to understand the object of study on its own terms, but also to decide on its relative merits and drawbacks, and to formulate what they feel to be a more appropriate response to the questions involved.

The active approach of present-day Chinese universities has not always been compatible with the teaching styles of the older professors. There is too great a discrepancy between the traditional detachment of scholarly analysis and the intense involvement of class struggle. Moreover, the students' rejection of the concept of "scholarship free from politics" has contributed to the undermining of professors' authority in the classroom, and opened the way for an increase in the students' contribution to the learning process. Criticism sessions among professors and students are an accepted, almost institutionalized means of effecting change, and challenges in the classrooms to statements made by professors—out of the question in old China—are now not uncommon.

The reactions of the professors have naturally been mixed. The teacher in one of my classes complained of being "oppressed in my own classroom." In the case of another instructor who was criticized for delivering a lecture lifted almost verbatim from the reading material, he might have felt the same way, but went back to do some research, lectured the next session on the same, reinterpreted topic, and later wrote a self-criticism of the gaps in his understanding of the new educational concepts.

Establishing the primacy of working-class values and ideology in academic affairs has not been easy. Inexperience and the lack of a precedent have often led to extremist measures in examination policies and admissions procedures. These have alienated portions of the academic community. I sometimes came away from conversations with older intellectuals amazed by their juxtaposition of support for socialist objectives and contempt for the new educational system. One professor bitterly complained to me about the preference given by Peking University's admissions policy to applicants of worker and peasant background. He was disgusted with the idea of admitting students with less than middle-school education into the university. "What can I do with them?" he complained. "If you give me a plot of land with weeds growing on it, maybe I can get rid of the weeds, but if you give me barren wasteland, it's hopeless."

Many intellectuals resent their subordination, first to the workers who have participated in the administration of the universities since the Cultural Revolution, and then to the politically conscious worker-peasant-soldier students. In particular, they resent the attitude which prevailed for many years after the Cultural Revolution that intellectuals are still fundamentally bourgeois in their outlook despite their years of socialist education. In some cases, this resentment has given rise to a general disgruntlement and disinterest in the politics of education. The withdrawal of this group of intellectuals has hurt the movement to revolutionize the universities and poses a major problem for the future.

There is a special difficulty in realizing "politics in command" in an academic environment. In the countryside and factory, the political cadres are as a rule born and raised on home soil, and are therefore as wise or wiser in the ways of production as the technical production leader. The campus worker or Party Secretary or incoming student, on the other hand, is often a stranger to much of the content of academic life. In a community that has traditionally awarded respect only for scholarly achievement, the sharpness of the distinction between the political "layman" and the nonpolitical "expert" intensifies an already difficult struggle over means and objectives.

A Personal Look at Chinese Students

My eighteen-month stay in China was the most personally satisfying experience of my life, in large part because of the examples set for me by my Chinese classmates in their own personal lives. Their perception of themselves as active participants in the political struggle forms the basis of a personal sense of responsibility, integrity, and selflessness, which greatly impressed me.

I sometimes tried to explain to my Chinese classmates the attitudes of many U.S. students who have lost faith in the educational process. I discussed with them the disillusionment of students who feel the irrelevance of the content of their education to their future job responsibilities. I tried to convey to them the pain of foreign students who come to America hoping to acquire useful skills, and who discover, upon returning to their own countries, the uselessness of both their capital-intensive technology and their changed lifestyles. My schoolmates knew something of what I meant. They cited cases of severe depression and suicide to show that both disillusionment and pain were common reactions in students attending Peking University before 1949.

By contrast, my classmates seemed confident that it is now the values and objectives of the working-class people which direct the educational process, and which will ensure that their education will not be meaningless. They felt strongly that to be lax in their studies would be to betray the people's trust in them.

For Chinese students, constant self-evaluation and self-improvement take place in criticism sessions. Many of these are spontaneously organized by the students themselves. Their motivation may be trivial or significant: quarrels among roommates as to when the lights should go out at night; a student who seems to be developing a disparaging attitude toward a classmate; someone who's becoming lazy about getting up for morning exercises or attending political meetings; a student cadre who has been acting superior toward other students. All these are occasions for students first to discuss matters among themselves, and then to gather on the bunk beds in someone's dorm room at night to hold a criticism session.

Criticism sessions are difficult for those outside of China to understand or imitate. Perhaps this is because they presuppose a unity of purpose and ideology. Even in China, feelings get hurt, and "face" has to be considered. Students and intellectuals in particular seem much less willing to be criticized than do workers and peasants. Despite the fact that the Chinese have developed a rare talent for suiting the harshness of the criticism to the sensitivity of the one being criticized, my own response to early criticism sessions was too often one of "offense as the best defense."

At first, my classmates criticized me for things I could ignore, like leaving my door unlocked or wearing torn or dirty clothes, the argument being that such actions reflected an ultra-leftist, romanticized concept of revolution and the present state of Chinese society. But in the early seventies "ultra-leftist" still seemed like something of a backhanded compliment and it was only after the Chinese gently but persistently began to draw the lines between ultra-leftism and personal as well as political immaturity that their criticisms became mortifying, and eventually motivating.

Whatever disagreements I had with the Chinese, I could not deny the power of their belief in the potential and responsibility of individuals to better themselves. It is a belief that motivates an almost frightening rigor and honesty in their criticism of themselves and others, and that made my experience in China both personally oppressive and profoundly liberating.

The goal of criticism is to help others overcome their faults so that they may better contribute to the common cause. Many of the discussions in criticism sessions center on the degree of the individual's commitment to the political struggle. One of my roommates was criticized by her class-mates for an overly active ego, a preference for working on papers on her own rather than in groups, and a disdain for compromise. Afterwards she conceded that even in political work that demanded persuasion and ac-commodation, she thought in terms of establishing the correctness of her own thinking rather than working to influence the thinking of others. It was to her an indication of an insufficient commitment to the revolution-ary cause, which is necessarily a common struggle.

There is no adequate way to describe the unselfishness of the Chinese, except possibly to say that an American visitor to China would almost certainly find the entire population hopelessly masochistic. Living with a Chinese roommate means constant pressure to be the first to take the thermoses to be filled with hot water, to be the quickest in making each other's beds, to be the most willing to help the other with her studies. The start of a physical labor session is a race to grab the most difficult work.

Unselfishness can be disturbing. I felt uneasy about it especially when I saw basketball games in which the good players deliberately allowed the less competent to take more shots, or when I came back to my room to find my quilts and clothes washed by some anonymous friend. (I felt they should understand that I needed the practice in using a washboard.) Students obviously are sincerely concerned for each other's welfare, but at times I wondered whether they were perhaps being selfishly selfless.

The Chinese people believe a life of selflessness to be the most glorious possible, in terms both of contributions made and of emotional returns to the individual. Knowing this, I felt recurring doubts as to the motives behind the self-sacrifice commonplace in China, even while I conceded the remarkable nature of a society in which the dilemma could arise. I reasoned that over any extended period of time, the difference between true selflessness and self-indulgence must necessarily manifest itself in some objective divergence in behavior. I looked for examples of class-mates making unnecessary but self-satisfying sacrifices, or depriving themselves even when it might be detrimental to the willpower or charac-ter of those around them. Instead, I found that sacrifice is meant to be in response to objective need, and in some ways imposes a responsibility on others to respond in kind. (When I finally got around to washing a friend's quilts, she acted as if she had been expecting it all along.)

I would like nonetheless to see among young people a more critical attitude toward the act of self-sacrifice, and by extension, toward revolu-tionary acts in general. For the past generation, an underlying message of Chinese politics has been "the more revolutionary, the better." It has been, and continues to be, a message of strength and determination. Yet I think it has also unwittingly encouraged a potentially dangerous loyalty to the veneer of revolution, in some cases even at the expense of its substance. The reluctance of many people to criticize even the excesses of the Cultural Revolution, the readiness of some young people to deny personal emotions such as love, the overwhelming emphasis on sacrifice —all these seem to me examples of a tendency to support automatically whatever is the current "leftist" political line.

Summing Up

The educational process in China derives its meaning from the needs and directions of the country's political and economic struggles. This seems to imply that the universities follow the political, emotional, and intellectual patterns set by the rest of the society. In a sense, I believe this to be the case. The status of women in the university illustrates the point.

The Chinese sometimes seem amused by the hypersensitivity of Western visitors on the question of women's liberation. When I first started studying at Peking University, I was wary of this amusement. It is true that women in China now have almost equal representation in the student population, and that they hold positions of responsibility at every level of the university structure. On the other hand, I was disturbed to find male students casually asserting, and women wryly agreeing, that "It's inappropriate for women students to be troop leaders since they'd have to march around barking out orders," or that "Men think more creatively than women."

The status of Chinese women needs to be placed in the perspective of the society outside the university. As the students themselves argue, the liberation of women (and of the Chinese people as a whole) is only relative, implying a comparison with the pre-Liberation past, and perhaps also with the Western present. The crux of the question lies in the relative change in women's economic status; but that change is difficult to appreciate in the setting of universities that are still relatively remote from the production process.

It was only after I went to the countryside that the change became clear to me. Women in the village talked of how they had been customarily cowed or beaten in the old society into docile servility, or how they had been barred from the threshing ground because it was thought the grain would sicken from their presence. These same women are now indispensable to the agricultural production and growth of the village, and their role in production has given them respect and authority in matters of administration as well. They have formed their own "Iron Women's Team," not because they have been excluded by the men, but because they feel pride in demonstrating their physical and political abilities.

Faced with the confidence of the Chinese peasant women, I realized how esoteric the question of ideological sexism must seem to working men and women alike. What is important, what will decide the future, is not the vestiges of prejudice but the fact that the basic obstacles to women's liberation have been surmounted. Women are actively involved in work, actively engaged in that realm of practice whose effect on thinking is so valued by the Chinese. The remaining ideological blinders will be gradually discarded in the face of proven ability. It seems fitting that total liberation for women, as the intellectual defines it, will probably be won first at the commune and factory, and come only last to the university.

Living in China, I was impressed most of all by the people's vitality and optimism, that sense of progress and hope that often seems to have been lost in American society. Even with this confidence, however, the Chinese people have not forgotten the pitfalls in working to realize their socialist ideals. The shock of what they perceive to be the demise of Soviet socialism and the emergence of "class enemies" within their own Party has served to demonstrate that not even the Communist Party is an absolute safeguard against revisionism. The deciding factor in the future of China is seen to be the political consciousness of the people, and in particular, the young people.

One achievement of the undermining of the authority of teachers in Chinese classrooms has been to encourage young people to exercise their own analytical powers and political judgment. And yet, skills of analysis and judgment acquired in the classroom are not enough. As the struggle to move toward communism continues, distinguishing between right and wrong becomes increasingly difficult, and in the end, it is often experience and emotional allegiance that determine an individual's political stand. In contrast to the older workers and peasants in China, young people lack direct experience of exploitation and oppression, and their fervor in denouncing the old ways and in supporting the new is consequently diminished. For some, the "sweetness of the present" has undoubtedly eroded their interest in the political struggle. The Chinese point out that the inarticulate, uneducated old peasants often work the hardest and display the soundest political sense, whereas the eloquence of young people is not always matched by their performance in either political struggle or production.

Yet the young people I lived and worked with in China displayed a commitment to hard work and struggle that refutes the concept of the inevitable deterioration of political will. Worker and peasant youth in particular emphasize that the relative comfort and security of their present lives are a consequence not of the gradual development of China's technological and production capabilities, but of a continuing revolution, which has transformed them into the "masters of society." Maintaining their present status therefore requires a constant vigilance against back-sliding as well as a continuing involvement in the political process.

When I first went to China, I felt some ambivalence toward the values of the Chinese people. I recognized the material achievements of the Chinese government, and admired the determination of the people to continue the socialist struggle, but worried over the seeming sterility of their daily existence. By contrast with China's apparent singlemindedness, the United States appeared certainly morally and politically deplorable, but also perversely satisfying in the stimulation and challenge it provides of individual choice, complexity, and confusion.

As I learned more about the university, factory, and commune, I came to the opposite conclusion. I feel that for U.S. observers to condemn the monotony of existence in China is simply to deny the complexities of an outlook on life alien to them. In the process of participating in the movement to revolutionize the university, I found that political involvement as it is understood in China calls for a most rigorous examination of one's personal values, hopes, and beliefs, as well as a profoundly emotional struggle to accept new ideas and to correct the weaknesses of one's own thinking. The Chinese see politics as determining the future well-being of their country and of themselves as individuals, and respond to political issues with a passion and commitment rarely found in the United States. This is far from sterility. And an experience of it happened to bring out what I feel to be my own best thinking and actions.

Politics and the Citizen

RICHARD BAUM

Richard Baum assesses the various political attitudes to be found among the Chinese people. He raises for the purpose of his discussion some common stereotypes of the PRC, including China as a dictatorship over blue ants and China as a quasi-religious band of brothers. Baum contends that no stereotype carries the whole truth. To draw up a balance sheet, he asks three questions of the political life of the Chinese: How do they view the political system as a whole; what do they think of particular national leaders and issues; and what is the meaning to the citizens of the nonstop local participation in politics?

Baum brings together evidence from all sorts of sources to address these questions. The core values of the system are much supported, he believes. On national politics people are less passionate than is often supposed and escapism has been growing. The local level he finds to be a caldron of complexity, with much jostling of interests and quite a degree of dissembling. The total picture is far from being one of harsh regimentation, or of a new paradise of political athleticism (if that would be a paradise). One clear lesson of Baum's essay is that the PRC is on a treadmill of constant change and that new generations tend to bring surprises in China as elsewhere. The revolution is getting a bit tired, he concludes, in an analysis that can be read as a counterpoint to Erica Jen's.

Richard Baum's books include China in Ferment: Perspectives on the Cultural Revolution *(1971),* Prelude to Revolution: Mao, the Party, and the Peasant Question, 1962–66 *(1975), and* China's Four Modernizations: The New Technological Revolution *(1979). He received a PhD from the University of California at Berkeley, and is now professor of political science at the University of California at Los Angeles. Baum visited the PRC four times since 1975 as a member of cultural exchange delegations.*

—R.T.

In the three decades since the culmination of the Chinese Revolution in 1949, casual observers of the Middle Kingdom have been exposed to a variety of highly stereotyped images of political life in the PRC. Ranging from Orwellian nightmares of Big Brother, newspeak, and double-think to equally extreme utopian fantasies of perfect harmony, cooperation, and social justice, these stereotypes have encompassed all manner of assumptions about the nature of China's contemporary political system and the underlying values, political attitudes, and aspirations of the Chinese people.

One commonly encountered stereotype, widely purveyed in the 1950s and 1960s, portrayed the Chinese people as a faceless horde of docile "blue ants," laboring slavishly under the ruthless and all-pervasive scrutiny of Chairman Mao and the CCP. In this view, political power was absolute, arbitrary, and all-encompassing, while individual (or familial) privacy, autonomy, and discretionary freedom were virtually nonexistent. All forms of dissent and nonconformity were severely proscribed by the Party and, if they occurred, were severely punished—either physically (through arduous "labor reform") or, more brutalizing and insidious still, psychologically (through "thought reform," known widely in the West as "brainwashing").

According to this draconian image of Chinese totalitarianism, the Communist regime was by definition illegitimate. Given free choice in free elections, the Chinese people would surely opt to throw off the yoke of their oppression.

Or would they? Alongside this early totalitarian stereotype, there appeared in the mid-1960s a new view of Chinese political life under communism. Spawned in the feverish atmosphere of China's tumultuous Great Proletarian Cultural Revolution, the new image drew its inspiration from the radical—and often bizarre—exploits of China's youth, the Red Guards.

From 1966 to 1968, tales of rampaging Red Guards filled the Western media, to the point where many outside observers speculated that China had gone collectively mad with revolutionary fanaticism. Throughout this period the spectacle of millions of young Chinese students spitting, beating, and shouting obscenities at their elders (and at each other), reading aloud from their "little red books," and invading state organs to seize power from alleged "bourgeois authorities"—all in the name of passionate devotion to a deified and infallible Chairman Mao—served to reinforce the image of a nation of ideological zealots.

In the early 1970s yet a fresh vision unfolded. With the swing of a Ping-Pong paddle and a U.S. presidential pilgrimage to Peking, the prevailing stereotypes were once again shattered and replaced by a new set of images—captured live on network television and in the flowery prose of a steadily expanding stream of visiting journalists.

The new imagery portrayed neither a passive, coerced populace nor a massed phalanx of militant fanatics, but rather a nation of diligent, self-confident people struggling valiantly and cohesively to overcome their inherited economic backwardness in order to build a new socialist society. Where before the Chinese people had appeared either as oppressed victims of a malevolent Stalinist devil or as hysterical disciples of a mystical Maoist god, they now appeared as rational, self-disciplined masters of their own socialist destiny. The "mass line" was no sham—it really worked. The people supported their government, approved of their leaders, and had a real and effective voice in the formulation and implementation of policies directly affecting their lives. Political conviction was not madness but meaningful commitment. The "thought of Mao Tse-tung" was not metaphysical cant but a practical guide to problem solving.

Almost overnight, China had thus "changed" once more. No longer a living hell, China was now, it seemed, a virtual paradise on earth.

Or was it? More recently, in the mid-1970s, a backlash set in against the type of euphoric imagery represented by the "I have seen the future and it works" school. Fueled by the bizarre incidents that followed the deaths of Chou En-lai and Mao Tse-tung, fed by a new series of spectacular political purges, nourished by mounting evidence of systematic political persecution of large numbers of Chinese artists, writers, and scientists, and reinforced by recent reports of widespread economic failure, educational breakdown, and worker unrest, this backlash witnessed an ironic recrudescence of the earlier totalitarian image of Chinese political life.

As if to lend credence to this image, China's post-Maoist leaders instituted a series of liberal political reforms in 1977 and 1978. A new State Constitution was promulgated, providing legal safeguards against arbitrary search, arrest, or harassment of citizens.* Tens of thousands of erstwhile "counterrevolutionaries" and "rightists" were given a clean bill

*See Cohen's discussion, pp. 240 ff.—R.T.

of political health. And new—albeit limited—freedoms of speech and assembly were introduced via the extraordinary mechanism of Peking's "democracy wall." Such reforms led some observers to predict the whole-sale democratization of politics in the PRC, and coincidentally spawned yet another potential stereotype—that of Jeffersonian China.

It is not my purpose to argue for or against the relevance of one or another of the prevailing stereotypes of Chinese political behavior, nor to disparage the utilization of stereotypes as such. Rather, I wish to suggest that each of the distinctive images of Chinese politics outlined above—the totalitarian, the mass fanatic, and the participatory demo-cratic—while capturing the essence of a particular aspect of contempo-rary Chinese political reality, grossly oversimplifies that reality. In order to answer the question, What really makes China tick?, it is necessary to go beyond simple stereotyping to examine the multifaceted political orientations and behaviors of actual individuals and groups of Chinese citizens under actual conditions.

Orientations Toward the Symbols of Revolution

At the broadest level, political behavior includes the subjective orienta-tions of a citizenry toward the political system as a whole: its history, symbols of statehood and authority, constitutional mythology, and basic principles of governance. Such orientations serve to define the legitimacy —the basic "rightness" or "wrongness"—of the political order in the eyes of its citizens.

In China, there appears to be a rather high level of positive attachment to the core values and symbols of the Communist Revolution. Whatever else they might feel about individual leaders, specific political institu-tions, or particular government policies, most Chinese, most of the time, seem to display relatively strong feelings of loyalty to the system of governance established in 1949.

Older Chinese citizens frequently speak of their "liberation" by the CCP with a certain amount of genuine pride and patriotic sentiment. For members of this older generation, who experienced firsthand the priva-tions and physical insecurities of pre-1949 Chinese society (and who comprise roughly 30–40 percent of China's present population), revolu-tionary legitimacy derives in the first instance from feelings of a personal identification with the liberation struggles initiated and led by the CCP.

For members of the younger generation, who never directly encoun-tered the miseries of pre-Liberation society (and who comprise over 60 percent of China's present population), on the other hand, the legitimacy of the present system derives less from a keenly felt sense of personal emancipation than from the sustained processes of ideological indoctrination and political socialization that begin in early childhood. Just as American children are indoctrinated at a very early age with larger-than-life tales of the heroism of the Founding Fathers, the honesty of Abe Lincoln, and the greatness of the American Dream, so too are China's "children of the Liberation" continuously exposed to the mythology of the Chinese Revolution and to the legendary exploits of Chairman Mao, the CCP, and the PLA. This socialization process, reinforced by a certain amount of tangible socioeconomic progress achieved since 1949, has resulted in the fostering of a generation of Chinese youth with a strong sense of idealistic commitment to the core values of the Chinese Revolution—including socialism, egalitarianism, self-reliance, and "serving the people."

If China's revolutionary political system is thus regarded as legitimate by the majority of older peasants and workers as well as by most members of the younger generation, what then of basic opposition to the system? Does it exist? And if so, where is it to be found; how widespread and significant is it?

Foremost among those who have rejected the symbols and values of the revolution are the so-called class enemies, individuals and families who, by virtue of their past political behavior or economic status (e.g., former landlords, wealthy merchants, supporters of the Nationalist Party, common criminals, and other assorted "bad elements") have been labeled as "counterrevolutionaries" and subjected to the coercive constraints of the dictatorship of the proletariat. At a rough estimate, there are some 40–50 million such class enemies, comprising approximately 5 percent of the Chinese population. They have been deprived of their rights as citizens and exposed to varying forms and degrees of punitive discipline, ranging from intermittent political surveillance to intensive labor reform and long-term imprisonment. In addition, an indeterminate number of unrepentant criminals and unreformed counterrevolutionaries (perhaps on the order of 2–3 million) have been executed by the state since 1949, with the vast majority of these executions occurring during the early years of Communist transition, from 1949 to 1953.

Aside from the obvious alienation of designated class enemies, pockets of opposition to the Communist Revolution are also encountered—albeit less frequently—among certain segments of the peasantry (primarily in poor villages that have experienced little or no economic growth in recent decades); among some members of the "bourgeois intelligentsia"; among the so-called rusticated youth (urban students permanently reassigned to the countryside since the early 1960s); and among certain minority nationalities (e.g., in Tibet, where Communist power was coercively imposed, and rather widely resisted, in the 1950s).

For most of the remaining 80–90 percent of the Chinese people, however, the symbolism of the revolution has been more or less effectively internalized in the form of subjective attachment to the system. It is in this sense that we speak of Chinese communism as being basically "legitimate" in the eyes of its citizens.

Orientations Toward National Issues and Leaders

While it is evident that the Chinese people by and large support the general norms and symbols of their political system, it is less clear whether—and to what extent—they support specific political institutions, policies, and leaders. How do ordinary citizens perceive China's governing elites and political organs? How do they respond to central political authority? And how are they affected by political debates and factional conflicts at the national level?

Contrary to popular impressions in the West, for most Chinese, most of the time, national politics does not seem to hold particularly great interest; and there appears to be a certain amount of contemporary relevance in the traditional peasant adage which holds that "Heaven is high; the emperor is far away." Although the Chinese mass media have an extremely high political content, and although the vernacular has been suffused with political terminology, limited attention is normally paid to nonlocal political issues in the daily lives of the Chinese people.

Indeed, the level of political erudition and sophistication of the majority of China's 700 million peasants appears to be quite low. For example, more than a year after the beginning of China's Cultural Revolution in 1966, peasants in many villages continued to be both uninformed about and uninvolved in the new revolution—despite widespread propaganda coverage in the mass media and the nationwide peregrinations of several million Red Guards.

One former Red Guard recorded his amazement when he interviewed a young peasant woman in a mountain village in Fukien Province in 1967:

> I asked her what was in heaven. She said that Mao Tse-tung was in heaven, constantly watching over everybody. He would know whoever was not working hard and have him punished. . . . Then I put a whole series of questions to her. I asked her how large China was. She shook her head. I asked her if there were any other countries besides China. Again she shook her head. I asked her if she knew the earth was round. She shook her head. Finally, I could only shake my head with her.*

While such parochialism is undoubtedly exceptional, the illustration should serve to remind us that even in China—ostensibly the most highly politicized nation on earth—the penetration of the traditional social

*Ken Ling, *The Revenge of Heaven* (1972), pp. 317–18.

order by the modern political apparatus of Party and state has been limited and imperfect. And for the majority of Chinese peasants, the most pressing questions of daily life apparently concern neither the latest power struggle in Peking nor the latest edict of the Politburo, but rather the perennial agrarian concerns of wind, water, weather, and work points —in other words, the problems of economic subsistence and livelihood.

Sometimes, however, such fundamentally apolitical peasant concerns may become translated into political realities, particularly when the material livelihood of the peasants is affected by the outcome of a national political issue. For example, during the Cultural Revolution the peasants in one village reportedly preferred Liu Shao-ch'i to Mao Tse-tung, "because they identified Liu with the private plots which gave them a chance to put some savings (aside) and move up the ladder. To them, Mao meant only compulsory grain deliveries, long hours of work for little reward, and [mass] movements which wasted the nation's time and money."*

Although urban workers are generally more politically sophisticated and well informed about national politics than their peasant counterparts, there is some evidence that among workers too politics is of relatively limited salience in everyday life. Thus, a number of former Chinese industrial workers, interviewed in Hong Kong, reported that they and their co-workers participated only infrequently and perfunctorily in the political life of the factory.** And when workers do become politically involved, such involvement tends to be congruent with the pursuit of their own self-interest. During the mass campaign to "restrict bourgeois rights" launched by the Gang of Four in 1975, unskilled and apprentice workers who occupied the lowest rungs of the industrial wage ladder were the most active and ardent supporters of industrial wage equalization, while skilled workers and veteran workers with the highest seniority (occupying the top rungs of the wage ladder) tended strongly to oppose such equalization.

Since the pursuit of material self-interest is regarded in China as a manifestation of "bourgeois mentality," such pursuit must of necessity be rationalized in terms of officially sanctioned principles. And in a society that routinely requires renunciation of the self and public obeisance to "correct" ideological principles, one possible result may be the generation of a certain amount of public cynicism.

When Mao Tse-tung and Lin Piao promulgated the slogan: "Let politics take command (of economic work)," in the mid 1960s, one provincial official, concerned over his province's poor showing in grain production

---

*Gordon Bennett and Ronald Montaperto, eds., *Red Guard: The Political Autobiography of Dai Hsiao-ai* (1971), pp. 213–14.
**See Martin K. Whyte, *Small Groups and Political Rituals in China* (1974), esp. chapter 8, and Parish's essay in this book.

in previous years, irreverently responded: "Let *politics* take command? Better to let *fertilizer* take command! Fertilizer solves problems." And when Mao's unpopular wife Chiang Ch'ing initiated a movement in Shanghai musical circles to introduce piano accompaniment to Peking opera in 1966, a wall poster appeared in the Shanghai Conservatory of Music that proclaimed in large characters: "Smash the piano!" A final illustration of political cynicism is provided in the autobiography of a former Red Guard, who reported that during the Cultural Revolution, "the Central authorities constantly urged: 'Take along the Mao quotations; study them whenever there's time.' What we did was take along the cards and play whenever there was time."

Of all the sources of political cynicism in China, however, perhaps the most common is the repetitive cycle of mass campaigns and top-level political purges. In China, yesterday's orthodoxy all too often becomes today's heresy, while today's sainted leader becomes tomorrow's tainted villain. In such fashion, a succession of high-level political leaders— including Liu Shao-ch'i, Lin Piao, and Chiang Ch'ing—have virtually overnight turned from Chairman Mao's "close comrades-in-arms" to "lifelong political swindlers" and "renegades." And at least one current leader—Vice-Premier Teng Hsiao-p'ing—has survived two major descents into political purgatory, only to return again each time with enhanced authority.

Such manifest contradictions, often unacknowledged by Chinese authorities, have tended to create a certain credibility gap among the Chinese people. As one alienated young Chinese intellectual put it, "It wasn't the injustice so much as it was the way that the leaders denied its existence."*

So too have many people become visibly annoyed with the repetitive campaign cycle that periodically punctuates the tranquility of daily life in China. One peasant refugee confided to me that he had frequently fallen asleep during daily group study sessions that accompanied the initiation of each new campaign in the countryside. Another peasant rhetorically inquired, "How can a country be run when so much time [is] spent in movements and in plans like the Great Leap Forward?"

Despite such manifestations of apathy, cynicism, and alienation, however, some national political events do evoke sentimental, affirmative responses in large numbers of Chinese citizens. For example, the death of Premier Chou En-lai in January 1976 apparently resulted in widespread spontaneous expressions of genuine grief. When public mourning for the late premier was briefly sanctioned in the spring of that year, there was a considerable outpouring of emotion—resulting in a widely publi-

*Bennett and Montaperto, eds., *Red Guard*, p. 227.

cized riot in Peking when the mourners were prohibited (reportedly by agents of the Gang of Four) from placing commemorative wreaths at the foot of a public monument. And when the Gang of Four was arrested in the fall of 1976, there were widespread reports of public jubilation in numerous Chinese cities, indicating that the Gang, led by Mao's wife Chiang Ch'ing, was rather unpopular throughout China.

Despite periodic high intensity, then, and contrary to official propaganda, politics is apparently not uppermost in the minds of most Chinese most of the time. While some groups (e.g., Party members, activists, and administrative cadres) are more closely attuned to the subtleties of national politics than others, political issues, which are often only dimly perceived by the citizenry at large, on the whole run a poor second to the material realities of everyday life in commanding public attention and interest. In this sense, politics has failed to "take command" in contemporary China.

Local Political Participation

Chinese citizens relate to their political system on yet another level: as active participants in local politics. This occurs through membership in the Communist Party and Youth League, mass organizational activities, performance of "activist" roles in schools and work units, participation in local elections, and periodic meetings of political study groups. Indeed, some form of political participation is virtually inescapable for most citizens in contemporary China.

At the center of China's political system stands the CCP. Comprising about 3–4 percent of the total population (with 35 million members in 1977), the Party is the hub of all political activity, both local and national. Because of the rigorous standards of Party recruitment and the high prestige generally attached to Party membership, CCP members form a true sociopolitical elite in Chinese society.

As the youth auxiliary of the Party, the Communist Youth League (CYL) has as its main function the politicization of young people aged fourteen to twenty-five. CYL members are generally recruited in schools, with each class in any given school having its own Youth League branch. Like the parent CCP, the CYL recruits members according to the twin criteria of class origin and political behavior.

Relations between Party members and non-Party members (as well as between CYL members and nonmembers) have varied from place to place and time to time, depending on the vicissitudes of local socioeconomic conditions, the personal character of individual Party members, and the general popularity or unpopularity of specific policies being implemented by the Party at any given time.

Periodically, there have been reports of CCP members and cadres using their Party authority and official perquisites to promote special interests; and this has occasionally served to strain the Party's credibility with the masses. Thus, for example, relationships were visibly exacerbated in many Chinese universities and cultural organs in the mid-1950s, at a time when many Party officials were reportedly assuming bureaucratic airs and adopting sectarian attitudes toward the masses. As one non-Party teacher in a Chinese university complained during the course of the "Hundred Flowers" Campaign in 1957,

> . . . a man is judged not by his virtues or abilities, but by whether or not he is a party or youth league member. . . .
> Why are vainglory, fame, and profit in the thoughts of the young? This has something to do with the existing system. Some party members rushed to join the party in order to enjoy the resultant privileges. Those who do not join the party have no future. . . .*

Other reports of Party members and cadres using their official positions or personal connections to promote their interests, reward their friends, and punish their enemies have frequently cropped up during periodic political campaigns, such as the Socialist Education Movement (1963–66), the Cultural Revolution (1966–69), the "Criticize Lin, Criticize Confucius" Campaign (1973–74), and the movement to repudiate the Gang of Four (1976–78). In the campaign to criticize Lin Piao, for example, Lin and a number of his erstwhile "sworn followers" within Party organizations in various places allegedly committed the unproletarian sins of "lording it over others, living in comfort . . . and leading the life of an official. . . . They approach friends and relatives for favors. . . . They expropriate things by unlawful means. . . . They vie with others in 'being generous' and 'showing off.' . . ."

Such unproletarian conduct on the part of a minority of Party members and cadres tends to strain relations, and is the source of a great deal of official concern in the PRC. Strain also is generated insofar as there are times when even the most conscientious Party members and cadres are required to promote policies and programs that run counter to the immediate interests of their friends, neighbors, and co-workers. In such cases, friction may arise and Party members may find themselves temporarily isolated from the masses. Indeed, so unpopular among the peasants were some rural Party policies during the Great Leap Forward that a number of local officials in the countryside actually resigned from office rather than conscientiously implement the offending programs.

One further source of strain is the periodic "open door" rectification campaign, wherein the masses are encouraged to air their grievances

*Quoted in Dennis J. Doolin, ed., *Communist China: The Politics of Student Opposition* (1964), pp. 31–2.

against Party members and cadres. During the Socialist Education Movement, for example, Party officials in some rural areas were heavily criticized by local peasants for various alleged acts of petty corruption and incompetence; and in some cases, the accused officials retaliated against their critics by giving them undesirable labor assignments, reducing their oil or cloth rations, or—in a few extreme instances—actually beating them up. And during the Cultural Revolution, numerous cases of Red Guard harassment and physical abuse of Party officials were reported, as the "revolutionary little generals" of Chairman Mao were given virtually unlimited license to seek out, expose, and struggle against alleged "bourgeois powerholders" within the Party.

One such putative "bourgeois powerholder" was Fukien Province Party Secretary Yeh Fei. The Cultural Revolution struggle against Yeh is described in vivid detail by a Red Guard participant:

> At 9 A.M. sharp . . . more than 1,000 [Red Guards] arrived at Yeh Fei's residence. . . . We rushed directly into the living quarters. . . . Yeh Fei [and] his wife, Wang Yu-keng . . . were at the breakfast table. . . . As we entered the dining room, Yeh Fei's face turned white. . . .
>
> "Yeh Fei, Wang Yu-keng, stand up! You are under arrest! We are the commandos of the August 29 General Headquarters!" . . .
>
> Pushing Yeh and Wang aside, we began our search [of their quarters]. It was past noon when we finished; Yeh Fei and Wang Yu-keng had been on their feet for more than three hours. . . . At about 1 P.M. we took Yeh and Wang back with us to headquarters. . . . It was decided to hold a mass meeting on the following day to struggle [sic] Yeh and Wang. . . .
>
> [The next morning] as we put Yeh and Wang into a sealed food truck, obtained from the Foreign Trade Bureau, I said to them, "I hope you don't die during the struggle." . . .
>
> [At the struggle meeting] we could not stop the surging crowds. . . . [They] did not quiet down and listen until they heard the announcement that Yeh and Wang had been dismissed from their duties.
>
> [We] asked Yeh Fei and Wang Yu-keng, "Do you know that being paraded in trucks on streets today represents your dismissal?"
>
> "Dismissal is for the central authorities to decide."
>
> "Fart! This is the peerless authority of the people! We, the August 29 General Headquarters, have the power to represent the people of Fukien and pronounce the verdict." . . .
>
> But the best way for us to convince the public that the youths of August 29 had indeed toppled Yeh Fei . . . was to have everyone see them paraded through the streets subserviently bowing their heads and confessing their crimes.*

*Ling, *The Revenge of Heaven*, pp. 135–45.

Although such incidents involving Red Guard confrontations with Party officials were not uncommon in the emotionally charged atmosphere of 1966–67, they are not normally representative of Party/mass relations in the PRC. To the extent that tension in these relations does exist, it is as often a result of status and authority differentials (and the consequent envy and resentment involved) as of blatant misconduct on the part of Party members.

Normally, the Party and Youth League recruit new members from among the ranks of proven "activists" in schools, factories, and villages. In every basic-level organization, Party members and cadres are on the lookout for individuals who, by their exemplary behavior, are regarded as potential targets of cultivation as activists. Once they have been identified and cultivated, such activists (usually a handful of people in each classroom, factory workshop, or rural production team) perform a vital function as a link or conduit between the Party and the masses. They normally take the lead in implementing Party policies, work longer hours than their peers (including frequent volunteer labor after hours or on weekends), and set a good example in political study. They also serve as informal "opinion leaders" in small group meetings, which are regularly held among the members of all basic-level organizations.

Although many if not most activists in China are probably genuine idealists with high socialist consciousness, there have been frequent reports of individuals becoming activists for selfish, opportunistic reasons. Since political activism is seen by many young Chinese as a possible avenue toward upward social mobility (i.e., a path to a good job, Party membership, or college entrance), there is considerable incentive for some individuals to manifest dissimulative, or feigned activism—a phenomenon that has been openly acknowledged and strongly criticized in the Chinese mass media. As one Chinese intellectual put it,

> Since [Liberation] there have emerged, encouraged by the "desire to better oneself," a group of activists who seek every opportunity to get a position, who praise and please their superiors obsequiously, who know how to read their superiors' minds . . . and who attack others.
>
> Their state of mind is understandable for, as the saying goes, "Every man has a desire for profit." There are many privileges and material incentives that tempt one to seek promotion to the nobility! . . .
>
> Of course, those who really wish to devote their whole lives to the building of communism deserve our respect and admiration. However, behind this we can smell more the aroma of cooked rice and broth. . . .*

One obvious example of dissembled activism was related to me in Hong Kong by a young peasant refugee. This young man had tried to

*Quoted in Doolin, ed., *Communist China*, pp. 46–7.

escape from his native village to the nearby city of Canton three times in the early 1960s. Each time he was apprehended by the public security police and returned to the village, where he was subjected to harsh criticism and organizational discipline. In 1966, when the Cultural Revolution began, this unhappy and thoroughly alienated young man adopted new tactics. He threw himself into the study of Mao's "little red book," and in less than two months he had memorized the entire volume of quotations, chapter and verse. He then entered—and handily won—his commune's Mao-study competition, thus earning the praise of his fellow villagers. Believing that he had turned over a completely new leaf, they issued him a travel permit and some spending money, and sent him off to Canton as the local entrant in the province-wide competition among activists in the study of Mao's thought—whereupon he used the money to buy passage to Hong Kong aboard a smuggler's fishing boat.

The problem of dissembled activism, while by no means universal in contemporary China, is nonetheless endemic to a system in which concrete rewards and benefits frequently accrue to those who are able to demonstrate their "overconformity" to officially prescribed norms of political and social behavior.

Nonactivists frequently distrust activists and tend to keep the latter at arms length. As one former middle-school student recalled, "We didn't want the [activists] to hear our personal talk because we were afraid they would report to teachers." Another student echoed this anxiety with the observation that

> When I was introduced to [an activist] my first reaction was to speak carefully, to avoid politics, and to try to speak less and talk about harmless, small things. When activists approached me, I would just ignore them until they went away. . . . Ordinary students didn't criticize activists because they would remember it in their hearts and make trouble for you when you did something wrong.*

In addition to political activism, local elections constitute a second major form of citizen participation in China. Within each rural commune, individual production teams (small subvillage units of around twenty to thirty families) elect their own administrative cadres each year. The most common method of nomination is by the next higher level of commune administration, the production brigade. In this method, a list of candidates is drawn up by the brigade leaders and passed down for consideration by the team. Normally there are more names on this list than cadre positions to be filled, thus providing some (albeit limited) scope for choice by the local peasants.

*Susan Shirk, "The Middle School Experience in China," unpublished PhD dissertation, Massachusetts Institute of Technology, 1974.

In theory the criteria of political consciousness and class origin are paramount in the nomination of candidates, but in reality emphasis seems to be given to the more practical, instrumental qualities of production experience, relations with the peasants, and fair-mindedness. Indeed, the relative stress on such qualities has been so great that many production teams elect cadres who lack political sophistication and ideological commitment, and who operate more in the style of Confucian patriarchs, ruling over the "extended family" of the village in the manner of traditional village elders, rather than in the style of model Communist activists.

Once the candidate list is passed down from the brigade to the team, an election meeting of team members is held. Sometimes team members will propose additional cadre nominations at the election meeting. Alternatively, they may reject one or more of the listed nominees handed down by the brigade, and propose substitutions. Such occurrences are rather rare, however, because the existing brigade and team leaders are generally united behind the prepared slate, and ordinary peasants do not often wish to risk incurring the displeasure of these authorities.

Once the nominations are completed, voting is done either by secret ballot or by a show of hands. The second method has been criticized by some peasants on the grounds that it results in intimidation by brigade authorities, who frequently sit in as observers during team election meetings. As one peasant put the problem: "Team members worry that brigade cadres will come and see. If we raise our hands against brigade wishes, we run the risk of encountering brigade displeasure. . . . Therefore, brigade lists of nominees are often passed."*

In the relatively rare event that nonlisted candidates are elected by the production team, the names of the unlisted electees are forwarded to the brigade for approval. If brigade authorities disapprove, the individual(s) in question may be denied cadre positions—despite their having been duly elected. However, if the nonlisted electees are highly popular within the team, brigade authorities may feel constrained to approve their election in order to retain the goodwill and cooperation of the peasants.

Brigade officials also have the authority to dismiss team cadres and appoint replacements between elections. Such authority is used sparingly, for it smacks of "commandism" and may tend to alienate the peasants. One example of alienation occurred in a production team in Kwangtung, where a highly popular elderly team leader was summarily dismissed by brigade officials for having resisted a Party order calling for peasants to relinquish their privately operated fish ponds and bamboo

*John P. Burns, "The Election of Production Team Cadres in Rural China: 1958–1974," unpublished paper presented to the workshop on the pursuit of political interests in the PRC, Ann Arbor, Michigan, August 1977.

groves. A tough young cadre was appointed in his place, and attempted to implement the Party policy, whereupon the team members registered their disapproval by cutting down all the bamboo, and catching and eating all the fish in the ponds. For the next year the peasants openly defied the new team leader; and at the subsequent election meeting they refused to reelect him, giving their votes instead to the deposed village elder. Eventually the higher authorities capitulated to the peasants and restored the former team leader—as well as the fish ponds and bamboo groves.

Such incidents of conflict notwithstanding, competition for election to team cadre positions is generally rather minimal, and the electoral process is thus usually devoid of intense partisan campaigning. Indeed, it has been widely observed that many, even most team members are normally unwilling to serve as cadres. For one thing, being a cadre involves sacrificing leisure time (which might otherwise be spent cultivating one's private plot) in order to attend meetings, organize production tasks, supervise accounting and work-point allocations, and so forth. Second, being a team-level cadre involves very little supplemental income or other material "fringe benefits." Third, a cadre sometimes has to implement unpopular policies, and is frequently involved in resolving disputes among team members in such areas as labor assignments, work-point assessments, and so on. Rather than risk uncomfortable and potentially alienating confrontations with their friends and relatives, many peasants simply avoid "running" for office. Finally, being a cadre involves undergoing periodic investigation—and possible severe criticism—during political campaigns.

Because of the relative paucity of qualified individuals willing to serve as administrative cadres in the countryside, and because of the widespread persistence of traditional social attitudes and behavior patterns among the peasantry, the Party and government continue to tolerate a substantial amount of old-style patronage and Confucian-style paternalism in the administration of rural production teams. Relations of kinship and friendship are frequently more important to peasants than those of proletarian comradeship; and for this reason, higher level authorities have often been constrained to downplay their own criteria of "correct" leadership styles and cadre behavior as the price of continued peasant support and cooperation at the grassroots level.

Perhaps the most ubiquitous form of grassroots political participation in contemporary China is the small group. Such groups—generally comprising eight to fifteen members—are found in all types of basic-level organizations, including school classrooms, factory workshops, rural production teams, and administrative offices. Small groups meet periodically (normally a few times each month, but during intensive mass movements as often as several times a week) for various purposes, such as study of Party and government documents, mutual criticism and self-criticism, newspaper reading, and discussion of the group members' personal and work-related problems.

Small groups tend to elicit compliant behavior through the exertion of subtle but strong influences toward group conformity within a carefully controlled social milieu. Ideally, the small group format induces conformity by isolating the potentially deviant individual, who perceives himself or herself to be "out of synch" with group norms. If the isolated deviant values the acceptance and support of the group, and if his or her unorthodox views fail to gain substantial reinforcement within the group, the pressure toward submission and compliance will be quite high.

In practice, small groups in China run the gamut from highly effective socializing agents to formalized (and ineffective) political rituals. In some cases, small groups function as genuine open forums for the expression and mutual support of members' norms and values, while in other cases the groups are so highly politicized by their leaders that members carefully avoid revealing their true feelings and attitudes, lest they render themselves vulnerable to criticism. Here there tends to be a ritualistic dissemblance on the part of group members. Thus, in one recent research report it was noted that "group members carefully search for cues as to what public statements are required of them and make them, no matter what their public views and reservations are. Such sessions can become empty charades that group members feel they must engage in."*

Indeed, the phenomenon of group members cursorily going through the motions of "spontaneously" airing their views and criticizing themselves—and their comrades—is perhaps the most frequent deviation from the ideal process of small group politicization in the PRC. This common deviation is similar to the phenomenon of dissembled activism noted earlier. An extreme example is provided by a former inmate of a Chinese prison, who describes how eager he and his fellow inmates became to please their captors:

> The only way we could demonstrate our revolutionary ardor was to confess well. Our sessions . . . became more and more charged with verbal signs of devotion. We chatted away our platitudes like Stakhanovite parrots. . . . Like everyone else, I wanted to have my confession accepted as quickly as possible. . . . When my zeal was rewarded with definite signs of approval, I responded favorably. I gave myself more and more easily into long ram-

*Martin K. Whyte, "Small Groups and Communications in China," unpublished paper presented to the conference on Communication and Cultural Change in China, East-West Center, Honolulu, Hawaii, January 3–7, 1978.

bling discourses about imperialism, Soviet revisionism, serving the people, or whatever other subject was in vogue for the moment. . . . I had simply accepted the bargain that my life in [prison] tendered to me: Follow the path marked out for you, don't make trouble, and you will be comfortable. I fell into it. It was easier.*

In addition to dissembled or cursory activism, another rather common deviation is the phenomenon of passivity, or withdrawal. Such passive withdrawal from participation in group activities may stem from one of three sources: apathy, alienation, or fear of criticism. As an illustration of the first, several peasants whom I interviewed in Hong Kong stated that they often played cards, gossiped, dozed, or otherwise "goofed off" during study group meetings.

The second type of passive withdrawal, stemming from group members' alienation, is illustrated by the case of an Anhwei peasant who recalled an occasion when his study group met to criticize Teng Hsiao-p'ing in the spring of 1976. Because Teng was quite popular with the peasants, the group leader's admonitions to the peasants to repudiate Teng as an "unrepentant capitalist roader" fell on deaf ears. "Nobody said a word," recalled the peasant. "The discussion group leader just sighed in desperation, closed his books and left the room. We all assumed that he made up something for his report to his supervisors. He had to protect himself and the rest of the village."**

Passive withdrawal based on fear of criticism is exemplified by the case of a former Red Guard leader who describes his retreat from group politics during the Cultural Revolution: "I was so afraid of making a mistake and subjecting myself to censure that I immediately resolved to play a passive role. . . . I had concluded that in a society like my own, it was safer to do nothing."†

Despite the existence of several notable gaps between the theory of small group politicization and the practical realities of group behavior in contemporary China, the technique of face-to-face communication through small groups has nonetheless been effectively used to secure the "voluntary" compliance—whether active or passive, spontaneous or dissembled—of large numbers of Chinese citizens. At its best, the small group technique resembles the type of peer-oriented consciousness-raising experience common to "encounter" groups and "sensitivity training" in the West (albeit of a more highly politicized nature). At its worst, the group process may devolve into a mere hollow exercise in ritualistic

*Bao Ruo-wang (Jean Pasqualini) and Rudolph Chelminski, *Prisoner of Mao* (1976), pp. 69, 285.
**"Chinese Peasants Resist Directives," Los Angeles *Times*, May 7, 1978.
†Bennett and Montaperto, eds., *Red Guard*, p. 209.

affirmation, devoid of true commitment or a change in internalized values. In either case the goal of securing at least overt social and political conformity without recourse to physical coercion is enhanced, even if the resulting behavioral changes may well be only superficial or temporary in many instances.

Conclusion

In examining the symbolic political attachments, attitudes toward political authority, and patterns of political participation of various individuals and groups of ordinary Chinese citizens, we have witnessed a complex reality that tends to belie the simple one-dimensional stereotypes introduced at the outset of this essay. Although we have seen evidence of certain elements of totalitarian control, ideological extremism, and participatory democracy in different spheres of Chinese political life, such elements clearly do not suffice—either singly or in combination—to comprehend the full richness and multidimensionality of the Chinese political order.

It is apparent that although most Chinese to some degree support their political system (measured in terms of symbolic allegiance to the dominant values of the revolution), such popular support may be—and in some cases already has been—subject to erosion over time. Unless a popular legitimacy is periodically and cumulatively reinforced by visible material progress and improved living standards, there is a potential for increased alienation.

Most young Chinese have never experienced firsthand either the deprivations of pre-Liberation society or oppression by former class enemies. For these post-Liberation generations, who already comprise a substantial majority of the Chinese population, the CCP's perennial appeals to "recall past bitterness" and "compare it with present sweetness" do not seem to be particularly effective techniques for regenerating emotional commitment to the revolution. As one official report put it,

> Youths of this generation do not know the evils of the old society. . . . Some of them do not even understand what landlords and capitalists are. . . . Many other youths hold the belief that in a socialist society everyone will have good food and good clothes and can go to school in the cities. . . . Thus, they are not prepared ideologically for class struggle . . . between capitalism and socialism.*

*Quoted in Richard Baum, *Prelude to Revolution: Mao, The Party, and the Peasant Question, 1962–66* (1975), p. 38.

In the eyes of the young, the future legitimacy of the system may well hinge upon the regime's ability to deliver on its oft-repeated promise of a better material existence, rather than upon the continuation of what are increasingly perceived as essentially pointless class struggles against long-vanquished enemies. Indeed, a realization of the increasingly contingent nature of popular support would appear to underlie recent decisions by the Hua Kuo-feng regime, (a) to grant a virtual across-the-board pay increase to China's industrial workers (the first such general wage hike since 1956); (b) to produce a greater variety and better quality of consumer goods for domestic distribution; (c) to permit workers and peasants to augment their incomes through spare-time self-employment; (d) to speed up the pace of agricultural mechanization; and (e) to ease the burdens and hardships endured by China's 15 million or so "rusticated intellectual youths" in the countryside. Such measures, if effectively implemented, should help to boost the trust and confidence of important segments of Chinese society.

There is substantial evidence that many Chinese citizens have successfully adapted to the rather rigid constraints imposed by a highly ideologized, highly authoritarian political system. Far from being the docile tools of an all-pervasive Party-cum-state, many Chinese have cushioned themselves against the excessive demands of the system and used the system to promote their own interests, becoming rather adept at manipulating their political environment. While such self-serving behavior is by no means universal, it is a frequent and recurrent response to a political system that demands of its citizens a great deal of self-denial and manifest devotion to the cause of "serving the people."

It is also evident that the ideological extremism manifested by certain groups in Chinese society is as much a function of the calculated pursuit of self-interest as it is a result of true devotion to the cause of proletarian dictatorship. Thus, for example, large numbers of Red Guards, political activists, and young unskilled workers have at various times cloaked their self-aggrandizing behavior in the legitimatizing mantle of current ideological slogans and rhetorical hyperbole. Such practices—known as "Waving the red flag to oppose the red flag"—are a constant source of concern to Party leaders in China.

This is not to say that all popular manifestations of ideological commitment in China are contrived or spurious; it is simply to note that in a society that rewards overconformity and applies persistent pressure to discourage deviancy, there may be substantial incentive for individuals and groups to wear their devotion (real as well as feigned) on their sleeve.

Certain elements of democratic participation in politics are clearly evident at the grassroots level in the PRC. Yet, as we have seen, the process of nominating and electing local cadres is often subject to indirect manipulation and even—in some cases—authoritarian preemption from above. This does not mean that all local elections in China are a sham, but only that there are significant, often highly subtle constraints on the exercise of free political choice at the grassroots level, where the operative ethos frequently seems to be, "If you want to get along, go along."

It appears that a great many Chinese citizens, particularly in the countryside, are rather apathetic and uninformed about politics. Despite almost three decades of intensive efforts on the part of the regime to politicize the peasantry, most rural émigrés continue to report a general atmosphere of political disinterest and laxity in the villages—except during periodic mass campaigns. Indeed, many traditional social practices—including arranged marriages, feudal religious rites, female subservience, and clan-based factionalism—continue to flourish in China's rural hinterland. And local leadership in the countryside is often in the hands of traditional village elders rather than model political activists, a fact that tends to reinforce the persistence of pre-Liberation behavior patterns and social mores.

Despite the apparent politicization of virtually all organized social activity in contemporary China, and despite the extremely high ideological and political content of the Chinese mass media, educational curricula, and even the vernacular language itself, it is evident that there is a substantial gap between political ideal and behavioral reality in Chinese society. While such a gap may be perceived to exist in virtually all societies, it seems particularly great in China, where continual demands for revolutionary orthodoxy in thought and action have been superimposed, in a very brief span of time, on the world's oldest and largest continuous civilization.

In many ways, China is truly a revolutionary society. The regime's commitment to fundamentally altering the political, social, and economic structure of the nation is indisputable. Yet the ordinary Chinese citizen may be substantially less revolutionary than his leaders would care to acknowledge. Though he may be sentimentally committed to the symbols of Liberation; though he may not yearn to throw off the "yoke" of communism; and though he may routinely speak the language of proletarian dictatorship and "serving the people," the ordinary citizen's political behavior bespeaks an imperfectly transformed individual. Just how different are the Chinese? Just how different is different?

The View from the Factory

WILLIAM PARISH

William Parish offers a field report on work life in China. He wrote it in Hong Kong, where he had been interviewing scores of industrial workers who have recently left the PRC for Hong Kong. They are by no means all anti-Communist, or enamored of capitalist Hong Kong (this fact might caution us against a black-and-white view of the moral difference between China and non-Marxist societies). But they have much to teach us on the issue that concerns Parish: What keeps the Chinese worker up to the mark?

Without quite likening the Chinese factory to the U.S. Post Office, Parish finds it to be a relaxed, cozy, low-powered place. Malingering can be found but strikes are very rare. There are many similarities to work life in America: not everyone is equal by any means, and extra effort generally wins extra rewards. But Parish finds that the differences are far greater. Life is more secure, money does not rule; seniority counts more heavily.

The shocks that come are political ones. But the valuable concreteness of Parish's information enables him to conclude that the political crises of the past decade or so, though convulsive by American standards, have not had as much impact on work life as is sometimes believed—and claimed by Peking.

The Chinese factory, all in all, gives us a fascinating glimpse of how individual and collective interests are harmonized without market forces or a competitive ethic.

William Parish, associate professor of sociology at the University of Chicago, has visited the PRC twice and lived in Hong Kong and Taiwan for a total of five years. He is the author of numerous journal articles, and co-author of Rural Small-scale Industry in the People's Republic of China *(1977) and* Village and Family in Contemporary China *(1978).*

—R. T

In any society there is great concern about how to organize a system of work rewards that both induces high levels of performance and secures equality, freedom, and other social values. This problem is of particular concern in socialist societies like China that strive to eliminate such Western labor problems as high unemployment, inflation, and alienation of laborers both from their work and their fellow workers. Three major questions arise: Is the Chinese worker simply an economic person, responding to economic incentives much like workers in the West? Do the Chinese work more in response to pure ideological appeals? Or does the Chinese laborer work more out of a strong sense of social solidarity and identification with his or her own work unit?

The Chinese debate over proper incentives as seen in the official press and in interviews with émigrés in Hong Kong provides data for an initial analysis of Chinese responses to work incentives and how these responses differ from, or coincide with, those common to the Western world. The émigrés include both "illegal" refugees (often youth who swam all night to reach the peninsula of Hong Kong) and legal emigrants (Overseas Chinese who returned to China from Southeast Asia in the 1950s and early 1960s only to apply for legal exit in the 1970s). Twenty-one out of the total one hundred people interviewed worked in Chinese factories before their departure. In the British colony of Hong Kong, churning out consumer goods for the Western market, these émigrés encounter capitalism in some of its starkest forms. Their frequent ambivalence about this new world and about the world they left, as seen in some of the quotes below, helps to build confidence in the truth of what they have to say. Many émigrés remain fond of certain parts of the world they have left, and some of the legal ones go back regularly for visits and even entertain thoughts that they might go back permanently if things don't work out in Hong Kong. Our confidence in their reports is further strengthened by the coincidence between such interviews and the official Chinese newspaper reports on the last decade in Chinese industry, although at this stage much of what we say must be taken as hypothesis awaiting further analysis. My emphasis is on the full-scale state industries that have been the focus of much of the Chinese debate over work incentives in recent years.*

Economic Incentives

Initially, many aspects of Chinese payment systems in both industry and agriculture would seem to convince us that, much as in the free market economies of the West, incentives to work are based simply on economic reward. The greater the worker's skill and effort, the higher his or her pay. The Chinese themselves give some support to this conclusion in emphasizing that they are not yet at the stage of communism where people will be paid "each according to his need," but rather still in the transitional stage of socialism, in which people are paid "each according to his work."

The wide spread in formal pay scales also suggests a heavy reliance on economic incentives. In industry, the ratio in pay between the lowest and highest paid regular workers is about three to one, a figure not too different from that found in many free market economies. The inclusion of apprentices, temporary workers, and other irregular workers who have few of the regular worker's fringe benefits gives an even larger ratio. Technicians, engineers, and managers are on separate pay scales, rising to a potential salary ten times as great as that for the most poorly paid regular worker. In formal regulations, then, there is ample room for differential reward proportional to skill and effort. The link between material reward, skill, and effort has been brought even closer in the last few years with most industries restoring the material bonuses that were common before 1966, and a few selected industries even returning to piece rates in place of time rates.

Similarly, in agriculture there is a close correlation between skill, effort, and level of pay. Many villages (production teams) pay members according to task rates—each field plowed or unit of rice transplanted earns the worker a set number of work points. The faster, more skillful worker earns more. Even in those villages that pay by time rate, the time rate is reassessed yearly, with women, young, and old earning less than ablebodied males in their prime years. In villages, families with more ablebodied workers, especially able-bodied males, earn more and live a more comfortable life than families not so well endowed with labor power. In

*For purposes of argument, I am dealing here with state industries in general, ignoring some significant variations among industries with different technologies. Factories have been grouped into small (less than 100 employees), medium (100–499 employees), and large (500+ employees).

both industry and agriculture, then, things appear familiar to the Western reader.

Much of this familiarity is deceiving, however. On closer examination, one finds that there are as many dissimilarities as similarities between the Chinese system and that of the West. In industry, although the potential range of salaries is much larger, in fact most workers are squeezed into the range of U.S. $20 to $37 a month, giving an effective salary range of less than two to one.* Though potential salaries are much higher, virtually all technicians, engineers, and managers are restricted to no more than $75 a month. Many get only $40 to $50 a month, no more than some older skilled workers make. And both skilled and unskilled workers are eligible for work clothes, cool drinks, and other supplements that help narrow the differences between technicians, managers, and workers. As one worker from a watch factory notes, "The cadres [administrative personnel] say that it is difficult to be a cadre. One's benefits are lower, and besides the workers are always complaining about one's work." The effective range in salaries and benefits for most workers, technicians, and managers, then, is much narrower than in Western societies. Differences in types of work do not lead to major differences in levels of pay.

The link between skill, effort, and pay is further weakened by the fact that most promotions are based heavily on seniority. Prior to 1966, skilled workers could take exams to get promoted more rapidly. There were no such exams in the decade following, and both before and after most workers got salary increases only in nationwide promotions around 1963, 1971, and 1977. The 1971 promotions were the most extreme, using seniority as the only basis for promotion. But all promotions have emphasized that low-wage workers with several years seniority should be promoted before anyone else. In each major promotion campaign, a considerable proportion of those making $20 or $25 were promoted to making $25 or $30 odd. The 1977 promotions were somewhat more clearly based on performance. After the low-wage, high-seniority workers had been taken care of, a small group was promoted on the basis of skill and effort. But even this group could not be promoted too much, being limited to a maximum wage of $55 a month. Promotions based heavily on seniority are known in the West as well, but the Chinese system in recent years has gone much further in stressing this principle and in limiting it to low-wage workers.

*The exchange rate followed is 1 Chinese yuan = U.S. $0.61. The Chinese "poverty line," below which a state worker gets a hardship allowance, provides some perspective on these salaries. The line runs from $20 to $34 for a family of four, depending on the worker's city and factory. These are subsistence amounts. A more reasonable living standard requires more; hence the pressure on most wives to work.

Even stranger to the Western eye is Chinese industry's inability to fire or even demote incompetent employees. At first glance, it would appear that Chinese industries and the larger state apparatus have unlimited control over employees. For all practical purposes there is only one employer—the state. One might think that workers would be intimidated by this one employer, fearing that they would either lose their job or be transferred to a menial one in the city or countryside. The option of going without work and living on the earnings of one's spouse is not attractive for either men or women, since it usually takes two wage earners to feed, clothe, and house a family. But in practice factory managers almost never fire their employees except for serious criminal and political offenses, and even then workers are not so much fired as carted off to labor camp by public security. Demotions are only slightly more common.

In this situation, the more effective threat has been to accuse a person of political crimes in a major political campaign, dragging him or her before a factory mass meeting, to stand bowed at the waist and submissive in the face of insults and political harangue for a number of hours. Even this device could be applied only against a selected few, and most of the time life in factories has been relatively secure and unthreatening. A particularly articulate worker from a small lock factory reports on his experience:

> There were quite a few lazy ones, at least during and in the wake of the Cultural Revolution. . . . People would arrive late and then go out to shop once they were there. . . . We had study meetings daily after work for about half an hour. In these meetings the work group head would sometimes bring up the name of someone who was constantly late and lagging on the job. Occasionally, even the Party Secretary for the whole factory would look up someone who was lazy and have a little personal talk. Nevertheless, if one's name were brought up just in a study meeting after work one wouldn't worry about it, for most workers already having worked many years felt secure in their job. My name was brought up several times but more for problems of backward political thought than for laziness. Even if the Party Secretary talked with one, one would not worry about it.

Private and small group criticism, then, had little effect. Criticism in mass meetings had rather more:

> If one's name was brought up in a meeting before the whole factory, however, one would definitely be worried. For then one was on the verge of becoming a target of criticism in a political campaign and that was definitely hard to take. Once one's name was mentioned in a public meeting, one's behavior would change immediately. In my factory, two to three

names were mentioned per year in public meetings. The names tended to be those of bad class origin and those active in the radical Red Flag faction in the Cultural Revolution.

Some of these two to three names were the same old political targets who kept being mentioned over and over again, and in large factories an even smaller percentage of all workers would ever be subject to public criticism.

Coercion does have a role in Chinese factories, but it has had more to do with political attack than with the threat of being fired or demoted. And even the threat of political attack applied only to certain workers who happen to have come from the wrong (capitalist, landlord) family background, who committed errors in some earlier political campaign, or who continued to flaunt their uncooperativeness in the face of repeated warnings. For most workers life has been secure, in that they could expect eventual promotion with increasing seniority and freedom from fear of demotion or dismissal. We approximate such a system in the U.S. federal government; the Chinese are different in extending it to most industrial employees as well. Given this security and the difficulty factory managers have in controlling employees without using harsh measures that are inappropriate against the average employee, one must ask whether ideological commitment has not been substituted for economic control.

Ideological Commitment

Value commitments in work are not totally alien to the Western world. Max Weber and some other observers argue, indeed, that what set western Europe off from the rest of the world in the early stages of industrial growth was a peculiar commitment to the Protestant work ethic. Nevertheless, any intense tie between work and a theologically formulated Protestant ethic has faded. The remaining attempts to combine intense commitment and work in the West are restricted to a few small, utopian communes. The Chinese are unique in the modern world in trying to combine ideological commitment and work on a society-wide basis.

The attempt to bring political commitment to the Chinese worker is a massive one. On the average, groups of a dozen or so workers in a single work group under a single group leader meet two or three times per week for an hour to half-hour's study after work. Every month or so the whole factory assembles for a meeting, led by the factory's Party Secretary and factory head. In both the factory meetings and the work group meetings, the worker hears at least as much about the latest policy line from Peking as about practical production problems. Though many workers are not interested in the details of these policy lines, a few political activists can be counted on to pick up current political themes and discuss them vigorously. Even the more reticent are forced to join in at times. "Usually, only a few would do most of the talking and others would just listen," said one worker from a moderately large scrap steel plant, but "periodically everyone would have to speak out on what their understanding of an article was." Even if the worker's expressed "understanding" is just a rehash of yesterday's editorial in the *People's Daily* or the Party Secretary's speech from the day before, new policies are quickly disseminated to the entire factory population. The Western world knows no system quite so effective in distributing messages from the central government.

When this system has worked well, workers have been concerned as much about building a strong nation and a new way of life as about their individual economic welfare. This appears in a comparison with the conditions of work in Hong Kong made by our informant from the lock factory. "Hong Kong workers have no aspirations other than earning more money," he says. "Chinese workers pay much less attention to money. Prior to the Cultural Revolution, being influenced by Communist thought, young workers in China were much more concerned about the collective good, the future of the nation, and so on. They were very idealistic." Similarly, Overseas Chinese informants who have come back out often report that in the difficult Great Leap Forward years of 1959–61, when they seldom had enough food to fill their stomachs, they nevertheless served contentedly because of a sense of participating in a common cause of building a new nation.

Still, political commitment as a work incentive can be carried only so far. Intense political commitment fades with age and time. The older Chinese workers seem to be less committed than the younger ones—or, to the extent that they remain or ever were committed, their commitment is a much more passive, nondoctrinal one. Even more problematically, political appeals can be carried to excess, especially when they emphasize class struggle in which one group of workers must attack another. The Chinese government now judges the extreme emphasis on political campaigns and ideological commitment of the last decade to have been a failure. The decade started in 1966 with Cultural Revolution attacks on leaders such as Liu Shao-ch'i for promoting "bourgeois" practices in all areas of life, including factories. The Cultural Revolution was essentially finished in 1968, but in the following years there was a succession of centrally directed political campaigns—mass media and organizational movements that attacked "class enemies," corruption, Lin Piao, Confucius, bourgeois rights, and so on. It was in these campaigns that some workers were publicly ridiculed before factory meetings.

Informants in Hong Kong agree with the post-1976 official assessment that the atmosphere of this decade was counterproductive. For one, workers detested leaders who got their position on the basis of political expertise alone. The workers in one restaurant had a poor impression of the new Party Secretary, an army veteran appointed to the restaurant in 1966. His problem was that "he couldn't talk without politics spilling out, while at the same time he had no understanding of concrete work problems." In a medium-sized water plant, the old Party members who had entered the Party before 1966,

> . . . were the backbones of production. They had a lot of prestige among the workers. The workers relied on them to solve all sorts of production problems. But those joining the Party after the Cultural Revolution were all unacceptable. They were political upstarts, who got into the Party mostly by attacking others in political campaigns. We thoroughly disliked them.

This feeling was exacerbated by many of them being former peasants whose only qualification was that they had served for a time in the People's Liberation Army, where they acquired political legitimacy but not the technical competence so respected in factories. Political skills divorced from technical skills are not respected—a reaction the Western worker would appreciate as well.*

Besides placing unrespected political figures in charge of production, the successive political campaigns of the 1966–77 decade tended to create factionalism and distrust among workers. During the most severe years of 1967–68, struggle among workers in different political factions actually slowed down production, causing a drop in national economic growth. By 1970 there was no longer active struggle in most factories. Yet some of the effects of the preceding years remained. According to our informant from the lock factory:

> Prior to the Cultural Revolution there were no serious conflicts among workers. They not only were very cooperative and helpful to one another but also very open with one another. Today, they are still helpful. . . . But since the Cultural Revolution there has been a lot of mental pressure. Workers have come to fear that in the next political campaign, old historical political problems will be dragged up and fear that errors that they themselves did not commit but were committed by their parents and siblings will be brought up and held against them. Because of this, people will not say what is in their heart. The Cultural Revolution had a lasting effect, which was to make people very cautious of what they said to one another. Every-

*Erica Jen's experience in the countryside led her to a different conclusion; see page 151–52.—R.T.

one began to think before they spoke and refused to say what they really felt. A distance grew between workers.

What effect did this withdrawal and tension plus the failure to provide regular promotions have on industrial production? The Chinese government's answer is that the last decade was debilitating, with workers engaged in rampant factional quarrels and frequent breakdowns in production in the last few years of the decade. Some Hong Kong informants report this bleak situation in a few large, centrally run factories in cities such as Peking and Shanghai. But in the great majority of not so large, provincial and city-run industries, which are the dominant kinds of industries in China and the industries from which most of our informants come, the situation was not nearly so bleak. At least after 1967–68 there were almost no stoppages in production in these factories. Although insidious, the problems that persisted were of a more subtle sort, having to do with the pace and fervor of work. With no promotions throughout the late 1960s and promotions only on seniority in the early 1970s, workers saw no point in working hard. Our informant from the lock factory notes,

> Productivity in Hong Kong is much higher than in the factory where I worked in China. Since Hong Kong is a capitalist society emphasizing competition, both the boss and his laborers must be fast to keep up. The pace of work is fast. By contrast, in state factories in China, outside of political campaigns, most workers just soldier through their daily eight hours [literally: play a day's monk, beat a day's gong]. This is because the pay is set and how much one does has no effect on one's income.

Also, much as in the U.S. Post Office in recent years, generous health benefits gave Chinese workers ample opportunity to malinger. In the scrap steel plant,

> After the Cultural Revolution many people were taking a day off from work —some were taking off on their own affairs, some for illness, some were just lazy. Some with medical acquaintances got [dubious] sick certificates. . . . One gets full pay for sick leave only after eight years of work. . . . [But] if one uses just two hours in going to see a doctor, there is no deduction in pay. So many workers who were late for other reasons would simply say that they had been to see a doctor.

Other informants describe a similar situation in their factories, particularly among young workers. The labor problems of most Chinese industries in the last decade, then, have had more to do with the pace of work and malingering than with full stoppages in production.

Collective Solidarity

One reason why problems have not been more serious over the last decade is that Chinese workers find other sorts of satisfactions in their job. That workers should get and expect many satisfactions other than pay is a frequent theme in Western theory and research. One line of reasoning, stemming from Marx, holds that such satisfaction will be higher in socialist societies because workers in such societies have more control over their work. They have a better chance to be whole people, with a closer attachment to (an absence of alienation from) their product, their factory, and their workmates. As visiting foreigners have discovered, the Chinese do not share the Western concern about alienation from work stemming from overspecialization of labor. As long as efficiency is improved, the Chinese leaders are happy to let a worker be the left-fender bolt tightener on a continuous assembly line.

However, the Chinese are quite concerned with reducing differences between leaders and led in industrial enterprises. The question is whether the adopted mechanisms have been all that effective. Informants report that the widely touted three-in-one technical groups—including managers, technicians, and workers—tend to have been formalistic. If they functioned at all, they brought together skilled repair workers and technicians who would have been talking to one another anyway. Only a few workers have been recruited into management, and once there, they tend to have become so busy with office and lab work as to have lost regular contact with the laborers from whose ranks they came. The attempts to have managers work periodically on the factory floor have been more successful, with managers in many factories coming down every week or so for a little production work. When these leaders tackle actual production problems, wear patched clothes, and avoid bureaucratic airs, there is frequent admiration from the workers. But the irony of this politically inspired program is that many nonpolitical managers who did not necessarily have good political credentials were already at work on the shop floor. It is the political managers, the Party Secretaries and their like, who must make a special effort to come to the shop floor to live up to this policy. The other irony is that some political managers are able to do so little real production work that workers begin to think of their leaders as hypocritical, when otherwise there would have been no expectation that executive officers should do such work.

Besides the issue of whether workers identify with their product and management, there is the question whether they identify with their fellow workers. This issue is raised not only in Marxist writings about alienation, but also in Western social science research which suggests that work motivation depends as much on informal social groups among workers as on pay incentives. Informal work groups can provide satisfaction. They can also turn against production, setting low output norms and sanctioning any worker who tries to deviate from these norms.

Even in the face of recent political campaigns, Chinese industry promotes solidarity among its workers. Workers are assigned to jobs not by their own volition but by the state labor bureau. Once in a job they are not free to leave, and most will spend their full work career in a single factory. This long history of work in a single place, and security from being fired, allows the workers to become well acquainted with one another. In many factories such mutual acquaintance begins in an initial two- to three-year period during which new workers are apprenticed to an older "master." Except for exceptional personality conflicts and occasional political conflicts when a politically hyperactive youth is assigned to a more moderate master, master-apprentice relationships are close. The two sometimes visit each other's homes, go on trips together, and exchange meals and gifts on major holidays even after the apprentice graduates. Among other workers as well there are often close relations, with people helping one another, for example when a family member is sick or dies. Some informants working in factories in Hong Kong report that even though they are happy to be out from under the political pressure of Chinese factories, they miss the old personal relationships. Our scrap steel worker notes, "Things are more comfortable in China than in Hong Kong. There is no piece rate there to make one work hard and there is no threat of being laid off tomorrow or the week after as there is in Hong Kong. True, there is more political threat, but there is still less pressure than in Hong Kong and interpersonal relations are less tense." And the lock worker, who evaluates Chinese factories negatively in several other respects, agrees: "There is more human feeling in China than in Hong Kong. If one's child is sick all one's co-workers will be concerned about it, asking what they can do to help and continuing to ask until the child is well." Most informants concur in this sort of assessment.

Research on Western factories suggests that this same solidarity, though good for promoting satisfaction, can slow down production if the workers all agree informally to control output and hide their full productive capacity. Some of the same tendencies are seen in Chinese factories, with workers speeding up when management is present but otherwise holding to a steady pace and punishing those who break this pace. In a medium-sized metal works factory,

> Every work group had a set amount it was supposed to produce each day. If the group fell short, the leaders might call the group into a meeting to discuss why they fell short. But in their hearts everyone knew the number

they were supposed to complete, and once through they would start drinking tea, telling jokes, and so on. The group leaders didn't care much as long as the daily quota was met. . . . Since there was no longer any bonus, there was no reason to keep working past the quota. Every day we would just produce a little more or less than the quota so as to average out around the quota or just slightly above it. . . . When we got near the end of the year, there were meetings to discuss the work quotas for next year. Workers were not willing to report too high a level since this would make it hard for themselves. So it took several meetings to hammer out an agreement.

And in the textile factory, "The factory set output quotas per group and per person. The workshop head kept a record of personal output. But the quotas were fairly easy to meet and some would stretch out their work so that they just did the quota and no more."

The problem for the managers is how to break this pattern. One Chinese technique that is unavailable to Western factory managers is to use political activists who side with management rather than their fellow workers. In the scrap steel plant, in which our informant estimated that about one-fifth of the workers were Party members, Youth League members, and other activists, "the activists were faster workers than the others. . . . Except for production drives, things are pretty calm, but when the factory starts a production high tide the workers speed up, not because they are personally enthused but because when one's neighbor speeds up one will look politically backward if one does not keep up with him. And one doesn't want to stand out as a potential target."

The work of the activists can make them sufficiently unpopular to be excluded from normal social interaction, so that their personal influence is weakened. In the scrap steel factory, "We were more careful in talking when the activists were present." And in the metal works factory where workers tried to keep quotas low, "There were some activists calling for higher quotas [at the end of the year], but with others not supporting them they couldn't get agreement on this. They were somewhat isolated."

The key to a manager's success in a Chinese factory is to skillfully balance off the satisfactions found in group solidarity with the potentially divisive role of political activists and the political campaigns to which these activists are attached. This balancing act sets the Chinese factory distinctly apart from the Western factory, even though some of the problems of informal work norms are similar.

Another potential way to deal with solidarity against management is to support it by a greater emphasis on collective incentives. This would make Chinese factories similar to the large Japanese factories, which tend to provide lifetime employment, ample fringe benefits, and a close identification between worker and factory interests. Already Chinese workers are much more tightly tied to their factory than workers in the West. The Chinese laborer's work unit is his or her most important source of official identification. Work cards (about 3 by 3 inches before being folded in half) are used somewhat like a driver's license in the United States: in getting a package from the post office, buying a train ticket, identifying oneself to the police, and so on, the easiest form of identification is simply to whip out one's work card. In a late-night household registration check or a search for pickpockets on a bus, say, a person without a work card may be questioned for hours while one with a work card is immediately let go.

Being attached to a state work unit and holding a work card gives one a respectable niche in society. One must go to one's work unit before any other unit for permission to marry, and the answer will not always be yes if a worker is not yet in his or her late twenties or is a potential Party member proposing to marry someone of "bad" (landlord, capitalist) class origins. The work unit is the best source of housing (which is extremely scarce) for a young couple. It is the work unit that enforces the limit of two children per couple, and sometimes even says in which year the two can be born. It is the work unit that has to approve one's divorce—more often than not refusing.

To the Western eye, informants seem remarkably amenable to this level of control, perhaps because in other spheres the work units are considerably more generous. One's work unit provides hardship allowances, medical benefits, and a pension. Its leaders visit your home each lunar New Year when you are retired, they visit you when you are sick in bed, and often organize and pay for your funeral when you die. The bigger factories have canteens with subsidized meals and nurseries for the very young. Youth in their teens and late twenties can sometimes escape rural assignment by taking over their parent's factory job when he or she retires. Truly, large Chinese factories do provide cradle-to-grave protection, and blessed is he or she who happens to work for a really wealthy and munificent one. Westerners have approximated this level of factory intervention in personal life only in the rare factory town. The Chinese have applied it to a whole society, or at least to much of the urban part of that society.

Yet, in the midst of all this enveloping care, personal identification with one's work unit seems strangely missing. Unlike the large Japanese enterprises, there are no company songs or other ceremonial symbols linking workers to their unit. Although some older workers may take pride in the success of their enterprise, most remain ignorant of the exact progress and success of their unit and emotionally unattached to that degree of success.

A final comparison with Chinese collective agriculture is instructive here. In contrast to Soviet collective agriculture, the Chinese system is quite efficient. It begins by providing a rather close correlation between skill and effort and the size of one's slice (as measured in work points) from the production team's income pie at the end of the year. As in industry, the differences in pay between any two individuals may not be all that great, particularly between any two adult males, adult females, or teenagers; but they are sufficient to indicate differential reward for differential skill and effort. Most important, these individual rewards are backed up by collective rewards and a collective identity. One identifies with one's production team because teams are based on old villages and neighborhoods of thirty to forty households each. Usually the families in a team have been neighbors for generations, and in South China they are often members of a single lineage, all descended from a common ancestor. Finally, the team is the basic income-earning and income-sharing unit in the countryside. It owns its own land and machines, and at the end of the year it divides profits among all members. A member's income is determined as much by the size of the unit's profits as by his own work points. So he or she is concerned as much with the size of the total pie as with the relative size of the cut. (The contrast with industry is immediately apparent in interviews; the village informants are far more knowledgeable about all the details of village finances and accounting.) In production teams, then, individual interests are melded with collective interests in a process strengthened by old village and kin solidarities and by the small size of that unit.

It is this melding of individual and collective interests that is so difficult to bring about in Chinese urban enterprises. Some aspects of the team experience, such as generations of residential proximity, kin ties, and small size, could never be replicated in industrial enterprises. Yet one could envisage giving workers more economic and symbolic ties to these enterprises, much as in Japan. Or one could envisage giving Chinese workers more economic interests in and administrative power over enterprises, much as in the Yugoslavian pattern of worker-managed, autonomous enterprises. In the spring of 1978 several articles in the Chinese press appeared, giving very approving descriptions of Yugoslavian industrial management. And the pre-1966 policy of allocating part of above-target production to the workers' welfare fund was reaffirmed. It is very unlikely that the Chinese would be willing to release central control over prices and market forces to the extent needed in the full Yugoslav model. Nevertheless, the other options for increasing efficiency—increasing pay differentials or a return to intense political pressure—are so ideologically repugnant or counterproductive that some movement toward greater autonomy and control by the workers may be inevitable.*

In sum, there are some things in Chinese industrial work settings that are familiar to Western readers. In both the West and China there is a common need to give some kind of graduated economic reward to differential skill and productivity, a common need for gradual income increases to give people a sense of accomplishment and progress, and a common role for informal work group pressures on the pace of production.

Yet the differences are more striking than the similarities. In China, economic rewards are less steeply graded than in the West, particularly for technicians and managers. There is a much greater role for ideological incentives. Even though pure ideological incentives cannot be pushed too far, activists who internalize much of the government's program or who simply want to curry favor with political managers can sometimes act as levers for disrupting informal work group resistance to higher production norms—a lever that is missing in the West. Finally, with minimal job mobility and a feeling of job security bolstered by numerous social benefits, Chinese workers have the possibility of a high degree of collective solidarity—a solidarity that could either turn against Chinese enterprises, or, with proper collective economic incentives, as in Japan or Yugoslavia, be turned in favor of higher economic productivity. All in all, the mix of incentives in Chinese industry is quite different from anything known in the capitalist West.

---

*By late 1979 these tendencies were proceeding apace. Some state enterprises had forged a much closer link between worker bonuses, benefits, and the success of the enterprise. And, in a manner reminiscent of Yugoslavian practice, small, urban collective enterprises responsible for their own profits were cut loose both to vary incentives in line with profits and to compete externally with the state sector. This competition, aided by the deregulation of prices on many consumer goods, was to provide an additional check on state worker performance, since no longer could state workers assume a steady market for their products.

The Hand of the State

Universal Values and Chinese Politics—A Balance Sheet

DONALD W. KLEIN

↑

Donald Klein, planting his feet firmly in the camp of internationalism, believes that China shares important values with the West. He argues that China's modern experience has put her within reach of the democratic revolution that has shaped the modern West. Klein guides us through the constitutional forms that show Peking to be committed to many rights and goals to which America is also committed.

Klein is mainly concerned with testing the PRC's performance in living up to its apparent commitments. In the sphere of economic justice, he gives high marks to Mao's China; and similarly in areas of social progress. On the political aspect of the democratic revolution, he finds the PRC sadly lacking. He makes an important distinction, however, between participation, where the picture is not unredeemed—but perhaps not also capable of being sustained as the years go on—and civil rights. Taking a more negative view of the latter than Victor Li's later essay does, Klein finds the central problem to be that not all the people are "people." At the end he confines himself to hope, rather than venturing into prediction.

Donald Klein took his PhD at Columbia University and is now associate professor of political science at Tufts University. He is co-author of Biographic Dictionary of Chinese Communism (1971) and of Rebels and Bureaucrats (1976). He visited the PRC in 1973 and 1979 and has lived a total of nine years in Hong Kong, Korea, and Japan (his wife's homeland).

—R.T.

Visitors to Peking's famous Gate of Heavenly Peace gaze upon five enormous portraits. One face is Chinese. The other four are Western—two Germans and two Russians. Mao Tse-tung's portrait holds pride of place in both location and size, yet the faces of Marx, Engels, Lenin, and Stalin personify more than a partial meeting of East and West. They symbolize something even larger for China: the acceptance of a broad range of values that has been slowly and painfully universalized since ushered in by the democratic revolution in the West two centuries ago.

But how do we define this "democratic revolution" without drifting off on lofty clouds of rhetoric? Do we refer to a secular world religion that offers its rewards on this earth? Do we mean the conviction that every human being is entitled to a life of dignity? Do we mean the rule of law? Or justice? Or liberty and freedom? Or is equality preferable, and if so, do we mean equality of opportunity or equality of result? Do we prefer the ringing slogan: "Liberty, equality, fraternity"? Or the equally ringing: "From each according to his abilities, to each according to his needs"?

There is what might be called an official definition. The United Nations-approved Universal Declaration of Human Rights (1948) reads, in part: a "recognition of the inherent dignity and of the equal and inalienable rights of all members of the human family" as "the foundation of freedom, justice and peace in the world."

If none of these words or phrases is acceptable, we all recognize the lip service paid to them in an era made distinctive by the emergence of the masses in history. One may better appreciate how far we've come in two centuries by considering a remark made just before the French Revolution by Catherine the Great: "Society requires a fixed order. There ought to be some to govern, and others to obey." She might as well have said: "Only elites have rights, the rest have duties." In either case, these are reasonable descriptions of human history—in East and West, in word and in deed—prior to the democratic revolution launched by the American and French revolutions.

A contemporary negative example is provided by two pariah nations: Rhodesia and South Africa. Why are they so easily identified? The answer, simply, is that both deny a most elementary aspect of the democratic revolution. Indeed, the denial of racial equality in word is in a sense more shocking than the well-known denial in fact.

In a positive vein, countless documents or statements demonstrate that the democratic revolution is not merely an ethnocentric invention of the West foisted upon the balance of mankind. Witness the scores of affirmations in the United Nations Charter, or the fervent third world backing for the UN's International Convention on the Elimination of All Forms of Racial Discrimination (unanimously adopted, one should add). Or Soviet Russia's recently adopted constitution, embodying in words at least the ideals of the democratic revolution. The Euro-Communist manifesto of 1975 even goes beyond the conventional civil liberties to include the right to "travel in and out of the country."

My view can be simply stated: there is virtually worldwide acceptance of a rough justice or equality that can be further divided into three types —economic justice, social justice, and political justice. Moreover, the People's Republic of China accepts these approximate categories.

Did the CCP, when organized in 1921, emphasize political, social, and economic justice? Or, as seems plausible in view of Marx's priorities, did it center almost exclusively on economic issues? In fact, the first Party manifesto most emphatically emphasized all three categories. Specifically, the manifesto proclaimed freedom of assembly, speech, and the press; equality for women; compulsory education; prohibition of child labor; universal suffrage; and a progressive income tax. Indeed, the entire program would seem old hat to contemporary social democrats.

During its early years, the CCP deliberately subordinated itself to Sun Yat-sen's Nationalist Party. Sun's party, it is worth noting, was guided by his "Three People's Principles." These principles (nationalism, "people's rights," and "people's livelihood") may not be the quintessence of the democratic revolution, but they are surely within its mainstream. And to this day, Sun the man and Sun's principles are portrayed by the Communists as part of China's revolutionary heritage. This is nowhere more vivid than in Canton, Sun's power base a half century ago. Visitors today find a city that seems as much "Sun Yat-senist" as "Maoist." It abounds in memorials and parks dedicated to Sun, and the main boulevard bears his name.

After Sun's death in 1925 and the bloody Communist-Nationalist break in 1927, the CCP was too occupied with the deadly game of survival to institute many progressive measures. Instead, two aspects of communism stood in the forefront: Party building and discipline (the Leninist component), and the establishment of the Red Army (the Trotskyist component). To be sure, programs were launched in Communist-held areas that harmonize with the democratic revolution. Concerted efforts, for example, were made to educate illiterate peasants and to draw them into the political arena. But all such attempts faced the brutal truth that the Communists' South China stronghold was under ferocious attacks from Chiang Kai-shek's forces. As a result, many so-called reforms spelled terror for innocent people, a process something akin to phases of the French Revolution.

Later, in Yenan, the Communists acted with greater moderation. Visitors to Yenan were deeply impressed by efforts to help the downtrodden —rudimentary education for peasants; Party cadres sharing the hardships of the most humble peasants; a rough implementation of Sun Yat-sen's idea that "to the tiller belongs the land." Much of this egalitarianism has been wildly romanticized (the "agrarian reformer" myth), and we should not ignore the fact that creative artists wore an art-must-serve-the-people straitjacket. Yet we must recall too that these favorable evaluations were made less in the framework of a sweeping "democratic revolution" than as a contrast to the flagrant abuses found in areas ruled by Chiang Kaishek. I have not dwelled upon the point, but an aspect of the democratic revolution is a kind of puritanism. And for many observers, "Yenan China" symbolized simplicity, unpretentiousness, and incorruptibility. To these same people, Chiang Kai-shek's "Chungking China" spelled court intrigue, ostentatiousness, and shameless corruption.

In a word, "Yenan China" went far toward the fulfillment of social and economic justice. And impressive strides were taken toward the realization of at least one aspect of political justice—mass participation in the overall political process. As for the other side of political justice—freedom of speech, of the press, etc.—there was little pretense of its existence, except from the most servile camp followers.

Communism in Power

When the Communists took power in 1949 they quickly began a wide range of programs, many of which concentrated on economic and social inequities. Such public health measures as epidemic control received great attention on the social front. Gross abuses of economic equity in rural areas were tackled under the Agrarian Reform Act of 1950. Perhaps the most notable early social legislation was the 1950 Marriage Law, more fittingly described as China's "women's liberation" act. By focusing on the cornerstone of traditional China, the family, the Communists took the first large step in the still unfinished task of giving equality to women and —as a substantial byproduct—youth.

It is hard to find two more "disadvantaged" groups in traditional China than women and youth. Both had very low status in a rigid hierarchy. The injustice to women, in particular, is best symbolized by the twin atrocities of foot-binding (which hobbled women physically and psychologically) and the high incidence of female infanticide.*It is no coincidence, there-fore, that women's and youth "mass" organizations were among the first and most important established in the PRC.

In the early years the Communists also inaugurated steps leading to a government constitution. Some eight thousand people took part in draft-ing the document, and then 150 million people discussed the draft—surely participatory politics with a vengeance.

Many governments, of course, readily subscribe to a rough brand of freedom, equality, and justice in their constitutions, and just as readily abuse them. The anguished history of the twentieth century offers ample testimony to this fact. By the same token, however, constitutions codify values intended to undergird the political process in everyday practices and indicate long-range goals for the entire political system. It is there-fore mistaken to dismiss constitution-making as a mere legalistic act, a task intended to placate unrepentant, bourgeois lawyers. It is, rather, very much a political act. We call the 1936 Soviet constitution the "Stalin Constitution" for good reasons. Proof of the pudding in the Chinese case is the deep involvement of her most senior leaders. Mao wrote a commen-tary on the draft constitution, and Liu Shao-ch'i (then the number two man) delivered the official report when the document was adopted.

Peking was closely wedded to Moscow when the constitution was adopted in 1954, and thus one might have expected an offspring of the Soviet constitution. And so it was. But one might also have expected drastic revisions when new constitutions were adopted in 1975 and 1978, for in the intervening years Peking's marriage to Moscow had ended in an unruly divorce.**More important, China had undergone two tumultu-ous social, political, and economic convulsions: the Great Leap Forward and the Cultural Revolution. The latter, after all, is held by some observ-ers to be a whole new concept of government—something unique to Mao and China.

Yet neither the break with Moscow nor programs launched by the Great Leap Forward or the Cultural Revolution seem to have had much impact on the broader ideas of the democratic revolution. In fact, a comparison of the earlier with the latter two constitutions reveals far more similarities than contrasts. Women, for example, are unequivocally declared in all three documents to have equal rights with men. All three constitutions call for equality among all nationalities; i.e., Mongols, Tibet-ans, and a few dozen other minorities (numbering some 50 million peo-

*Foot-binding may seem terribly remote to us today, as though we were reading about the France of Louis XVI. Yet I know a Chinese-American student who visited China in 1977 to see her family, one of whom was an elderly aunt with bound feet.
**On a 1973 visit to China I asked an official if we were flying in a Soviet-built airplane. She wryly answered: "Yes, but it flies better in China."

ple) are put on equal footing with the so-called Han Chinese.

In the area of civil rights, the three constitutions are living testaments to the democratic revolution. There is to be freedom of speech, press, assembly, association, as well as procession and demonstration. Moreover, the 1975 and 1978 constitutions offer a new right, the right to strike (added at the suggestion of Mao himself). All three documents declare that the freedom of person is inviolable.* Similarly, private homes are held inviolable, as is private correspondence. Religious freedom is guaranteed, to which the new constitutions add the "freedom not to believe in religion and to propagate atheism."

The 1975 and 1978 constitutions add a new interesting twist, clearly derivative from the Cultural Revolution: the right of citizens to "speak out freely, air their views fully, hold great debates and write big-character posters." China's famous wall posters now have constitutional sanction! In his 1975 trip to China, Ross Terrill found a vivid example of this from a wall poster prominently displayed in the heart of Shanghai. The poster (translated in *The Future of China*) is especially interesting because it was written not by someone who wanted the system overthrown but by a worker who clearly regarded himself as a patriot. He simply wanted to air his grievances about a wayward official, and to complain that an earlier poster had been wrongly removed by this same official. The worker correctly invoked Mao's name as a backer of wall posters, and he was even sufficiently aware of his "rights" as a citizen to note that the freedom to write posters was now a constitutional guarantee.

In the socioeconomic arena, the three constitutions declare citizens' rights to own lawfully earned income, savings, and houses. And all three documents go far beyond many other governments' constitutions in declaring as "rights" the right to work, to education, to rest, and to receive material assistance in old age, illness, or disability. The ancient struggle against bureaucracy is even reflected in articles asserting citizens' rights to lodge written or oral complaints against government officials who transgress the law or neglect their duties.

The few changes in the 1975 and 1978 constitutions mainly reflect new conditions since 1954, most notably the collectivization of various aspects of Chinese society and politics. For example, the rights of capitalists and handicraftsmen to own their "means of production" are absent from the 1975 and 1978 documents, as is the right to inherit private property.

More ominously, the 1975 and 1978 constitutions are silent on the earlier provision that citizens should "enjoy the freedom of residence and freedom to change their residence." The situation concerning the free-

*But see Jerome Alan Cohen's discussion on the crucial matter of arrest, pp. 240–41, 253–55.—R.T.

dom to engage in scientific research or literary and artistic creativity is more complex. In 1954 these were flatly asserted to be rights; but in the 1975 version such matters were not placed in the articles devoted to rights. Instead, science, literature, and art "must all serve proletarian politics, serve the workers, peasants and soldiers, and be combined with productive labor." This focus, presumably, was the work of Mao's wife and her now discredited Gang of Four. A balance seems to have been struck in the 1978 constitution. One article mentions again the idea of "productive labor," but scientific research and literary and artistic creativity are reinstated under an article dealing with citizens' rights.

Even allowing for minor changes from 1954 to 1978, all three documents closely embrace many of the means and goals traceable to the democratic revolution. More specifically, and more historically, the three constitutions go essentially beyond the nineteenth-century emphasis of the democratic revolution—which tended to stress political liberties—to encompass quite fully the twentieth-century focus on social and economic rights (e.g., the right to work).

Setting aside for a moment the implementation of these rights, a question arises: Should all these rights lead to happiness? Indeed, is this a government function, or is it a monopoly of naïve Americans who cherish those lines in the Declaration of Independence about "life, liberty and the pursuit of happiness"? The worldly-wise may scoff at the notion that tough-minded Chinese Communists would inscribe this into their basic document. Idealists will hope it to be true, but scarcely believe their eyes in reading it. In fact, the idealists are correct. The 1954 constitution does not merely suggest happiness as a goal, it guarantees it: "The system of people's democracy ... guarantees that China can build a prosperous and happy socialist society." Each of us can gauge the significance, if any, in the fact that happiness is unmentioned in the 1975 and 1978 constitutions.

PROMISE AND REALITY

Economic Justice

Economic statistics and eyewitness accounts testify to the enormous strides made since 1949. In an era when anti-pollution and "zero-growth" advocates abound, it is well to remember that the fairest distribution system ever invented can make only tiny improvements if the economic pie is simply too small. The Chinese have, to say the least, embraced economic growth with the gusto of a French gourmet, and today the economic pie is vastly larger than the best pre-1949 years. More important for our concerns, the distribution of these economic benefits is by any standard fairer than at any past time. One sees this plainly up and down the small streets of Chinese cities. Vegetable and fruit stands are everywhere, and there are many shops selling such simple but sturdy consumer goods as furniture, clothing, and athletic equipment. Just as clear is the fact that these goods are not solely for a privileged class or for even more privileged foreigners. And blessedly, unlike the Soviet Union, customers are not forced to stand in endless lines.

Virtually everyone is employed, even if underemployment is widespread in some sectors. Underemployment is seen by many economists as inherently pernicious. Yet, given current Chinese conditions, underemployment rather than unemployment is as much a political choice as an economic one. And, one can argue, underemployment may be among the wisest—and most just—policies adopted by the PRC. In any case, it clearly accords with the constitutional guarantee of the "right to work."

There have been a few bad periods, but the food situation has been good for the past two decades, and thus health is generally good. Clothing is frightfully drab, but nonetheless adequate. Stylishness seems closely linked to politics. In Peking, the city of commissars, drabness is *de rigueur,* but in the atmosphere of Shanghai or Hangchow, I saw subtle touches of color. Everyone has shelter—however modest, seedy, and crowded. Considering China's staggering population (of nearly one billion), these are no mean achievements, which contrast vividly with those of most developing nations.

But none of the above should suggest that everyone receives the same pay. Visitors to China are quickly awash in statistics from officials who make no pretense of a perfect egalitarian pay scale. In a word, China is still in the "to each according to his work" stage, as she marches toward the alleged finality of "to each according to his needs." Or, as it is bluntly put in the 1978 constitution: "He who does not work, neither shall he eat," and: "from each according to his ability, to each according to his work."

There are of course some weaknesses for which there are neither easy nor short-term solutions. Urbanites, for example, get industrial goods in more abundance and more quickly than rural dwellers (who constitute 80 percent of China's population). Like the United States, China is a huge country with rich and poor areas. Just as the rich crop lands of Iowa stand in stark contrast to the shriveled farms of Appalachia, so too in China the visitor sees the parched lands of North China in contrast to the lush green land of the Yangtze River Valley. But unlike the United States, China still has a very rudimentary communications network that prevents the easy shipment of many goods from rich to poor sections of the country.

In brief, then, whatever the current shortcomings or inequities, there is broad movement toward economic parity.

Social Justice

No form of social justice would mean much if the health of the populace were poor, as in so many underdeveloped nations. The Communists gave top priority to public health, with an emphasis on preventive medicine, and this may be China's greatest single achievement. It gladdens the heart of anyone to see youngsters with strong teeth, shining hair, and good muscle tone—no distended bellies or ugly sores on arms and legs.

An extensive birth control program is part and parcel of the public health effort. I saw charts in rural infirmaries, listing in elaborate detail which woman used what birth control devices. It's tempting to see tidy and efficient results. Yet Edgar Snow's conversation a few years ago with Mao Tse-tung illustrated the human and cultural dimensions. Snow allowed that "Now at least no one objects to birth control." Mao shot back that Snow had been "taken in." As paraphrased by Snow, in *The Long Revolution*, Mao continued: "In the countryside if a woman's first child is a girl, she wants to have a boy. If the second is a girl, again she wants a boy. The third one comes, a girl again, and she still tries for a boy. Soon there are nine of them, all are girls, by then she is already forty-five. . . ."

It was probably skepticism of this sort that led Mao to insist that public health officialdom should focus on rural China—or at least give it equal billing with the cities. From such thinking came the famed "barefoot doctors" (actually, they are paramedics), who have done much to give China an effective rural health delivery system. Nor should one ignore an exceptionally unusual achievement, the apparent eradication of venereal disease. (Who can possibly believe that there is absolutely no pre- or extra-marital sex in China? Yet few can doubt that China has come closer to the goal of eliminating venereal disease than any nation in modern times.) In short, whatever the problems, the overall public health advances are a stunning achievement.

Two other aspects of social justice are notable. As mentioned earlier, women and youth were at the bottom of the hierarchy in traditional China. Efforts to improve their lot are, of course, slow. Male chauvinism (not to mention patriarchial chauvinism) is as much a part of China as elsewhere, yet there have been striking advances. Personal observation of schools at all levels bears out the statistics that women now receive an education equal to men, and employment opportunities are relatively open to all. Careful studies by sociologists, however, demolish any euphoric judgment that women and youth have anything resembling "perfect equality" with men and older people. In the case of marriage and the family, for example, variant forms of "matchmaking" still exist (probably more so in rural China), and the woman still leaves *her* home to live with the husband in *his*. Nor, to say the least, are parents without a substantial voice in many aspects of their children's lives. Communist officialdom has not really tried to destroy parental authority (except for a brief period during the Great Leap Forward) in a sociological as distinct from a political sense.

In short, the Chinese record on social justice ranges from good to excellent. Further changes are clearly desirable. These same changes are frequently discussed in the Chinese media and, more important, they are being acted upon in a forthright manner.

Political Justice

Assessing political justice in China is at once quite easy, and yet in some ways more difficult than measuring economic or social aspects. Political participation and civil rights should be separately distinguished here.

In terms of participation, most Chinese must surely feel more "involved" in politics than in any past period. Referring again to the current constitution, Article 15 demands that all organs of state must be a "three-in-one combination of the old, the middle-aged and the young." Visitors to China testify to this combination. In those countless briefing sessions, one invariably encounters the "three-in-one" representation, even if it's soon apparent that the old-timer has a bit more to say than his younger colleagues (who, not incidentally, always seem to include a woman).

"Participation" can come in unexpected forms. I was being briefed by a "three-in-one combination" at a Hangchow factory when a question about worker benefits stumped the troika. Suddenly, without a trace of self-consciousness, the young woman serving us tea interrupted her work to supply the answer. Nor was it a one-word answer—she took two or three minutes to explain the case. None of the officials looked in the least put off by an act that would be regarded as taboo in many societies.

China's entire educational process puts a premium on participation. It is also well known that all Chinese must and do belong to some organization, which means a political organization. Sometimes this "belonging" is defined in terms of work place, sometimes by residence, and sometimes by both. But belong one must. Passivity is regarded as political dissidence. Activism is the prescribed norm which, for example, can take the form of attendance at innumerable study sessions, or gatherings at which one criticizes oneself or someone else.

"Political dissidence" can easily suggest struggles at the rarefied levels of the Party Politburo. But most Chinese live far from such concerns, and thus a more homely example better illustrates the difference between activism and passivity. The Chinese press once reported a meeting of street vendors. One noodle vendor always ended his rounds at six o'clock sharp. After attending several meetings he was made to realize that six o'clock coincided with a local factory's closing hour, and thus the factory workers were denied the chance to buy a bowl of warm noodles after work. The young man then realized that his "passive" attitudes were antisocial, and that the proper, the "activist" attitude would be to adjust his work hours slightly and encourage his fellow vendors to do the same. In a word, he began to practice the dominant slogan of China: "Serve the people."

Evaluating participation for most citizens can, of course, depend upon personal viewpoints. For those who see the glass half full, China is a participatory Utopia; for those who see it half empty, it is a participatory nightmare. What is also clear, and what surprises no one familiar with the great sophistication of Chinese in handling personal relations, is that participation becomes a kind of national sport. To steer clear of trouble, one must participate just enough—but not too much.* To scale the political ladder, the same rules apply. Willy-nilly, Chinese citizens must be ever vigilant about the endless zigs and zags of Party policies. Russian citizens face similar problems, but they have found a means of temporary escape from political participation: drunkenness. Alas for China, it is a nation of eaters, not drinkers.

It's also useful to look briefly at participation of women and youth in the higher reaches of politics. Without doubt, women have made significant advances. For example, a mere 4 percent of the Party Central Committee members were women in 1956, but now over 12 percent are. (Without pretending that the Central Committee and the U.S. Senate are perfectly analogous, note that the Senate has one.) Party scribes always pridefully point to the number of women at major political gatherings, as for example at the Eleventh Party Congress in 1977 when 19 percent of the delegates were women. The trend seems clear. At the highest level, however, the Party Politburo is and has been virtually an all-male act. Only three exceptions exist: the wives of Mao, Lin Piao, and Chou En-lai. When Lin, the former defense minister, fell from power in 1971, his wife simply disappeared from public life; Mao's wife,

*See the essays of Baum and Parish, pp. 178, 190–91.—R.T.

Chiang Ch'ing, was ousted in late 1976 as part of the so-called Gang of Four. Chou's wife endures.

There is, clearly, a sense of youthfulness about China. But has youth ascended to the political peaks? In short, no—not significantly. Two briefly summarized case studies illustrate the point. Back in 1953 the Communist Youth League's Central Committee consisted of 199 full and alternate members. Given the emphasis on the League as the "youthful arm" of the CCP, one might logically and fairly assume that many of these young people would have advanced to the Party Central Committee by 1977 when, of course, the 1953 Youth Leaguers must have been around fifty years of age. In fact, only 3 of the 199 former youths were elected to the 1977 Central Committee (and 2 of those 3 were already seasoned, and much older, "youths" even back in 1953).

Secondly, only two "young" men have ever reached the Politburo. One was about forty when he ascended to the Politburo in 1969, while the other was about thirty-five when he reached it in 1973. A month after Mao's death in 1976, these two found themselves constituting 50 percent of the Gang of Four which, as noted, included the wife of Mao.

Notwithstanding these two case studies, it is clear that since the Cultural Revolution of the late 1960s more younger people are Party Central Committee members. Perhaps even more important in the sense of participation is the fact that for the first time in 1969 many obviously humble workers and peasants were elected to the Central Committee. Even if only symbolic, and even if there has been a bit of backsliding since Mao's death (the full evidence is not yet available), this does seem to indicate a trend for the future.

Turning to civil rights, the story is largely a sad one. A root problem is that not all the people are "people." India has her non-people among the castes. The non-people in China are defined largely by class designations ("landlords," for example), or by ad hoc ones ("bad elements"), which effectively deny them even the theoretical right to enjoy civil rights. The very cloudiness and ambiguities of the definitions are a form of injustice. For example, is the child of a landlord or rich peasant numbered among the ranks of the people? There has been no consistent answer since 1949. At times there seems to be a broadly charitable view from the top: it is one's attitudes and not one's class background that count. Yet at other times—times of political intensity—the same offspring will be pilloried for his or her family background. The situation, obviously, can be one of great stress for the individual.

The Long Revolution contains a telling anecdote that Edgar Snow recounts in approving tones. Interviewing Ch'en Yung-kuei, a much-touted model peasant, Snow inquired about the number of deaths in 1964 in Ch'en's work unit.

> "We didn't lose anybody," [Ch'en] said. Not even a great-grandfather? He scratched his head. He remembered that one old landlord had expired. "If you call that a death," he said. "He hadn't been able-bodied for years!"[*]

Was he a good landlord, a bad landlord, or perhaps a repentant landlord? It never seems to have occurred to Snow to ask, let alone Ch'en to elaborate. A trigger word had been uttered; discussion was unnecessary. Landlords are non-people.

The leader who spelled out these distinctions back in 1954 when he gave the official interpretation of the constitution was at least forthright. "Some foreign commentators," said Liu Shao-ch'i,

> find it strange that while we strive to safeguard the people's democratic liberties and rights, we also suppress all treasonable and counter-revolutionary activities and punish all traitors and counter-revolutionaries. Of course, anyone who expects our Constitution to ensure freedom for the activities of traitors and counter-revolutionaries is bound to be disappointed.

A dozen years later, Liu found himself labeled a traitor (without due process, we should note). Liu, of course, had much company. In a word, no one publicly defended him, because there is no real free speech. No one wrote a letter-to-the-editor, because there is no free press. And if anyone prayed for him, he didn't do so within the framework of his right to exercise religious freedom. At best, Liu can hope for what is lamely called a "reversal of verdicts," that is, an admission of unjust treatment. Did Liu harbor this hope before his death? We don't know. There are no obituaries for non-people.

Official Chinese spokesmen (not to mention apologists) counter such points by invoking the doctrine called "democratic centralism." The idea, in a nutshell, is that when policies are being formed (and, to some degree, being administered) there can be genuine "democratic" debate. Afterwards, the minority must obey the majority. According to Liu Shao-ch'i: "We permit no one to impair the interests and freedom of the majority. . . . Our state does fully concern itself with and care for the interests of the individual. The public interests of our country and society cannot be separated from the interests of the individual."

If this sounds somewhat tortured, it is at least worth remarking that it

---

[*]Snow, *The Long Revolution* (1973), p. 45.

contains a significant gesture toward a basic tenet of the democratic revolution—majority rule. There are, in addition, other features of Communist rule that might be seen as partial substitutes for some aspects of civil liberties—provided, of course, one does not get too starry-eyed about the matter. For example, Mao always put a premium on what he called spontaneity "from below" (i.e., ordinary people). He was a tough disciplinarian, yet he knew that overcentralization could cause apoplexy at the center and anemia at the extremities. Still, for individual Chinese, the situation is similar to that of the shifting interpretations of class background. Today's spontaneity could be tomorrow's treason.

There is also a kind of redemptive process, seemingly unique to China. This too can be seen as a partial substitute for conventional civil liberties. Under the Maoist rubric of "curing the sickness to save the patient," a properly repentant sinner can gain grace again. Teng Hsiao-p'ing, today one of China's top leaders, is a classic example. Teng was attacked during the Cultural Revolution in language that, transformed to Soviet Russia of the 1930s, would have meant certain death. Yet Teng returned—not once, but twice (the second time after Mao's death). It's almost as though Trotsky had returned to Moscow in 1940 instead of being axed to death by a Stalin assassin.

Liberties and freedoms are usually seen as positive acts: one *makes* a speech, one *signs* a petition, one *practices* religion. But notwithstanding all the civics courses in the Western world or all the "study sessions" in China, there is a "passive" side that may be more important: the freedom of silence or the freedom to stand aloof from all politics. In short, the right to be left alone. But in China, such silence, such aloofness is, to repeat, equated with dissidence.

Finally, whether viewed as a positive or passive right, there is the issue of migration. America is a nation of immigrants, yet we seldom ponder whether migration may not be the ultimate freedom—the freedom to wake up one morning and say, "I don't like this country. I'm leaving." The point is made mournfully and eloquently by Robert L. Heilbroner in *An Inquiry into the Human Prospect.* He writes of "the damning fact of the continuous efforts [of citizens of socialist countries] of all levels of society to emigrate to capitalist nations, and the equally damning refusal of their authorities to permit the free entry of ideas." Without question, the description fits China.

In brief, the Chinese record in terms of political justice is mixed. Even on the more positive side, citizen participation often runs headlong into the privilege of remaining aloof from politics. Regarding civil liberties, we can and should take note of Mao's gradualist approach, described in a 1954 constitutional commentary: "We write into our constitution what is feasible now and exclude what is not. Let us take for instance the material guarantees for civil rights. They will certainly expand when production grows in the future, but the wording in the constitution is only 'gradually expand.' " Having granted this, the general record is grim.

An Overall Assessment—and the Future

Why has China captured the imagination of so many people? The "exotic" China of yesterday is surely not what commands our attention, not for long anyway. Innovations in this or that program would fix our gaze on China only temporarily. Even China's famed "self-reliance" has its limits of appeal, especially as people increasingly accept the necessities of interdependence. But what *has* captured world attention is a Chinese system that is perceived as having achieved—or is moving toward—greater fairness for the bulk of its citizens.

Within my framework of three forms of justice, I would argue that China can claim remarkable accomplishments in the economic and social spheres. In the former, China has probably reached a plateau, and further advances can only come gradually. The reason is simple: China, in gross terms, is still a very, very poor country. To change metaphors, further advances toward social justice, most notably those involving the role of women, must struggle against an undertow of traditional conservatism. Even a cursory glance at the Chinese press reveals that Peking is quite aware of this fact. Indeed, for all the rhetoric, it appears that China is fully prepared for a long, slow pull against this undertow.

In terms of political justice, two box scores are necessary. In one block, that of political participation, a fairly high mark is merited in that the people are involved. In a sense, the Chinese find themselves in the same stage the West was in a few centuries ago. It might be dubbed the stage of military metaphors. The West had its "fighting saints"; China has her "fighting cadres." Both found it necessary to mobilize the populace against the forces of evil—the Devil in the West; traitors and sundry other "bad elements" in China.

It is unlikely that China can long sustain this militant, mobilized "againstness." It wears thin. It bores. It can create corrosive cynicism. The Russians have learned at no small cost that "involvement" has its limits. And even in China there are some signs of public apathy, work slowdowns, and related phenomena.

Regarding more conventional civil liberties, the record is sad. Far too many people are under the sway of a mindless cultural relativism, yet if none but the naïve can believe that China is a land of civil liberties, we must grant the generations it took to make substantial advances in Western democracies. And, indeed, only the morally blind can argue that these same democracies are today without grievous inequities. We can also recall that just as Hobbes wrote *The Leviathan* against a background of civil war, so too did the Chinese Communists confront that eternal tension between authority and liberty. Even passionate civil libertarians can understand a post-1949 focus on economic and social priorities before the most elementary civil liberties were considered. As Lewis Feuer has put it, "When a large part of society begins to experience the sheer harsh threat of foodlessness, history becomes a tale told in the language of economic anxieties."*

To the domestic economic and social chaos we must add the fact that the PRC has always seen itself as a besieged state, sometimes by the United States, sometimes by the Soviet Union, and sometimes by both. China is probably unique in that she is apparently the only nation threatened at one time or another by nuclear assault from *both* superpowers. In such an atmosphere, civil liberties must be fragile, to say the least.

Are there any signs of a growth in civil liberties? Unfortunately, very few. By perhaps overly charitable interpretations, one might point to a seemingly increased use of wall posters to air grievances, plus a few strikes in recent years. And optimists can point to the "spontaneity from below"—people may become more accustomed to airing their views at lower levels, and in time these practices will gradually take hold in broader areas. Historians can point to past ages when "opposition" views were dexterously voiced in literary parables. Such devices are not unknown to post-1949 China. Optimists of a legal bent may suggest that Chinese will increasingly call upon authorities to live up to the terms of the constitution. (The Soviet Union offers a parallel. Well-known dissidents there, to a surprising degree, accept the "rules of the game"; what they object to is the perversion of these rules.)

Still other optimists can see interdependence as the wave of the future, and argue that sooner or later new ideas will permeate China, at which time Chinese will learn more about a somewhat better civil rights record in, say, Yugoslavia, or about the proclaimed civil liberties of the new-born Euro-Communists. But perhaps the most optimistic of all are those who point to the worldwide tide of rising expectations—a phenomenon by no means divorced from the democratic revolution. We hear evidence of this every day from third world spokesmen who bluntly articulate their "rising expectation" that rich nations "owe" the poor ones a more just life. Related to this is the thought that justice is contagious. If you have it in one area, you're more likely to want it (and ultimately demand it) in others. If there is merit in this view, average Chinese citizens may one day witness the delicious irony that their rulers grant them more freedom.

Finally, at the broadest level, we may be living in an as yet unrecognized

*Lewis S. Feuer, ed., *Marx and Engels: Basic Writings on Politics and Philosophy* (1959), p. xix.

Age of Convergence. I have preferred to see Marxism as a substream of the larger democratic revolution. Others, with considerable cogency, can see Marxism as a parallel river. In either case we have a kind of mirror-image situation. We can hope that there will be a convergence of the strengths of the socialist systems (economic and social justice) with the strengths of the capitalist systems (in political justice). There are, of course, too many imponderables and problems to have great confidence about such a development. "Doubt," said Voltaire, "is not a very agreeable state, but certainty is a ridiculous one."

Human Rights in a Chinese Context

VICTOR LI

Victor Li raises arresting new questions about the basis for judging how human rights fare in China. He insists on the importance of the context of rights, and on the variety of possible and defensible relationships between political rights and economic rights. He warns us that we often mistake American norms for universal norms, and that a profound search for the latter has hardly begun.

In discussing how China and the United States handle deviancy, Li shows how law and society relate to each other quite differently in the two countries. We espouse the "fall from the cliff" approach; the Chinese favor a "gradual slide to the bottom" approach. Li believes that the PRC's progress over thirty years must have required a high degree of willing cooperation from the people, and so he sees a genuine will of the people operating through the groups that bulk large in Chinese life. The absence of formal law bothers him less than it does Klein. Rather boldly, Li accepts the prior claim of class distinction, even today, over that of equality before the law, though he expects its validity to fade with time. Li finds China different, but not substandard.

Victor Li, born in China in 1941, grew up in New York City. He majored in mathematics at Columbia College, and later took a law degree at Columbia Law School. He also holds an LlM and an SJD from Harvard Law School. At present Li is Shelton professor of international law at Stanford University. He is the author of Law Without Lawyers *(1977) and* Law and Politics in China's Foreign Trade *(1977). In 1972, 1973, 1975, 1978, and 1979 he revisited China.*

—R.T.

The Scope of Human Rights

Discussions of international human rights tend to focus on political and civil matters. Some bow is made to the importance of securing economic and social rights, but this aspect is usually given short shrift. Yet it is clear that human rights encompasses a wide spectrum of economic, social, and cultural, as well as political and civil, concerns. Indeed, for the poor and developing countries of the world, economic and social rights may be much more important than political and civil rights. It is hard to think about freedom of speech in Bangladesh when the essential problem is human survival.

Consequently, a sense of process must be introduced into our analysis. Each society must set priorities according to its own particular needs and conditions. In the course of doing this, perhaps one human right might have to be restricted or delayed so that another one of higher priority can be achieved. For example, a number of countries have imposed martial law or other limitations on freedoms, ostensibly to improve the livelihood and security of the population: that is, reducing political and civil rights in order to enhance economic and social rights. We cannot simply condemn all such political restrictions. We must weigh costs and benefits in the light of the needs of that society.

How much loss of political and civil rights is worth how much gain in economic and social rights? Even if economic and social benefits result, is there some point beyond which political and civil rights should never be restricted? Or is the attainment of certain rights, especially in the basic economic area, so vital that it supersedes all other considerations? How should improvements in economic and social conditions affect political and civil restrictions imposed earlier?

While we may be unable to establish a complete framework for answering such questions, we can at least confront some of the problems of political and cultural diversity that must be taken into account in making cross-cultural evaluations about international human rights. In the United States, we are generally well beyond the problems of hunger, illness, and physical survival. Consequently we can place, or, if you will, have the luxury to place, greater weight on political and civil rights. But in what way is the American experience applicable to countries still struggling for individual livelihood and national survival?

It should be noted that even in wealthy Western democracies, political and civil rights are viewed as relative rather than absolute. When the perceived degree of danger is low, we tolerate much dissonance and go to great lengths to protect an individual against possible wrongful incursions by the government. Thus, American lawyers often say that "it is better for one hundred guilty men to go free than to have one innocent man unjustly imprisoned." But when the perceived degree of danger is high, the amount of leeway allowed is considerably reduced. The internment of the Nisei during World War II is an egregious case in point; the public and judicial response to rising crime by reducing various protections for persons accused of crime is a more recent example. More generally, the unfettered liberty of a person or group to act often is restricted to achieve other social goals: for example, antitrust restrictions or environmental protection. The specific balance between individual freedom and collective benefit depends on a society's perception of its needs and conditions.

A related major problem in discussing international human rights is that we sometimes make incorrect assumptions about the universality of certain principles, institutions, and processes. Of course, we are past the point of crude cultural chauvinism whereby the acceptability of another society is measured simply by its similarity to our own. Yet some matters are so deeply ingrained in our own practice that we are unable or unwilling to accept the validity of different approaches taken by other societies.

For example, Americans hold strong beliefs not only concerning the importance of law, but also about the manner in which the legal process should operate. Thus, in handling deviancy, we rely on written laws to define what can and cannot be done. The legal process is centered on a public trial, presided over by an independent judiciary that decides guilt or innocence and also supervises the work of the police. The right to counsel, a speedy trial, and other protections help to ensure that an accused person has an adequate opportunity for defense.

When looking at another society, our usual assumption is that law plays or should play an essentially similar role. But what happens if that society handles deviancy in a very different manner? In China, the quantity of written material that could be labeled "law" in the Western sense hardly fills a modest bookcase. There are very few formal trials, and even when these take place, much of the decision making appears to occur elsewhere. There are virtually no lawyers, and hence no defense counsel.

Does this lack of familiar legal institutions and processes mean that there is no justice in China? To argue that it does, we would have to demonstrate that such institutions and processes are absolute preconditions for fairness or orderliness; we cannot simply assume it. On the other hand, if we are willing to say that some vastly different approach to law could produce justice, we still must describe a series of standards by which that different system is to be measured.

International Human Rights Standards

Most of the specific legal norms contained in international documents concerning human rights reflect Western, and especially American, values and institutions. This is not surprising, since the United States was the major world power after World War II when contemporary concepts of international human rights took shape. This effort drew upon earlier religious and natural law ideas that implied the existence of certain universal standards and aspirations from the fact of the common humanity of all mankind. The drafters of these human rights declarations hoped to establish these universal norms as the core of a new international legal order.

At the same time, American constitutional law was going through a period of expansion. Initially, the Bill of Rights applied only to federal officers and to actions taken in federal courts. Beginning in the late 1930s and 1940s, a series of major cases held that the "due process" clause of the fourteenth amendment made the provisions of the Bill of Rights applicable to state courts and officers as well.* To accomplish this result, the Supreme Court, particularly Justice Felix Frankfurter, suggested that many of the practices embodied in the Bill of Rights were universally applicable. Frankfurter described these rights as "the very essence of a scheme of ordered liberty," and matters "that a fair and enlightened system of justice would be impossible without," as well as involving "the meaning, the essential implications of liberty itself." This language provided the basis for making federal due process protections applicable to state courts; but at the same time it also was highly suggestive of universal standards applicable to all societies—that is, a set of international standards of human rights.

It is interesting to note that the U.S. Supreme Court subsequently moved away from the idea of universal standards. The State of Louisiana, which has a French legal tradition, allowed jury trials only for capital cases. In a 1968 case, a defendant demanded a jury trial for an offense punishable by up to two years imprisonment, basing his claim on the fifth amendment. The Court agreed with his position, but had to back off from the earlier language that had suggested this constitutional protection was universally applicable, since most countries of the world do not use jury trials. Instead, the Court argued that "trial by jury is fundamental to the

*See Gerald Gunther, *Cases and Materials on Constitutional Law* (9th ed., 1975).

American scheme of justice" (my italics).* Thus the Supreme Court, which contributed heavily to the concept of universal standards, has recognized the difficulty of a cross-cultural application of legal rules, and has begun to limit these "universal" standards to the Anglo-American cultural context. Yet on the international level, scholarly and political dialogue continues to assume the universality of many Western-origin legal concepts.

Human Rights in the Chinese Context

The problems facing the Chinese leadership after 1949 were enormous. China had gone through more than half a century of continuous civil and foreign war. The resulting social disruption, loss in production, and breakdown of governmental control had left the country in chaos. China also was populous and poor, lacking capital, skilled manpower, and many material resources. In addition, threats to national security increased the sense of urgency: first, the Korean War and the danger of war with the Nationalist forces on Taiwan, then the Vietnam conflict and the presence of American forces there, followed by the positioning of forty Soviet divisions along China's northern border.

The CCP asserted that in order to overcome economic and social problems, as well as to maintain national security, drastic steps had to be taken. A revolution was needed to produce a thoroughgoing change of the social system; gradual incremental reform could not bring about major and immediate improvement in the livelihood of the common people. In the course of the revolution, the former members of the elite lost their property and many suffered physical injury or death. In Mao's famous words,

> A revolution is not a dinner party, or writing an essay, or painting a picture, or doing embroidery; it cannot be so refined, so leisurely and gentle, so temperate, kind, courteous, restrained and magnanimous. A revolution is an insurrection, an act of violence by which one class overthrows another.

The manner in which the members of China's former elite were handled certainly poses human rights issues. Indeed, revolution in general causes severe intellectual and emotional difficulties for us. The Western approach is a basically liberal one of gradual social reform and change.

---

*"[In earlier cases inquiring into whether some particular procedural safeguard was required of a State] the limitation in question is not necessarily fundamental to fairness in every criminal system that might be imagined but is fundamental in the context of the criminal processes maintained by the American states. . . . A criminal process which was fair and equitable but used no juries is easy to imagine. It would make use of alternative guarantees and protections which would serve the purposes that the jury serves in the English and American systems"—*Duncan* v. *Louisiana,* 391 U.S. 145, 149 (1968).

This may be because our present conditions are not so oppressive as to require drastic change, or because our institutions are capable of bringing about change at an acceptable rate, or even because we fear being the targets of revolution.

Some persons may reject out of hand any resort to revolution on the grounds that it relies on violence directed, often indiscriminately, against members of a particular class. I would pose the issue differently. Although we may not wish to choose revolution for ourselves, was China's taking of a revolutionary path, given her needs and conditions, an unacceptable choice? The human rights of the former elite may well have been violated, but the human rights of the majority of the population were substantially enhanced. In balancing these gains and losses, it obviously is important to consider just how many persons were hurt or benefited. On the whole, I cannot conclude that the use of revolutionary force in the dire circumstances faced by China in 1949 violated some sense of minimal human decency, any more than did the French Revolution in its violent overthrow of one group by another in the name of social justice.

One other issue of a factual nature should be mentioned. The Chinese often use the argument that "95 percent of the population support the Revolution" to describe their popular base of support. Many Western writers concentrate on the other 5 percent, suggesting that 40 to 50 million persons—a number larger than the population of most countries of the world—have suffered or are suffering violations of their human rights. That figure of 40 to 50 million misdirects one's attention: it speaks only to the size of China. If it is indeed true that 95 percent of the population has benefited substantially to the detriment of the other 5 percent, that is not a record any society should be ashamed of. Moreover, at least in theory and probably to some degree in practice, the disadvantaged 5 percent could reform themselves and become full members of the new society.

Cultural Differences

Differences in cultural background cannot explain away every difference in approaches to problems, nor can they be excuses for everything occurring in China with which we might disagree. Nevertheless, as we understand more of Chinese cultural attitudes and predilections, we might find that things that feel awkward or unpleasant to us may be much more "natural" and comfortable to a Chinese. In addition, we must come to intellectual terms with the problem of how to derive universal standards for societies that, over the centuries, have developed substantial variations in habits and institutions.

And clearly there are major differences between the American and

Chinese cultural backgrounds and attitudes that affect our views of contemporary problems. Thus, while the United States does not deny the importance of the larger group and community, the primary concern is the individual—whether in terms of legal status, personal fulfillment, or religious salvation. Consequently the American system stresses individuality, privacy, diversity, and protection of the individual from undue outside interference. We begin with the premise that a person should have freedom of action, and then ask under what circumstances this freedom may be restricted.

The Chinese approach has historically been quite different. Chinese culture appreciates the importance of individuals but places greater emphasis on how a person functions within the context of a larger group. The Chinese language provides insights into both the historical past and the modes of thinking for the present. There is no Chinese word for "privacy." Pause on that point for a few moments. What would be other key attributes of a culture that lacks a term for privacy? How much importance might a contemporary Chinese attach to privacy, or, indeed, how would he think about such a concept? More relevant to our inquiry, how can universal standards be drawn when the Chinese lack a word for one of the West's most important values?

A related observation about the Chinese language is that the term for "self" often has carried a connotation of selfishness, and frequently was used in contrast with the term "public," which implied the "public good." This preference for the larger collective unit over the individual continues into the present day, although of course groups in the People's Republic are defined by loyalties other than kinship and hold to Communist rather than Confucian ideology.

Nor was there a clear sense of a concept of "rights" as that term is used in the West. On the contrary, the emphasis was on the idea of duty. Phrasing obligations in this manner affected the means of enforcement. The principal remedy was subjective, in the sense that a person was made to feel through social pressure that he must perform his duty. The general community was involved by showing disapproval through methods such as gossip or ostracism. There was far less emphasis on giving an aggrieved party a "right" that could be formally enforced in a court or elsewhere against the person failing to perform.

The Handling of Deviancy: A Cross-Cultural Framework for Human Rights*

Having discussed the difficulties of trying to apply international standards of human rights, let me try to describe a cross-cultural framework

*For a more detailed discussion of this subject, see my *Law Without Lawyers* (1978).

for examining an actual problem: the handling of deviancy. Obviously this subject is only one aspect of human rights; in particular, it deals only peripherally with the problem of political participation and political dissent—a major topic in itself. Nevertheless, the system of criminal justice is a crucial subject for study because it is pervasive and touches upon the life of everyone. Historically, this aspect of law has been used as a principal criterion for judging the adequacies of other societies. And most importantly for our purposes, it clearly concentrates our attention on the underlying intellectual issue of how to find common ground when dealing with societies with vastly different cultural backgrounds and social conditions.

Pictorially, the Western approach to the handling of deviancy resembles falling off the edge of a cliff. Long before a person commits a crime, such as an assault or a robbery, he would have manifested unhappiness or antisocial behavior in various minor ways—being sullen or aggressive, avoiding employment, or associating with undesirable persons. Such minor "deviations" from the desired norm are protected from official interference on the grounds of privacy, freedom, or individuality—several of our most important values. On a social level, friends and neighbors occasionally intervene, but the extent is limited by the same considerations of privacy and freedom. Moreover, if a person did not want such interference, the law would support his demand that others keep their distance. Thus, at the early stages of a problem, a person is given little help by the state, and may use the legal system to rebuff informal offers of assistance from others.

The situation does not basically change as a person's deviations grow more serious—becoming a bully or a neighborhood troublemaker—and he comes closer to the edge. At some point, he deviates too far and falls off the cliff—i.e., commits a crime. Then the formal legal system is invoked, and the full majesty of the criminal law descends upon him.

The top and the bottom of the cliff are two distinct worlds. The top is the province of the individual. Police and other legal officials generally are not present and sometimes are not permitted to enter. The rules of conduct are permissive, and activity usually takes place around one's home or place of work. At the bottom of the cliff, an entirely different process takes over. This world is populated by its own distinctive set of actors: police, prosecutors, judges, lawyers, and the like. Because much of the activity takes place at inconvenient or intimidating sites such as police stations and courthouses, people from the top of the cliff generally do not take part, or even are excluded from taking part, in what happens at the bottom.

In addition to such practical considerations, our legal theory supports the idea that these two worlds should be separate. Juries and sometimes judges and others who have personal knowledge about the defendant or the offense frequently are not allowed to participate in a case. Except for sentencing procedures, other actions and attitudes of the defendant not directly related to the offense in question generally are regarded as irrelevant. For example, a defendant's past criminal record usually cannot be introduced as evidence in a criminal trial. The partial exclusion of persons having personal knowledge of the defendant, and the isolating of a single event from other actions committed by the defendant, are thought to be important guarantees of impartiality in our criminal system.

The state, by virtue of its size and access to far superior human and material resources, possesses great power in dealing with a criminal case. The question then arises how the exercise of this power should be regulated so as to ensure that an accused person is not simply overwhelmed by the state. Thus the fourth, fifth, and sixth amendments provide protection from unreasonable searches and seizures, and guarantee the right against self-incrimination and the right to a speedy and public trial. An accused person also is provided access to legal counsel. This is especially important since in the American system a layman generally stands little chance against a trained prosecutor. Moreover, in theory the defense attorney is fully cognizant of the rights of the accused and has the freedom and incentive to make certain that these rights are implemented.

Such institutions and rules help to ensure at least a minimum level of fairness in the operation of our legal system. They also form the core of the standards used by Western commentators and international human rights documents for measuring the adequacy of the legal systems of other societies. When applied to the Chinese system, however, these standards do not fit very well.

As opposed to falling off the edge of a cliff, the Chinese approach to handling deviancy much more resembles a gradual slide to the bottom. As in the Western case, the first antisocial act is not a crime but some minor matter. However, as a person deviates a little from the general norm, he is not left alone. On the contrary, anyone who notices a sullen complainer or an aggressive bully is supposed to "help." The duty of one person to help another is as basic to the Chinese social system and philosophic beliefs as the concepts of privacy and individuality are to the Western.

In China, an intricate social fabric is made up of "small groups" of people who work or live together. These groups serve as a principal mechanism through which help is offered. At the early stages, help generally takes the form of discussion by the group about the root causes of a person's problem and possible solutions. Being immediate neighbors or co-workers with whom one deals constantly, group members obviously know a great deal about the individual and subject matter involved, and can exert considerable peer pressure.

If a person does not respond, but persists in antisocial conduct by becoming even more disagreeable and disruptive, the amount of help given is increased in both quantity and intensity. The Chinese sometimes describe the process by the term *shuo-fu,* "to persuade by talking." This may take the form of wide public discussion of the problem and lead to offering suggestions or criticisms that grow increasingly pointed. If the difficulties continue, additional persons become involved. Elected neighborhood leaders, factory officials, or the local policeman might be asked to join in the discussion. Their presence not only increases the pressure on the person being criticized, but also provides some check on the actions of the group.

In carrying out these prolonged discussions, the local people work with the offender for a long time, trying to improve his conduct and gathering detailed information about his actions. As the policeman and others join in, the attitudes of the group are conveyed to the officials and, indeed, help shape the official view. Even after the formal legal system takes over, legal officials come to the group members for additional information. In a real sense, these local people make the basic determinations of fact in the case. It is immediate neighbors and small group members rather than legal officials whom one must first convince of one's position. And what one's peers decide is unlikely to be overturned during later formal legal proceedings. Without drawing the analogy too far, this system has some resemblance to the early English jury which, until the end of the fifteenth century, was composed of witnesses who had personal knowledge of the case and could swear to the veracity of a party's claim rather than impartial finders of fact.

Two other comments should be made about this gradual slide to the bottom. First, it takes quite a bit of doing to hit bottom. In some cases, a troublemaker might truly be convinced by the proferred advice and help; in other cases, it might be easier to conform to the socially desired norm than to continue to face criticism and pressure from close peers. Only the rare and extreme situation would require invoking the formal criminal process.

Second, the slide from the top to the bottom is basically a continuous process. Until fairly near the bottom, the principal actors are one's friends and peers, and the process is carried out in the familiar surroundings of one's place of residence or work. Even at the bottom, the legal officials have had considerable prior involvement with the community concerning the case; they also keep in close touch subsequently. The extensive participation of the public throughout the entire process is the essence of the "mass line" in legal work. With so many lay helpers, it is not surprising that the size of the legal establishment in China is relatively small. This approach requires a great deal of the public's time and labor, but these are assets China has in abundance.

Given this very different approach to the handling of deviancy and crime, how do we begin to measure the adequacy or fairness of the process? To begin with, it is clear that most of the standards articulated in such Western documents as the International Covenant on Political and Civil Rights envisage a judicially supervised system of public trials that is not readily applicable to the Chinese setting. The important aspect of the Chinese legal process is the small group discussions, especially the stage where they move from ordinary conversations to more intense criticisms. The guarantee of a speedy and public trial focuses our attention on the wrong place, because most matters are resolved at the peer group level. Even where a person slides all the way to the bottom and the case is handled by the formal legal system, most of the decisions will have been made well before the defendant reaches the courtroom. Guarantees against self-incrimination also make little sense since at the beginning of the slide one could hardly refuse to engage in conversation with one's peers. The concept of right to counsel must be reshaped so that rather than referring to a defense attorney taking part in the formal legal process, it looks to whether there are mechanisms or procedures to ensure that an individual is not simply overwhelmed by the greater power and resources of the group.

I would like to suggest some alternative measures for evaluating how well the Chinese system works. These standards are also procedural in nature, but this time are designed to fit the Chinese process.

A person being criticized and sliding toward the bottom must have the right to be heard. If he is not allowed to speak or no heed is paid to his explanations, then this condition is not fulfilled. Moreover, in the course of the decision-making process, the strengths of the various parties should not be so unequal that one side simply overwhelms another.

The decision makers must articulate reasons for actions taken, stating their premises and reasoning process. This helps to ensure more responsible action both by improving the quality of group discussions and by enabling some outside source to review later what transpired.

The premises and reasoning processes articulated must in turn be reasonable and rational, even if one disagrees with the eventual decision. They must be consistent over time, and adequate reason must be given for any changing of rules in midstream. Finally, there must be some opportunity for a degree of outside review of group actions.

Evaluating the Chinese System

What kinds of evaluation, then, do we make of the Chinese system for handling deviancy? Some areas do not pose much of a problem. It would appear that China's peer group sanctioning system provides considerable access to a person being criticized. In addition, at the beginning of the slide—which I think is the crucial stage—the parties generally are similar in strength, since the group consists of one's peers and neighbors. The disparity in power increases as one slides further toward the bottom, and particularly after some official has joined in; but this is to be expected and does not invalidate the process. (See also the discussion of class justice in the next section.)

But several much more fundamental issues are involved. At one end of the spectrum, one could reject the entire Chinese approach to handling deviancy on the ground that the lack of formal institutionalized rules and processes, in and of itself, makes the risk of injustice and oppression by the group against one member intolerably high. The implications of this position, however, should be made explicit. It suggests that people are so unreliable or lacking in ability that they can operate properly and effectively only in the context of certain specific institutions—a serious indictment. At the other end of the spectrum, one might consider the Chinese approach to be the model of participatory democracy. Law should indeed be everyone's business, and not a social function that is the exclusive province of legal specialists.

My own conclusion is somewhere in between, but considerably closer to the second position. To begin with, I would return to the earlier point regarding the great improvements in economic and social conditions in China. While we might lack the data to describe in detail how the peer groups actually operate, we can say with confidence that the progress of the last several decades would not be possible if these groups were acting in a confused or chaotic manner, or were producing a high degree of dissatisfaction.

The fact that members of a group must continue to deal with each other on many matters, over a long period of time, tends to limit blatantly unfair or extreme actions. Forbearance and responsible action by a person on one occasion help to ensure that the same consideration will be reciprocated later. Moreover, the group as a whole has an interest in reducing disruptive conduct that damages its ability to work together.

But most importantly, the evaluation of the adequacy of the Chinese process depends on one's philosophical beliefs concerning the nature of man. If one has a Calvinistic view of man as being basically evil, then the Chinese approach to handling deviancy described above would be especially troublesome. The "mass line" style of legal work places too much power in the hands of individuals and groups. But if one believes that the nature of man is good, or at least can be made good through adequate education, then people can be expected to act responsibly most of the time, and can consequently be entrusted with power. Some outside checks or reviews of the actions of the small group would be required, but these need not be very extensive. It may be that participation by local officials toward the bottom of the slide, or administrative review within the bureaucracy at the bottom, might be adequate, although we do not know enough about what actually happens to judge with any certainty.

Still, in theory an adequate outside review could be carried out without necessarily resorting to formal judicial action. For example, the practice of "people's reception" provides widespread access to officials. All letters and telephone calls must be answered. A time is fixed, usually on a weekly basis, for officials to "receive the masses"; many government offices follow the rule that the reception period continues until every visitor has been met by an official. Wall posters and letters to the editors of newspapers are additional means by which a person can draw public attention to some matters. Finally, rectification campaigns are conducted within the Chinese bureaucracy every few years. During a campaign, officials are expected to examine their actions and attitudes and to carry out self-criticisms when necessary. The masses are supposed to assist the officials in this exercise by evaluating their prior actions. These campaigns play a crucial role in providing a channel for voicing complaints and ensuring some regular degree of official accountability.

Few Westerners today still believe that man is basically evil; indeed, my guess is that most would assert an optimistic view of human nature, even though our actions often contradict this view. In any case, Calvinistic doctrines were very much in force during the formative years of Anglo-American common law. Legal rules and institutions were thought to be needed not only to restrict the power of the king, but also to curb man's natural evil tendencies. Even after philosophic views began to change, the feeling remained that human nature is not altogether reliable and that the rule of law must prevail over the rule of man. This feeling is reinforced by the fact that over time the public has delegated more and more of its direct involvement in the legal process to an expanding bureaucracy. Law now is hardly the business of the general public, but rather the business of lawyers and their associates. The kind of process I have described for China would be impossible in the United States, both on philosophical grounds and because our historical development has created a probably irreversible commitment to formal law.

For myself, I place great faith in education and in the human mind. There is no question that literacy and education are being actively promoted in China. I believe that this kind of intellectual development inevitably takes on a life of its own and grows of its own accord. Having taught a person to think and having given him tools with which to acquire more knowledge, the state cannot, I believe, readily turn him off at a later date.

The Role of Class Background

In reviewing the Chinese system, I find troubling one problem that does not concern subtle cultural differences or disparities in economic and social conditions, but rather fundamental beliefs about the nature of society: To what extent should a person's class or family background affect the manner in which he or she is treated? One premise of Western liberal democratic society is that all people are equal and should be treated equally. We may not always practice this principle, and social and economic disadvantages may produce severe and possible permanent distortions. Nevertheless our theory holds firmly to the concept of equality, and at the very least, it remains the ideal to which we aspire.

The CCP, and Marxists generally, view society in class terms. There are the exploiters and the exploited; the socialist revolution aims to remove the former and thereby enhance social justice for the latter. Given such a view, class enemies should not be treated the same way as the common people. Chairman Mao was quite explicit about this. He divided members of society into "enemy" and "people," and called for the exercise of dictatorship by the proletariat over class enemies. His rationale was that the small number of exploiters caused much suffering in the past and must be restrained if the great majority of the people are to gain their proper place in society. In this calculus, the restriction of the rights of the exploiters leads to far greater aggregate justice for society as a whole.

One could simply reject this "class analysis" of society and insist that all people be treated exactly the same. Yet I do not think the method of class analysis is so unreasonable as to fall below the minimum standards of human rights. First, much of the world analyzes society in Marxist class terms. From a different perspective, our own spotty record of implementing equality for all should make us hesitant about insisting dogmatically upon absolute equality as a legal standard. Likewise in traditional China, every person had a theoretical right to take the governmental examinations that qualified one for entry into officialdom. But when only an extremely small percentage of the population was literate and the cost of education was high, this theoretical right of equal opportunity did little to penetrate the self-perpetuating power of the elite.

At the same time, I believe that the consequences of class analysis must be handled with the greatest care. I can understand why the former elite had to be restrained, particularly in the early years after Liberation, since they might have attempted to recover their earlier positions. The fear of war, whether with the United States or the Soviet Union, and the perceived need for rapid and drastic domestic social change, would have increased concern about the need to control enemies at home.

It also is possible that the children of the former elite might have been corrupted by their parents' attitudes or resented the treatment of their parents, making this second generation somewhat suspect. But as time passes, the reasons for treating descendants of the former elite (i.e., persons with bad class backgrounds) differently from ordinary members of society should decline, and at some point it should disappear entirely.

Until the Cultural Revolution, discrimination against persons with bad class backgrounds was gradually diminishing. Then class background again became a major issue. Among other things, it was argued that the former elite had never really been removed since their children and grandchildren were entering higher education, and hence moving into leadership positions, at a greatly disproportionate rate.*

Far more recently, a number of important steps have been taken to reduce the stigma of bad class background. Education and employment opportunities increasingly are based on intellectual and professional rather than political criteria. Legal restrictions are placed only on those persons of bad class background who continue actively to oppose the regime. The Gang of Four has been criticized for stressing a person's objective (family) class background instead of examining his or her subjective beliefs and personal actions. These efforts to deal with each person on his own merits are welcome developments. A fundamental human rights issue could be raised if the descendants of the former elite become a permanent caste of second-class citizens.

Dealing with Differences

The Chinese are not just like us; neither are they so completely different that we have virtually nothing in common. The task here is to account for the similarities and differences between American and Chinese societies, and then make a valid assessment about what we find.

Let me add that I think it is proper to try to assess another society in this way, so long as we proceed with care and a fair degree of humility. At some point one must go beyond the merely descriptive and begin to evaluate. Asking what we like or dislike about China, and why, renders our approach to the study of that country far more explicit. In addition, an important byproduct of examining the values and performance of

*Cohen's essay (see p. 245) discusses the additional problem of "newborn" class enemies. —R.T.

another society is that one inevitably is forced to rethink one's own values and performance.

By what criteria do we evaluate norms or processes that are used in China but not in the United States? We might ask whether we would make the same choices for our society as the Chinese leaders made for theirs. In general, this is the wrong question. The United States and China are so different that one should not expect methods suitable for one society to be appropriate for the other.

A second line of inquiry is whether we would make the same choices for China as the Chinese leaders did. Aside from intrinsic arrogance, this approach basically sheds light only on the beliefs of the questioner.

In this essay, I have used a third criterion, which gives weight to the individual characteristics of each society while maintaining the concept of common needs and aspirations. Are there aspects of Chinese cultural background and philosophical beliefs that violate some minimal standard of decency by which human beings must treat each other? And if not, given China's conditions and needs, is what her leaders have done so unreasonable as to violate those same standards?

Due Process?

JEROME ALAN COHEN

Jerome A. Cohen puts a lawyer's finger to the pulse of China after thirty years of Marxist rule. Believing passionately in the importance of law to human welfare, he inquires into the relationship of the individual to the state in China. Dismissing the cultural relativists, Cohen asserts that "due process" is a measure of the health of any society. He applies it as a lens to Chinese theory and practice in a most illuminating way. We are given the best analysis to date of the 1978 constitution of the PRC, and of other recent legal developments. Cohen offers some reason for hope about the future of due process, but plenty for caution as well.

Jerome A. Cohen is professor of law, director of East Asian legal studies, and associate dean at the Harvard Law School. He holds an AB and LB from Yale University, and his broad experience includes years as a law secretary for the Supreme Court, under Chief Justice Warren and Justice Frankfurter. Cohen is the author of The Criminal Process in the PRC, 1949–1963 *(1968) and the co-author of other books, including* People's China and International Law *(1974) and* China Today and Her Ancient Treasures *(1974). He visited the PRC in 1972, 1973, 1977, 1978 and 1979, and has also spent considerable time in Hong Kong and Taiwan.*

—R.T.

Once a head is chopped off, history shows that it can't be restored, nor can it grow again, as chives do, after being cut. If you cut off a head by mistake, there is no way to rectify the mistake, even if you want to.

—Mao Tse-tung

Do Chinese care about "due process of law"? Is it a matter of indifference to citizens of the People's Republic if their government arbitrarily arrests, imprisons, tortures, or executes them? If officials, scientists, teachers, or workers are stigmatized and deprived of their jobs without notice of charges, opportunity to defend against them, or review of the decision, do they feel a sense of injustice? Does the Chinese government claim the power to take such actions? What does it do in fact?

The current concern over "human rights" embraces many aspects of the individual's relation to the state. Whether every government—regardless of its country's history, traditions, socioeconomic circumstances, political system, or ideology—has an obligation to provide its people with minimum economic, social, and educational benefits and allow basic freedoms of expression are much-mooted questions. Yet the very nub of what Americans ordinarily mean when they resort to the shorthand phrase "human rights" is the set of values that has slowly evolved in the West over two millennia—those elements of fundamental fairness that the state is expected to observe prior to inflicting serious harm upon individuals and groups.

Some American specialists on China have claimed that such due process values, as we call them, are irrelevant to China. Their argument is one of extreme cultural and political relativism.* The Chinese, we are told, are completely different from all other peoples, except from those on their periphery—in Korea, Vietnam, and Japan—whom they profoundly influenced through the reach of Confucian civilization. Traditional China, it is said, emphasized not law but morality, not rights but duties, not the individual but the group. Moreover, the argument contin-

*Readers of this volume may detect a modified version of the argument in the essays of Fairbank and Li.—R.T.

ues, given the impoverished circumstances of the world's largest population, contemporary China's rulers have had to choose between assuring survival through economic development and recognizing individual human rights, and not surprisingly they have opted for survival. Happily, it is said, this choice has won the natural acceptance of a collectivist-minded people who never experienced Roman law, Magna Carta, and the English, American, or French revolutions that emphasized the rights of man. They do not miss what they never had. Thus, the conclusion emerges, it would be dangerously self-righteous demagoguery—indeed, cultural imperialism—to suggest that Chinese, like other people, might wish their government to observe minimum standards of fundamental decency in dealing with them.

Is this argument correct? No question could be more pertinent to understanding China today. It has been widely discussed in the wake of the overthrow of the Gang of Four, and in the course of the adoption of a new Chinese constitution in 1978. One of the most striking attributes of this constitution is its attempt to symbolize renewed government respect for some of the values embraced by our phrase, "due process."

Among the new charter's most significant changes is its restoration of the procuracy as an organ of government. According to the constitutional system established in 1954 under Soviet influence, the procuracy was charged with responsibility not only for prosecuting criminal cases but also for overseeing the legality of the conduct of all government officials, as well as ordinary citizens. During the "anti-rightist" campaign of 1957–58, the procuracy was severely attacked for repeatedly refusing to approve arrest warrants and prosecutions sought by the police. Procurators were accused of maintaining a "favor the defendant" mentality by ordering the release of detained persons on a variety of technical grounds: that the action in question did not amount to a completed crime, or that it was not committed with the required intent, or that it had not resulted in serious consequences. Like the courts, the procuracy was subsequently subjected to closer control both by the police and the Communist Party apparatus. The Cultural Revolution of 1966–69 witnessed an even graver onslaught upon all three of the political-legal organizations—the police, the procuracy, and the courts—and upon the Party itself. Each of the organizations was crippled, but only the procuracy was abolished. The 1975 constitution, which was a compromise between the so-called moderates who now rule China and the so-called radicals later branded as the "Gang of Four," formalized the demise of the procuracy and allocated its functions to the police.

The elimination of the procuracy left the police to investigate the legality of their own conduct, an inadequate safeguard in any society. Moreover, no longer were the police required to obtain approval of an external agency—either procuracy or court—before formally arresting a suspect; under the 1975 constitution they could simply decide on their own, thereby rendering hollow that document's continuing guaranty of the personal freedom of citizens. The restoration of the procuracy in 1978 put an end to the unfettered arrest power of the police because the new constitution also reinstated the 1954 constitution's requirement that they obtain approval of the procuracy (or the court) prior to making a formal arrest.

In his March 1978 Report on the Revision of the Constitution, Yeh Chien-ying, chairman of the standing committee of the National People's Congress, made clear the significance of the procuracy's revival, which he attributed to "the extreme importance of fighting against violations of the law and discipline." He admonished Party and government officials that it was strictly forbidden to confine people arbitrarily. "Detention and arrests must follow legal procedures and the system of checking and approval must be strictly observed in this regard," he said.

The 1978 constitution also made potentially major changes concerning the trial of an accused. The 1975 constitution had omitted from its truncated section on the judiciary virtually all of the protections granted an accused by its 1954 predecessor. The 1978 constitution reestablished several of these. The most fundamental provides that "the accused has the right to defense"—a proposition so elemental that one might have thought it impossible to eliminate from any legal system. In addition, "all cases in the people's courts are to be heard in public except those involving special circumstances, as prescribed by law." Not only are cases ordinarily to be tried in public, but representatives of the masses are to participate in such trials as assessors, joining a full-time judge in administering justice.

Although Yeh Chien-ying's report did not tell us how, in light of these specific changes, trials are to be conducted, it did emphasize the importance of carefully investigating, analyzing, and weighing the evidence. And it prohibited extracting confessions from an accused through compulsion and relying on any coerced confession as proof.

Yeh linked the abuses of the Gang of Four to this renewed interest in institutional and procedural protections for accused. According to his report, the Gang raved about smashing the three political-legal organizations, and "put their words into action, seriously undermining the state apparatus of the dictatorship of the proletariat. They went so far as to exercise dictatorship within the Party and the ranks of the people."

During the period between the overthrow of the Gang in October 1976 and promulgation of the new constitution in March 1978, Party propagandists had spelled out many accusations of the Gang's violations of individual rights. For example, in recounting how the deposed leaders allegedly sought to conceal their criminal past, editorial writers claimed that: "They also sent people disguised as Red Guards to ransack the homes of those in the know and even had them arrested on trumped-up charges, kept them in jail for a long time and cruelly persecuted them to the point of murder to prevent divulgence of their secrets." Party officials arranged for a famous opera star—a member of the National People's Congress—to tell visiting American journalists how the Gang detained her incommunicado for three years of political investigation, subjecting her to the psychological intimidation of "struggle sessions" and middle-of-the-night interrogations that coerced her false confession. And personnel of the Supreme People's Court charged that the four "privately set up the 'Gang's' law, arrested and imprisoned people freely, conducted private trials, treated human life as no more than grass, provoked struggle by force and practiced fascist terrorism." The Gang, it is alleged, sought to usurp the state's judicial powers by replacing the courts with their own institutions.

The currently voiced concern in China for the return of "socialist legality" reflects more than abuses of the criminal process, horrendous as they apparently were. Statistically even more numerous were administrative sanctions that apparently resulted in loss of employment and reputation for hundreds of thousands of officials, scientists, technicians, and teachers. As the time-consuming task of restoring these victims to their jobs and reputations proceeds, the media repeatedly lecture both the bureaucracy and the public on the evils of relying on hearsay, speculation, false testimony, and coerced confessions.

To those of us who hope for the growth of due process values in China, events since the downfall of the Gang of Four have, on the whole, been rather encouraging. But how far will the trend go and how significant is it likely to be? On the basis of almost three decades' experience since the founding of the PRC in 1949, a healthy skepticism would seem our best attitude.

First of all, one has to recognize that the constitutional changes recited above may simply remain paper reforms. In 1978 the Party has been much slower than in 1954 to mobilize an effective national campaign for the study and implementation of the constitution. Second, even if a sustained effort is made to implement the changes, these provisions are likely to be interpreted as they were during the period 1954–57, the previous era when socialist legality was China's goal. At that time the police frequently circumvented the law that required them to seek the procuracy's approval of an arrest shortly after a suspect was detained. To the extent that the public trial ordinarily guaranteed an accused actually took place, guilt or innocence was not genuinely an issue; the proceedings merely rehearsed the record compiled during the often lengthy pre-trial investigation and interrogation process and, at most, the sole question in controversy was the precise sentence to be meted out. The people's assessors, who were supposed to decide the case together with a judge, were generally mere ornaments to the proceedings; and the right to make a defense meant that the accused, who invariably confessed, could plead mitigating circumstances in an attempt to reduce the severity of his sentence. Indeed, in June 1978 I witnessed precisely such a criminal trial in Shanghai.

It is important to note that the 1978 constitution did not bring back all of the 1954 constitution's provisions bearing upon the criminal process. Most obvious is its failure to reincorporate Article 78, which stated that in adjudicating cases the courts were to be independent and subject only to the law. During the mid-fifties that principle had been invoked by certain judges and scholars in an unsuccessful effort to free the courts from Party control of their decision making in specific cases. The "anti-rightist" movement of 1957–58, however, left no doubt that the demands of legal professionalism had to yield to those of the political struggle. And the 1978 constitution made no change in this position, treating the judiciary as simply one of a number of state agencies under the supposedly all-powerful National People's Congress. Moreover, unlike the 1954 constitution, it identified the Party as "the core of leadership of the whole Chinese people" and the vanguard that exercises leadership over the state in behalf of the working class. This is the significance of Yeh Chien-ying's call for strengthening the unified leadership of the Party over the courts as well as the police and procuracy.

The new constitution did not reassert the 1954 constitution's promise that citizens "are equal before the law." Legislation had spelled out the meaning of this principle by stating: "In the adjudication of cases by people's courts, the law shall be applied uniformly to all citizens irrespective of their nationality, race, sex, occupation, social origin, religious belief, level of education, property status, or duration of residence." Until 1957, at times when the masses were not being mobilized in one campaign or another, Chinese commentators occasionally admonished law-enforcement officials to overcome the "subjectivism" revealed by their tendency to detain and convict suspects largely because of their "bad" class background. But, as in the case of judicial independence, the anti-rightist movement witnessed the repudiation of the principle of equality before the law, in both theory and practice, and no mention was made of it in either the 1975 or 1978 constitutions.

It is common ground between the Gang of Four and their captors that, following the Maoist line, the dictatorship of the proletariat means dictatorship over "the enemy" and democratic centralism within the ranks of "the people." Both groups thereby invoke Mao's famous distinction between the two kinds of contradictions: those "between the enemy and ourselves" and those "within the people." This basic dichotomy has been taught to every criminal justice administrator, although there has been considerable debate over how to determine whether a suspect should fall into one category or the other, and what are the specific implications of the categorization.

In some cases, of course, it is easy to determine, without regard to a suspect's class status, that a given act reveals "a contradiction between the enemy and ourselves" and deserves severe punishment. If, for example, an individual assassinated an important official while shouting "Down with communism!" there would be no difficulty, whatever his class status, in convicting him of the crime of counterrevolution and sentencing him to the death penalty. But many cases are not so simple. If a peasant is caught stealing a few bowls of rice from a commune granary, the authorities may be puzzled. Should he be treated as an enemy or a member of the people, and with what consequence? Although other factors are also considered, in such cases the suspect's class status often proves decisive. If he is classified as a "poor peasant," he may simply be released after some private criticism-education or criticism and self-criticism before members of his production team. If he has "landlord" or "rich peasant" status, however, he may be prosecuted and sentenced to five years of reform through labor for the counterrevolutionary crime of sabotaging socialist production. Because he is a member of one of the "reactionary classes," evil intent can be attributed to him, even though he may actually have been motivated by hunger. Surely there is at least a presumption to be overcome.

These class labels were attached to everyone in the nation at the time of the Communist takeover a generation ago. They do not connote any current economic status in an economy that has been collectivized for two decades, and are often inherited by children and even grandchildren. Actually, the labels have not remained constant. The constitutional definition of reactionary classes has expanded over the years. The 1954 constitution listed "feudal landlords" and "bureaucrat capitalists" as the only politically disfavored classes; but both the 1975 and 1978 constitutions, reflecting the intervening theory and practice, refer to all landlords, add the category of "rich peasants," substitute the broader term "reactionary capitalists" for "bureaucrat capitalists," and then add, as a catch-all, "other bad elements."

The category of "bad elements" is not a class at all but a hotchpotch of miscellaneous offenders. In a famous 1957 speech "On the Correct Handling of Contradictions Among the People," Mao made clear that "bad elements," like counterrevolutionaries, were to be lumped with "the enemy" and treated as objects of the dictatorship of the proletariat. He stated: "In order to protect the social order and the interests of the vast [number of] people, it is also necessary to put dictatorship into effect over robbers, swindlers, murderer-arsonists, hooligan groups, and all kinds of bad elements who seriously undermine social order."

Mao conceded that many people confused the two different types of contradictions, and he admitted that "it is sometimes easy to confuse them," and that "[i]n the work of liquidating counterrevolutionaries, good people were mistaken for bad." He went on to say that "such things have happened before and still happen today. We have been able to keep our mistakes within bounds because it has been our policy to prescribe that there must be a clear distinction between the enemy and us and to prescribe that mistakes should be rectified."

The challenge of keeping mistakes within bounds persists. This is why the Preamble to both the 1975 constitution and its successor emphasized the importance of correctly distinguishing and handling the two kinds of contradictions. As we have seen, the Gang of Four itself went "so far as to exercise dictatorship within the Party and the ranks of the people." Its successors seem well aware that they would risk endangering their society if they allowed unrestrained use of the criminal law as an instrument of the political warfare called "class struggle." Yet they believe that it would be premature to follow the Soviet example by announcing an end to class struggle, especially in view of the present ever more intense contest for power in Peking and the purges that this periodically generates at every level of government.

In one sense the 1978 constitution even compounds the problems of keeping mistakes within bounds; for, in what Yeh Chien-ying calls "an important change," it adds yet another category of targets to "the enemy." These are the so-called newborn bourgeois elements, who have been singled out, Yeh notes, "in conformity with the present situation of the class struggle in our country." Yeh's definition of this term may elude some officials, for he states that:

> It refers to those newly emerged elements who resist socialist revolution, disrupt socialist construction, gravely undermine socialist public owner-ship, appropriate social property or violate the criminal law. Not a few of the embezzlers, thieves, speculators, swindlers, murderers, arsonists, gang-sters, smash-and-grabbers, and other evildoers who have committed seri-ous crimes and offenses against the law and discipline or disrupted public order in our own society belong to this category of newborn bourgeois elements. . . . To exercise dictatorship over them is very necessary.

It should be pointed out that Yeh did not content himself with adding to the disfavored categories, but also stressed the possibility of restoring to the ranks of "the people" those who have reformed. He stated that:

[W]ith regard to those who after remoulding and education have really behaved well, we should remove their labels as landlords, rich peasants, counter-revolutionaries or bad elements and give them citizenship rights with the consent of the masses on the basis of public appraisal and approval by a revolutionary committee at the county level.

It was subsequently reported that some 100,000 persons who were declared "rightists" in 1957–58 have had their "caps" removed. There have also been reports of recent efforts to curb discrimination against the children and grandchildren of individuals who retain "bad" labels, a policy endorsed by the *People's Daily* itself.

Surely the growth of due process values will be deterred by the Party's continuing insistence on political control of judicial decision making and harsher treatment of disfavored groups. Yet some progress is taking place, and more appears to be on the way. Yeh Chien-ying's report announced that "[i]n accordance with the new Constitution we shall revise and enact other laws and decrees, as well as rules and regulations for the various fields of work." The Gang of Four has been repeatedly denounced for inciting anarchism and slandering all laws, rules, and regulations as revisionist and capitalist. It is clear that efforts are taking place to "strengthen the socialist legal system," as editorial writers frequently exhort. The director of the Institute of Legal Science within the new Academy of Social Sciences has announced that codes of criminal and civil law and procedure, as well as economic legislation, will actually be promulgated before long. Moreover, summaries of judicial decisions are being edited for publication in order to provide further guidance for both officials and the public.

For the Party, of course, the advantage of a better articulated set of laws is that it will provide, as Yeh put it, "a deterrent to, and a restraining force upon, law-breakers and offenders; for enemies who sabotage socialist revolution and construction it is a merciless iron fist; but for the masses of the people it is a code of conduct which they voluntarily observe." Yet the nationwide campaign to publicize the constitution and educate the people about law for which Yeh called—and the development of the habit of rule-following it may produce—may reinforce the ferment that already exists over the importance of government itself observing the law and adhering to notions of fundamental fairness. This in turn may stimulate demands for further reforms.

Support for such a trend may come from other sources. Legal education, which ceased during the Cultural Revolution and has been hobbled since its resumption in the early seventies, has taken on new life at Peking University. Legal research—in virtual abeyance since 1966 and seriously restricted prior to the Cultural Revolution—is reportedly resuming.

Criminal law and procedure and constitutional law are said to be among the subjects that will be pursued at the graduate level under the auspices of the new Academy of Social Sciences. In the mid-fifties some legal scholars and legal officials vainly advocated interpretations that would have transformed a variety of vague constitutional provisions into due process safeguards. And many bureaucrats who had been trained to apply the rules and procedures established by the regime opposed the efforts of the more Maoist-minded to eliminate the restraints of the system; this in turn produced much of the frustration that the radicals vented on the procuracy, the courts, and even on important elements within the police.

It is possible that the PRC may eventually reintroduce "people's lawyers," as one member of the National People's Congress privately predicted in mid-1977. During the period of law reform that began with the 1954 constitution and ended with the anti-rightist campaign, "offices for legal advice" were established in large and medium-sized cities, and their lawyers—successors to the bourgeois lawyers whose functions had been abolished after the Communist takeover—played a role in both criminal and civil cases. To be sure, they were only called into a relatively small number of criminal cases, and then only after the pre-trial investigation and interrogation of the accused had been completed. Furthermore, their courtroom duties were usually confined to pleading mitigating circumstances in an effort to obtain a lenient sentence. But the participation of these lawyers seems to have provided an additional stimulus to the government to observe its own rules and muster sufficient evidence to justify conviction of the accused under the charges lodged. Those Party leaders who presided over the introduction of a Soviet-style legal system into China in the mid-fifties—and Teng Hsiao-p'ing, perhaps the most powerful current leader, was prominent among them—permitted explanations to be published, for the benefit of other Party leaders and the public, concerning the necessity for a Communist government to employ lawyers, who are often thought to be a bourgeois excrescence. That this educational effort failed became clear when the "offices for legal advice" fell casualty to the anti-rightist campaign, long before the procuracy was abolished.

For two decades China, a country of almost 1 billion people, has had no organized legal profession. After the demise of "people's lawyers," Peking claimed that they had been unpopular, a claim that contradicts the earlier propaganda in their behalf. In any event, it is said that they became unneeded as the populace became better educated and therefore able to handle its own legal problems. The return of the lawyers would be an important signal that Party leaders were preparing to take another step in the direction of legality.

Other potential sources of due process values are the systems devised for disciplining Party members and government functionaries. Once the current preoccupation with "reversing the wrong verdicts" has passed, to what extent will the treatment of the country's elite continue to set standards of fundamental fairness that may eventually be applied to the imposition of sanctions against ordinary people, if not disfavored elements? The 1977 Party constitution, for example, reviving a provision of its 1956 predecessor that had been omitted by the 1973 version, states:

> When a Party organization takes a decision on a disciplinary measure against a member, it must, barring special circumstances, notify the member that he or she should attend the meeting. If the member disagrees with the decision, he or she may ask for a review of the case and has the right to appeal to higher Party committees, up to and including the Central Committee.

The 1956 law regulating dispensation of disciplinary sanctions against state employees, which has presumably been revived by the current government, similarly required that, before the imposition of serious sanctions, the official must receive notice of the charges, a hearing before the decision-making unit, and an opportunity to review the decision.

If these standards are consistently observed in practice, it is possible that, when members of the elite impose sanctions of equal or greater severity upon other people, they may see the need for granting them similar procedural protections. Surely such niceties would be appreciated not only by those enmeshed in the criminal process but also by those against whom nominally noncriminal, yet severely punitive, sanctions are applied. Many of the hundreds of thousands or millions who have suffered "rehabilitation through labor," which consists of long confinement in a labor camp in conditions not substantially very different from those suffered by convicted criminals, received no notice of any charges, no hearing, and no chance for appeal. The same is true of the far larger number who have received the equally stigmatizing but generally less severe "supervised labor," which does not separate the recipient from society but keeps him or her employed for an indefinite term under restrictions far more stringent than those applicable to criminals on parole or probation in the United States. If the Party's current concern for applying strict standards of proof prior to imposing criminal or administrative sanctions reaches these two major categories of "noncriminal" cases, this will constitute a major reform; for more offenders are undoubtedly dealt with by means of these categories than through the criminal process, and in some periods they have assumed far greater importance than criminal sanctions.

Some of the stimuli for due process reforms comes from abroad. The fact that the PRC is now represented in the United Nations means that it is caught up in the slow but inexorable multilateral efforts to formulate international legal norms to regulate nation-states' treatment of their own nationals. Because it has long opposed UN invocation of "human rights" as a means of influencing China's domestic affairs, even while appreciating the opportunities that this vehicle offers for influencing the domestic affairs of other states, the PRC has attempted to tread carefully in what is becoming a legal minefield.

Peking has not directly criticized the UN General Assembly's Universal Declaration of Human Rights, which proclaims, "as a common standard of achievement for . . . all nations," principles including equality before the law, the right to an effective judicial remedy for violation of one's legal rights, freedom from arbitrary arrest and detention, the presumption of innocence, and the right to defend oneself against criminal charges in a fair and public trial by an independent and impartial tribunal. Yet the PRC has never endorsed the Declaration, despite the fact that the PRC has accused the colonial and racist regimes of southern Africa of violating it. Peking's pretext for failing to endorse it is that, because the Republic of China had participated in its adoption, the PRC "reserved its right to comment on that Declaration." The real reason, plainly enough, is the inconsistency between the Declaration's content and the norms applied by the PRC at home. For the same reason Peking has failed to comment on the International Convention on Civil and Political Rights, which goes beyond the Declaration in spelling out Western-style procedural guaranties.

Although the PRC has not chosen to sit in the UN Commission on Human Rights, it is represented in both the Commission's parent body, the Economic and Social Council, and the Social, Humanitarian and Cultural Committee of the General Assembly, as well as in the Assembly itself. Thus it has had to react to various human rights proposals that have come before these bodies. Apart from questions of colonialism and apartheid, Peking generally prefers to abstain or not even participate in the voting and to be as silent as possible. For example, it appears to have purposely absented itself from the Assembly's 1976 vote on a resolution concerning the protection of human rights in Chile.

Nevertheless, it has voted for Assembly resolutions that condemn torture on the basis of the Universal Declaration, the International Covenant on Civil and Political Rights, and other internationally articulated standards. Yet the PRC has opposed most Assembly efforts to call upon states to: report laws and administrative and judicial measures that prohibit torture; give urgent attention to developing an international code of ethics for law-enforcement agencies; and approve the Standard Minimum Rules for the Treatment of Prisoners adopted by the First UN Congress on the Prevention of Crimes and the Treatment of Offenders, which guarantees an accused the presumption of innocence, the right to be informed of the charges, and a proper opportunity to make a defense.

The PRC did not object to the Assembly's adoption by acclamation of the "Declaration on the Protection of All Persons from Being Subjected to Torture and Other Cruel, Inhuman or Degrading Treatment or Punishment," even though that Declaration called upon states to: provide appropriate training for law-enforcement personnel; undertake systematic review of interrogation practices; make criminal all acts of torture; and establish complaint and disciplinary procedures. It is not clear whether the PRC voted favorably or merely abstained regarding an Assembly resolution entitled "Human Rights in the Administration of Justice," but in committee Peking approved a draft version of the resolution despite the fact that it indirectly called on states to consider, when formulating national legislation, draft principles that are completely at odds with those endorsed in China, such as an independent judiciary, access to legal counsel, and a privilege against self-incrimination.

It is difficult to reconcile the PRC's actions on these last two resolutions with its general sensitivity about international interference in China's domestic affairs. To be sure, PRC scholars have long maintained that General Assembly resolutions are not legally binding but merely recommendatory. Yet this has not prevented the PRC from opposing or not taking a position on other resolutions that endorse principles contrary to those prevailing in China. It is possible to explain Peking's support for simple anti-torture resolutions on the ground that their provisions are not inconsistent with the norms of China's criminal process, which explicitly ban torture. But this cannot explain Peking's acquiescence in those parts of the 1975 Declaration that go beyond condemnation of torture, and surely the administration of justice resolution is at odds with the PRC's domestic system. Perhaps China did not wish to appear to be the only country unprepared to endorse these humanitarian standards. Whatever the explanation, enough has been said to suggest that the People's Republic is now enmeshed in a complex web of international negotiations that should heighten its sensitivity to the criminal process and add to the pressures favoring increased protections for the individual.

Perhaps even more of a prod than the relatively unpublicized international legislative process is the intense, unremitting propaganda war in which the PRC is engaged on two fronts. Peking's rivals in Taipei and Moscow, although conscious that "human rights" is a two-edged sword that can be turned against them as well, have sought political advantage by enhancing foreign interest in the situation on the mainland. ROC propagandists never lose an opportunity to charge PRC leaders with having "wrongly imprisoned, tortured and killed millions of their own people," and having failed to enact codes of criminal law and procedure. Taipei also injected this "human rights" question into the American debate over whether the United States should establish formal diplomatic relations with the PRC. Many American opponents of normalization stressed the lack of due process and free expression in China. Even some proponents of normalization stated that those Americans who favor making human rights an important component of U.S. foreign policy have no reason to support normalization. Certain other proponents argued that human rights should not enter into any discussion of normalization.

Ever since 1964 the U.S.S.R. has been openly critical of the PRC's departure from the Soviet model of socialist legality. Commentators in Moscow had a field day ridiculing the excesses of the Cultural Revolution and the lack of formal protections in the 1975 constitution. And after the fall of the Gang of Four, they claimed that, in order to eliminate its pernicious influence, China's new leaders "adopted methods used by the Gang of Four." According to Moscow Radio, beamed to China in Mandarin, "many people have been executed and detained" and "[t]he public security organs are running rampant everywhere," extracting coerced confessions and creating frameups, even while the new leaders are condemning the Gang of Four for such practices.

More objective works circulating in the West, such as the publications of Simon Leys, Jean Pasqualini's *Prisoner of Mao,* Chen Jo-hsi's *The Execution of Mayor Yin,* and Ross Munro's widely read series on human rights in the Toronto *Globe and Mail* and other papers,* have begun to put the People's Republic on the defensive.

Peking has sought to deflect the increasing foreign interest in human rights in China by a variety of techniques. One is to denounce "the so-called 'human rights' issue" as "nothing more than a hypocritical farce" staged by the rival superpowers, "a regular slanging match with each letting the other's skeleton out of the closet." A second is to claim that China "is the country where human rights are best observed," that more than 95 percent of the Chinese people enjoy them, and that the rest can also, "if they are receptive to reeducation."

China's third technique is more to the point for our purposes. This is to divert attention by indicting the U.S.S.R.—in domestic Chinese newspapers and radio broadcasts as well as foreign-language media—for imposing "a police tyranny" and "inquisitorial persecution" that "can arbitrarily take people into custody and interrogate them for long periods, and use chains, handcuffs, or even guns to suppress those who dare

*See also Jerome A. Cohen, "Human Rights in China," Washington *Post,* April 23, 1978, and Susan Shirk, "Human Rights: What About China?" *Foreign Policy* (Winter 1977–78).

resist"; for frequently confining political dissenters in mental hospitals, isolating them, and depriving them of all rights including an open trial; and for maintaining more than 1 million other prisoners in over 1,000 labor camps, where they are said to be tortured and inhumanely treated in a manner reminiscent of Hitler's concentration camps.

What do Chinese think when they hear and read such accusations against the U.S.S.R.? Do they think, as PRC propaganda suggests they should, that in the U.S.S.R. not merely intellectuals but also workers and peasants are oppressed, and therefore the Chinese people are much better off? Or do they think that the situation in the PRC is similar to that in the U.S.S.R.? Certainly the "intellectuals"—and in China anyone who is a high-school graduate is considered an intellectual—and the disfavored classes can be forgiven if they see the similarity. (Actually, since the late 1950s, Soviet accused have generally been allowed legal protections far greater than those available to their counterparts in the PRC.) The 1956–57 campaign to "Let a Hundred Flowers Bloom" revealed unexpectedly broad dissatisfaction with the administration of justice, at least among the educated. Subsequent widespread abuses, especially during the anti-rightist movement, the Great Leap Forward, and the Cultural Revolution, obviously magnified this feeling. Perhaps the most spectacular protest by intellectuals concerning socialist legality was the unusually long big-character poster put up in Canton in late 1974 under the pen name "Li I-che." It called upon the National People's Congress to plainly prescribe measures to punish the high officials who committed the heinous crimes of knowingly violating the law while enforcing it, fabricating cases, using public prosecution to avenge personal grudges, establishing their own jails, and resorting to unrestrained corporal punishment and murder.

The demands voiced by the famous Li I-che poster, which reportedly led its principal author to labor camp,* presaged the charges lodged two years later against the Gang of Four. Those charges, of course, have left no doubt that the abuses of the criminal process have affected not merely intellectuals and people with "bad" class background, but also many officials of the Party and government and broad segments of the masses. Even before the Gang's downfall, indications of ferment among the masses on this score had filtered through the Bamboo Curtain. Some Red Guard newspapers published during the Cultural Revolution condemned arbitrary acts of the political-legal òrgans. More recently, demobilized soldiers complained about illegal beatings inflicted by the police and their assistants. Factory workers protested against the unjust rape conviction of a colleague. And co-workers in an organization intervened to save

*The chief authors of the poster were released in early 1979.—R.T.

an innocent comrade from imprisonment for allegedly trying to escape to Hong Kong.

In these circumstances it is doubtful whether thoughtful Chinese needed Radio Moscow to point up the irony of the new leadership's condemning the Gang of Four for abuses of due process even while committing similar abuses in an effort to weed out the Gang's followers.

What about the case of the Gang of Four itself? In a curious way the enormous publicity generated about its alleged crimes has focused world interest upon China's criminal process. None of the previous PRC leadership struggles—surely not the purge of President Liu Shao-ch'i and other "capitalist roaders" during the lawlessness of the Cultural Revolution— so explicitly directed foreign attention to legal factors. To the Western observer, the handling of the case demonstrates the extent to which the administration of justice in the PRC departs from the world community's evolving notions of universal minimum standards. The accused have simply been detained incommunicado, with no opportunity to defend themselves against the dossiers compiled and circulated against them, even though, as we have seen, they have been charged with subjecting their political opponents to the same kind of defenseless incommunicado detention that they now suffer. This undoubtedly contributes to the relative lack of interest and even frequent cynicism that have greeted the 1978 constitution abroad.

Do thoughtful Chinese have a similar view? Because of the barriers to learning "public opinion" on any issue in China, we cannot know. Many Chinese must be aware of the inconsistency between how the current leadership says cases should be handled and how it is dealing with the Gang. Yet many undoubtedly recognize that special considerations often attend the handling of a case involving a nation's highest leaders, and a large number probably believe that the Gang is so thoroughly wicked that the ordinary rules of fairness should not apply.*

In any event Chairman Hua and company confront a genuine dilemma in seeking to chart an appropriate way to dispose of the case. Is there to be a formal "show trial" reminiscent of the Stalin purge trials of the 1930s? An ordinary trial under the newly reestablished rules of the mid-fifties? Can Mao's widow and her cohorts be relied upon to confess in public or would they seize the occasion to defend themselves and attack the regime? Can they be shown to the country and the world after long months of intense interrogation and confinement? Would it leave a better impression to detain them indefinitely without any form of adjudication

---

*Yet one of the demands made by the extraordinary crowds that gathered at Peking's freshly minted equivalent of "Hyde Park" in late November 1978 was for an open, fair trial of the Gang, televised to the whole nation!

as was apparently done in the cases of many previously deposed leaders? Should the government simply announce that they have been found guilty and sentenced? There is no easy way out for the victors, and the case seems sure to provoke further concern about China's criminal process, both inside and outside the country.

Perhaps the key question concerning due process that confronts Chinese leaders today is the extent to which, in major political cases and in ordinary cases, it can afford to alter the PRC's long-standing incommunicado interrogation practices, practices that none of the changes in the new constitution is likely to affect if the experience of the mid-fifties is any guide. In China in all but minor cases a criminal accused is detained and cut off from any outside contact while police interrogation and investigation run their course. He sees no lawyer, no friends, no family, even if processing of his case takes years. Usually he is given only a subsistence diet that leaves him slightly hungry and on edge. He is frequently kept in a cell with other prisoners who seek to improve their own prospects by mobilizing group and other pressures to urge him to make a full confession and to reveal the involvement of others. And he is subjected to interrogation, often for long periods and late at night, by officials who have been taught to use intimidation, ruses, and various psychological techniques to elicit his cooperation. There is no presumption of his innocence but the presumption, rather, that he would not have been detained unless he had done something wrong, and it is up to him to tell the police all about it instead of awaiting specific accusations. Not only does he possess no privilege against self-incrimination, but stubborn refusal to talk can even result in the application of leg irons or handcuffs or a turn in solitary confinement. Overt torture, however, is forbidden, although angry cellmates have been known to assault the obdurate. The fate of the accused is entirely in the hands of his jailers. There is currently no effective outside institutional restraint upon either the duration or conditions of police detention, whether by procurators, judges, legislators, or others.

Thus the accused in the PRC confronts what may well be the nearest thing to the Inquisition in the contemporary world. In dealing with those suspected of being "class enemies," the leadership of the Chinese Communist Party, like the Inquisition, views the criminal process as an official inquiry into an evil that must be stamped out. In these circumstances it would be absurd, China's leaders believe, to conduct that inquiry as a contest between equals, with the judiciary playing the role of umpire to make certain that if the prosecution violates the rules, it loses the game. The state cannot be neutral in the struggle against evil, they maintain; all of its agencies must cooperate in, not interfere with, that struggle. If the "class enemies" were permitted a host of procedural protections, they would take advantage of them, refuse to reveal the truth, and thereby frustrate the investigation.

China has no belief that it is better to let many guilty people go free than to convict a single innocent person. This is not to say that the Chinese are indifferent to accuracy; they are not. Their criminal law seeks to identify and punish offenders, isolate them from society when necessary, rehabilitate all those who are susceptible, and deter and educate the populace. To the extent that the guilty go free, these purposes cannot be achieved. Nor can they be achieved to the extent that the innocent are convicted. The Chinese are aware that the coercive atmosphere of their inquisitorial process increases the likelihood of eliciting not only true confessions but also false ones. But they believe that through outside investigation and repeated careful interrogation of the suspect, followed by internal review within the police and verification now by the procuracy as well as the judiciary, there is, on balance, a higher probability of reaching accurate results than if they employ a more adversarial, more public process that offers the suspect greater procedural safeguards.

Should this rationale for subjecting "the enemy" to an inquisitorial process also apply to members of "the people" who are detained by the police for criminal investigation? The system of dictatorship does not apply to "the people," Chairman Mao maintained, and one might therefore suppose that even in a criminal case different procedures would apply in dealing with "a contradiction among the people" than in dealing with "a contradiction between the enemy and ourselves." Yet they do not. One reason for this, of course, is that often the proper classification can only be made after the process has been completed. Moreover, according to PRC ideology, there is no fundamental inconsistency between the interests of the Chinese state and those of the people. Unlike the situation in bourgeois countries, there is thus no need to protect a suspect by means of rules that are based upon mistrust of the state. A member of "the people" who is detained for investigation should simply cooperate and tell all. He can be confident, the Chinese Communists claim, that the state will do the right thing, for it has his interests at heart.

After all, if a parent returns home to find that his children have destroyed the furniture, he doesn't say: "Children, you are under suspicion, but you are under no obligation to tell me anything about what happened, anything you say may be used against you, and you have a right to counsel and a public trial." In this kind of situation parents often privately interrogate their children, comparing the answers and demeanor of each with those of the others and drawing appropriate inferences if anyone refuses to answer. In other words, if parents want to know whether a child has done something, they ask the child in circumstances calculated to elicit a response. Because parents have the best interests of the child at heart and the child is supposed to know this, our society generally accepts the practice as a reasonable way to proceed. This is the attitude that the People's Republic adopts toward apparently wayward citizens.

The attitude is not a new one in China. Traditionally the family was taken as the model for relations between government and people, and the county magistrate, the imperial official closest to the people, was called the *fu-mu kuan*, "the father and mother official." Sir George Staunton noted in 1810 that "[t]he vital and universally operating principle of the Chinese government is the duty of submission to parental authority, whether vested in the parents themselves, or in their representatives. . . ."*

Indeed, one is struck by many similarities between the contemporary criminal process and its Manchu predecessor. The conception of judges as ordinary civil servants rather than special officials independent of political authority, the frequently long detention of a suspect in a coercive environment, the presumption of his guilt, the lack of a privilege against self-incrimination, the absence of counsel, the inadequate opportunity to make a defense, and the emphasis upon confession are all as noticeable today as they were to the first Americans to visit China almost two centuries ago.

Yet, despite these similarities, it would be quite wrong to overgeneralize and assume that China's legal tradition is wholly without support for due process values. As one might expect of the nation that invented bureaucracy two millennia ago, as early as the seventh century A.D. the T'ang Dynasty produced a legal system that was then the world's most sophisticated and that served as a model for neighboring Korea, Vietnam, and even Japan. Although we lack sufficient records to generalize with confidence about the actual application of the law to specific cases in that distant era, the Manchu Dynasty that began a thousand years later and endured until the revolution of 1911 has left us a vast sample of its judicial decisions. To be sure, the Confucian heritage preferred moral indoctrination to legal coercion as the principal means of running the empire; nevertheless, these cases—and the comprehensive criminal code that they interpret—make clear the large extent to which the imperial system relied on law to reinforce the dominant moral values and to make people conform to the state's needs. The elaborate distinctions of the legislation, the reasoned opinions that judges were required to write in support of their decisions, and the lengthy review procedures in cases involving major sanctions, all reflect an overriding concern to curb arbi-

---

*Sir George Thomas Staunton, *Ta Tsing Leu Lee: Being the Fundamental Laws, and a Selection from the Supplementary Statutes, of the Penal Code of China* (1810), p. xviii.

trary actions in the administration of justice. The Chinese tradition emphasized the group and the government rather than the individual, and duties to society rather than individual rights; but the legal system was an institutional and intellectual construct that plainly recognized and enforced limits beyond which officials were not permitted to go in dealing with suspected offenders. Even torture, which was allowed in court but not elsewhere to extract a confession from an obdurate accused, was carefully regulated both in duration and the types of instruments that could be used.

The theory that underlay these restraints was not a philosophy of individualism and the rights of man but one that focused on the needs of good government. Yet it was premised on certain beliefs about what was fair, just, and acceptable to the Chinese people. Indeed, many cases reveal how strongly held Confucian notions of justice infused the application of legal principles. Although the code expressed duties rather than rights, those duties created obligations on the part of officials to behave properly according to the prevailing standards and thus created expectations on the part of the populace that officials would live up to those obligations.

Of course, like any other legal system, that of imperial China was not in fact congruent with the norms and procedures found in its statutes and reported decisions. Corruption and arbitrary departures from prescribed practices often plagued the administration of justice, especially during periods of dynastic decline, as nineteenth-century China made foreigners all too aware. Yet the records reveal continuing concern over this situation and periodic efforts to improve it. Moreover certain institutions, particularly the censorate, which enjoyed a roving mandate to inspect the legality of official conduct and which must have made the concept of the procuracy easier for contemporary Chinese to understand, were designed to cope with these problems. And a carefully articulated code of administrative punishments existed to deter arbitrary official actions.

It was the duty of a censor to admonish even the emperor if he departed from the standards associated with his role. Although the emperor theoretically enjoyed absolute power to interfere in the administration of justice and was under no technical legal restrictions, a considerable body of institutions, procedures, moral principles, and inherited role expectations actually circumscribed his discretion. According to the Confucian ethic, an emperor was to act like an emperor, just as a county magistrate was to act like a county magistrate, that is, each was to fulfill his obligations to those he ruled. In theory even the emperor had to be mindful of supervision from above. Ever since the earliest recorded dynasty—the Shang of 3,500 years ago—China's rulers have had to live with the idea that government must be benevolent toward the people. From this devel oped the doctrine that emperors inherited from their imperial ancestors the duty to rule wisely and fairly, and that a sovereign who treated his subjects arbitrarily risked losing the Mandate of Heaven that justified his right to rule. And, in fact, widespread dissatisfaction with the administration of justice proved to be one of the classic signs of dynastic decline, as contemporary China's historically minded rulers and people are well aware.

Interestingly, the People's Republic is at the moment popularizing the more positive aspects of imperial Chinese law rather than its repressive features. All over China, on both stage and screen, the traditional-style Chinese opera *Fifteen Strings of Cash*—banned by Mao's wife for a decade—is again delighting audiences with the dramatic story of how an upright judicial official reversed the unjust conviction of innocent persons from whom false confessions had been extracted through torture. On two separate 1978 visits to China I witnessed performances of this opera before large and enthusiastic audiences. On different occasions, I asked a number of Chinese whether any contemporary significance should be attached to the recent revival of this superb entertainment, which had been seen and approved by Chairman Mao and Premier Chou En-lai in 1956, shortly after it had been created to contribute to the law reform atmosphere of that era. Their answers were similar. As one put it: "Isn't it obvious? It means that the Chinese people will no longer tolerate arbitrary official acts, that torture is wrong, that confessions may not be coerced, that officials must go down among the people to get the facts and must weigh evidence carefully."

Of course, this theme ties in with the campaigns to discredit the Gang of Four, to popularize the new government's asserted respect for fundamental fairness, and to check abuses of power by corrupt and arrogant officials. Undoubtedly there is an element of scapegoating to the attempt to make the Gang exclusively responsible for the widespread abuses during the past generation. What we are witnessing is a de-Maoification process that is less disruptive than de-Stalinization was for the U.S.S.R. Whatever the accuracy of the claims that only the Gang and its followers violated the rights of the Chinese people, these accusations plainly acknowledge that governments should not behave in this way and that people have a right to complain about such treatment.

This recent official preoccupation with curbing arbitrary rule is plainly a response to the demands of the articulate segments of the population, who have experienced a great deal of arbitrariness. Peking's current leaders are engaged in a comprehensive effort to restore the morale, enthusiasm, and productivity of these people, whose active participation is essential to China's fulfillment of the ambition to become a modern, powerful socialist state. Not only intellectuals but Party and government administrators and workers want reassurance about their personal security. So long as fear of arbitrary action persists—and PRC media now concede that such fear has been rampant for years—one cannot expect officials to take bold initiatives, scientists to innovate, teachers and researchers to present new ideas, and workers to criticize bureaucracy and inefficiency.

The current leaders have made it clear that in their view the relationship between economic development and individual rights is not an either-or proposition, and that even in a poor country that has China's distinctive tradition and circumstances certain minimum guaranties of individual rights are essential to promote development. Stalin's heirs acted on a similar premise, and this Soviet reaction to Stalin long ago led some observers of China to anticipate a similar trend there after Mao's passing. Despite its distinctiveness China, it turns out, is not totally different from the rest of the world in either human or economic terms. This is why the People's Government has again begun to use the term "human rights" in the due process sense of protecting individuals against fundamental unfairness, as it did during the law reform era of 1956–57 and as the Chinese Communists did prior to 1949 when they sought popular support against Chiang Kai-shek's regime.

To be sure, Peking is not on the verge of adopting the "rule of law" in a Western sense. As a Foreign Ministry official told me in early 1978: "Yes, the present liberalization is very exciting, but please remember that we will not go as far as many Western friends would like." Yet if the present Party line persists, enhancing economic development, educational progress, and international contacts, it is possible that the Chinese government may gradually demonstrate increasing respect for minimum due process standards.

The fact that a Chinese is poor and that his ancestors lived under Confucianism does not mean that his sense of justice and our own are wholly different. And posthumous rehabilitation, a practice that is now in vogue in China as the government seeks to make amends for many arbitrarily caused deaths, offers too little solace. As Chairman Mao recognized: "If you cut off a head by mistake, there is no way to rectify the mistake, even if you want to."

Culture

The Performing Arts

ROXANE WITKE

Roxane Witke takes us into the Chinese theater. She explains the way Chinese have traditionally viewed the theater and looked upon actors. It becomes a window onto the mentality of China. The theater has a purpose: to inspire people to better social behavior. Looking at the changes since 1949, Witke tells us much about the state of movies, opera, and plays. She has an especially keen eye for the ups and downs of women in these art forms. The fights over culture in recent years are broached. But Witke believes that the CCP's entrenched "totalism," not merely the ultra-leftism of the Gang of Four, is the real barrier to greater subtlety and individual self-expression on the Chinese stage.

Roxane Witke had a unique glimpse behind the scenes of the Chinese performing arts in meeting Chiang Ch'ing in 1972. The long talks between the two women were the basis for Witke's Comrade Chiang Ch'ing, *which has been translated into twelve languages. A graduate of Stanford (BA), Chicago (MA), and the University of California at Berkeley (PhD), Witke had already made contributions in the field of Chinese studies before her encounter with Chiang Ch'ing, and she had spent the year 1966 in Taiwan. Her essays on the arts and the position of women in modern Chinese history have appeared widely. After teaching at several universities, she resigned to write. At present she is a research associate at the East Asian Institute of Columbia University. Her next book will be about Shanghai in the 1930s.*

—R.T.

Talk about national characteristics is always risky. Still, there are certain qualities that seem to distinguish the Chinese, and some of the most fascinating come through the performing arts. The Chinese have always loved spectacle. They adore dramas large and small. Their Communist Party has not let them down.

Whether in small groups or in mass demonstrations, the behavior of the Chinese is often theatrical. Over the last quarter century or more they have grown accustomed to a nearly total orchestration of their lives by political authority. Few remain to be stunned by the slogan, "All art is politics." As various essayists in this volume point up, the vast majority seem to believe that the leaders are correct in programming, monitoring, and censoring most of the national and local culture. They are used to the fact that culture, which includes the performing arts, is not only controlled by the Party's Central Committee and its numerous organs, but also is judged by them and only them—in public at least.

As we compare ourselves to the Chinese we must remember that their country allows no journalism or other publishing that is independent from the Party. The types of magazines we take for granted do not exist for them. Privately sponsored journals of cultural criticism and review, show-business publications, dance news, or movie magazines are prohibited. There is nothing on the order of *People* or *Us* to keep them up with the doings of the stars. The only showcase personalities are to be found among the top political leaders.

The span of China's performing arts is astonishingly broad. Besides the ancient and modern operas, ballets, choral and symphonic music, national and minorities dance, cinema, and government-controlled radio and television, there is the equally important theater of daily life. Political skits, songs, and dances professing love for the Party Chairman and the Party, or touting the latest campaign, are performed regularly in schools, factories, and communes across the nation. What foreign visitor can forget the schoolteacher at the May Seventh Cadre School (for reforming intellectuals and bureaucratic types) who sings of the sweetness of collecting "night soil"? Or the cunning kindergarten children who ring out paeans to Chairman Mao or Chairman Hua one day, then deliver lyrical poison to the Gang of Four the next?

Role play, we find, governs much of daily life. Hardly entertainment for its own sake, art has become a way of expressing merit. Done by amateurs or professionals, painting, writing, and acting are used to demonstrate political rectitude. Conformity to the prevailing orthodoxy is to be expected. But on rare occasions the brush or pen, or the words of the actor, will express dissent.

As the source of all orthodoxies, the government is far less concerned that art imitate life than that life imitate art. Success in theater is not measured commercially, by what makes money, but politically—what makes people behave well.

The aim of this essay is to discover some of the human values conveyed by China's performing arts. We must remember that the question of "human values" is foreign to contemporary Chinese discourse. By their adopted Marxian standard, it is repulsively bourgeois. So we must maintain our own perspective. We may first remind ourselves of the ways of actors and the ranges of themes in China's past. Such comparison will show up some of the human—and inhuman—features of both Chinese theater and everyday life.

Tradition

The theater has evolved over the centuries and continues to do so under the present regime. In the dynastic past dramas had religious as well as secular significance. Styles ranged from the broadly popular to the esoteric. All forms of music, dance, and drama, including opera, were regionally specific. They used the local dialect and expressed the history, legend, and popular imagination of the area that fostered them.

In China more than in America and other parts of the West, government and theater have long been affiliated. China's political patronage goes back at least to the eighth century, when the emperor Ming Huang set up his favorite actors in his palace Pear Garden. The term Pear Garden remained in the language, referring metaphorically to the ruler's troupe, or to periods when the emperor personally or through his ministers guided the evolution of operatic models.

Mao Tse-tung was always mindful of and sometimes playful with tradition. From the late 1930s through the mid-1940s he gathered his own Pear Garden in his northwest retreat in Yenan. There the strongest component of the famous Lu Hsün Academy of Literature and Art was the Drama Department, which existed only on account of Party patronage. At that Academy the Communists' first revolutionary operas were born.

Even now at the Imperial Palace in Peking the ornate Ming-style elevated stage that the Empress Dowager Tz'u Hsi had built for her private theatricals still stands. But this may be less a proud reminder of the tradition of imperial patronage than a symbol of her personal indulgence. She kept more than ten troupes in her palace. Their fanciful masques were shared with court favorites, but not with the people at large.

Past rulers never controlled the nation's theater so thoroughly as have Communist Party chairmen. Yet the governments have always recognized that the people are susceptible to its influence. Along with art and literature, theater affects public morals, for good or for ill. In the past the court and its bureaucratic representatives throughout the empire promoted works designed to instill Confucian morals in the populace. "All dramas should encourage good and punish evil," it was said. Theater should "correct the feelings of the people and safeguard their customs." Particularly valued were plays that heightened respect for fathers, magistrates, and elders, and propounded loyalty to the emperor.

Since they lacked railroads, airlines, radios, and telephones for obtaining and relaying information, the emperors never enjoyed a total censorial command over the theater. In order to contain "bad" influence from repertories produced beyond their control, they simply excluded vulnerable types from theater audiences. Women were among those barred. During the last dynasty so were the elite corps of Manchu Bannermen, who might have been led astray by the mischievous entertainment of the Han Chinese.

Actors

In China as in other cultures, professional actors used to be the least respected of all artists. Their mobility and autonomy diminished their prestige. As wanderers, vagabonds, and gypsies without stake in communities, they easily slipped through the fingers of the law. Some were "bohemians," who could not be bothered with Confucian precepts or other social conventions. Thus popular opinion grew to assume that the women were promiscuous and the men possibly homosexual. Hence the government, which protected the Confucian underpinnings of the state, legally restricted their social mobility. Those caught transgressing the law were punished more severely than the rest of the community. Actors and their progeny were forbidden to sit for the examinations for the civil service—the only road to high status, wealth, and power.

Of course there were exceptions to the vast majority of actors whose lives were depressed. Each era had several great performers, often male specialists in the opera's stock female character. Such stars could aspire to the life of the prima donna. Scholars or wealthy merchants patronized them, and homosexual love sometimes was part of their relationship. A patronized actress might serve as a courtesan. Such favorites would be showered with gifts of silk, gold, and jade; parties were thrown for them, and many maintained their own mansions.

Exclusion from political assignments did not prevent actors from controlling much of their product. They organized their own troupes. Those who had permanent theaters were likely to manage them. If forceful, a great performer's personal style could establish a new "school" of acting that would be passed on to a son (though feudal filiation in China was less formalized than among *kabuki* actors in Japan) or to other apprentices. An actor's updated production of a familiar opera could be absorbed in the dramatic tradition. Playwrights and musicians enjoyed similar freedoms to modify tradition.

Although considered contemptible as a class, certain of China's best actors paradoxically were esteemed for their exemplary "human" character as well as for their artistry. Some are remembered for having assumed patriotic stances at moments of national peril. Since Liberation, the Communist leaders have charged all actors with serving as political paragons in their personal as well as their artistic lives.

As the Communists established political power in the early 1950s, they "nationalized" the theater, gradually dissolving private companies and severing lines of patronage by the rich, who were violently overthrown. They ended the practice whereby poor parents sold children of seven or eight to itinerant troupes, where they were often abused and exploited for menial labor. They also forbade the training of boys to play girls and implemented across the board the Western custom of recruiting actresses for the female parts.

The rationale for nationalizing the theater was spelled out at the Yenan Forum of 1942.* At the conclusion of the debates among diverse cultural and political figures brought together at the northwest capital of the Red Army, Mao laid down a hard, Soviet-style line: hereafter writers and artists should serve as cogs in the revolutionary machine. They were to be "engineers of the human soul," he said, using the epithet Stalin had borrowed from Gorky. Playwrights should put a stop to their wavering bourgeois sensibilities. They should not miss the libraries or entertainments of the cities, nor hanker after the high culture of the past, nor crave that of the West. Intellectuals should stop writing merely to satisfy themselves or to impress each other. Their duty henceforth was to "serve the people"—the "workers, peasants and soldiers" designated as their main audience.

In the early 1950s the government assumed authority over hundreds

*Discussed on pp. 287 and 311.

of thousands of actors, singers, composers, and musicians, assuring them a more secure livelihood and respectable status than most had known in the past. The arrangement also had its restrictions. Theatrical people were bound to recognize the Party's prerogative to invade their professional circles. Writers were ordered to render the Party's political messages as popular entertainment. Actors were expected to propound the new orthodoxy and to confine their performances to repertories approved by the Culture Department of the Party's Central Committee.

So far I have spoken only of professional actors. Also targeted for political conversion were the amateurs, men and women whose tradition was unparalleled abroad. Usually these were affluent men, who performed for intimate or public groups. Most were aesthetes who simply relished theater. But during the period of national disaster after the turn of the century, numerous amateurs—both men and women—were compelled to show their conscience by taking political stands. Scattered performances attacking the Manchus directly or indirectly hastened that dynasty's demise.

Amateur acting thrived during the May Fourth era (peaking in 1919), among the young especially. Chou En-lai and other future Communist leaders were among the schoolchildren and college students who flocked to the streets to fire up citizens against the thrall of Confucianism and the threat of Japanese imperialism. More sophisticated amateur groups mounted performances on a spectrum of national and radical issues during the 1930s.

The theater of propaganda soon spread to the military. From its early years the Red Army underwrote troupes of amateurs to advocate their causes. Succeeding the Red Army after Liberation was the People's Liberation Army, which sustained Mao Tse-tung's teaching that soldiers were obliged to fight cultural as well as military warfare. The army was a "seeding machine" that spread propaganda through music and theater. Some thought that was going too far. After Mao died and his inheritors sought to make the military more professional, Chiang Ch'ing was blamed for having tried to transform the PLA into a company of actors and actresses who merely pranced around with bayonets!

Since the Communists rose to power, the civilian population has also devoted much of its energy to performances. During the Cultural Revolution, Party authorities complained of amateur troupes that spent so much time putting on shows that their productive labor on farms and factories fell behind.

The Party has also worried that professional actors (or writers or artists for that matter) should not exploit their official patronage by forming a new privileged class. To avoid such Soviet-style revisionism, the revolutionary press published glowing reports of how professional actors, notably the troupes committed to the model theater, voluntarily farmed on the side, which meant gardening—raising fruits and vegetables near their studios.

Women as Artists

Chinese women are just coming into their own as performing artists. The tradition from which they evolve is not proud or strong. There has always been a minority of actresses and courtesans who won high patronage, but on the whole their artistic skills were never on a par with Japan's geisha, for example. China's most numerous female entertainers were the most debased—the so-called sing-song girls, whose coy posturing and wailing tunes finally wended their way into our clichéd imagery of "the Orient." But we should not overlook the fact that their establishments, which sometimes served as brothels, provided the setting for much public performance up to the nineteenth century.

There also used to be a few acting troupes composed entirely of women. Perhaps the most famous in modern times was the Shaohsing theater, where women played male parts. Although many relished their twist upon a male-dominated tradition, Chiang Ch'ing banned them during the Cultural Revolution. Women who take male parts "ruin their looks," she told me. Also unsuited to revolution was the fact that their repertories naturally featured more romances of love than of military heroism.

Like most world theater, Chinese opera has always had stock characters. The scholar, the military hero, and the buffoon used to be favorite types. After Liberation they were gradually displaced by stereotypes forged from revolutionary experience. Several of the traditional and modern female stereotypes are worth mentioning because they reflected popular views of women.

One was the ingénue, usually a daughter or daughter-in-law of a family of social rank. In the classical theater she was submissive and coy—"oppressed" by the standards of today. In the modern theater spurred by the West she began to rebel. Chinese productions of Ibsen's *A Doll's House* were immensely popular among the young intellectuals of the Republican era, and actresses vied for the part of Nora.

Another stereotype was the older woman, the matriarch or mother-in-law who could be both formidable and absurd. Her tyrannical rule over the family was a form of revenge, a release of aggressions pent up from youth, when she was bossed around by old women and most men. One of the most memorable matriarchs emerged from dramatized versions of the eighteenth-century family saga *Dream of the Red Chamber.* Her only surviving example on the revolutionary stage is in the ballet *The White Haired Girl.* The point of her awful presence, say Party authorities, is to remind the young, whom the revolution saved from domestic tyrants, of how their parents and young people perennially suffered in the hands of termagants who had gained seniority.

A more attractive figure populating traditional literature and the performing arts was the woman warrior. Her parallels with our contemporary Wonder Woman and Bionic Woman are remarkable. Late Victorian observers of China had noticed in her shades of Joan of Arc. Her Chinese stereotype was built upon the sixth-century figure of Mulan. The daughter of an aging general, Mulan was admirable for her Confucian mores: she went out to fight the Huns in place of her father. What has always been fascinating about her was that she was the obverse of the prevailing Confucian ideal of the submissive ingénue, who led a thoroughly domesticated life. She was also a female version of the prototypical male warrior. A glamorous but aggressive strategist, she was the equal of or superior to a man. The revolutionary theater preserves her prototype by updating it. In ancient theater and modern motion pictures she fought for father, clan, or country. Today she defends the Communist Party and the proletarian class. As with male warriors, demonstrations of starlike individual heroism are toned down. In the revolutionary ballet *The Red Detachment of Women,* the female soldiers of the Red Army dance largely ensemble.

Another favorite character of traditional and modern theater I'll call the transvestite: the domestic but clever girl who decides to win over the man she loves in the masculine territory of scholarship. She disguises herself as a comely young male student and entices him by matching wits. Once he is charmed, she sheds her disguise and commences a love affair that is fancifully implied. Most likely this will be ended by her outraged parents. The Communists have also terminated her female stereotype. Education has ceased to be a male prerogative, and even the most delicate seductions are shunted from the stage.

There was too the clever maid who might act as the go-between for lovers whose parents had obstructed their encounters. In her revolutionized version she may exchange messages between Party activists during wartime. Other new heroines will be considered in the context of the model operas and ballets initiated in the 1960s.

Plays*

Of all the performing arts available to the Chinese, the drama imported from the West articulated most explicitly the change of values and mores that came about in the twentieth century. Translated and original works

---

*The word for a play in Chinese is *hua-chü,* meaning "talk play," because it relies on speech, eliminating the music, acrobatics, and symbolism of traditional opera.

broadened the experience of young Chinese actors by allowing them to read new scripts and to try out—or I should say try on—new parts. Dramatized versions of *Uncle Tom's Cabin* and *Camille* were among the earliest foreign works. Isolated from origins, their reflections on American race relations and the French aristocracy were impressive but overblown.

Later Sinified productions of Ibsen, Strindberg, O'Neill, and others expressed in universal terms the ways in which the human lot is problematical. The unbroken dialogue, clash of personalities, and contests of ideas enriched the conceptual vocabulary of young Chinese intellectuals, who were determined to free themselves from the straitjacket of their old culture. The diversity and daring of the foreign-style drama made it the most avant-garde genre of the New Culture Movement of the 1920s. Common themes were the challenge of the individual against society, youth against age, children against parents, women against men, reason against superstition, rationalism against religion, and anarchy against authority. Such heady theater belonged to a stage of cultural revolution that was generated from below. Most of those themes were banned after Liberation, when dilemmas were dictated from above, especially after the Great Proletarian Cultural Revolution of the 1960s.

Communist policy on the modern theater and film derived from the West was ambivalent, if not outright hostile. On the one hand, many of the foreign works and their Chinese knock-offs exhibited an advanced consciousness of the problems of women, youth, and the poor that responded to Marxist goals. But so often included in the plays and films was what the Communist Party termed "decadent, bourgeois" concern for individual consciousness, for moral choice, for the right to challenge *any* political authority—and for the glamour afforded by materialism. Hence much of the modern repertory—and with it modern consciousness—was banned.

During the 1950s the external source of drama shifted primarily to the Soviet Union. Gogol, Chernyshevsky, and Ostrovsky were high on the list. Repertories of Chinese opera eliminated "superstitious," meaning religious, themes, as well as tales of the marvelous, the so-called ghost plays. Slowly new "socialist dramas" were forged. Stanislavsky's theories of drama were much discussed and written about. But his accordance of initiative to the actor, and his emphasis on the subjective power of the ego, clashed with the Party's demand for conformity and its Russian-inspired standard of "socialist realism." After 1957, the year when Mao retaliated against the intellectuals' and artists' surfeit of Hundred Flowers, the publication of foreign dramas was abruptly terminated. China's concept of the drama became increasingly national and provincial.

Since Chiang Ch'ing had begun her career in the modern drama movement, we might have expected her to promote it after she came to power. Instead she destroyed it, and in so doing drastically shifted the course of development of modern Chinese culture.

When I quizzed her on this point during our interviews in the summer of 1972, she offered complex reasons. The ideological ones for rejecting modern theater had been learned; the personal ones would never be forgotten. To the public she represented Mao and the ideals of proletarian dictatorship, which in the arts were paradoxically conservative. In zealous addresses to the masses during the years of the Cultural Revolution, she condemned most modern trends in foreign drama and cinema: naturalism, nihilism, anarchism, bourgeois decadence, and sickly melancholy—all so poisonous to the Chinese people. But during our private discussions, other motives were revealed. She was furiously resentful of T'ien Han, Hsia Yen, and a host of other (actually brilliant) modern dramatists whom she believed had scorned her when she had been a fledgling actress, and later had misrepresented her early political career. Armed with power during the Cultural Revolution, she finally avenged herself by directing the nation to mount a hate campaign against them and diverse leftists who, like her, had fought the former regime. T'ien Han died during the Cultural Revolution. Hsia Yen, among other once-famous dramatists, returned to the public eye only after the wheel of fortune turned against her.

Despite Chiang Ch'ing's fall and the release of thousands of political prisoners, the former momentum of the modern drama movement has not yet been restored. But in the future there may be a revival of the "old" modern themes: romantic love, sexual struggle, resistance to the rise of industrial civilization, illusion and disillusion, anomie, "inward migration," opposition to bureaucratism, an emphasis on the value of nonconformity, and the pursuit of a true democracy. And after didactic decades, artistically independent satire and comedy may return as well.

Cinema

Before Liberation, the moving picture was China's main channel of information about exotic lands and peoples. The foreign imagery and values absorbed through the film are incalculable. From the late 1920s several nations marketed films in China, but Hollywood's were the most popular among the urban Chinese of most classes.

Partially equipped and financed by American companies, the Chinese began producing their own silent films in the 1920s and talking ones in the next decade. And during the 1930s filmmakers joined dramatists, novelists, and graphic artists in getting away from sentimentalism and bringing a new political consciousness to their media. Several studios in

Shanghai produced films of considerable artistry and thematic complexity. Social reform, women's rights, the rise of the working class, and resistance to Japan were among the chief issues.

Japan's attack on Shanghai in 1937 shattered the film industry. Talents fled throughout the country and abroad. Subsequently the Communists, who were meagerly equipped, began to use film for documentary and propaganda purposes in Yenan. As they established national authority at mid-century, they tried, for ideological reasons, to put an end to foreign "dumping" of films on their market and began the reconstruction of their own film industry for the promotion of socialism.

Looking back to the 1930s and 1940s reminds us of a level of artistry and expressiveness that was barely sustained in later years. Although the ruling Kuomintang was censorial, issues that mattered to the people were aired on the screen. Among these were conflicts between old-fashioned parents and modern children, antagonism between mothers-in-law and daughters-in-law, and freely chosen love affairs that challenged arranged marriages. Some of the most popular melodramas were pessimistic: the young lovers were defeated at the end. Others projected a more aggressive view of the future: without political revolution the old sexual and generational conflicts would never be eased. There were also fantasy solutions. *Liang Shan-po and Chu Ying-t'ai* was one of China's most exquisitely wrought and popular film stories of all times. The young lovers— the girl was of the "transvestite type"—were forbidden to marry. When they died, they were metamorphosized into a pair of butterflies. This was but one of hundreds of historical romances whose feudal ambiance, sentimentalism, and otherworldliness would be suppressed by the new order of proletarian purism.

During the early years of the People's Republic, surviving film companies were either disbanded or reemployed by the state. Bureaucrats in the Ministry of Culture attempted to generate a new socialist cinema from on high. And throughout the 1950s Soviet filmmakers stationed in China had a hand in China's industry. Only after the anti-rightist movement of 1957 and the departure of the Soviets in 1960 did some of China's great filmmakers, who had first flourished in the 1930s, come into their own. In 1961 Hsia Yen described the period as one when the leaders were free to make clarion calls, but the writers were also free to make choices. Creative work, he wrote, was "a sort of spiritual production which is different from material production; it is not so simple as the production of thermos bottles or teacups." None should be subjected to coercion or oppression, nor be obliged to write a script on a "fixed topic, fixed persons and fixed time." His film *The Lin Family Shop* was one of the most sensitive and popular of those years.

But in the mid-1960s Hsia Yen and a host of other great film talents were struck down by Chiang Ch'ing and her pilot group of cultural revolutionaries, and did not regain their public voice until 1977. As has become customary in a hate campaign, they were accused of "bourgeois," "revisionist," and "counterrevolutionary" motives—to name but a few. Many were taunted by Red Guards, imprisoned, or put under house arrest. On the eve of the Cultural Revolution practically the entire film industry ground to a halt.

Until very recent times the few Chinese films that have reached this country have been seen by small, somewhat cultish American audiences. Excluded from commercial channels, most arrive through political agencies, mainly "friendship" groups that foster cultural propaganda. Decisions on what films to export—even through commercial channels—are made at the highest levels of Chinese government. Few of those chosen are old; most are current and notable for their illustration of the current political line. Set in the famous oil fields of Ta-ch'ing, *The Pioneers* presents a story of how to drill in the proletarian style. *Spring Shoots* spells out recent debates over education. Pekingologists have read the former as a veiled show of rivalry between the so-called radicals (Chiang Ch'ing and her group) and Chou En-lai, and the latter as a struggle for prominence between the revisionists once led by Liu Shao-ch'i and the revolutionaries led by Mao and his lieutenants, the now-discredited Gang of Four. If subtitles exist, they usually are poor. Dramatization and acting are wooden by our standards; the didacticism is offputting; and the Aesopian (sometimes imaginary) references to the leaders are grasped by few.

Such political programming may work for Chinese viewers, but it often fails to resonate in the world outside. We miss the "bourgeois" qualities to which we've grown accustomed: revelations of individual psychology, of intimate family details, of love affairs, tensions between generations, struggles against male—or female—chauvinism, or personal tragedies that can find no political redemption. And of course the nakedness and pornography so prevalent in Western films are absolutely out.

There are stylistic reasons too for our alienation from the human aspect of Chinese films. In China the camera has always been used as a static instrument. The cameraman stands back from the action, allowing his equipment to observe. In keeping with ancient tradition (excepting some Buddhist imagery), close-ups of the human face are rare. Conditioned by our own cultural tradition, we may search in vain for flickers of individual rather than official thought or emotion behind the "masks" that sometimes project the hyped-up style of the classical opera.

The Chinese used to be up with our film world. From the 1920s through into the early 1950s the names of Douglas Fairbanks, Greta Garbo, Clark Gable, Hedy Lamarr, Shirley Temple, and others were easily recognizable in China. But in recent years most Chinese would be hard put to name a contemporary American or other foreign film star. Since Mao died, a few cautious glimmers have been shown. On New Year's Day 1978, *People's Daily* carried a "Little Tramp" photo of Charlie Chaplin (Mao had been among his fans), who died on Christmas Day. The brief account of his life commended his "profound compassion for oppressed and exploited humanity," and his films were lauded for their "deep ideological and social meaning." The next year *Modern Times* and other Chaplin films were revived.

Although the masses have been insulated from the stimulation of foreign films, the leaders have not been blinded. From Liberation if not before they have built up various archives of foreign films. Obviously they and their favorites have been free to screen these privately. One might assume that this was for mere entertainment. But Chiang Ch'ing, who was an addict, said that she and her colleagues studied them to learn their good technical points, which they could then apply to their own fledgling industry.

After Mao's death Chiang Ch'ing was accused of constructing films as instruments of power struggle, to forward her "plot to usurp Party and state power" (of course any recent Chinese film has been designed to promote the Party and its present leaders). *Spring Shoots* allegedly took two or three years to shoot because she redid it two or three times (not shocking by our professional standards), and it cost over half a million U.S. dollars. Apparently, others trying to make movies faster and cheaper were scorned by her for "following the theory of productive forces," which means thinking like capitalists. Recently it was alleged (though it is not necessarily true) that the Gang of Four refused to implement Mao's order to produce enough films annually for people to see a new one each week.

Opera

Opera is the most ancient form of theater that still flourishes in China today. Most elements of voice, instrumentation, dance, and acrobatics existed during the Han Dynasty more than two thousand years ago. The operatic form began to be perfected during the Mongol Dynasty of the thirteenth and fourteenth centuries. Playwriting became a diversion for scholar-bureaucrats left underemployed by their alien rulers, and some of the works carried subversive political meanings.

In the past opera had religious as well as secular significance. Styles ranged from the broadly popular, which could be crude or refined, to the esoteric, favored by cultish scholars. Regardless of class appeal, operas always had a regional character. There were at least three hundred local types with their own myth, music, and dialect. Cantonese and Peking opera were vastly different. The southern style had as many as fifty short acts that trailed on all day, while the audience moved in and out, nibbling and chatting, and zeroing in on favorite scenes. Since Canton was a port city open to trade, its opera was the first to pick up traits from the West. After the turn of the twentieth century the ancient costumes, which were typically lavish, might also be loaded with imported sequins or illuminated with hundreds of tiny light bulbs. Occasionally a singer would don contemporary Western or Chinese costume. Influenced by Hollywood films, some singers affected Bing Crosby's crooner style. To the small Chinese orchestra were added the violin, electric guitar, and saxophone.

Association with the capital made Peking opera (known as *ching-hsi*, literally, "capital theater") more austere and classical. The incorporation of admired regional traits also made it cosmopolitan. But not until Chiang Ch'ing took over did her addition of Western instruments and sets begin to bring the Peking opera into international fashion.

Regardless of regional type, the old opera variously combined spoken and sung voice, instruments, gesture, dance, acrobatics, and swordplay. The musicians sat to the side of a stage that was bare of screens and had only the minimum of props, such as a chair or a table. The acting was mimetic and symbolic. A headdress with long feathers signified a general, a fan a scholar; showing an oar meant rowing a boat. Flicking a riding whip with silk tassels indicated the presence of a horse; an upward kick meant mounting him. Pacing about the stage showed taking a journey. A person dressed in black was meant to be invisible.

Reform of the opera was a terrible ordeal in the 1960s, when the performing arts became more obviously than ever functions of the Party and state. In the first round, the choice was always between doing things in the old Chinese or in the new foreign way. For the Chinese, a people of immense cultural pride, doing things in the foreign way cost "face," unless there was a fine way of rationalizing it. Historically, the import of material goods and the mastery of foreign technology have been far less upsetting to the Chinese than the adoption of foreign culture or the incorporation of foreign values. The late-nineteenth-century reformer Chang Chih-tung laid down a rule that became famous: "Chinese learning for substance and Western learning for function." By that he meant that it was all right to import foreign hardware, but not to adopt foreign values, namely, political institutions, religion, and culture. However, subsequent reformers and revolutionaries would find that segregating the two was nearly impossible.

The leaders of each episode in China's modernization have had to wrestle with problems of cultural balance. Mao Tse-tung's experience of the West was limited, yet he wrote numerous essays trying to make Chinese sense out of the foreign political theory of Marxism. Mao had sought not only to industrialize China, but also to transform its human nature: to create by cultural devices a "new communist man." His defenders of the early 1960s seized control over the arts world and all the media in order to bring that about.

While Chiang Ch'ing might have made primary use of the modern film and play, instead she turned to opera—the most ancient and most popular form. She had decided that if she stormed this "strongest citadel" (her apt metaphor for the classicism and rigidity of opera), plays, film, and music, as well as literature and the graphic arts, eventually would capitulate to her lead and conform to her theatrical models.

Naturally she discovered that she could not create a new proletarian culture on the sole strength of China's past. The goal of reforming the opera entangled her and like-minded politicians and cultural figures in the essential dilemma of modernization: How to use foreign techniques and traditions to update the opera without corrupting or destroying the essential Chineseness of its form. The slogan, "Make things foreign serve things Chinese," justified a selective infusion from the West. Yet the basic character of the old opera would be preserved, "face" would be saved, and the feeling of rootedness in the past not lost.

In the mid-sixties, "Destruction must precede construction" became one of the most widely quoted slogans. All "feudal" and "bourgeois" signs of the older superstructure were obliterated to make way for the "newborn things," in essence Chiang Ch'ing's model theater. This push from one cultural era to the next entailed the most monumental purge of people and legacy in all of Chinese history. The entire canon of traditional and modern opera (updated before the Cultural Revolution), plays, cinema, old Chinese and foreign music was struck down. From the rubble slowly arose the new "jewels" of the superstructure: the model theater. Among the best promoted were the revolutionized Peking operas *The Red Lantern, Taking Tiger Mountain by Strategy,* and *Shachiapang,* all three depicting idealized facets of Communist Party history.

As the opera was reformed, each element was reconstructed in the proletarian class interest of the audience, and ultimately of the masses nationwide. A self-made authority in music, Chiang Ch'ing ordered composers to prepare scores that would orchestrate the will of the people to accomplish new tasks. The job was frustrating, she explained in our interviews, because the Chinese musicians were very conservative. Music was either Chinese or foreign to them. The old folk and esoteric melodies they simply played over and over again, and the Western music (which some also played) they regarded with awe. Few had attempted a mix. Flashing Mao's slogan, "Weed through the old to bring forth the new, and make things foreign serve things Chinese," she insisted that certain old Chinese tunes could be woven into Western orchestration. For only the latter, she thought, was bold, militant, and thus conducive to revolutionary action. For the score of *Taking Tiger Mountain by Strategy* (of which she was especially proud) she added Western timpani to the Chinese percussion section. Foreign violins, violas, and cellos were combined with the Chinese stringed instruments. The oboe, clarinet, trumpets, and French horns joined with the Chinese flutes. Thus the original group of eight operatic instruments became thirty. She made similar amplifications in *The Red Lantern,* and to the horror of Chinese purists she added the piano!

Also adopted from Western drama and motion pictures were realistic backdrops, mobile stages, sophisticated stunts and spotlighting, and more dialogue interspersed with the song. Still, much of the traditional was preserved, including dramatic poses and electrifying frozen stares.

But the themes in the model theater were entirely new to China's performing arts: demonstration of class struggle, subordination of individual to group interests; respect for the absolute authority and infallibility of the Party; absolute loyalty to the Party Chairman; demonstration of ideal proletarian character; raising consciousness of oppression; and directions on political retribution, which is called "settling blood accounts."

Each of these arduously wrought syntheses of history, politics, and art illustrated an episode in the rise of Chinese communism, presented from the perspective of Mao's orthodoxy. Building upon styles of the Soviet Union (and to a lesser extent of Nazi Germany, picked up through the media of the 1930s), China's leaders employed socialist realism and revolutionary romanticism to stimulate the masses to action. Human types were idealized in beauty and boldness. National pride and limitless optimism were on display. The model works showed ideology in action—political doctrine with a human face. They were the most effective propaganda: colorful, clever, and entertaining.

The new pantheon of heroes and heroines were archetypes of working-class men and women. The drabness and defeatism by which laboring people had been known in the past were termed "negative" and dispensed with. The new heroes and heroines were "positive": colorful, resolute, glamorous. *The Red Lantern* illustrates how the legacy of political struggle passes down through generations. Set during the resistance war against Japan, the opera's model characters, who have subtle family connections, show the proper working of three generations. Dauntless Granny Li is the paragon for senior citizens. Li Yü-ho, the handsome railway switchman, is in his prime when finally martyred, along with Granny Li. Lively young T'ieh-mei inspires the youngest generation by vowing to avenge her family history of torture and execution at the hands of the Japanese and to dedicate her life to the Party.

The virtue of the new hero was to quicken the dialectic between theater and life. In the early 1960s Chiang Ch'ing had gone around telling actors, "To act a revolutionary you first must be a revolutionary."* She urged them to get out of their academies and live among the rural people and minorities in order to get the feel and flavor of their actual lives. Although that process of "gathering raw materials" and "broadening world views" became the subject of tedious propaganda, the rationale was much the same as when Marlon Brando went down to the docks to prepare for *On the Waterfront,* or Jon Voight spent weeks among paraplegics in a veterans' hospital to educate himself for *Coming Home.*

A Different Drummer

The Cultural Revolution radicalized the performing arts with the goal of ameliorating human nature by making it proletarian. Whether that was accomplished remains to be seen. We do know that the strain of conformity upon performers and the masses was unspeakably great. No one had the strength or courage to complain while Mao was alive; but as soon as he died, his chief defenders were locked up and labeled the "Gang of Four." The winners who emerged from this swift power struggle now bid for mass support by raising the banner of cultural liberalization.

Chairman Hua's moves to liberalize culture naturally have been politically calculated. From the beginning he has had to smear the Gang of Four while saving the face of Mao, who had authorized their cultural leadership, now condemned as a "fascist dictatorship over the arts." Daily doses of printed propaganda and recitations throughout the land deplore the Gang's "reign of terror," which endured for a "black decade."

But how should popular opinion of the former regime's model works be reshaped? Because they did indeed monopolize the stage, their stories and characters have become incorporated into the consciousness of the people. To discredit them absolutely would have been too shocking. Instead, history was readjusted. Although it was common knowledge that Chiang Ch'ing and her colleagues had organized and directed the model theater, the new explanation was that it actually had been Chairman Mao

---

*In an interview of 1967 the actress who played T'ieh-mei of *The Red Lantern* put the formula for making real life imitate political art: "The process of playing a heroic character is also one of learning from that heroic character. To play a heroic character well on stage, one must at the same time learn from the heroic character off that stage. . . . To propagandize the thought of Mao Tse-tung on the stage . . . I simply shorten the distance between myself and the proletarian heroic character I play." Though conceived for actors, the formula was intended to apply to audiences as well.

and Premier Chou who had fostered them. Chiang Ch'ing had only "meddled" (could a "fascist dictator" be so marginal?). Her taking over scripts written by others (universal practice among producers) proved that she "stole the fruits of the people."

The vilification of the Gang of Four that has saturated the Chinese press and the public language of the people from October 1976 to the present reveals the brutality of life at the top. Although our distance from their reality makes it difficult for us to pass judgment on the accused or accusors, certain charges are fascinating because they point to the link between theater and political power in China. The Gang is criticized for having concocted infallible heroes who never showed a moment's hesitation in their pursuit of Party goals. Such absolutism in the drama contradicts the Marxian idea that correct ideas come from practice. In other words, their absurdly stereotypic characters masked the reality that people learn in the course of living, and that the lessons can be shown on stage. Strongly implied is the message that the black-and-white characterizations of the old opera and its revolutionary versions may have their place, but must not prevail over the drama as a whole.

More meaningful to the power struggle is the charge that the Gang used their theory of the "three stresses" to raise their heroes high above other positive characters in the model works. That elevation revealed the Gang's craving for personality cults of themselves and their "sinister plot to seize ultimate Party and state power." But there is also ample evidence that Hua's present regime uses theatrical characterization as an instrument of political power.

How much liberalization will follow from the Gang's fall remains to be shown. In some ways the fear of political contamination from traditional Chinese and foreign culture has already eased. Though costly to produce, a few old operas have been restaged, as have some of the earliest revolutionary operas created in Yenan in the 1940s. More folk or classical music of China can be heard live or on the radio, and Beethoven, Schubert, and Chopin are no longer dismissed as mere excrescences of the foreign bourgeois or imperialist mentality.

Because the experience of music is aural, some may consider it less seductively political than films. To protect the people from distraction by visions of alien styles of life, access to foreign films and drama will be restored far more cautiously. Some Eisenstein films from the 1930s have been screened again, as have a few Soviet and Chinese films of later dates. Translations of Shakespeare (and various foreign novelists) are back in the shops and selling fast. The chance for intellectuals and students to read the "great books" is bound to improve.

But the gap between what intellectuals may read and what the people must see is still vast. Since Hua Kuo-feng rose to power, there have been thousands of propaganda musicals about how millions of hearts beat in unison to celebrate him, and of ardent arias to Mao, Chou En-lai, Chu Te, and other late revolutionary leaders. As a slap in the face of Mao's final and most politically active wife, several hundred ballads, dramas, and operas were churned out on the life of Mao's second wife, Yang K'ai-hui, martyred in 1930 for her association with him. *Red Hearts,* a play of 1975 about a physician's noble struggle against the Gang of Four, was a hit when it first appeared in Peking in 1978.

Few will dispute that the former regime was harshly repressive and its theater meager. Still, there are no signs of a "thaw" of the magnitude of that experienced by the Soviet Union after the death of Stalin. In the fall of 1977 the new minister of culture declared to the Central Committee that his office would continue to serve as censor and that it would ban all materials contradicting the Party's interest. The art of knowing when to add pressure for conformity and when to lift it will long be with the Chinese. Thousands of cultural figures victimized during Mao's anti-rightist campaign of 1957 and his Cultural Revolution of the next decade have been released, but the experience of prisons and labor camps will have broken most in body and spirit. For example, of the national and minorities dances now being restaged, some sent abroad, are dated, revisionist in substance and style. Such familiar numbers as the *Lotus Dance, The Bowl Dance,* and *Militia Women of the Grasslands* are redolent of China's half-hearted imitation of Hollywood entertainment imported through films in the 1940s and 1950s.

A regeneration of Chinese culture cannot depend solely on rehabilitated artists, or on their students, for they had none. And since the present regime has made material modernization the goal of this century, scientific intellectuals will be more generously supported than humanistic ones.

The Chinese want to enrich their culture and to make it more humanly significant. The dilemmas they now face are common to leftist and totalitarian regimes in their established years. They also raise questions. For example, how *are* human values to be fished from the pool of class consciousness? How persistent is cultural tradition even when overlaid by imported ideology? Like the Confucians before them, the Communists use literature and art to instill a sense of duty so that people will fulfill designated social and political roles. But the constant stress upon conforming to an assigned station distracts from the exploration of individual potential and the exercise of individual rights. Before assuming that the Chinese will always be this way, we should remind ourselves of the diversity of Chinese tradition, and of the fact that it has been jolted by modernism. Twentieth-century Chinese dramatists and filmmakers have demonstrated that concern with individual potential and rights is not merely a foreign affectation, but an aspiration that can be and perhaps should be universal.

Revolutionary theater throughout the world has sought to create the illusion of having solved the universal conflict between personal gratification and public duty. Already in the 1930s critics of Soviet and other Communist literatures were pointing out the dangers of making art represent an imagined totality, of trying to bring everything into relation with everything else. Man becomes a cog in the machine, a part in the predestined whole. He who fails to play his assigned role will be torn off the page, ripped from the picture, shunted to the wings, and dumped into a Marxian nether world. So it will be until writers and performers in China question the notion of totality and dare to reconsider their predicament in a changing world.

Literature in Fetters

HARRIET MILLS

Harriet Mills describes the literary scene. Her starting point is the principles that Mao Tse-tung laid down for writers in a series of talks at Yenan in the 1940s. She spells out the strategies that the CCP used to harness Chinese literary tradition for its new purposes, including the reinterpretation of old stories in socialist terms, the use of old forms to tell a new story, and (occasionally) the transformation of old forms into a genuine new style. Introducing the themes and plots of individual stories, Mills weaves a rich tapestry of the efforts of Chinese novelists and playwrights to keep literature alive in the years of the CCP in power. She believes it has been something of a dance in fetters. Mao insisted that all conflict and emotion is based on class; this simply does not seem as true in the China of the 1970s as it did when the revolution was still unfolding.

Mills sees the period of the Cultural Revolution as a disaster for literature, and she is not sure that the period since—even after the fall of the Gang of Four—has really solved the fundamental problems. A controlled literature means just that, and will do so while the CCP rules China. Chinese writing remains very separate from literary trends in the rest of the world.

Harriet Mills was born in Japan and grew up in China. Back in the United States she took her AB at Wellesley College and her PhD at Columbia University. From 1947 she was a Fulbright student in Peking. During that period she was arrested for alleged espionage and spent four years (until 1955) in detention in the PRC. Mills, now professor of Far Eastern languages and literatures at the University of Michigan, has also taught at Columbia (1959–60) and Cornell University (1964–66). The author of Intermediate Reader in Chinese (1967), she revisited China in 1976.

—R.T.

In May 1942, in his *The Yenan Talks on Literature and Art*, Mao Tse-tung laid down the fundamentals of his still dominant policy on literature and art: literature was to serve politics; the Party, not the artist, would set the standards for content and style.

Two factors prompted Mao. First, Communist experience in Kiangsi and later in Shensi had proved the value of the popular arts in mobilizing peasant support for the revolution. Second, the Party was then under attack by a group of Party and non-Party veterans of the leftist literary movement in Shanghai of the thirties. As refugees in Yenan, these largely middle-class idealists had found not the paradise they sought but disappointing evidence of laziness, incompetence, and special privilege, as well as an intolerance of free discussion and criticism. Hoping to promote reform, they spoke out as friends in satirical tones only to discover, to their dismay, the dilemma of the artist who must serve a Party, not a personal muse.

Mao, an educated man appreciative of China's literary tradition, saw this tension not as conflict but as a struggle for synthesis. He viewed history as the continuing struggle between oppressor and oppressed. For him there was no universal human nature or human sentiment that could transcend these lines, only class love and class hatred. Throughout history, writers and artists had reflected the values of the privileged, ignoring the needs of the peasants, workers, and soldiers whom art and the revolution must now serve. Thus the revolutionary artist must undergo a long and painful ideological remolding until the proletarian view displaced his own and his work was able to reflect the concerns of the masses and be accepted by them.

To this end, Mao insisted, writers of bourgeois background must live among the people and learn from them. They must study popular art and use it to spread the revolutionary message, to expose domestic and foreign enemies, and to portray heroes of all sorts as models for emulation. For the time being, the new art was to be popular enough for workers, peasants, and soldiers to enjoy. Yet it must avoid the "empty, cut and dried dogmas and formulas" of a "poster and slogan style," because works of art, no matter how politically correct, are "powerless if they lack artistic quality." Only art that penetrated the basic contradictions of life had the power, Mao argued, to arouse the masses in the battle to push history forward. Later, out of the fusion of popular forms with progressive foreign and Chinese elements, higher forms would emerge. "Thus," he concluded, "the political character of our art becomes entirely at one with its truthfulness."

Finally it was the responsibility of the artist, Mao emphasized, invoking the Soviet doctrine of socialist realism, to see the future in the present, to discount current failings as remnants of a past already doomed to failure by the process of history. Ridicule and satire should be aimed at enemies, not at the people or the Party.

The main architects of the tremendous development of popular arts that followed Mao's talks were local folk professionals and a new group of young local writers. The veterans, many of whom were harshly criticized in the campaign that followed Mao's speech and sent for periods to live among the masses, played a less significant part. For many of them the tension between loyalty to their art and loyalty to their interests in the revolution remained unresolved, resurfacing periodically, with unfortunate results for them personally, during the next thirty-five years.

Three basic strategies for utilizing popular culture emerged. The first was the reinterpretation or modification of traditional stories. Basic to the old fiction and opera, to the storyteller and the ballad singer, was a core of tales about emperors, ministers, generals, scholars, and their ladies that for centuries had taught the illiterate peasant the little he knew of history. From them he had also absorbed the fatalistic Buddhist doctrine of *karma,* which held that suffering in this life was retribution for transgression in an earlier existence, an attitude the rulers of the past had manipulated in order to ensure their control of the countryside. In all these stories common folk appeared only as clowns, servants, or extras. Now, in their adapted versions, ordinary people had roles of dignity and responsibility more consonant with the philosophy of the new society. The luster of the old heroes faded as story themes were also recast. Thus one play about personal enmity between an imperial guardsman and a traitorous minister emerges as a timely instance of patriotic resistance to domestic and foreign enemies. The essential character, plot, and music, however, remain largely intact. Such reshaping was the basic strategy that underlay the reform of the Peking opera in the early years after Liberation.

More common and important was the adaptation of traditional forms to modern themes, the putting of new wine into old wine skins. The various types of local opera, storytellers, and ballad singers, as well as the episodic pre-modern novel, all began to tell stories on contemporary topics like guerrilla warfare and landlord brutality, the wonders of land reform and the new marriage patterns, or the sterling qualities of model workers, peasants, and soldiers.

Finally there was the creative transformation of a popular form into something entirely new. The now famous *yang ke* opera form, of which *The White Haired Girl* (the original, not the later ballet version) is the most famous example, evolved in less than a decade from an earthy, satiric, and erotic harvest dance by incorporating folk songs, dance, and operatic elements. Reportage—a lively new form of journalism that resembled the best of background reporting without the investigative dimension—was likewise developed as an amalgam of traditional narrative and the modern short story by both local and refugee writers. Although originally focusing primarily on ingenuity and heroism in the war against the Japanese, it is today a major prose genre accepted on any front. These were the first of the new fruits Mao had promised.

Thus by late 1948, on the eve of final victory, the Chinese Communist cultural program was in place. Policy had been defined; a pattern of cultural organization with writers' groups and touring dramatic ensembles had been set. There was a new generation of writers experienced in the popular tradition. And it had a huge, satisfied audience of 90 million in the Liberated Areas. But what had worked so well in the less sophisticated provinces was to encounter problems in the new urban environment.

In July 1949, three months before the new government was founded, a national conference of literary and art workers was convened in Peking to organize the cultural world. Mao's Yenan talks and the Yenan experience were explained to representatives from the newly liberated parts of China. An administrative structure for culture and propaganda was established, consisting of experienced refugee cadres, younger Yenan writers, and sympathetic supporters from the May Fourth generation. Writers' groups were organized; publishing channels proliferated; performances of Yenan drama and reprints of Yenan fiction introduced the new mode. It was an exciting time.

But there was a price. The various forms of urban fiction that had been the mainstay of lowbrow illiterates would be no more and a crude censorship so devastated the traditional opera that by the mid-1950s the theaters were almost empty. Most of the older May Fourth writers went silent, although Lao She, a well-known popular humorist and author of *Rickshaw Boy,* wrote a few plays extolling government efforts in sanitation and other areas.

Two basic problems have adversely affected literary output under the new regime. First, writers knew how to deal with the past but not with the present. Once the struggles against clearcut enemies like the Kuomintang, the Japanese, and the landlords were over, writers were at a loss as to how to depict—with ideological safety—the tension between backward and progressive elements in the ranks of the people. For example, should peasants who were slow to accept the virtues of agricultural collectivization be sympathetically or critically portrayed? How does one handle the reform of the industrial or commercial world? Such uncertainties have meant that virtually all novels and a very large percentage of the short stories of the past thirty years have dealt with history—with the revolutionary struggles against the Kuomintang, the Sino-Japanese War, and land reform.

The second problem has been government control. Ever since 1942 there have been voices demanding that the author must be free to describe things as he sees them, not as he is told to see them. In 1942 it was the group around Ting Ling, China's major woman writer and the first to explore female sexuality in the mid-1920s, who roused Mao's ire. They bowed but never really surrendered. In 1948 it was Hsiao Chün, another of the group best known for his 1934 novel *Village in August,* about guerrilla warfare in Manchuria against the Japanese, who raised the issues again. For his intransigence he was sentenced to hard labor in Manchurian coal mines. In 1953 it was Ting Ling's old friend Feng Hsueh-feng, who insisted that curbs on free expression not only lowered artistic standards but made writers timid lest artistic error become political treason. For this he lost the editorship of the *Literary Gazette,* one of China's chief literary journals. In 1955 Feng's associate, the outspoken Hu Feng, who also objected to Party control of literature, to the worker-peasant-soldier orientation of literature, and to socialist realism that required putting a bright face on grim reality, was declared a counterrevolutionary and imprisoned.

The top literary bureaucrats, people like Chou Yang and Mao Tun, were of course aware of these problems. Both were sophisticated men, students of world literature and veterans of the Shanghai literary scene in the 1930s. Chou had made his mark as an ideologue, an accommodating literary policeman, liberal or orthodox as the times demanded. Mao Tun, now eighty-two and a major figure in modern Chinese literature for almost six decades, is a popular novelist and long-time Communist sympathizer.

It was these men who in the early years of the new regime repeatedly complained that the current literature was boring, its technique crude and its plots predictable. The heroes, they said, were stereotyped and colorless, the themes too few, and life's complexities were reduced to arid formulas. Where were the stories about state-owned enterprises, students, or intellectuals? Writers, they acknowledged, seemed afraid to portray the shortcomings of the masses. The verdict was clear: What passed in rural Yenan no longer sufficed.

One does not have to read far to verify the charges. Agricultural stories usually show how a "holdout" is convinced to join a collective. The failure of his crops, the success of the collective, and the gentle persuasion of the Party representative always win him over, leaving the impression—which Mao Tun regretted—that the profound issues of the countryside could be "solved in a morning." Novels, even with their broader scope, did little better. The characters in Chao Shu-li's *Sanliwan Village* are a conscientious roster of various conflicting points of view, but he never feels free to use them to explore the distrust and dissatisfaction then plaguing the reform process in the countryside. The result, Chou Yang complains, is too simple.

Industrial stories, as one wag commented satirically, always had "nine chapters." They pit the triumphant ingenuity of the common worker against experience and scientific expertise. Military stories, like the Yenan prototypes, are tales of superhuman valor and determination. Even stories that their authors no doubt intended as tributes to the way Communists always triumphed over difficulties were criticized by Chou and Mao as lacking "positive" characters and too prone to probe for "negative" traits. Chou was particularly upset by one in which a model Communist worker serving as a volunteer in Korea is helped to overcome his unseemly fear of American bombs by his non-Party father. How, Chou Yang asked, could imperialists scare a Party member? How come physical, not political, elements determined his behavior? And how come his father, not the Party, solved his problem?

The basic problem with the new literature, Chou and Mao Tun declared, was that the ideological level of the authors was too low. Writers were still too prone to see the "rot of the present" rather than the "seeds of the future." They must go to the masses and raise their political consciousness. But simply living among the people, they were warned, would solve nothing. They must work hard to learn how to "extract the essence of contradictions," and thus acquire the "political and artistic courage" to reflect the struggle between old and new in its true colors, not as some sort of "petty quarrel or expression of personal eccentricity." They urged writers to study the popular models of the national heritage and the language of the people, remembering always that ideology was primary, technique secondary.

To be sure, there were still gay and charming tales in the innocent manner of the earlier era, which could be read like fairy tales with an amused smile. K'ang Chuo's *My Two Hosts* is the artfully disingenuous confession of a Party worker about how slow he was to realize that the odd behavior of his young associates was the work of the demon love! But penny candies lose their charm and one needs more solid stuff.

By the end of 1955, despite the progress of the early years, the economy was in critical straits. The talents of intellectuals who had been disheartened by the Hu Feng campaign were once again needed. And so in an effort to allay their fears, the Party in early 1956 called for free discussion and criticism from all segments of society: "Let a Hundred Flowers Bloom and a Hundred Schools of Thought Contend!"

The older writers who had been through the earlier if less dramatic drives were understandably slow to respond. The Party's shock came as younger authors of the Yenan and post-Yenan generation voiced the old demands of their elders, calling for more freedom, higher artistic standards, and release from the official dogma of socialist realism which, they said, made it impossible to reflect life as it really was. Although they did not directly attack the Party's right to control the arts, they did object strongly to the ignorant and arbitrary conduct of some literary bureaucrats. Stories by young writers in their early twenties handed down scathing indictments of the Party's administrative style. In one, an eager new employee finds that though right may be on his side, powerful officials cannot be brought to account because no one dares to point a finger at them.

The impact of the "Hundred Flowers" Campaign on literature was limited. Although for a few months the hold of dogma was relaxed and there were stories about daily and family life, even stories with love themes, the real legacy of the Hundred Flowers was the fear created by the subsequent anti-rightist campaign. Shocked by the nature and depth of the criticism that surfaced in 1956, the Party halted the discussions and in 1957 and 1958 turned against its critics.

Among the older writers, the severest punishment went not to those who had recently spoken out but to Ting Ling and Feng Hsueh-feng, prominent symbols of the group that had been critical of the Party's policy on literature since 1942. Ting Ling was sentenced to menial if not hard labor and, though still alive, has not been rehabilitated. In the younger generation it was Liu Shao-t'ang, a popular figure among students and author of some of the sharpest fictional criticism of the Party, who had to be discredited. Otherwise writers were told they could write on any subject they wished, so long as they did not go against the interests of the state or the people.

Both the Great Leap Forward of 1958 and the frenetic rush to communize China that followed in 1959 dramatized Mao's turn back to the masses away from the intellectuals and writers he had come to distrust. The masses were held to be superior to the educated elite in all things, including the writing of literature. Thus, amateur and spare-time writers among the masses were encouraged. There was an emphasis on collective rather than individual effort. Mass meetings of peasants composed hundreds of millions of "poems," which were culled and edited for publication. Production was the order of the day. Like ordinary workers, the country's professional writers were assigned work quotas.

It was into this atmosphere that Chou Yang, in Mao Tse-tung's name, introduced the doctrine of "revolutionary realism combined with revolutionary romanticism"—an updated version of the old socialist realism. The new formula, which was intended to increase emphasis on the positive and encourage optimism, is reflected in the brisk gloss of the 1958–60 short stories. They are slick, often amusing, but totally without depth. Difficulties are glossed over; reason prevails too easily; the Party Secretary, Mao Tun observes wryly, is venerated like an omnipotent Buddha. He calls for satire.

The work of Li Chün, one of the best of the post-1949 writers, is in many ways typical. Reading his stories of women under the commune system, one would never guess at the profound struggle that still continues over the gradual emancipation of women. In one cheery story, the Jade People's Commune purports to be delighted with its new female meteorologist. In another, Mom is assigned to run the commune distillery. In a third, when an old-fashioned father-in-law pockets the earnings of his daughters-in-law, orders them about, and refuses them any say in family matters, the question is handily redressed by the Party Secretary. Most famous of all is his "Li Shuang-shuang," which has now become a classic of stage and screen. Li Shuang-shuang is bored with housework and anxious to participate in the Great Leap Forward. Her husband keeps putting her down, but she is too keen and witty to stay down. Eventually she organizes a canteen, mechanizes its operations, and proves herself twice the man her husband ever was.

Among the novels of the 1958–60 era that were too long in the making to reflect the current scene, three very popular works deserve special mention. All are historical. The first, Yang Mo's semi-autobiographical *Song of Youth,* traces the transformation of a young bourgeois woman into a revolutionary in the course of the Communist-led student movement in Peking between 1931 and 1935. It is a unique work in that woven through the story of those years runs a personal thread of loneliness, ambivalence, and love. This has made the book a favorite with readers but an easy target for the Cultural Revolution.

A second, Ch'u Po's *Tracks in the Snowy Forest,* is a fast-moving novel of action and suspense based on the author's experience of guerrilla warfare. In many ways it is like a traditional Chinese novel. There are three objectives to be captured: an impregnable mountain fortress, a bandit lair, and a wily, retreating enemy band. Each attack requires a different strategy by the small Communist detachment, which has little to rely on but guts and ingenuity. The first is achieved with superb physical skill, the second with the incredible bravado of impersonation, and the third by a combination of psychology and virtuoso skiing.

The third novel, Liu Ch'ing's *The Builders,* portrays the devoted efforts of a poor peasant saved by the revolution to build a mutual aid team in the early 1950s. The strength of the book lies in its description of opposition to collectivization by several different kinds of decent if misguided persons. The real enemies that the hero faces are not so much plots by wealthier landholders as the peasants' ignorance, fear of innovation, greed, and timidity.

The years 1960–62, when the withdrawal of the Soviet advisers in 1960 and the ensuing natural disasters compounded the economic dislocation of 1958–59 and threatened China with collapse, are known as the "bitter years." The leadership, although bitterly divided over the wisdom of Mao's radical economic policy, recognized that the crisis required a softer policy toward intellectuals—including writers—who might help salvage the situation. Thus began the brief respite of 1961–62 that called a temporary halt to the cruder aspects of the literary dictatorship about which writers had complained.

Under the new relaxation, although art was still construed as the servant of politics, there was a call for diversity of subject matter, theme, and style, and for less emphasis on a mechanical interpretation of class struggle. Family problems, love affairs, and even tragedy (hitherto taboo) were seen to be of potentially positive significance. There was a revival of discussion on beauty and aesthetics, on the difference between artistic truth and fact, and on the depiction of truly typical (not formula-defined) characters. There was renewed emphasis on the Chinese heritage and freedom to reinterpret historical figures. Despite the anti-revisionism of China's official anti-Soviet political stance, concern with the humanistic values so characteristic of nineteenth-century Russian literature briefly resurfaced. Authors once again pondered man's human as against his class nature, the individual dilemmas and eternal values that transcend class.

In one short story a young man reared by an older brother returns after a long absence to discover his relative is now a profiteer and class enemy. The older man, infuriated by his brother's attempt to change his thinking, knocks the younger unconscious with an iron spade. When the young man comes to, he remembers all that he owes his brother and forgives him. Eventually the older man mends his ways, transformed—as a later hostile critic would sneer when humanism was no longer tolerated—by "nothing but Christian 'forgiveness,' 'compassion,' and a 'bourgeois appeal to human nature.' "

Of the sixty-odd novels published in the 1961–62 period, only about half a dozen deal with anything other than the now standard revolutionary struggles or the pre-Great Leap period in agriculture. Three of these pioneer previously neglected subjects: the transformation of a capitalist in the early 1950s, the life of university students, and the revolutionary struggle of the Uighurs in Sinkiang. (Indeed writing by and about minorities has become a new dimension in Chinese literature.) The other three are happy pictures set in (but not really about) the Great Leap and communes.

But the most welcome works were still historical. *Red Crag* by Lo Kuang-pin and Yang Yi-yen—by all odds the most popular modern Chinese novel ever published—tells the story of the struggle of Communist prisoners incarcerated in Chungking in 1948 in the Sino-American Cooperative Organization's notorious Pai House and Coal Pit prisons where the authors themselves were held. Their incredible tale of betrayal, deceit, torture, courage, and hope gives the work a stamp of authenticity that is compelling.

Welcome as the respite of 1961–62 was, most writers at the time did not realize the extent to which the literary world was becoming entangled in the factional political struggle. At an August 1962 conference, two longtime Communist writers turned literary bureaucrats blasted the government's agricultural policy in the most scathing terms and demanded remedial action. They called on writers to reflect, not whitewash, the misery and tragedy of the countryside, where, they claimed, the Great Leap had destroyed the ideals of socialism. Shao Ch'üan-lin, Yenan veteran, protégé of Chou Yang, and a hatchet man of the Hundred Flowers Campaign, argued that since most people still did not fully support the revolution—being men-in-the-middle torn between old and new, hope and fear—literature should describe such characters and stop depicting flat heroes with red faces. It was a political challenge in a literary context.

A second voice came from the theater. In 1961 several plays, the most famous of which was *The Dismissal of Hai Jui* by Wu Han (a historian, not a professional playwright), resorted to the time-honored practice of historical allegory to protest not only Mao's dismissal of P'eng Te-huai for his opposition to the commune policy but the policy itself (P'eng was posthumously honored with a memorial service in late 1978). These plays warned that unless peasant suffering and grievances were relieved, the government's days were numbered.

Mao Tse-tung could hardly let such challenges pass. In September 1962 he remarked, "The use of the novel for anti-Party activities is quite an invention!" He hinted that it was also counterrevolutionary. The overthrow of political power, whether by revolutionary or counterrevolutionary forces, he declared, required the support of public opinion—in the shaping of which, he had always maintained, literature played a major role. In late 1963 and mid-1964 Mao repeatedly warned the Peking literary authorities about the dead wood, revisionism, haughtiness, and obstructionism in their midst. Apparently backed by high-level opponents of Mao, they responded with various protective maneuvers. But their tactics failed. Shao Ch'üan-lin was among those who fell in the autumn of 1964. By April 1965 Mao Tun and other major veterans of the literary movement of the thirties were down. Chou Yang too came under attack and was eventually dismissed. In late 1965 Mao Tse-tung left Peking for Shanghai to plan an attack that would smash the Party hierarchy and make it more amenable to his dreams. In November of that year Yao Wen-yuan, the Shanghai literary critic soon to win fame as one of Chiang Ch'ing's Gang of Four, launched the first attack on Wu Han's play, which four years earlier had dared attack Mao. The literary world was now caught up in the dispute over whether the radical policies of Mao or the more gradualist approach of his opponents would guide the future development of China—a dispute that resulted in the Cultural Revolution.

As one might expect, none of this is even hinted at in the literature. Short stories stick to their old formulas and novels follow a predictably historical line. Ai Ming-chih's *Seeds of Flame,* the story of the plight of workers in Shanghai shipyards between 1918 and 1927, concentrates less on the momentous political events of this decade than on the personal lives and attitudes of the workers, and the quirks of fate and personal motivation that led them into an American business enterprise, the Kuomintang, or the Communist Party. Chih Hsia's *Railway Guerrillas* and Ai Hsun's *Thundering Yangtze,* both published in 1965, give detailed and exciting accounts of Communist-led guerrilla activity during the Sino-Japanese War. The first is an excellent picture by one who was there of how a small detachment with few resources other than daring and intelligence disrupted Japanese and puppet-controlled rail lines. The second, much broader in scope, is a vivid account of how an initial group of six men managed to outwit the Kuomintang and the Japanese and build a large base area in the Lo River Basin north of the Yangtze between the winter of 1939 and the spring of 1941. Even *Bright Sunny Skies,* by Chiang Ch'ing's protégé Hao Jan, deals with the problems in the 1951 movement for agricultural cooperation rather than with more recent developments.

One work, *The Song of Ouyang Hai*—the story of a model soldier crushed under a train in 1963—deserves mention more for the circumstances surrounding its production than for any intrinsic merit. It is an army product, a symbol of the increased involvement of the military in national cultural life under Lin Piao, who had succeeded the dismissed P'eng Te-huai. Lin founded an Army Arts Institute and expanded military theatrical companies to play to both military and civilian audiences. And in 1963 he even formulated a creative theory, which Chiang Ch'ing later adopted. Under his formula, the leadership selected the theme of a work, assigned an author, and sent him to "investigate." His resulting draft was then criticized by the masses and changed according to their suggestions. It was under these circumstances that Chin Ching-mai, an obscure army cultural worker, struggled with his book on Ouyang Hai. He has written disarmingly of how difficult it was to make his view of what the book should be conform to what the army wanted and of how many criticisms and revisions the manuscript underwent. The end result is saccharin and flat. Between 1965 and 1972, due to the disruption of the Cultural Revolution, no new novels seem to have appeared.

The Cultural Revolution was the black decade when Chinese literature and art were nailed to the ground and told to smile. Driven by a desire to reshape culture as Mao had reshaped the countryside, and suspicious of anything foreign or complex, Chiang Ch'ing and her supporters banned China's classical heritage as feudal or worse, foreign works (including most proletarian and third world literature) as pernicious, Western music as yellow, Chinese literature of the thirties (even left-wing literature) as reactionary, and the literature of the 1949–66 period as the product of a black conspiracy.

Their control was so tight that for the first time in the history of the modern Chinese movement a decade passed in which the endemic tension between literature and politics could not surface. Not content to proscribe and censor, they hounded and persecuted authors, editors, and performing artists—some even to death. Lao She was driven to suicide. Pa Chin, for decades the novelist most popular with Chinese youth, was put on public trial and for four years forced to wash bathrooms in the Shanghai Writer's Union over which he had previously presided.

Veterans and newcomers alike fell in wave after wave of denunciation. Ideology cloaked the vicious pursuit of private vengeance and prejudice. Mere mention of Mao Tse-tung's martyred wife was enough to send Chiang Ch'ing, his current spouse, into a fury of jealous reprisal. Virtually all, if not all, of the authors and works discussed above suffered, except for those under the group's direct sponsorship. Royalty payments were stopped. Writers' organizations were dissolved, and after mid-1966 the national literary magazines ceased publication, although newspapers and certain army and local organs continued. Even direct sale of movie and theater tickets to the public was stopped in favor of organized distribution to ministries, factories, and like groups, as one more measure to facilitate control over literature and art.

Naturally there was opposition. Although Chou En-lai, who tried to blunt some of the Gang's moves, was too powerful for the Gang to attack directly, themes close to his heart, such as the Taching oil fields, were banned from stage and screen, much to his, and later even to Mao Tse-tung's, annoyance.

Mao was also irritated that some of his statements on literature that did not accord with the group's position were suppressed or their release delayed. He did not like having plays he enjoyed banned. "Model operas alone," he is supposed to have remarked, "are not enough."* He complained that writers came "under fire for the slightest fault." People were afraid to write or produce plays; there was "nothing in the way of novels or poetry." Make literature better, he urged. He was much too sophisticated to stomach programs like one offered at the 1976 May Day Theatrical Festival that featured two ballads, "Fight to Defend Chairman Mao and the Party Central Committee" and "Defend the Victories of the Chinese Revolution"; a dance, *Reversing Correct Verdicts Goes Against the Will of the People;* a Peking opera, *Beat Back the Right Deviationist Wind;* and a special children's item, *Denouncing Teng Hsiao-p'ing.*

Chiang Ch'ing and her group persisted with their program. First, they increased the emphasis on nonprofessional writing, both individual and collective. Second, they adopted the three-in-one collective "authorship" pioneered in the army by Lin Piao. Third, they appropriated ideas Yao Wen-yuan had advanced in late 1963. In still another rewrite of the "revolutionary realism–revolutionary romanticism" formula, Yao had called on literature to praise "light . . . the revolutionary class, revolutionary persons and revolutionary ideals." Literature was to deal solely with major problems of the day, with struggles on the class, scientific, and production fronts. It was not to concern itself with the inconsequential trivia of daily or family life. The social background of each character must be clearly indicated. Heroes were to be heroic, villains villainous—there were to be no men-in-the-middle. Contradictions among the people must be resolved and class enemies punished.

Fourth, they endorsed Chiang Ch'ing's doctrine of the three prominences, which held that in any work positive characters must be more prominent than ordinary ones, the heroic more prominent than the positive, while a superheroic paragon presided over all. And finally, it was decreed that there were to be no love stories. Nor were heroes allowed to die or make mistakes.

The literature of the Cultural Revolution was more manufactured than created. Product specifications were rigid. Proposals for new products were submitted to management; upon acceptance or revision, a sample was produced, then market-tested and changed as often as necessary to ensure acceptability. No wonder that one author referred to a short story of his that had undergone eight revisions as "a thousand-man cake."

What emerged was a poster literature, ideological and impersonal, its face too bright, its grin too forced. More than before, stories tended to be political lectures or pep talks that substituted ideological rhetoric for

---

*"Model operas," a distinctive Cultural Revolution form, are discussed by Roxane Witke on pp. 78–80.—R.T.

normal conversation. Listen to Swallow and Dawn, two sisters-in-law to be. Swallow, envious of Dawn's superior skill as a crane operator, seeks advice about her own balky crane:

> "Well, sister," said Dawn, "when something goes wrong with the crane, it means there's an internal contradiction. So check to find the principal aspect of that contradiction. Rocking means . . . either a bent shaft or faulty wheels."
> "Yes, you've applied dialectics to maintenance work and spotted the trouble so quickly," Swallow was full of admiration for her future sister-in-law.
> "Hard work and study, that's what makes people smart. We have to use our heads and accumulate experience through practice. . . . But we must study theory too. Then we can use dialectics to guide our work."

Other stories are curiously defensive in tone. They seem to argue as if trying to justify the views they seek to impose. In the name of fighting "revisionism"—a catch-all term for policies the Cultural Revolution opposed—such stories denounce commune hiring of outside labor or the use of "material incentives" to increase production. Difficulties in current factory production are likewise attributed to the pernicious persistence of "revisionist" tendencies. Some cadres are described as suffering from "revisionist" haughtiness and insensitivity, as though to justify the Cultural Revolution's wholesale attack on the Party hierarchy. Stories about education not only support the anti-intellectual system of the post-1966 era, but ridicule the more traditional one it displaced. The teacher who is hurt while seeking herbs that will enable a girl to walk again is contrasted with her pre-Cultural Revolution predecessor, whose only legacy is said to be a few pieces of chalk in an empty classroom, the symbol of useless book learning.

In the literature of the Cultural Revolution, Mao's thought is the source of all wisdom and inspiration. Appropriate quotations from the Chairman, printed in big black characters to contrast with the sayings of ordinary mortals, provide the magic key to the solution of all problems. The automatic guarantee of success that invocation of his words signals mechanizes and flattens the narrative. No wonder that one longtime resident of Peking recently told me the sentiment in his circles during the Cultural Revolution was: "I may have to buy the stuff but I sure don't have to read it!"

The fall of the Gang of Four in autumn 1976 may well have been the most welcome day in the history of the People's Republic. Nowhere was their eclipse greeted with more relief than in the literary world.

Long-banned books—foreign and Chinese—began to be republished; uncut versions of favorite operas and stage plays were produced; libraries dropped their borrowing restrictions. The rehabilitation of persecuted authors began as some were released from silence, supervision, the countryside, or confinement. For others it was too late—for Lao She and Feng Hsueh-feng there was only reburial in the Cemetery of the Martyrs of the Revolution.

But tensions remain. The Gang's supporters have been difficult to dislodge. Some writers still wait for redress. Many fear to write; the scars are too deep, the future too uncertain.

Official statements on literary policy are disappointingly conservative. The emphasis is not on possible loosening of Party control but on getting back to the *status quo ante*. Hua Kuo-feng has stated that literature will continue Mao's worker-peasant-soldier orientation and his Hundred Flowers policy. All kinds of literature may compete freely, it is declared, so long as they: (1) accord with Mao Tse-tung's "six criteria" in regard to benefiting Party leadership, socialist construction, socialist revolution, and the worker-peasant-soldier masses, and (2) are helpful in the modernization of industry, agriculture, science, technology, and national defense. Writers are told to "strive for the unity of revolutionary political content and the highest possible perfection of artistic form," that is, to continue the "marriage of revolutionary realism and revolutionary romanticism."

Ostensibly criticism is to replace censorship. "Fragrant flowers" of proletarian socialist literature and art are to be energetically cultivated, not in an isolated hothouse but in strenuous competition with "poisonous weeds." Such weeds will not be banned, but neither, we are warned, will they be allowed to run wild. They are to be curbed by "facts and reason," not "administrative decree." One would feel more assured if Hao Jan, a very gifted storyteller and Chiang Ch'ing's protégé, were not now under attack.

The conservative pattern is reflected in the literature itself. Out of some twenty-three 1977 novels surveyed by *People's Literature,* eighteen still deal with the revolutionary struggle, with the army, or with land reform and economic construction. Only one of the remaining five tackles a fresh topic—reform in the financial world. Much the same pattern holds for shorter fiction in 1977 and early 1978. Most stories are on history or the army; the rest still focus on social attitudes, good and bad. The majority decry such evils as resistance to technical innovation, prejudice against women, selfishness (a farmer schemes to enlarge his courtyard at the expense of the commune), concern for the welfare of one's own unit to the detriment of the whole, and unfounded suspicion of one's colleagues (moral: Don't rush to judgment). A minority lauds positive qualities like honesty in refusing to accept unrealistic production quotas, or job devotion above and beyond the call of duty. Mercifully the Party Secretary now makes only an occasional low-key appearance. Ritual invocation of the Mao gospel has ceased.

There is a revival of love interest in fiction. Classical and modern works in which love is featured are being reissued. New stories reassure the young that, contrary to the assertions of the Cultural Revolution years, attraction to the opposite sex is normal and the enrichment of life which love brings makes for better workers and citizens. There are of course no scenes of passion and no explicit sex; hand holding is about all we see. In general the tone is one of wry amusement like that of a musical comedy. Some stories warn against marrying for material advantage; others relish sentiment—often for a long-martyred revolutionary lover.

The note of honest passion in some post-Cultural Revolution literature attacking the Gang of Four is refreshing but should not be interpreted as a sign that Chinese literature has become open and critical. Rather it derives from the current congruence of popular sentiment and government policy.

The dialogue theater, which suffered severely in 1966–76, is again flourishing. Two themes predominate: the misdeeds of the Gang of Four and the heroic lives of revolutionary leaders and martyrs. Some combine the two. *Red Hearts* shows how the Gang of Four obstructed a family of doctors in their study of coronary disease, a program funded by the Gang's enemy, Chou En-lai. A smash hit, *Where the Silence Is,* depicts the opportunistic betrayal of a family friend by a Gang follower. The fugitive, who is wanted for his part in the "counterrevolutionary act" of editing and printing a selection of poems honoring Chou En-lai, goes to prison like a hero, confident of ultimate vindication.

In the current political struggle, as in literature, Chou En-lai has become an anti-Gang symbol with anti-Mao overtones.

Chou is the emotional center of Li To's short story "A Wreath of Music." In a small room not far from T'ien-an-men Square where memorial demonstrations to Chou are going on, a sick old musician plays at a piano on which rests a picture of the late Premier. In his youth the musician had been inspired by a Chou lecture. Now many years later his master composition, "The Red Crag Concerto," has been declared a "poisonous weed" like the book from which it took its name. But today he is defiant. When police charge in and try to make him surrender his only master score, he shouts: "Over my dead body," then collapses. As the police beat a temporary retreat and an ambulance is called, the musician asks his young friend (the narrator) and a little neighborhood girl who have witnessed the scene to turn his score into a memorial wreath. Three days later, at his request, they take it to T'ien-an-men Square, where as they join the silent thousands approaching the Martyrs' Monument with their wreaths, the air is suddenly filled with the music of "The Red Crag Concerto."

One puts the story down with mixed feelings. The tribute to Chou is very real, but its too obvious combining of "revolutionary realism" with "revolutionary romanticism" almost makes one wince—albeit with sympathy.

Very different is Liu Hsin-wu's "Class Teacher," an agonized look at the tragic impact of the Cultural Revolution on the mind of China that has attracted considerable attention. It finds no one exempt from responsibility, no one free from the effects. What, it asks, shall be done with victims of all kinds, but especially the youngsters it has ruined?

Hsieh Hui-min, the Youth League secretary for the ninth grade and a typical product of the Cultural Revolution years, is a sort of automaton who cannot and will not think for herself. She is rigid and totally devoid of imagination. Even on the hottest day she will not wear a skirt because to do so is decadent and capitalistic. She cannot understand that mountain climbing might be a more suitable group activity for healthy ninth graders than the study of official government documents, which she indignantly complains, seems to put them to sleep. No amount of persuasion can get her to read a book the press has not officially recommended. Chang, the narrator and her ninth-grade teacher, asks in despair: How can she be led beyond slogans and quotations to learn to read, analyze, and think?

Sung Pao, the other young victim in the story, is sullen, scared, and ignorant. In the Cultural Revolution he had heeded the cry against education, quit school, joined some ruffians, and stole books from the closed school library to sell. When that failed, he and his friends had no better use for the volumes than to amuse themselves by drawing mustaches on the illustrations of women. Just released from a period of police detention, Sung is visited by Chang, who has agreed to take him in his class. Chang is shocked by the boy's awful blankness, the emptiness of his mind, and his illiteracy. Suddenly Chang realizes that Sung and Hsieh are alike in that neither cares to or knows how to think. Both are stunted and hollow. Hsieh is afraid of being poisoned by books; Sung has been poisoned by a disdain for them. How, Chang asks, can China build for the future on such a foundation? Adapting Lu Hsün's famous line, he cries: "Save, save the children ruined by the Gang of Four!"

There are two other characters, the first a fortunate girl whose family has kept their library and their sanity during the dark days just passed. She has been secretly brought up on Lu Hsün, Mao Tun, classical poetry, and assorted foreign works. Today she is happy, self-confident, nurtured as a child of China should be. The other is a teacher who, though he hated the debasement of education in the Cultural Revolution, now feels no obligation to help its victims. For him, Sung is a rotten apple who will spoil the barrel and should therefore be relegated to some special school for kids like him.

And finally there is the narrator, the real hero of the story, a symbol of enduring decency and concern. He is furious at those who in the years just past dared tamper with the minds that are the future of China. He is also disgusted with himself. Why, he asks as countless thousands must have, did he not stand up during those dark years? Can he now find the strength to make up for his failures? Can he help the Sungs and the Hsiehs to "heed the broader world, to take an interest in the fruits of all human civilization, to acquire higher powers of analysis," so that they can help move China ahead? He knows he must try.

What of the future? Now that China is firmly set on a crash program to become an advanced industrial society, will the relaxing of constraints against science and technology free literature as well? I doubt it. Despite the homage paid the arts, they are in fact today of less than crucial importance. Where science and technology can change the parameters of society, literature and art can only explain and support. It is scientists, not artists, who are being sent abroad for training. To be sure, the cultural realm, the bastion of the now fallen Gang of Four, is not so unimportant that the government can afford to tolerate known antagonists therein— hence the continuing campaign to dislodge gang supporters. But the fact remains that the thaw in culture has been much slower than in the critical technological areas. Furthermore, as the Chinese leadership well knows, too free an intellectual enviroment can be dangerous. And so, as long as there is a Communist Party government in China, I do not expect to see successful open challenge to the right of that authority to control literature. As the process of de-Maoification continues, literary formulations associated with Mao's name may be modified, even replaced. Yet whatever comes next will, like what went before, derive its sanction from the central political authority.

As time goes by are we likely to get psychologically oriented literature such as we know in the West? I do not believe so. Why should we? The basic Chinese tradition does not concern itself with the individual psyche as such. People have always had specified roles to play rather than themselves to find.

Some may ask whether technological and social change in China and her ever closer integration with the outside world will alter the traditional

Chinese view of the individual's role in society. I am inclined to doubt it. I look for a literature built on Chinese values for a Chinese audience, not one in the international mode like certain modern Japanese writing. Chinese literature of the future will, like "Class Teacher," give us a better picture of China than of man.

Values Through Art

MICHAEL SULLIVAN

In the realm of art China has always seemed very different from the West. Michael Sullivan is first concerned to make clear what traditions lie behind China's art today. There was Confucian art, which upheld a conception of the public good; and there was Taoist art, which gave play to the individual imagination.

We see that much of the past has sunk without trace. The social base of art has been vastly expanded by thirty years of Maoist rule. At the same time Sullivan stresses many continuities—birds and flowers are painted in the old way—and he insists that the past has been subtly dealt with, not merely rejected. Nature still bulks large, as it always did. Realism is given a rather relaxed meaning that owes more to tradition than to Marxist realism at its crudest.

Sullivan does not believe that a single world standard exists for judging contemporary art, and he sees a fluidity on the Chinese scene that allows him to think the West could learn from the painters of the East. Behind the simplicity of today's peasant painting lies the possibility, at least, that just as social change produced this hearty peasant art, so further social change may sharply raise its horizons and lead to greater sophistication in the art of the masses.

Michael Sullivan, Christensen professor of Oriental art at Stanford, is a leading authority on the art of China, where he lived for five years in the 1940s and which he revisited in 1973 and 1975. Educated in Great Britain, he holds a LittD from Oxford University, a LittD from Cambridge University, and a PhD from Harvard. Sullivan's books include: Chinese Art in the Twentieth Century *(1959);* The Birth of Landscape Painting in China *(1962);* The Cave Temples of Maichishan *(1969);* The Meeting of Eastern and Western Art *(1973);* The Three Perfections: Chinese Painting, Poetry and Calligraphy *(1974); and* The Arts of China *(revised edition, 1977).*

—R.T.

The first question often asked by people interested in modern China is not what has happened to Confucianism and Taoism, but what has happened to the great artistic heritage? Not because people respond to Chinese art as they never could to Confucianism and Taoism, but because they cannot conceive how this refined, philosophical, and somewhat elusive artistic tradition could survive the assault of Western, and particularly Marxist, realism. For when we think of the typical Chinese painting, we think of towering mountains in the mist, of aged scholars lost in contemplation of a waterfall, of the idle fisherman, of poets and recluses —a world removed from everyday life. Many of these pictures, the artist's inscription tells us, were painted in the manner of the old masters, for Chinese painting drew its inspiration as much from its own past as it did from nature itself.

The values that traditional Chinese painting embodied were those of the Confucian scholar or of the Taoist recluse—at one extreme intellectually and socially elitist, at the other rejecting society in the artist's solitary search for the truth amid the mountains and streams. The practice of fine art was in any case confined to a minute segment of society. For the mass of the people it might just as well not have existed. We could be forgiven for thinking that revolutionary China has utterly rejected this kind of art, and replaced it with an art of the people. A truly popular art is indeed being created, as we shall see. The key question is whether in the process of creating a new art the art of the past has been swept away, and with it the values that it expressed.

Ever since the time of Confucius, the Chinese have evoked the past as a standard by which to gauge the present, a source of lessons in what to emulate, what to avoid. Having no religious authority, history, and the way in which good and wise men have behaved in history, was the chief source of society's values. The past could be an inspiration; but it could also be a burden. Today—and this is one of Mao Tse-tung's greatest achievements—it is no longer a burden. It is an inspiration or a warning, or it is simply irrelevant.

So it is perhaps not surprising that the most ancient and the most modern Chinese ideas of the purpose of art and of the artist have a good deal in common. The bronze sacrificial vessels of the Shang and Chou dynasties were used in ceremonies that demonstrated the harmonious ordering of society: the very concept of "beauty" was first applied not to art but to the ancestral sacrifices and to the music that accompanied them, because they were an aid to, and an expression of, correct thinking and harmonious social action. Ancient frescoes on the walls of palaces and ancestral shrines, painted by anonymous craftsmen, depicted not only gods and spirits but virtuous rulers, loyal ministers, and sages of antiquity and their evil counterparts. The heir apparent would be conducted by his tutors through these galleries and made to contemplate the portraits as an essential part of his moral education.

Until the century or so after the fall of the Han Dynasty in A.D. 220, it would have been impossible to conceive of a pictorial art in China that was not magical or moral in content and purpose; that was not, in short, created for the better ordering of society. It could have been said then, as Mao Tse-tung said in 1942, that "There is no such thing as art for art's sake." Because it stresses the social and ethical role of art and the artist, we might call this the Confucian tradition in Chinese art, although it was born long before the time of Confucius and was not exclusively Confucian in content. After the Han Dynasty, Confucianism had to share with Buddhism this concept of art as essentially didactic, conveying its ethical message through the vehicle of the figure, human and divine.

But in the chaos that followed the fall of the Han a new concept of art and the artist emerged—a concept that we can loosely call "Taoist." For these painters it was in the contemplation of nature, and not at the ancestral shrine, that true order and harmony were to be sought. In discovering nature, the artist also discovered himself as a creative being, expressing his wonder at his power, as he put it, "to bring down a panorama of a thousand miles within a scant foot of silk." This "landscape experience" was an intense and private thing, to be shared only with like-minded men. Carried to its logical conclusion, it cut the artist off from society and turned him into a recluse.

Thus there came into being in China two conflicting ideas about the purpose of art and the role of the artist, Confucian and Taoist, social and individualistic. Some artists took one path, some the other, but there were few in whom the two impulses were not both at work. Often their lives were divided between public service and seclusion in the countryside: when they were at their desks they were dreaming of the hills and streams, and when in the hills a nagging conscience told them they should be at their desks putting their education to the public good. One thing, however, they had in common: they took it for granted that behind every painting lay a moral or philosophical message.

Gradually, from the eleventh century onward, among the scholar-painters the "Taoist" impulses triumphed over the "Confucian." Henceforward the great masters were almost without exception landscape painters. For while figure painting touched Chinese society at every level, from the scholarly studies of the literati to the pictures of demons and door-gods in the village shrine, landscape painting, as the vehicle for the expression of philosophical and poetic ideas, was the art of the gentry. Not surprisingly, this attitude to art and the artist has been strongly attacked in twentieth-century China as elitist and undemocratic.

Not only social attitudes toward art, but the very nature of the traditional Chinese aesthetic process, the way in which the Chinese artist "sees" the world and sets down what he sees, is vulnerable to the challenge of Western art. For what mattered to the Chinese painter was not that he should render accurately what was before his eyes at any given moment, but that he should capture the essential aspects of his subject: not Mount Hua seen from the east on a stormy winter afternoon, but Mount Hua as the typical embodiment of the very idea of a mountain, and as a visible manifestation of the life-giving spirit that animates nature. Although he may make studies of individual rocks and trees on the spot, the Chinese painter is not concerned in his finished work with the particular, or with accidents of time and place; he is making a general statement about nature in its eternal aspect. Such Western techniques as shading, cast shadows, and one-point perspective, which fix the time of day, direction of the sun, position of the viewer, by forcing him to particularize, would defeat his purpose.

It is not that the Chinese artist could not paint realistically if he wanted to. Up to the twelfth century, indeed, it might be said that his chief aim was to achieve a totally convincing effect, so that the viewer could almost imagine that he was not looking at a picture at all, but wandering *in* the landscape, a sense that the continuous perspective of the long handscroll makes compellingly real. But for a number of reasons—historical, social, psychological—painters of the gentry class abandoned pictorial realism centuries ago, leaving it to the court painters and professionals, in whose hands it eventually hardened into a set of dead pictorial conventions. By the fourteenth century, landscape painting at the upper levels of Chinese society had become very generalized, even abstract; it was also as personal in its expression as the scholar's own handwriting. For to these men, the purpose of painting was no longer to represent nature but to express themselves. They spoke of "playing with the brush," and of their paintings picturesquely as "prints of the heart." Their art, like their poetry and scholarship, was meant not for the public, who never saw it, but for each other.

The view that there was one superior kind of painting that was suitable for a gentleman, and another, inferior, for the professional, was to dominate art in China from the fourteenth century until well into the twentieth. Art was socially and stylistically polarized, a state of affairs that was perpetuated by the scholars themselves, who set the standards and wrote the art history and criticism, and were naturally interested only in the art of their own class. That anyone below the level of a scholar, or at the very least an educated man of the merchant class who consorted with scholars, might take up the brush and paint for pleasure was unthinkable.

As China decayed in the late Ch'ing period (1644–1911), so did her arts. She was living on her past, slowly consuming herself, when Western culture brutally pushed its way into her country. Yet Western art did not have an altogether easy passage, for it presented a challenge to China's most precious legacy. It was not that Western techniques were hard to learn, for the Chinese had always been adept at taking over what they needed from abroad. It was rather that the modern Western concept of art as an end in itself, and of the artist as an outsider, responsible only to his genius, dedicated to absolute personal freedom, was new and disturbing. There had been eccentrics and dropouts in China's past, but they had always been viewed with disapproval, even by their fellow artists.

Returning from Paris fired with romantic ideas of how an artist should behave, the young painters of the 1920s lived as best they could the life of the Latin Quarter in the French Concession of Shanghai, striking bohemian attitudes and painting in the manner of the École des Beaux Arts. The bohemian attitudes were soon abandoned in the stresses of the 1930s, but these painters, notably Hsü Pei-hung (1895–1953), had brought to China new techniques of painting that enabled the artist to forget his scholars and waterfalls and to depict the world as he saw it.

Hsü Pei-hung is a particularly important figure because he was not content simply to imitate the manner of the Salons (see Plate 1). Soon he took up his Chinese brush again to show how traditional techniques might be used to paint modern subjects in a realistic way. As with so much else in the culture of the PRC, the seeds of the new styles in art were sown in the 1920s and 1930s by men like Hsü Pei-hung, who shared the liberal-progressive outlook of the intelligentsia of the Treaty Ports, and were generally anti-Communist if they had any politics at all.

But while this cosmopolitan culture enjoyed its brief heyday, the writer and polemicist Lu Hsün (1881–1936) was teaching a growing band of young idealists in Shanghai that art, and the woodcut particularly—because it was Chinese and it was cheap—could and indeed must be used as a weapon in the struggle against the ills of modern society (Plate 2). Lu Hsün proclaimed a new art for the masses: the time had not yet come for an art created by the masses themselves. The artist must go to the people, feel with them, speak for them, and stir them to protest. For a few years the debate raged between the believers in these rival ideals of

Plate 1. Hsü Pei-hung: Horse. Ink and color on paper, 1940. Hsü Pei-hung injected a new realism into traditional Chinese brush and ink technique.

the aims of art. During World War II, patriotism and the common catastrophe briefly brought both sides together in a cultural united front. But this had already broken up before peace came in 1945, and the controversies raged again in the war's brief aftermath.

If I have sketched the background of stress and conflict at some length, that is because we can only understand the tensions in the arts under the PRC as arising inevitably out of this past.

With the establishment of the new regime in 1949 it may have seemed that, for the time being at least, all conflicts were resolved. For Mao Tse-tung had laid down in *The Yenan Talks on Art and Literature* (1942) the line that the arts must follow, and in the general wave of popular enthusiasm for the revolution there was little dissent. Besides, the policy of the honeymoon years of the early 1950s was comparatively liberal. The art magazines discussed Greek sculpture and Renaissance painting; aesthetic problems were debated; Dürer's religious paintings were reproduced, as were Hsü Pei-hung's academic nudes. Only "bourgeois formalism"—meaning essentially all the modern European and American movements since about 1890—was condemned as decadent.

But from 1958 onward the arts came under wave after wave of attack:

Plate 2. Li Hua: Refugees, Rich and Poor. Woodcut, about 1939.

the first from the backlash against the "Hundred Flowers" movement; the second during the Great Leap Forward; the third and most savage of all from the intolerance and hooliganism turned loose by the Cultural Revolution of 1966–69, followed by the more sharply focused and in its way equally vicious cultural dictatorship of Chiang Ch'ing, whose devastating influence on the creative arts can scarcely be exaggerated.*

Mao Tse-tung's dicta were enforced with increasing rigidity. The new art, he had said at Yenan, "should serve the toiling masses of workers and peasants who make up more than ninety percent of the nation's population," and "both the cultural and practical movements must be of the masses." There were to be no exceptions, no chance to escape to the hills and streams or into the privacy of one's own thoughts. Individualism was condemned, and during the worst times the work of art became as anonymous as had been the wall paintings in the ancestral shrines of the Han Dynasty.

But if the masses had never had an art of their own, on what was their new art to be based? China had had her peasant arts: the New Year pictures, for instance, the crude paintings and clay sculpture in village shrines, the flower decorations in Shansi peasant homes, the batiks of the

*See Witke's discussion, pp. 272 ff.—R.T.

Southwest Minority peoples; but delightful as these were, they were hardly enough on which to build a new national art. The masses were given some guidance, however. Long before, Lu Hsün had written that the aim of the modern Chinese artist should be "by selection to accept the historical legacy of Chinese traditional art: to absorb the best in style and technique from foreign art; and thus to establish a new national art in accordance with the demands and needs of the masses."

What is the best? How does one tell unless one applies non-Marxist criteria? Are the landscapes of the Sung Dynasty master Fan K'uan better than those of the eccentric Tao-chi, the figure compositions of Michelangelo better than those of Rembrandt? Mao Tse-tung dealt with this problem in purely political terms, and in so doing begged the question. Although he acknowledged that there was such a thing as aesthetic beauty, it must always, he insisted, be subordinated to ideological content, and he attempted to apply this yardstick to the art of the past: "To study the development of this old culture," he said at Yenan, "to reject its feudal dross and assimilate its democratic essence, is a necessary condition of our new national culture."

But where is the "democratic essence" in a painting by an old master such as Ni Tsan (1301–74), who painted dry ink landscapes with an ethereal, almost abstract atmosphere, and no human figures in them at all? In the Palace Museum in Peking his landscapes are labeled as "decadent." Outside the galleries stands a notice exhorting the visitor to take from the pictures on show what is good, and to reject the bad.

"What is bad about Ni Tsan's landscapes?" I asked my guide when I visited the museum in 1973. She was oddly unsure. "What is good about them, then?" I asked. "They accurately depict," she replied, "the daily life of the common people in those times." I pointed out that there were no common people in Ni Tsan's landscapes at all. "But," she replied, "the common people loved the landscape too." My guide's pride in her cultural heritage was at least as great as her dedication to Maoist ideology, and if by both exhibiting and criticizing the landscapes of the great traditional scholar-painters both ends are served, who are we to complain?

If we judge the state of art under the PRC by what is shown in national art exhibitions, by what is reproduced in official publications such as *China Pictorial* and the art magazine *Fine Arts (Meishu),* or by what the picture shops are willing—or in bad times permitted—to handle, then we must form the impression that all modern Chinese art is bright in color, explicitly or implicitly propagandist in content, positive in tone to the point of being naïve. Typical of this kind of art is Tang Ta-hsi's "Fruit from the People," in which a happy child in her mother's arms gives an apple to a PLA man on the march. All are healthy, clean, smiling; the harvest is abundant; peasants and soldiers, for the first time in history, are friends. The world looks good.

But not all art in China today is so obviously propagandist as this. There is, for one thing, a great deal of conventional traditional painting. Among the amateur works I saw in a factory art club exhibition in Chengchow in 1973 were bamboos, birds and flowers, landscapes, kittens with pink bows around their necks, that carried no discernible political message. It seems that much was done, even in the bad years, that Party ideologists overlooked, and that there are many artists who paint for their own pleasure and that of their friends in a manner quite different from that of the pictures they execute on official commission for public buildings and hotels. A first essential in understanding contemporary China is to be able to distinguish between what is officially said and written and what, at many levels, is actually done.

Now let me ask what, in art and in values expressed through art, the new China has taken from the old, what she has rejected, and what are the problems still to be solved. As I write (in the spring of 1978) a spirit of freedom such as has not been felt since the early 1950s has brought the arts to life again. But who can be sure that in the years to come the chill wind will not once more blow down from the north, to kill the flowers that are now in bud? What I have to say cannot but be provisional.

It is easiest to see what has been rejected. The whole social foundation upon which the art of the past was created has been swept away. Gone is the patronage of emperor and court, gone the elitism of the scholar class and the very scholar class itself, with its contempt for the professional and the artisan. Today the professional is the artist employed by the state, either on major projects such as the decoration of public buildings, or as a teacher in the art academies and in factory and commune art clubs, while the only true amateurs are the peasants and factory workers who paint in their spare time.

Gone are the great private collections to which only the gentry had access. The styles of the scholar-painters have been drained of their philosophical content and, in the spirit of Mao's slogan, "Make the past serve the present," have been put to new uses, given new significance. The idea that the purpose of art is, as the Sung Dynasty poet Su Tung-p'o had put it, "to give lodging to one's thoughts and feelings," smacks too much of selfish individualism to be tolerated in today's China—unless, of course, one's thoughts and feelings are "correct" and widely shared. Gone too is the obsession with the past, the conviction that only by painting in the manner of the great masters of Sung, Yüan, and Ming can one produce good pictures.

Gone is the very idea of the great master, the painter of genius. The artists who make the most significant contributions—whether they be men of the stature of Li K'o-jan, Huang Yung-yü, and Kuan Shan-yüeh, or the anonymous peasants of the Hu-hsien Production Brigade who, if the official accounts tell the whole story, seem to have created a new kind of art unaided—are held up as models to be emulated. But in no sense do they, or could they, constitute an elite in the old way, for the very concept of a cultural elite today is heretical. Finally, we do not need to look far beneath the surface of the art of modern China to see that, along with all this clearing away of old ideas about the role of art and the artist in society have gone the Confucian and Taoist philosophies that lay at the very heart of traditional painting.

The reader who has followed me thus far might be forgiven for thinking that nothing survives of the great artistic tradition but its styles and techniques. Some say that China's fine museums were built for the purpose of putting the artistic heritage behind glass, sterilizing it, lest it infect the masses with reactionary thoughts: it can safely be admired precisely because it *is* dead. But the great efforts made to inculcate into the masses the lessons of the past, through archeology, "teaching bitterness," conservation, and a Marxist interpretation of history, suggest that the art treasures are not dead by any means, but a potent influence upon the present.

It has also been said that China today is engaged in a "love-hate" relationship with her past. I think this is misleading, because it suggests an ambivalence that is not there. Rather, it is a "love-the-art-but-hate-the-system-that-produced-it" relationship, a much healthier attitude. It is precisely this confrontation of past and present, this refusal to deny the past, that makes the culture of contemporary China so dynamic.

There is no longer a scholar class in China to produce the incomparable works of a Shen Chou or Tao-chi; but to compensate, the basis from which art springs has been immeasurably broadened. The art materials counters of department stores are crowded, for millions of people are taking up the brush to paint for whom such an act, a generation ago, would have been unimaginable. Best known are the Hu-hsien Production Brigade paintings I referred to above.

The Hu-hsien district of Shensi has always been known for its decorative New Year pictures and colorful house decorations. In the last twenty years the local peasants have developed a new "school" of painting. Bright in color, showing a strong flat sense of pattern, their cheerful pictures reveal their own world, highly idealized (Plate 3). When they speak of their paintings as being "close to the truth," they are not speaking of life as it is (the existence of a North China peasant, even today, can be pretty grim), but rather of getting the details of a harvest scene or a tractor correct. As the modern painter Zao Wou-ki noted when he visited

Plate 3. Chang Lin: Diligence and Thrift. Ink and color on paper. By a member of the Hu-hsien Production Brigade in Shensi Province.

Hu-hsien in 1973, "They want to be sure their art is functional. They never use the words pretty or beautiful." In this respect, at least, their attitude to art is thoroughly traditional.

If the metaphysical union of man and nature no longer seems to animate the landscape paintings, this does not mean that the Chinese today love their mountains and streams any the less. The landscape painter still draws upon the symbols of nature to express his strongest feelings, although sometimes the meaning may have changed. The pine tree still stands for indomitable courage, but the bamboo, so far as I know, no longer symbolizes the pliant but unbreakable spirit of the scholar-official under a tyrannical ruler. The plum blossom in deep winter stands not only for the awakening of a new spring but also now, as it did for Boris Pasternak, for heroism, for the blood of the revolutionary martyrs red upon the snow. Red has always been a symbol of joy in China. When the Gang of Four was crushed, Huang Yung-yü expressed his joy in typical Chinese fashion in paintings of brilliant red lotuses. New, and more obviously political, is the symbolism of the red sun rising to bathe the land in its radiance.

As always, the landscape painting must mean more than itself. Landscapes, the painter Li K'o-jan has said, "are the artists' odes to their motherland and home." The fact that men and women are now transforming the landscape for the good of all, leveling hills, diverting streams, engages them in an even closer relationship with nature, for only by understanding it can they transform it. A metaphysical approach would be of little help. Yet, just as the Western biologist is discovering that man's prosperity, indeed his survival, depends not on "conquering" nature but on achieving a symbiosis with nature, so may this intense Chinese engagement with the natural forces contain the essence of a philosophical view, and thus bring into focus once more ideas about the eternal flux of matter, about energy, movement, space, and time, that are deeply rooted in Taoism.

For the figure painter there is likewise a shift in focus rather than a complete break with tradition. The content of figure painting is of course not Confucian but Marxist-Maoist, but the message is as uncompromisingly ethical as ever. Once it was the heir apparent who was paraded before portraits of the virtuous and the wicked. Today it is schoolchildren everywhere who are shown archeological evidence (one of the chief uses, indeed, of archeology) of the suffering of the slaves in ancient times and of the extravagance of their masters. It is the children who contemplate imaginary portraits of heroes and villains of past and present, of the selfless Lei Feng and Iron Wang who mixed the slurry with his own body, and who gaze at savage caricatures of Chiang Kai-shek, Lin Piao, and the Gang of Four (Plate 4).

In China the alternative, therefore, to one kind of ethical content is not a neutral or abstract art, but another kind of ethical content. Its expression, compared with that of the great figure composition of the past, is often obvious and crude, descending to the "slogan and poster" style that even Mao Tse-tung himself condemned. So long as those in power insist that art speak only to the masses, it is likely to remain so, for it is speaking to people to whom art has never spoken before and whose responses are unsophisticated. As the standards of performance and appreciation rise, however, we may expect these pictures to carry their message with greater subtlety.

There are limits beyond which we should not expect Chinese art to go. Even if China fully opens her doors there will be no painting of the nude, because to the Chinese a "nude" is always a naked body, an offense against personal modesty. Nor will there be any pure abstract art; not just because abstraction is Western, bourgeois, formalistic, but because the Chinese are not, and never have been, interested in an art whose content is just itself, and which is philosophically and morally neutral.

"Form alone does not constitute beauty," the modern critic Chu Kwang-chien wrote. The total effect of beauty, he says, is achieved by "form animated with content," and he cites the Chinese critics who from earliest times have maintained that the aim of art should be to unite form or body *(hsing)* with spirit or soul *(shen)*. What the Western abstract painters are doing, he maintains, is to spread the cult of soulless beauty,

Plate 4. Anonymous woodcut in the manner of the old New Year pictures. An ancient chariot burial, showing the extravagance and cruelty of the old feudal society. The banner reads "Criticize Confucius and Lin Piao!"

that is, beauty without any other content than form itself. This may seem a bit naïve to us; after all, form, in a work by Mondrian for example, *is* content. But to the Chinese, that is just not enough. Even the "pure" abstract art of calligraphy is judged by the quality of the personality of the writer it reveals, while a bad poem or a salacious text, however beautifully written, could never be admired as a masterpiece of calligraphy.

If Western influence is most obvious in the realm of realistic figure painting, that is because, unlike the landscape painters, the figure painters can no longer rely upon their traditional repertoire of scholars and idle fishermen. Already in the 1930s art teachers were telling their students to stop putting scholars into the street scenes they were drawing on the spot, and the helpless students were asking them for photographs of modern people that they could copy in.

Because drawing the human figure from a living model meant drawing in an entirely new, foreign manner, modern Chinese artists have shown greater interest in Western figure than in Western landscape painting. Yet even here it is not complete realism that they are aiming at. Model workers, soldiers, and peasants must be shown clean, with open shining faces, striking heroic attitudes some of which are borrowed from the conventions of the theater, for these icons are created to stir the masses to great deeds. This kind of art, which is as didactic and inspiring in purpose as the wall painting of the Han Dynasty, is called "revolutionary romanticism," and is best described in words of Mao Tse-tung's that sound strangely like Longinus on *The Sublime in Art* or the principles of Sir Joshua Reynolds. "Life as reflected in works of literature and art," Mao said at Yenan, "can and ought to be on a higher plane, more intense, nearer the ideal, and therefore more universal than actual everyday life."

Only in depicting villains and the bad old days are dark colors, heavy shading, and distortions permitted, and as a consequence these works are often artistically the most effective. One has only to compare the blandness of the average propaganda painting idealizing the new society with the high drama of *The Rent Collection Courtyard,* which recreates in lifesize clay figures the harrowing scene that took place every autumn in the mansion of a former Szechwan landlord (Plate 5). Much more of a challenge is presented to the artist by the dark side of the old society than by the unrelenting sunshine of the new. Milton was condemned for making Satan the most interesting character in *Paradise Lost.* The artist's dilemma is a universal one.

So accustomed are the Chinese now to the symbolic idealization of modern men and women that when a few years ago the Mexican government sent to Peking an exhibition of paintings by Rivera, Orozco, and other revolutionary artists, the Chinese authorities withdrew about

Plate 5. Anonymous team of sculptors: Detail from *The Rent Collection Courtyard*. Lifesize figures in clay, in the courtyard of a former landlord's mansion in Tayi, Szechwan.

twenty of them on the grounds that the public would not understand the distortions of the human figure.

Chinese officials requested the withdrawal from a recent exhibition of Australian paintings of some nineteenth-century works that showed the whites exploiting the aborigines. Both the theme and style of these thoroughly Victorian works were unexceptionable, but it was felt in Peking that such pictures would damage Australia's image in the eyes of the public. Here of course ideology took second place to power politics and diplomacy. Incidents of this kind suggest that the Chinese are more flexible and pragmatic in their attitude to ideology than Western observers often give them credit for.

The problem of realism in Chinese art, however, is not just political and ideological. Centuries ago painters distilled from their predecessors' experience a vocabulary of typical forms in nature, of hills and rock formations, of various types of trees and leaves, of waterfalls, houses, wandering scholars, which were eventually codified for the student's guidance in such books as the famous seventeenth-century *Painting Manual of the Mustard Seed Garden*. From such handbooks the young painter learned his technique and repertoire much as the pianist does by his exercises. We would expect that under socialism the painter would be told to abandon these conventions, go out into the countryside, and draw exactly what he sees. What has happened is far more interesting.

The critic, acknowledging that the old conventions are stale and no longer true to life, says to the painter, not "abandon them," but "go out into the mountains and check that your conventional brush strokes for trees and leaves, for the texture of mountains and rocks, are true to nature, or correct them accordingly." The painters have gone obediently, indeed willingly, out into the countryside, sometimes on long tours that have taken them to remote places hallowed by memories of the Long March; they have checked their vocabulary and made it livelier and truer to nature. Likewise, the conventional long-robed scholar is replaced by the equally conventional worker, peasant, or soldier, for whom idealized models can be found in the new artists' manuals.

The significance of this cannot be overestimated; for it shows that the Chinese have met the challenge of Western realism not by surrendering to it, but by revising, reinvigorating, and enriching their language of pictorial conventions. This confidence in the traditional way may be seen even in some of the propagandist figure paintings, where there is often no shadowing or cast shadows, no ground for the figures to stand on, while the use of empty space as an element in the composition is, again, thoroughly traditional.

This does not mean that the problem of realism has been solved, particularly when it comes to evaluating the art of the past. For how can one admire the landscapes of Yüan masters such as Ni Tsan, which are semi-abstract, individualistic, formalistic? The answer—if published discussions of this question are a safe guide—has been very simple: call them realistic anyway.

The early Ch'ing master Pa-ta Shan-jen (1625–c.1705) was a drunkard and a dropout, his paintings sketchy, careless, and expressionistic. Indeed, there seems to be almost nothing about him, except his rejection of Confucian orthodoxy, that was acceptable to the apparently uncompromising standards of post-1949 China. Yet, writing in 1964, the painter and critic Chang An-chih could claim that Pa-ta was a realist because "in a few strokes he captured the very essence of the subject he portrayed." Another critic calls Pa-ta's almost equally eccentric contemporary Tao-chi (1641–c.1710) "fundamentally a realist" because, in his *Essay on Aesthetics,* "he advocated that artists should take nature as their guide, but give their own interpretation of it." Realism, to Chang An-chih, is not visual accuracy but what he calls "essentiality." Most classical landscapes, he wrote in 1964, "are highly realistic in the sense that they are a synthesis of nature and the artist's feelings and ideas."

Such definitions of realism are purely philosophical, not to say metaphysical. They take no account of socialism or class struggle, and it is not difficult to see that if allowed to flourish they would lead inevitably toward art for art's sake. Not surprisingly, discussions of aesthetics at this level were abruptly halted by the Cultural Revolution, and have not been resumed since—or, if they are taking place, are not yet being published. Yet the artists who expressed these views include several who after suffering considerably during the Chiang Ch'ing dictatorship in the arts are now, as I write, flourishing once more.

While such debates may be going on in private, there is for the time being no challenging Mao Tse-tung's insistence that formal beauty must be subordinated to ideological content. The word "beautiful" is not today, and never has been, applied to pictorial art in China. This is, as we have seen, a traditional Chinese view. What is new is not the idea that art should serve society, but that it should do nothing else.

If authority has its way, there can be no exceptions, no recluses, no Taoists communing with nature in the privacy of their mountain cottages, no eccentrics. Only the Hundred Flowers may bloom, and all are red. The rest are poisonous weeds—to be encouraged to grow only so that they may be identified and rooted out. Never in Chinese history, except perhaps in the time of the first Ch'in emperor, whom Mao greatly admired, has there been such all-embracing pressure to conform. The fact that the pressure is moral as well as political—an appeal to the artist's selflessness—makes it all the more irresistible, particularly as China's achievements since 1949 would seem to justify the demands that are made equally on every member of society.

It is the response to this appeal that has brought about the almost total integration of the arts into the fabric of Chinese society. Today no longer must the artist compete for attention by being more daring than his rivals; extremism in any form puts him not at the head of the pack but out of the running altogether. So there is no avant garde in China today. If the painter claims that only in total freedom can he give full rein to his talent, and so best serve society, he is told that his attitude is selfish. All have talent for something; all must serve as the state directs; there can be no exceptions.

In the bad years—the Cultural Revolution, for example—he even lost his identity as an artist. His paintings were unsigned, and the seal, if there was one, often bore the simple legend: "Long Live Chairman Mao." Freedom may be a relative term, but the restraints under which many Chinese artists worked until very recently would be intolerable in New York, or even in Warsaw. The peasant painters of Hu-hsien no doubt feel themselves to be entirely free, and if they had the choice of painting in a more sophisticated way would have no reason to do so. The question of artistic freedom becomes acute when there is a choice. The urban, educated artists, some of whom are aware of artistic currents abroad, have felt the strain of conformity far more acutely.

One can stress the positive aspects of art under the People's Republic: its vast and ever-widening popular base, its freshness, its relevance to life today, its creative revitalization of the artistic legacy, its traditional insistence that the best art is that which promotes the harmony and well-being of society. The achievement is indeed remarkable. And yet this new art leaves whole realms of human experience and emotion untouched, unexplored.

I am thinking of religious and metaphysical experience, and of the unfettered play of the imagination, which have produced much of the great art of China's past. The inspiration of the painting of the scholars lay often in the communion of feeling between them, the love of friend for friend, the joy of meeting after long separation, the poignancy of parting and death.

Today the expression of these feelings is not encouraged, unless, as in the outpouring of deep and genuine emotion at the death of Chou En-lai, they are felt on a national scale. Does this suggest that the Chinese have been taught to switch their strongest and deepest feelings to the collective level? Perhaps this is what the authorities would have us, and them, believe. For my part, I find it very unlikely.

The very foundation of Chinese aesthetics, the vital spirit in nature that I spoke of earlier, presupposes a source of inspiration beyond the reach of the orthodox doctrines of Marxism-Maoism. Not only the landscape painter, but anyone wandering in the hills, enjoys ecstatic experiences that have nothing to do with the transformation of the land under social-ism. To ignore this, and to claim as some official critics have that the vitality in a landscape painting is "an expression of the prosperity of our socialist countryside," is absurd.

It is not that the extra-political sources of aesthetic inspiration are denied. They are simply not discussed, just as in writing about Buddhist art its religious content is never mentioned. But given the sense of history and the intellectual sophistication of a growing segment of the Chinese people, it is hard to believe that these deeper issues will remain beyond the pale forever; and when they are once more brought into the light of day, the words of Karl Marx may be remembered. "The writer in no way considers his work as a *means*," he wrote in 1842. "His work is an end in itself. It is so far from being a means for the writer himself and for others that he is ready to sacrifice *his* existence for *its* existence when the need arises."*

In view of the enormous pressure on the artist to conform, both in traditional and in Maoist China, it is not surprising that the number of free spirits has been few, particularly as most Chinese believe that their responsibility as artists is inseparable from their duty as citizens. The courageous behavior of a few artists during the "Hundred Flowers" Campaign of the 1950s, and even under the ascendancy of Chiang Ch'ing, suggests however that the conformity is less universal than it appears; while for years there has existed a small underground movement among artists and writers, who according to reports have produced satire, erotic fiction, and paintings full of hidden symbols, seen by only a few trusted friends. Political protest, in Chinese art and literature, is none the less effective for being clothed in allusion and allegory.

So the state of art in China today is complex. The reaction of the Western liberal observer cannot but be complex too; deploring the lack of freedom of the individual, the stylistic caution and timidity, the appeal to the mass cultural level; while at the same time envying the security of the artist, and admiring the solid ethical foundation on which Chinese culture today is based. Americans above all the Western peoples should be able to respond to the general lack of cynicism in the modern Chinese spirit, its optimism and dedication to the future, for these are attitudes upon which American society was built and they are not dead in America yet. If Western artists react to the art of contemporary China by saying that it is so conservative as to present them with no kind of challenge, one must ask in return: Why should the latest developments in environmen-tal, conceptual, or minimal art have any relevance in China today? Is there but *one* modernism, in New York, Paris, or Tokyo, that the art of the rest

*"Debates on the Freedom of the Press," *Karl Marx, Friedrich Engels: Collected Works*, tr. Dixon, Dutt et al. (1975), vol. I, p. 175.

of the world must follow? The idea, considered in the context of world history, does not stand up to examination.

The challenge that China presents lies, in any case, not in matters of artistic style or technique, but in the Chinese concept of the very purpose of art and of the place of the artist in a healthy society. It may not be possible, or desirable, for the Western democracies to achieve a state of such cultural integration as China finds tolerable. But her example should at least lead us to question many things in our own cultural life —in the broadest sense of the word "culture"—that we now take for granted.

I am thinking not only of the gross materialism of our culture, but of the commercialization and competitiveness of the art world, the anxious and artificial relationship that often exists between the artist and a public that seems to have no use for him. Is the choice then between the total freedom of the artist, and his total integration into society at the cost of his freedom? At times in the last thirty years China seems to have presented just such stark alternatives.

But already the climate is changing. Mao Tse-tung's aesthetic doctrines have, for the time being at any rate, become unfashionable, and the possibility of the reemergence of elites is not quite so unthinkable as it has appeared in the recent past. New contacts with Japan and the Western democracies are bound to stimulate new styles and techniques in the arts, although it seems unlikely that the values expressed through art will change very much, for they are deeply rooted in Chinese society.

Meantime, as the level of China's cultural life continues to rise, it may be that she will find a balance between total control and total freedom. Such a middle path would be well in line with the traditional Chinese view of the role of art and the artist in society.

Index

327